Slaves, Subjects, and Subversives

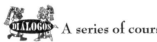 A series of course-adoption books on Latin America

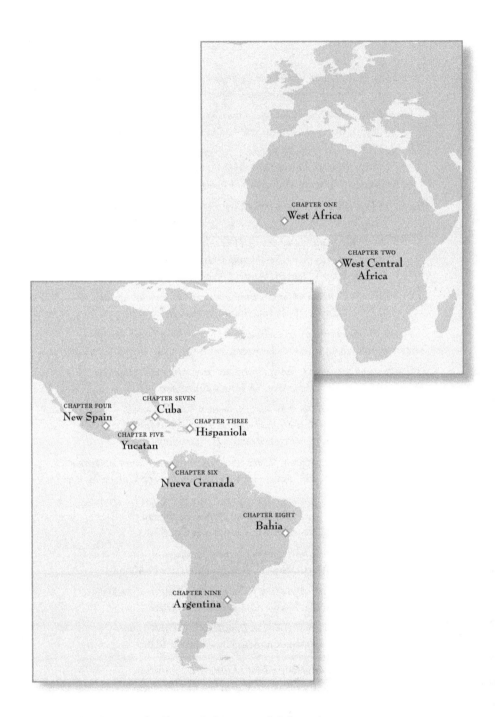

Geographical context for Slaves, Subjects, and Subversives.

Slaves, Subjects, and Subversives

Blacks in Colonial Latin America

Jane G. Landers, editor

Barry M. Robinson, editor

University of New Mexico Press · Albuquerque

Library of Congress Cataloging-in-Publication Data

Slaves, subjects, and subversives : blacks in colonial Latin America / [edited by]
Jane G. Landers, Barry M. Robinson.
p. cm. — (Diálogos)
Includes index.
ISBN-13: 978-0-8263-2397-2 (PBK. : ALK. PAPER)
ISBN-10: 0-8263-2397-9 (PBK. : ALK. PAPER)
1. Blacks—Latin America—Social conditions.
2. Blacks—Latin America—Ethnic identity.
3. Slaves—Latin America—Social conditions.
I. Landers, Jane. II. Robinson, Barry, 1975–
III. Series: Diálogos (Albuquerque, N.M.)
F1419.N4S53 2006
305.896'07308—dc22

2006017253

Book and cover design and type composition by Kathleen Sparkes
This book is typeset using Janson 10/13.5, 26P
Display type is Bernhard Modern
Ornaments are Type Embellishments

Contents

❧

Acknowledgments

❧ THIS VOLUME HAS BEEN TOO LONG IN THE MAKING, and I have accumulated many debts of gratitude to acknowledge. I would like, first, to thank our Diálogos Series editor, Lyman L. Johnson, whose idea it was to compile a collection of essays on the black history of colonial Latin America, and who invited me to edit a volume on this theme. With every apology I offered for delays along the way, Lyman responded that a good book was worth waiting for and David Holtby, recently retired as editor in chief of the University of New Mexico Press, was equally patient and supportive. Both of these fine editors have been wonderful to work with, and I am most grateful for their faith in this project. Maya Allen-Gallegos, managing editor, and Sonia Dickey, editorial assistant for UNM Press, have been unfailingly helpful while dealing with coeditors often located on different continents. Our copyeditor, Robin DuBlanc, rose to the challenge of editing a difficult manuscript based on often obscure sources in multiple languages—Arabic, Spanish, Portuguese, French, and English. She was a meticulous reader and we are in her debt.

My authors have also been supportive and patient, and when I pressed at the end to put the finishing touches on our collaboration, they interrupted their own busy schedules to respond to my final requests. Each is doing pioneering research in the field, and I hope to have the opportunity to work with them again. One of my deepest debts is to my coeditor, Barry Robinson, without whose impressive organizational and editorial talents this volume would have been even further delayed. I can only hope that the time he devoted to this volume and the lessons learned along the way will serve him well as he revises his own excellent dissertation on the conflicted roles of indigenous actors in the Mexican independence. My colleague and research partner, Mariza Soares, whose pathbreaking scholarship on black brotherhoods in Brazil I had hoped to include in this project, was visiting Vanderbilt when I was concluding this project and was a tremendous help in the final editing process. I could not have done it without her.

Renée Soulodre-La France was a critical assistant in the final phase. She helped me proofread this manuscript in Cusco and Lima.

Lastly, I would like to acknowledge the originators of the field on whom all of us have relied and whose cited works fill our endnotes. They set the example that inspired us all.

Introduction

Jane G. Landers

꒦ APPROXIMATELY 12 MILLION AFRICANS EXPERIENCED THE TRAUMA OF enslavement in Africa, loss of families and homelands, and the horrors of the Middle Passage. The great majority of those who survived to reach the Americas remade their lives in territories claimed, and nominally ruled, by Iberians—either Spaniards or Portuguese.[1]

This may surprise U.S. readers, who often assume that the African American history they learn in school is much more representative than it really is. In the U.S. canon the experience of Africans is often reduced to a single powerful narrative of bondage and suffering on nineteenth-century sugar, rice, and cotton plantations. Indelible images from popular media such as *Gone with the Wind*, *Roots*, and *Amistad* only reinforce the known and familiar.

The essays in this volume offer a corrective to this powerful but limited depiction of African American history. Drawing on a wealth of previously unused sources and new interdisciplinary perspectives, the authors demonstrate that the history of Africans in the Americas began in colonial Latin America more than a century before 1619—where too many U.S. history texts still begin the story of African American history. These essays also show that although plantation slavery was a horrible reality for many Africans and their descendants in Latin America, blacks experienced many other realities in Iberian colonies, not only as slaves but also as free subjects and as subversives who fiercely rebelled against their enslavement.

While numeric specificity is impossible, black Africans had formed sizeable populations in southern Iberia for centuries preceding Spanish and Portuguese colonization of the Americas, entering the peninsula via the trans-Sahara trade and with the Muslim occupation (711–1492).[2] Islam united West African and Iberian caliphates, and Paul Lovejoy's chapter one shows that so, too, did cultural, legal, and social traditions, including those surrounding slavery.

Once Portugal regained its territory from the Muslims in the fourteenth century, it launched into the Atlantic and initiated a systematic trade in African slaves. By the mid-fifteenth century Portuguese traders were importing about 1,000 African slaves into Lisbon annually; after 1490 that number had risen to 2,000.[3] From Lisbon, many Africans filtered into southern Spain. The notarial archives for Seville from 1501 to 1525 record the presence of 5,271 slaves, almost 4,000 of whom were listed as blacks or mulattoes. Muslims, white Christians, Jews, Canary Islanders (or Guanches), and American Indian slaves were also present in those records.[4] Southern Iberia was a multiethnic and multiracial world long before Columbus set sail, and over long centuries of African presence in the peninsula, Iberian law, custom, and society began to accommodate difference. After all, Iberians knew West Africans living below the Sahara had developed great cities comparable to many in their own lands, with important centers of learning. Sub-Saharan Africa was famous for its gold fields, its well-organized trading systems (including a trade in slaves), and great armies and cavalries that helped feed that trade. Aristotelian beliefs in natural lords and natural slaves were not race-based: great African rulers were worthy of respect.

Thus, race alone did not justify slavery, and medieval slave codes imbedded in the *Siete Partidas* (a codification of Spanish law compiled during the reign of Alfonso X, "the Learned," 1252–84) offered the enslaved many avenues out of bondage. By the fifteenth century a small, but significant, free black class could be found in most of Spain's southern cities. While retaining much of their African "national" culture, these free people also claimed several Spanish identities—as *vecinos* (recognized residents of municipalities) and as members of parishes, and religious brotherhoods, or *cabildos*.[5] Memberships in such corporations awarded useful legal protections and privileges that blacks as well as Spaniards enjoyed.[6] In early modern Spain, while Portuguese slavers were busy collecting slaves on the African coasts, free black *mayorales*, or stewards, arbitrated disputes in black neighborhoods and defended their charges in courts, while black officials administered the funds and responsibilities of black churches, hospitals, and social welfare systems.

Although Africans in Iberia seemed models of acculturation, they nevertheless preserved very visible cultural elements such as language, music, dance, and ritual association and ceremony and probably many less visible social structures as well. Assimilationist policies and the relative cultural freedom Africans exercised probably served the interests of Iberian authorities. One Spanish scholar compared early modern Seville to a chessboard with equal numbers of black and white pieces.[7] As far as we know however, Africans never revolted in southern Spain or Portugal nor staged any mass escapes, despite their relative proximity to Africa and their common employment as sailors.

Rather than revolt, many free and enslaved Africans joined in Iberian exploration, conquest, and colonization of Latin America. Their unpaid and wage labor built the cities, created the ranches, mines, and plantations that fueled Latin American economies, manned the wharves and ships that were the lifelines back to Spain and Portugal, and provided every imaginable service and craft needed to maintain the urban life Iberians preferred. The military skills of Africans and their descendants also helped Spain and Portugal defend vast American coastlines against their European competitors, put down indigenous revolts, and even track runaway slaves.

In Latin America, Iberians developed a two-tier system of African slavery. Spanish-speaking Catholic slaves known as *ladinos* filled a wide range of urban domestic, artisan, and lower-status economic roles, working in occupations as varied as tailoring to masonry. Urban slaves generally received better treatment than their rural counterparts, based on older metropolitan slave relations, on their access to legal and religious protections, and on their integration into a cash economy. They were allowed to work for themselves on Sundays and feast days and also to hire themselves out for an agreed-upon return to their owners. With effort, slaves could accumulate sufficient income to buy their freedom or that of their kin through a legal mechanism called *coartación*. Owners and the state also freed slaves for meritorious acts, and upon receiving their freedom all former slaves became subjects of the Spanish crown, equal, theoretically at least, to subjects of other ethnicities.[8]

Despite the fairly successful transfer of medieval patterns of manumission and incorporation to urban settings such as Santo Domingo, Havana, and Mexico City, the early numeric superiority of slaves imported directly from Africa, whom the Spaniards called *bozales*, triggered rebellion throughout Latin America. Lynne Guitar in chapter two analyzes America's earliest sugar regime, established by West African slaves on Hispaniola in the early years of the sixteenth century, as sugar cultivation in Morocco and other Mediterranean regions was declining. The grueling work on that island's mega-plantations led many slaves to flee to nearby mountains where they formed the hemisphere's earliest maroon communities. By midcentury Spanish colonists lived in dread of slave revolt.

From the Antilles, Iberian conquest and colonization moved on to the mainlands of Mesoamerica and South America, and so, too, did Africans. For the next three centuries, geopolitics and global economics propelled Africans through a wide variety of imperial regimes, landscapes, cultures, languages, and religions, both in Africa and in the Americas. Although most of their peregrinations were forced, the Africans studied in this volume also made choices about where they would go, how they self-identified, and what they used of their background in particular situations—much as they probably did when still on the African continent. The worlds and experiences that Africans moved through altered, but did not eradicate, their original identities. To borrow Ira Berlin's wonderful phrase describing such Atlantic creoles, they were individuals "of linguistic dexterity, cultural plasticity, and social agility."[9]

As Berlin and others have shown, creolization, in fact, began in Africa. In chapter three John Thornton emphasizes how quickly Central Africans adapted to elements of European culture, including the Catholic religion. Thornton shows that this acculturation became more pronounced after Portugal founded a large colony in Angola, and he argues that by the mid-seventeenth century Angola resembled contemporary Latin American colonies.

While the crowns of Spain and Portugal were joined (1580–1640), Portuguese traders shipped ever-larger numbers of Central Africans to Latin America from slave forts in Kongo and Angola. Many of these Central Africans were transported to New Spain, and Jane Landers analyzes in chapter four the varieties of rebellions they instigated in the seventeenth century. Angolan slaves in Mexico City turned medieval Iberian forms of association into vehicles for rebellion, and escaped slaves from coastal sugar estates proved so indomitable that the Spanish crown eventually had to accept their demands and recognize them as free Spanish subjects.

One reason that Spaniards were forced to treat with slave rebels was that European competitors were, from the beginning, unwilling to grant Spain and Portugal exclusive rights to the Americas. In the sixteenth century English and French pirates raided coastal cities and treasure fleets, and French Huguenots attempted, but failed, to establish colonies in Brazil and Florida. By the seventeenth century, French, Dutch, and English challengers had all established their own colonies in what was once a "Spanish lake." African slaves throughout the Americas quickly learned to read the political winds swirling around them and take advantage of the new geopolitics.

In analyzing the life of one eighteenth-century Afro-Yucatecan, Matthew Restall in chapter five finds what readers more familiar with an Anglo variant of slavery might consider a surprising degree of mobility for blacks in the circum-Caribbean. Like Berlin's Atlantic creoles, many black Yucatecans moved through the Spanish and English worlds with seeming ease. Restall's Manuel Bolio was born in the Kongo, married a Maya wife in Mérida, worked in Bacalar in southern Yucatan, and was finally prosecuted as a bigamist by the Cartagena Inquisition for marrying a second time—this time choosing a woman of African descent.

As Manuel was being tried in Cartagena, slaves on Nueva Granada's Jesuit haciendas were also facing a crisis. Renée Soulodre-La France analyzes in chapter six how geopolitics transformed their lives and identities when the Spanish crown expelled the powerful Jesuit order from Latin America in 1767. Facing sale and separation from families and friends the slaves, not surprisingly, resisted. Some chose flight, but others adopted their new status and identity as "slaves of His Majesty" to legally pursue corporate privileges and protections.

Black corporatism, which originated in medieval Iberia, survived well into the nineteenth century in various forms throughout Latin America and gave Africans and their descendents mechanisms and institutions through which to resist enslavement and hardening racial categories. In chapter seven Matt Childs analyzes the governance of Havana's black brotherhoods and finds that African-born individuals held the upper hand and the leadership of most of these nation-based corporations. Cuban authorities supported this bias, hoping to pit African-born members against creoles and thus divide and conquer, but despite their political disabilities, creoles joined the brotherhoods, hoping to preserve some sense of African identity as Cuba's slave regime increasingly defined them by color.

In chapter eight Stuart Schwartz analyzes a major Hausa uprising in 1814, showing that slave resistance was often organized corporately and along ethnic lines in Brazil. Although the large slave population of Salvador da Bahia was predominantly drawn from the Mina Coast, in the nineteenth century Muslim Hausas from the central Sudan flowed into Brazil. In Salvador, Africans of various origins regrouped and rebelled against their enslavement. Some organized themselves into religious brotherhoods and militia units, while maroons from the suburban *quilombos* ringing the city waged a virtual war against their former masters. In Salvador *quilombeiros* conspired with their urban compatriots as they gathered for ethnic drumming and dancing sessions called *batuques* or in religious houses of *candomblé*. Rebel leaders were often drawn from urban work crews or *cantos* that were also organized along ethnic lines. Like their contemporaries in Cuba, blacks in Brazil found meaning and utility in ethnic identities that, while altered or "invented," had at least some connection to African origins.

As Brazilian blacks found fraternity in African ethnicity, many blacks in Spanish America chose instead to identify themselves as loyal supporters of the Spanish crown in disciplined militias organized by the Bourbon reformers of the late eighteenth century. Then, as independence movements broke out, thousands of blacks joined armies on both sides—some fighting for the king and others for the would-be leaders of would-be republics. Seth Meisel in chapter nine shows how blacks in the young viceroyalty of La Plata fought to defend Buenos Aires from British forces in 1806 and how the "alchemy of military service could make slaves into patriots and patriots into free men." Slavery was already on the wane in Argentina, but four to five thousand male slaves won their freedom through military service. Grateful Spanish authorities staged theatrical public ceremonies in which they manumitted slave soldiers and incorporated them into the Spanish state as subjects. Subsequent governments would be similarly indebted and grateful, although abolition did not become final in Argentina until 1853. Meisel analyzes the tensions between black claims on citizenship and lingering racial prejudices.

Each of these essays is the result of painstaking archival research by the authors, and it would be a missed opportunity not to share some of the fascinating records they uncovered. The documents in our appendices are only a sample, but they underscore our argument about the variety of the black experience in colonial Latin America and about how geopolitics and the cultural traditions of Africa shaped that history. Over the course of more than three centuries, Africans and their descendants in Latin America suffered as slaves, lived as free subjects of Iberian monarchs, and rebelled against the indignities and injustice of servitude. Using medieval corporate traditions, legal and commercial processes, and their own force of arms, many freed themselves before finally helping to win independence for new nations throughout Latin America. We hope that this volume will help incorporate black history into the broader history of colonial Latin America and the black experience in Latin American colonial history into the larger history of Africans in the American diaspora. We also hope it will inspire other scholars to follow our lead and generate new scholarship in these fields.

NOTES

1. David Eltis, *The Rise of African Slavery in the Americas* (Cambridge: Cambridge University Press, 2000); Herbert S. Klein, *The Atlantic Slave Trade* (Cambridge: Cambridge University Press, 1999).

2. William D. Phillips, Jr., *Slavery from Roman Times to the Early Atlantic Trade* (Minneapolis: University of Minnesota Press, 1985), 162–63, 173, 180, 186–89.

3. C. de C. M. Saunders, *A Social History of Black Slaves and Freedmen in Portugal, 1441–1555* (Cambridge: Cambridge University Press, 1982), 17–25.

4. Alfonso Franco Silva, *La esclavitud en Sevilla y su tierra a fines de la edad media* (Seville: Universidad de Sevilla, 1979), 132–46. For data on slave sales and prices, see his *Regesto documental sobre la esclavitud Sevillana (1453–1513)* (Seville: Universidad de Sevilla, 1979).

5. The term *cabildo* most commonly referred to a municipal council but could also be used to denote a self-governing body within an ethnic group or fraternal organization. See chapter 7 for an in-depth discussion of how Africans in Cuba used *cabildos de nación* as a stage for defining and contesting ethnic identity.

6. José Luis Cortés López, *Los orígenes de la esclavitud negra en España* (Madrid: Mundo Negro, 1986), 151–76; Ruth Pike, *Aristocrats and Traders: Sevillian Society in the Sixteenth Century* (Ithaca, NY: Cornell University Press, 1972), 170–92; Diego Ortiz de Zúñiga, *Anales eclesiásticos y seculares de la muy noble y leal ciudad de Sevilla, metrópoli de la Andalucía*, 3 vols. (Madrid, 1796), 3:78; Vicenta Cortés Alonso,

La esclavitud en Valencia durante el reino de los Reyes Católicos (1479–1516) (Valencia: Publicaciones del Archivo Municipal de Valencia, 1964).

7. Antonio Domínguez Ortiz, "La esclavitud en Castilla durante la edad moderna," *Estudios de historia social de España* 2 (1952): 377–78.

8. Jane Landers, *Black Society in Spanish Florida* (Urbana: University of Illinois Press, 1999), chap.1.

9. Ira Berlin, "From Creole to African: Atlantic Creoles and the Origins of African-American Society in Mainland North America," *William & Mary Quarterly*, 3rd ser., 53 (April 1996): 263.

CHAPTER ONE

The Context of Enslavement in West Africa
Aḥmad Bābā and the Ethics of Slavery

PAUL E. LOVEJOY

⁂ IN 1592 AḤMAD BĀBĀ (1556–1627) OF TIMBUKTU WAS IN CHAINS, TAKEN across the Sahara to Morocco in captivity. Had he been sent west to the Senegal River, he might well have been sold to a waiting slave ship and taken to the Americas, where he would almost certainly have ended up in Latin America and been identified as a Mandingo, which is how Muslims from the western Sudan were labeled at the time. Aḥmad Bābā was no ordinary slave, however, and his destiny was not in the Americas. He was a political prisoner, the most learned and respected scholar in the schools of Timbuktu and indeed of the Songhay Empire, of which Timbuktu was the most important city. A Moroccan expedition from Marrakesh crossed the Sahara in 1591 in the brazen attempt to conquer Songhay and extend a Muslim Sharifian empire into the heart of Africa. Aḥmad Bābā's captivity was a consequence of this invasion. Many Songhay citizens were enslaved, and even more Songhay slaves were effectively reenslaved and taken to southern Morocco to work the sugar plantations that had been established there. Distinguished individuals like Aḥmad Bābā were held for ransom, enslavement befalling them should ransom not be forthcoming.

In fact, he eventually returned to Timbuktu, where he wrote his famous treatise, *Mi'raj al-su'ud—The Ladder of Ascent towards Grasping the Law concerning Transported Blacks*, which was based on his experience and his extensive knowledge of Islamic law.

Aḥmad Bābā's story needs to be placed in the context of colonial Latin America in the seventeenth and eighteenth centuries, for his scholarship had an important influence on the thinking of Muslims in West Africa, and thereby helped to shape the contours of the slave trade in West Africa and affected the movement of slaves to all parts of the Americas. By comparison with West Central Africa, relatively few West Africans were taken to the Americas before the late seventeenth century—they probably constituted less than a quarter of the total number—and fewer still from the Muslim interior, let alone from Timbuktu. Still, there were enough to be identified as Mandingo. As is suggested in this chapter, one of the reasons for the restricted movement of slaves from the interior of West Africa to the coast was that Muslims were generally opposed to selling slaves to non-Muslims, and specifically to Christians. The writing of Aḥmad Bābā on this subject not only represented this thinking but was in itself the basis of legal and political action that interfered with the sale of enslaved Muslims into the trans-Atlantic trade.

Although it has seldom been recognized, the legitimacy of enslavement was widely discussed in West Africa in the sixteenth and seventeenth centuries. The work of Aḥmad Bābā specifically addresses issues relating to the significance of racial and ethnic categories as factors in the justification of enslavement. This debate over slavery has been overlooked in scholarship that focuses only on Europe and the Americas. In West Africa, the debate over slavery relied on interpretations of Islamic precedent, which was invoked to protect freeborn individuals from enslavement. By extension, the debate influenced the flow of trade, since there was some attempt to restrict involvement in the trans-Atlantic slave trade on the basis of religious identification with Islam and the desire to avoid the sale of slaves to non-Muslims, especially Christian Europeans on the coast of Africa.

This internal discourse is revealed in Aḥmad Bābā's *Mi'raj al-su'ud— The Ladder of Ascent towards Grasping the Law concerning Transported Blacks*, which was concerned with distinguishing among those people who were known in the Islamic world as "Sudani"—blacks or people of the Sudan. He specifically refuted arguments that black Africans could be enslaved on racial grounds. Only "unbelief" was a legitimate reason for enslavement, and for this reason his treatise was intended to be an "Exposition and Explanation concerning the Varieties of Transported Blacks" that established the ethnic and political basis of identification with religious belief and social status. The treatise therefore expresses an indigenous West African perception of community and collective consciousness that is essential in understanding conceptions of ethnicity and how these may or may not have changed through limited interaction with the trans-Atlantic world. It is argued here that the internal debate within West African Muslim circles was a factor that limited the export of slaves to the Americas; slaves from West Africa were largely restricted to people often known as "Mina" and included various people speaking different languages but generally the Gbe languages from the coastal regions of the Bight of Benin.[1]

Demographic and Legal Context

Most of the enslaved Africans sent to the Americas in the seventeenth and eighteenth centuries came mainly from the Bantu-speaking regions of West Central Africa, comprising the Kingdom of Kongo, the Portuguese colony of Angola, and their hinterlands, perhaps amounting to 85 percent of the total number of displaced Africans in this period.[2] Of approximately 467,000 slaves sent to Latin America in the seventeenth and eighteenth centuries, 42,240 came from West Africa, 352,590 came from West Central Africa, 6,096 came from Southeast Africa, and there were 65,997 slaves whose origins in Africa cannot be specified. The number recorded from West Africa in the seventeenth century was just under 5,000, and for the eighteenth century almost 40,000. It should be noted that the number of slaves in the unspecified category was greater than the total for West Africa in this period, but even if all of this category were assigned to West Africa, the proportion of West Africans would still have been less than a quarter of the estimated departures from Africa of those whose regional origin can be established or estimated. The analysis is complicated because of the large number of people whose origins in Africa are unknown and hence have not been included in any of the regional totals; this figure amounts to approximately 124,000 for the seventeenth century and 1,329,000 for the eighteenth century. Of these, the database records about 19,000 slaves arriving in Latin America from West Africa in the seventeenth century and just under 35,000 in the eighteenth century. The two estimates based on regional origins in Africa and destinations in Latin

America are not the same since the first set of figures calculates departures from Africa while the large unspecified category includes arrivals in the Americas; estimated losses of slaves during the Atlantic crossing have to be remembered. Despite the problems with these estimates, it is clear that far more West Africans went to Latin America in the eighteenth century than in the previous century, but that relatively speaking many more came from West Central Africa. Since several thousand people also came from Southeastern Africa, the total population from Bantu-speaking regions, with their relatively similar languages and predominance of matrilineal societies, suggests a degree of homogeneity that was not found among those people who came from West Africa, who derived from a cultural and linguistic mosaic that was far more complex than the Bantu regions of West Central and Southeastern Africa. The West Africans included people who spoke very different languages, including the large linguistic subfamilies of Gur, Kwa, West Atlantic, and Mande. These people were often characterized as coming from the Guinea Coast, the Mina Coast, or simply the coast.

The strong Muslim presence in many parts of West Africa had an important influence on restricting the sale of slaves to Europeans on the coast. As I have argued elsewhere, West Africa appears to have sent fewer slaves to the Americas than otherwise might have been expected because of this influence.[3] This is not to suggest that Muslims were free from enslavement or that they did not engage with Christian Europeans for reasons of expediency. Indeed, the presence of Muslims in the Americas from the earliest days of the trans-Atlantic trade demonstrates the complexity of the situation in West Africa at a time when Spain and Portugal were consolidating their control of the Iberian peninsular and establishing empires beyond the shores of Europe. Moreover, the shifting alliances among Muslims after the Ottoman conquest of much of North Africa sometimes pitted Muslims against Muslims and inevitably resulted in the reduction of free individuals to the status of slave. One consequence of this political situation was an outpouring of legal opinion and debate on the legitimacy of enslavement and the proper relationship between Muslims and Muslims—and indeed between Muslims and Christians and other non-Muslims.

The legal opinions of Aḥmad Bābā both reflected and helped to shape the attitudes of West Africans on the legitimacy of enslavement and the permissibility of trading in slaves. In his important treatise, written in

1615 and subsequently elaborated upon, Aḥmad Bābā established himself as probably the most important Muslim commentator on slavery in West Africa before the early nineteenth century. His treatise outlined the categories of people who could be enslaved "legitimately."[4] His principal aims appear to have been to confirm earlier Islamic opinions that the only justification for enslavement was "unbelief," and he approached this complicated issue on both the personal level and the political. His ideas were developed at a time when there was considerable conflict among Muslim states in West and North Africa that was closely related to the conflict in the Mediterranean between Christians and Muslims. He clearly wanted to establish that racial factors were irrelevant in determining legitimacy. Moreover, he argued that it was illegal to enslave anyone who came from states that had Muslim governments or anyone who came from communities that paid tribute to Muslim states for protection. He specifically challenged the contemporary political situation that he encountered in West Africa during the last two decades of the sixteenth century and the first years of the seventeenth century. An understanding of this period in the history of West Africa provides a context for examining the peopling of the Americas through slavery.

Aḥmad Bābā's career overlapped with the Moroccan conquest and occupation of Songhay after 1591, which intensified the debate about the legitimacy of enslavement and about who could legally be held as a slave and who should be freed from captivity on religious grounds.[5] Although both Morocco and Songhay were Muslim states, Morocco's subjugation of Songhay revealed that legal opinion could be overridden for political reasons. Although the expulsion of Muslims from the Iberian peninsula in the late fifteenth century and the ongoing conflict between Spain and Portugal on the one hand and the Muslim states of North Africa on the other have been studied extensively, it is seldom recognized that the conflict among Muslims in the Maghreb was an integral part of this larger picture. The expansion of the Ottoman Porte to the western Mediterranean involved the conquest of Muslim states in an attempt to establish a pan-Islamic empire, but the Ottomans faced resistance from many Muslims, including the Sharifian dynasty of Morocco that was centered in Marrakesh.[6] The dynasty claimed descent from the Prophet Muhammad (as reflected in its designation as *shurfa*, pl. *sharif*), and hence they claimed to be the inheritors of the "caliphate" of the Prophet. On this basis, the regime not only resisted Ottoman hegemony and opposed the Qadiriyya

sufi brotherhood for its support of the Ottomans but also developed a
strategy to obtain the support of Muslim governments south of the Sahara
or overthrow any governments that opposed their claims to the caliphate.
According to Michel Abitol, the intention was to establish a large Muslim
state in the west that stretched from Borno in the region of Lake Chad to
the Atlantic and northward to include the Maghreb.[7] In resisting Ottoman
encroachment from Algiers, the Sharifian dynasty at times found an ally in
Spain, and after the defeat of the Spanish armada in 1588, in England.[8]
And, particularly ominous for the development of trans-Atlantic slavery,
the Sharifian dynasty relied on the export of sugarcane that was produced
on plantations worked by black slaves in the region of Sous for much of its
foreign exchange.[9]

As a member of the Timbuktu *'ulamā'* (scholarly community),
Aḥmad Bābā was adamantly opposed to the Sharifian invasion of
Songhay, and because he was also associated with the rival Qadiriyya
brotherhood, he was imprisoned and removed to Morocco along with
other captives who, without doubt, were devoted Muslims. Though he
was eventually released and returned to Timbuktu, his experience in captivity under conditions of dubious legality made him uniquely qualified
to write on matters of slavery, which is perhaps one reason that his opinions weighed so heavily in subsequent Muslim scholarship in West
Africa. Morocco's subjugation of Songhay pitted Muslim state against
Muslim state, and through captivity Aḥmad Bābā undoubtedly came into
contact with enslaved people of diverse backgrounds, an experience that
must have informed his commentary. Moreover, Songhay had promoted
enslavement of non-Muslims as state policy in the sixteenth century,
especially under Askia Dawud (1549–82), who settled large numbers of
enslaved people on agricultural estates along the middle Niger River and
also exported slaves to North Africa.[10] In both Morocco and Songhay,
therefore, the employment of slave labor on agricultural estates was part
of state policy. The importance of slave labor means that the legal opinions on who could be legitimately enslaved have special meaning in
understanding the role of ethnicity.

Aḥmad Bābā drew upon a long tradition of commentary on the subject of slavery, and he was well aware of the importance of slavery to
the economies of both Songhay and Morocco. Muslim scholars in West
Africa, as well as in North Africa, whom he quotes or summarizes,
had already examined the issue of legitimacy in enslavement. This legal

tradition predated European slaving on the African coast and the rise of the trans-Atlantic slave trade, and of course involved relations between Christians and Muslims, especially in the Mediterranean. Some scholars, and Aḥmad Bābā was one of them, argued that the non-Muslims in sub-Saharan Africa, although not Christians, should be treated in a similar fashion. That is, they were subject to enslavement, unless they were protected through the payment of a discriminatory tax *(jizya)*. It is argued here that this debate helped shape the contours of the European trade along the African coast that resulted in the settlement of enslaved Africans in the Americas. The connection between sugar production in southern Morocco in the region of Sous and the export of sugar to England especially has been noted above.[11]

An early fatwa on slavery in sub-Saharan Africa was issued by Makhluf b. 'Ali b. Salih al-Balbali of Tabalbala, who taught in Kano, Katsina, and Timbuktu, and who died sometime after 940/1533–34. He had studied in Fez and Walata and also had taught at Marrakesh and hence was well acquainted with the conditions of slavery in both sub-Saharan Africa and Morocco, and his work was well known among scholars in both the Sharifian state and in Songhay.[12] In his opinion the people from Muslim countries in sub-Saharan Africa, including Borno, Songhay, and the Hausa cities, should not be enslaved, and if individuals from these states were found in a state of captivity they should be freed without reservation. Another important influence on Aḥmad Bābā was his own relative, Mahmud b. 'Umar b. Muhammad Aqit, who was the *qadi* (judge) of Timbuktu between 1498 and 1548. He issued a legal opinion that anyone who had been enslaved and who was a Muslim or who came from a country that was considered to have embraced Islam voluntarily should be freed. Moreover, he accepted the testimony of the individual who was in a condition of slavery, placing the burden of proof on the owner, not the slave. According to John Hunwick, his ruling "required only that slaves should claim to be from such lands in order to be set free, without actually having to prove it."[13] These scholars wrote at a time when Songhay and Borno dominated much of the West African interior and were actively pursuing slave-raiding campaigns to their south in the quest of obtaining slaves who were clearly not Muslims. But in North Africa there was considerable confusion as to whether race and color of skin were enough to identify those who could be enslaved. As would later be true for the trans-Atlantic slave trade, those who had been enslaved were often identified with the place where they were first traded, in this case Songhay and Borno, which made it difficult to determine whether the enslaved were actually from those places or from somewhere else and only passing through these states. These early fatwa attempted to address the questions of legitimacy that affected the export of enslaved people to North Africa and the central lands of Islam, and their opinions were understood at a time when there was conflict in the Mediterranean between Muslims and Christians that often resulted in enslavement of the proponents of the opposing religion, and in the case of politics among Muslim states inevitably resulted in the enslavement of some people who were in fact Muslims. It is argued here that the debate among Muslims in West and North Africa with respect to sub-Saharan Africa was one factor that restricted the export of enslaved Africans to the Americas, with the result that enslavement for the trans-Atlantic slave trade was largely confined to the coastal areas of West Africa, where Muslims were absent or in a distinct minority and hence usually not affected.

In 1615, after returning to Timbuktu as a free man, Aḥmad Bābā set out his observations on the measures that needed to be established for the protection of Muslims from unjust enslavement. Building on earlier scholarship, which he cites, he addressed the issues of who could be enslaved and under what conditions. While condemning war between Muslim states, and specifically such unprovoked invasions as Morocco's of Songhay, he nonetheless condemned states whose Muslim rulers were lax in the defense of Islam and who tolerated "pagan" beliefs and relied on slave armies that readily enslaved Muslims. This criticism also appears to have been leveled at Sharifian Morocco. In his defense of Muslims in sub-Saharan Africa, moreover, he wrote a text that became part of the curriculum of Islamic education on matters of slavery and ethnicity for subsequent generations. Later criticisms of the militarist regimes of the Bambara states of Segu and Kaarta and of the Hausa states of Gobir, Kano, and Katsina focused on their tolerance of non-Muslim practices and their internecine warfare that inevitably resulted in the enslavement of Muslims, even though these states relied on Muslim merchants and sought the advice and services of an urban 'ulamā'.[14] These later critiques, in the tradition of Islamic scholarship, specifically referred to the legal authority of Aḥmad Bābā and the various authorities upon whom he relied.

FIGURE 1.1: *Sankore Mosque in Timbuktu. The mosque served as a center of Islamic scholarship for scholars like Aḥmad Bābā. Photograph by John Hunwick.*

Ethnic Categorization and the Slave Trade

This legal tradition was clearly set within the framework of Islamic scholarship and hence was largely irrelevant to the Atlantic world and the settlement of the Americas by enslaved Africans, but the categorization of
West Africa in ethnic and religious terms reflected a reality that seems to
have influenced the trans-Atlantic slave trade in several respects. First, the
ethnic identification of Africans was also a feature of the Atlantic world,
and there was concern to justify enslavement on the basis of legal and religious precedents that recognized ethnicity and race as factors in determining legitimacy. It seems that the assumptions underlying the identification
of ethnicity and religion as factors in justifying slavery were carried down
the Atlantic coast of Africa in the sixteenth and early seventeenth centuries.
Aḥmad Bābā formulated his views on the problem around the same time
that Christian theologians were also attempting to establish the legitimacy
of enslaving Africans. Father Baltasar Barreira, for example, wrote a treatise justifying the enslavement of Africans on the coast of Sierra Leone
in 1606 that also explained servility in terms of ethnicity and religion,
although it is virtually certain that he was unaware of the debate among
Muslims in the interior.[15] Nonetheless, it is significant that in the early
period of European trade along the African coast, a large proportion of the
enslaved population that was removed from Africa came from this region
where Muslims were absent or present only as itinerant merchants. In
absolute numbers the size of this population was relatively small, but those
who were taken to the Americas largely came from the upper Guinea Coast
in this period.[16]

Other contemporaries of Aḥmad Bābā, especially Alonso de Sandoval,
clearly recognized the ethnic diversity of enslaved Africans as well as the
presence of some Muslims among that population.[17] In his important study
of the backgrounds of the enslaved African population of Spanish America,
Sandoval also noted the ethnic backgrounds of the enslaved population
and discussed status in terms of ethnicity. Like Barreira, however, it seems
that Sandoval was also unaware of the debate among Muslims. The fact
that Muslims were among the enslaved revealed that the legal status of
individuals who were Muslims had been violated and that the legal network that had been designed to protect Muslims was not always effective.
Nonetheless, it should be recognized that both Muslim and Christian the-
orists were expounding similar concerns about the legality of enslavement
on the basis of religion and ethnicity, and the use of ethnic labels was often

similar enough to suggest a common basis for information on the origins and identification of Africans by ethnicity.

In his treatise, Aḥmad Bābā noted "that whoever now comes to you from the group called Mossi, or Gurma, or Busa or Borgu or Dagomba or Kotokoli or Yoruba or Tunbughu or Bubu [Bobo] or Karmu [?]—all of these are unbelievers, remaining in their unbelief until now," and hence their enslavement was legitimate. In one of his replies that elaborated on his treatise, Aḥmad Bābā identified those people whom he thought were undisputedly Muslims and those he considered non-Muslims, many of whom also had some Muslims resident among them. His list of Muslims included numerous, perhaps most, of the Mande patronymic clans, and hence his conception of ethnicity is also worthy of commentary.

> Praise be to God. I shall set forth for you the tribes of Muslims. Know that the best of the Muslims are Suwari and Darami, Fofana, Fadika, Dkukkur [Dukkure?], Kaba, Silla, Saysi [Cissé], Kalugh, Jaghayti [Diakhite], Jaghu, Sisaghu [Cissoko], Kakku, Ghanji, Saghanghu [Saghanughu], Kasam, Ghayas. Following them Ja, Samu, Nujadi, Andaw, Kay, Halu, Fay, Saghu, Tàk, Sunburu, Saghunbun, Kanabun, Bayan, Kayta [Keita], Wayan, Kayan, Jayb, Tur, Tarawari [Tarawiri], Baru, Kurugha, War.tay, Sughusu, Baghaka, Kamunti, Bafiri, Witrasib, Summir, Nakabi, Kunati [Konaté], Fasar.r, Suri [Sori], Wataka, Jighabi, Sanuka, Karma, Kuruba, Mara, Bankari, Bafay, Kusira, Kurahu, Kanbalu, Kanbal, Munud, Jawn, Tanu, Saghnu, Sanuka, Nayta, the makhzan tribe, Kabit, Jawar [Diawara], Kubati, Datiba, K.ruma'u, Kunnati, Kulkali, Danyugh, Danba, Katayugh, Kutuba, Sakalyugh, Sakaliba, Funt, Birthi, Janta, Dabu, Danbali, the tribes of Jani [Jenne], which are Wankara in the speech of Timbuktu, Nubughu [?], Nubi, Baghayghu [Baghayogho], Baghabughu, Baghba, Baluyugh, Balaba, Farala, Mati, T.k.r., Kanti, Dumayigh, Dumabu, Batayugh, Fatab, the tribes of Fullan, Jaghiti, Sidibi, Sankara.

The detail of his commentary extends beyond narrowly conceived definitions of ethnicity. His concern was to provide a means of identifying anybody who should not be enslaved, so that anyone who claimed an identity that was on his list might have recourse to what was considered to be wrongful enslavement.

Similarly, Aḥmad Bābā named those people whom he considered to be non-Muslims or whose Islamic practice was suspect and hence should not be protected against enslavement. He observed that there were Muslims among many of these people, reflecting the fact that there was a widespread network of Muslim-dominated trade in West Africa into areas that were considered "pagan" (majus).

> Know that Banbanu/i [Bambara] are more populous than all
> other majus, and closer to the lands of Islam. Tuma are majus,
> as are T.n.da, S.fi, Tasari, Kal.y.ni, Bunbun, Karunka, Yubu,
> some of whom are Muslims, but most are majus, Bulunka,
> so also Buna, Dak.n.b [Dagomba ?], Kur.si, Kay, Zaraklu,
> Turu. This is what I know about the tribes of the majus. As
> for the regions [aqalim], they contain many of them. Then
> I will detail [them]. And the first of the lands of Malli, border-
> ing the Arabs are Kat.k [K.n.k = Kingui], Baghunu. Among
> the towns of Kinki [Kingui] is Zara [Diara], the town of the
> wazir called Fari, who is one of the ministers of the sultan
> of Malli, under his sovereignty are Falka and Kusata and
> Kayaka [Kaniaga]. Those among the Arabs bordering them
> are the Awlad 'Uqba and Awlad Yunus and others. Among
> the towns of Kayaka is S.rin—these are all Muslims, they
> have not been mixed with smiths—Habak, Dami, J.yaghti,
> Kanti [who are] tribes of unbelievers—except for slaves
> [mamalik]. Other regions are Banbuk in the middle of which
> is a town called Jagha (or Jaghi), under whose dominion
> are twenty villages/towns, all of them Muslim unmixed with
> any unbeliever. There is also Kala, which is interpenetrated
> by Banbara [Bambara] who dwell there. Similarly Tunduki
> and Bal and Sibd.k [Sibiridugu?] and Kurbuduk, Jawma,
> Sankara, Dantala, Kamakara, Karaka, Buri [Bouré?]. As
> for Suruba and Kayara and Jafun [Diafunu] and Kunjur
> [Gundioro?] towards the land of S.n.b.lay, they are all
> Muslims in many lands [?], and in them are many Muslims
> and its habitation is a village, and [there are] types
> of unbelievers whose number is only known by God.

The ethnic terms in Aḥmad Bābā's writings and evident in later texts following his influence recognized a series of dichotomies—between the Central and Western Sudan, between Muslims and non-Muslims, between Fulbe and Bambara, between Bambara and Mandingo/Malinke, and between Fulani and Habe/Hausa in the Central Sudan.

While many of the terms that he used have not yet been identified, a few ethnic labels were also used in the Americas, thereby suggesting a link between the theoretical discussion within West Africa and the enslaved population in the Americas. The common ethnic terms included "Bambara," "Yoruba," "Mandinke," "Hausa," "Fulbe/Fulani" and others as well, which were clearly carried over into the nomenclature of the trans-Atlantic trade. The overlap with European terminology suggests an influence from this theoretical discussion whose significance has often been overlooked. Various studies in different parts of Latin America have identified the terms used for ethnic designations, but without noting the parallel between Muslim terminology in some cases and the lack of correspondence in others.[18] The extent to which the enslaved carried these distinctions into the diaspora is unclear, but there is considerable evidence that Muslims distinguished among themselves on the basis of ethnic categories that conformed to Aḥmad Bābā's terminology.[19]

In the seventeenth and eighteenth centuries, Islamic schools across western Africa taught the principles of slavery that derived from Aḥmad Bābā and the scholars to whom he referred, which suggests considerable continuity in thinking about the relationship between ethnicity and slavery in West Africa. Much of the educational system was associated with the Qadiriyya brotherhood with which he identified.[20] In the eighteenth century, for example, the Tuareg scholar, Jibrīl b. 'Umar, relied on this earlier tradition in advocating jihad to confront the violation of the free status of Muslims. His student, 'Uthmān dan Fodio, along with his son Muḥammad Bello and his brother Abdullahi dan Fodio, were strongly influenced by this literary tradition, and in their turn revitalized the arguments of Aḥmad Bābā in justifying jihad to protect Muslims from wrongful enslavement and to sanction the enslavement of the enemies of jihad, even if those enemies were Muslims. The many references in the writings of Sokoto leadership reveal the extent of the intellectual and ideological debt to the tradition of scholarship epitomized by Aḥmad Bābā.[21] This scholarly tradition had profound consequences for the later imposition of Islamic rule. Governments that were in fact ruled by

Muslims were declared apostate, just as Askia Muḥammad had earlier pronounced Sunni Ali's regime in Songhay in 1492–93 and al-Mansur had denounced the government of Songhay in 1591.

Military action was considered justified if it imposed a government that was perceived to be Muslim in its orthodoxy. As Islamic governments were reestablished in the western Sudan after the late seventeenth century, it became necessary to justify the results of victories that entailed large-scale enslavement, especially enslavement of freeborn Muslims. The parallel between the invasion of Muslim Songhay by Muslim Morocco and the jihad of 'Uthmān dan Fodio in his invasion of Muslim Borno revealed the contradictions in linking enslavement with religion. In both cases, Muslims attacked Muslim governments. Aḥmad Bābā denounced the enslavement of Muslims in the wake of the Moroccan invasion of Songhay, and Muḥammad al-Kānemī accused Sokoto of undermining legitimate Muslim government.[22] Borno had long maintained diplomatic and commercial relations with the Ottoman Empire and other Muslim states, and indeed had been an ally of Sharifian Morocco against Songhay in the 1590s. The 'ulamā' were fully conversant with the Islamic debate over slavery, but the intolerance of non-Muslim practices should be noted.

Hence relatively few Muslims were taken as slaves to Spanish America, or anywhere else in the Americas before the nineteenth century, despite the legacy of Christian and Muslim hostility and the struggle for control of Iberia and the coast of the Maghreb. In the sixteenth century, many people were enslaved along the upper Guinea Coast, and slaves were still acquired from this region throughout the whole period of the slave trade. Indeed, both off the coast at the Cape Verde Islands and also in the Bissau estuary and elsewhere along the coast, a Portuguese patois often served as the commercial language. But in the seventeenth and eighteenth centuries, it appears that relatively few enslaved people actually came from this area, especially after the dissolution of the dual Spanish and Portuguese monarchy. The slave trade voyage database compiled by David Eltis and his associates suggests an apparent anomaly in that northeast Brazil appears to have received a sizeable number of people from Senegambia in the eighteenth century, although no such concentration of Senegambians is recorded elsewhere in Spanish America, except in the Mississippi delta. In the nineteenth century, Muslims from the interior of the Bight of Benin became a significant factor in Bahia; their presence is particularly noticeable from the late eighteenth century, although this is not reflected in the voyage database.

It is important to observe that the majority of those enslaved Africans from West Africa who landed in the Americas, including Latin America, in the seventeenth and eighteenth centuries were not from Muslim areas, despite the presence of Mandingo and others who can be identified as Muslims. The largest number of people came from areas very near the coast, or on the coast itself, in areas south of the Muslim savanna.[23] Despite the likely inaccuracies in the voyage database, it can still be said that the enslaved came from three parts of the West African coast, including the interior of the Bight of Biafra, the Gbe-speaking region of the Bight of Benin, and the Akan area of the Gold Coast. This identification allows us to understand the backgrounds of the majority of West Africans from non-Muslim areas, although both the Akan and Gbe areas were connected by trade with Muslim areas, and Muslim merchants and craftsmen were known at the coast in the seventeenth century, if not earlier still. The history of Islam and Muslim traders in these areas is complex; Asante, Dahomey, and Oyo developed specific policies of their own in relation to Muslims. In Asante, by the end of the eighteenth century, Muslims were involved in the state chancery although the state was decidedly not Muslim, nor was the dominant Akan population. Moreover, the slave trade was heavily concentrated in areas in which people understood the same languages, or dialects thereof, and enslavement was a product of political struggles that were reasonably well known. Hence people came from areas in which there was relative ease of communication, and the issues that had resulted in enslavement were understood. The political history of the three most affected areas is relatively well known and attests to the importance of this linguistic factor, which also to a great extent reflected cultural similarities and hence laid the basis for ethnic identification across the Atlantic. The instructions of Aḥmad Bābā's treatise were in effect realized; people in non-Muslim areas and non-Muslims in general were more likely to be enslaved than Muslims. It appears that fewer people came from the interior than might otherwise be expected, at least in the seventeenth and eighteenth centuries. This preference within West Africa had the effect of restricting the trade, confining the victims to people who lived relatively close to the coast in the Bight of Benin and neighboring areas especially. It is these people who came to be known in Latin America as "Mina," and largely were Gbe-speaking people, but also probably some Akan and Yoruba.

In the first three-quarters of the seventeenth century there were very few West Africans transported across the Atlantic, relative to the numbers of the late seventeenth century and the greatly increased scale of the eighteenth century. Each European country involved affected the course of the trade, depending upon which colonies in the Americas it was attempting to supply, and the possibilities of acquiring slaves from different portions of the African coast. An examination of the origins of the enslaved population from West Africa cannot yet be done with precision, but it is still possible to separate West Africa from West Central Africa for purposes of analysis. An exploration of the movement of West Africans in terms of ethnic origins and the related political history thereby sets the parameters for future study when more detailed information on the movement of the enslaved population becomes available.

The areas of West Africa from which the enslaved population came included Senegambia and the upper Guinea Coast, north of modern Liberia, where there were a great variety of languages spoken, and where there was a strong and increasingly stronger Islamic influence that reflected the long tradition of Islam in the interior, where the empire Songhay held sway until its collapse in the 1590s. Despite this political upheaval, the Islamic tradition continued, and indeed expanded, through the operation of extensive commercial networks that stretched to the coast. By the eighteenth century, the Muslim presence was complicated by the development of a militant reform movement among Muslims that led to the outbreak of jihad in Futa Jallon, in the immediate interior of the upper Guinea Coast and Sierra Leone. Another jihad erupted in the Senegal valley, first in Futa Bondu and then in Futa Toro. In the Americas, people from this region can be identified quite early; material from the seventeenth century demonstrates a great variety of ethnic designations, many from areas immediately on the coast itself but some people from the interior, including Muslims, who were usually referred to as Mandingo, with variations in spelling.[24]

A second area from which enslaved Africans came included the region of the Gold Coast and Bight of Benin, often referred to in Latin America as the Mina Coast, the name originally derived from the Portuguese trading castle at Elmina ("the mine," from the Portuguese name Castelo de São Jorge da Mina), reflecting the importance of gold in trade, the gold coming from alluvial deposits in the forest region inhabited by the Akan, who constituted several small, centralized states and who in the eighteenth century were largely consolidated into the kingdom of Asante. Although these states were decidedly not Muslim, there was nonetheless Muslim influence through trade with the interior and because of the settlement of Muslim colonies in Asante, especially in its northern provinces that were conquered in the middle of the eighteenth century. In the seventeenth century, this region was a net importer of enslaved people, some of whom were brought along the coast by European slavers, where slaves were sold for gold. The wars of the first half of the eighteenth century, which resulted in the consolidation of Asante, reversed this flow, and in this period, large numbers of enslaved people who were captured during the Akan wars were sent to the Americas.

Many of the enslaved people from the Mina Coast came from the area east of the Volta River, the most important departure point being the beach at Ouidah, which witnessed the export of hundreds of thousands of people in the late seventeenth and eighteenth centuries. Ouidah was the most important port, first for the small kingdom of Huedah, whose capital was at Savi, a few kilometers inland, and then as the principal port for the larger kingdom of Allada, centered to the west of Lake Nikoue, which was fed by the Weme River and flowed into the sea along the lagoons behind the beach, entering the sea at Lagos in the east and Grand Popo in the west. As Robin Law has demonstrated, this lagoon system explains the location of a series of departure points for slaves in the Bight of Benin, from Petit Popo through Ouidah, Porto Novo, Badagry and Lagos, to mention only the most important.[25] When each of these ports was important in the trade, moreover, is explained through a consideration of the political history of the region, which focuses on the rise and fall of Allada, Dahomey, and Oyo. In the wars and campaigns that marked this political history, many people were enslaved and sent to the Americas, and the overwhelming majority of these people spoke one or more of the Gbe languages, including Ewe, Fon, Allada, and Mahi.[26] It should be noted, further, that wars in the Akan interior and in the Gbe region overlapped and effectively formed a continuous and contiguous power struggle, with the dominance of Asante in the west, Dahomey in the center, and Oyo in the eastern portions of this broad region.

The final area of West Africa from which a sizeable number of people came was the Bight of Biafra, and specifically the ports of Elem Kalabari in the Niger delta and Old Calabar on the Cross River in the seventeenth century, and especially from Bonny in the Niger delta in the eighteenth century. All three ports had a common interior, connected by river, which was settled principally by Igbo- and Ibibio-speaking peoples. While some people from this region were brought to Latin America in the seventeenth century, if not earlier still, most came in the eighteenth century, and often indirectly in English ships via Jamaica or Barbados, and from there to Vera Cruz, Cartagena, Portobelo, and then onward. The region of the interior of the Bight of Biafra was different from the areas further west in two important respects. First, there was no Muslim presence, as far as known, and second, there were no major centralized states in the area; rather, trade and society were organized through male secret societies that provided a network connecting the major ports with the Aro network of the interior.[27]

For reasons that are not clear, large areas of West Africa remained beyond the pull of the trans-Atlantic slave trade, a pattern that should not be overlooked in studying the movement of people across the Atlantic and the corresponding impact on West Africa. Hence the region between Oyo and the lower Niger River, including the Kingdom of Benin, was not heavily involved in the slave trade to the coast in the seventeenth and eighteenth centuries, while the heartland of the Igbo and Ibibio region became heavily involved in the trade only in the course of the eighteenth century; despite the presence of people identified as "Caravalí," "Carabalí," or "Calabar," the region was involved only marginally previously. Similarly, there were many areas near the coast in what is now Liberia and Cote d'Ivoire that were outside the Atlantic slave trade, and when involved at all were focused on several points near the mouths of rivers from the interior, and then for relatively brief periods.

The relative constraints placed on the trans-Atlantic trade by Muslim interpretations of legitimacy seem to have become less effective in the eighteenth century. There are two signs of this shift. First, the greatly increased demand for slaves in the Americas encouraged those who did not share Muslim views of legitimacy, and consequently, it was more difficult for Muslim scholars and legal structures to influence the contours of trade. Second, the reaction against the perceived illegality of enslaving those who were Muslims prompted a militancy that erupted in jihad, initially in the Senegambia region, and eventually spreading to the Central Sudan by the early nineteenth century. In this conflict, there was room for the enslavement of Muslims by those who opposed Muslim influence, since the non-Muslims involved in the slave trade were not interested in protecting the status of Muslims as free persons, and as in the period of Songhay, Muslims were enslaved if they opposed jihad. However, the great expansion in the numbers of enslaved Africans leaving West Africa, especially in the

TABLE 1.1. Ethnic Designations of Slaves in Bahia, 1775–1815

Designations	Number	Percent
Bight of Benin	44.3	
Gbe (Jeje)	104	
Yoruba (Nagô)	100	
Mina	40	
Mina Coast (Costa da Mina)	15	
Benin	4	
Savalu	1	
Central Sudan		10.6
Hausa	50	
Nupe (Tapa)	12	
Bariba/Borgu (Barbá)	1	
West Central Africa		45.1
Angola	167	
Benguela	93	
Congo	4	
São Tomé	3	
Mondubi	1	
Gabon	1	
Subtotal 596		100
Other		
Heathen from the Coast (Gentio da Costa)	270	
African (Africano)	13	
Coastal (da Costa)	2	
Total 881		

Source: Maria Inês Côrtes de Oliveira, "Retrouver une identité: Jeux sociaux des Africains de Bahia: (vers 1750-vers 1890)" (Ph.D diss., Sorbonne, 1992), 98.

second half of the eighteenth century, was still largely confined to non-Muslims, including Igbo, Yoruba, Akan, and others. This increase in the number of enslaved Africans from the Bight of Benin is reflected in data from Bahia (see table 1.1), where the proportion of slaves arriving from

West Central Africa fell dramatically by the end of the eighteenth century, declining to approximately 45 percent of individuals whose ethnicity can be identified. Between 1775 and 1815, the proportion of slaves coming from the Bight of Benin was 55 percent of the population whose ethnic background can be established, and of these Muslims from the interior of the Bight of Benin comprised at least 10 percent, and the proportion would rise even more in the nineteenth century.[28]

Clearly, not all ethnic labels used in the Americas were derived from the Muslim discourse within West Africa, but it is instructive that some were. Many of the terms for ethnicity along the upper Guinea Coast have been constant over time, as demonstrated by P. E. H. Hair, and therefore reflect local conditions in areas largely beyond Muslim influence and observation.[29] Similarly, the coastal peoples of the Bight of Benin and Bight of Biafra who comprised the large majority of enslaved Africans sent to the Americas in the eighteenth century were from areas of little if any Muslim contact or influence. This applies especially to the people in the interior of the Bight of Biafra, where Igbo and Ibibio appear to have constituted most of the enslaved population, but it also characterized the enslaved population leaving Bight of Benin, where various Gbe-language groups, including Ewe, Allada, Fon, and Mahi, were most common before the middle of the eighteenth century, and thereafter Yoruba as well. As argued here and supported by the work of specialists, these people were generally known as Mina. It is instructive that in Brazil and Hispanic America, those who spoke Yoruba and are now referred to as Yoruba were called Nagô and Lucumí, respectively, neither term being known to Muslims, who called these people by the term that has now become standard—Yoruba—as Aḥmad Bābā's treatise of 1615 establishes.[30] By contrast, the term *Mina* is not found in Aḥmad Bābā's writing, and hence like Nagô and Lucumí arose in the context of trans-Atlantic slavery. The term generally fell into disuse in favor of more specific linguistic designations. This nomenclature highlights a feature of the slave trade to the Americas that has been often overlooked— the important role of Islam in shaping the contours of slavery, especially in limiting the involvement of West Africa in the movement of slaves to Latin America in the seventeenth and eighteenth centuries.

As is clear from other studies of ethnicity in the Americas, enslaved Africans sometimes were clustered in such significant numbers that ethnic affiliation was a factor in identity and community. This ethnic factor was slippery in its application and significance, but still related to the African background and the necessary transformations imposed by slavery and migration. This study has isolated one cohort of the enslaved population, specifically Muslims and more generally people who came from areas dominated by Muslims in the interior of West Africa. In considering this factor, it can be seen that people were categorized on the basis of ethnicity, which was being used as a rough guide to determine who could be legitimately enslaved and who should not. This use of ethnicity as a means of identification was independent of the process of ethnic reformulation and interaction in the Americas under slavery, although it is suggested here that interpretations of ethnic transformation in the Americas emphasizing creative adaptation under slavery need to be placed in context. The scholarship of Aḥmad Bābā relates the issue of ethnicity to slavery in West Africa, demonstrating the importance of both literary efforts and self-regulation in matters relating to society and law. Moreover, the erudition apparent in the scholarship of Songhay predates the rapid expansion in slave-based production in the Americas.

Enslaved Muslims were taken to the Americas, despite Aḥmad Bābā's legal opinions, but generally the interior of West Africa was underrepresented in the slave registers of the Americas. Some enslaved Muslims, mostly men, did slip through the ideological net, as demonstrated in the concentration of Muslims in Bahia in the early nineteenth century, but in general slaves were retained within the Muslim interior of West Africa or sold into and across the Sahara to other Muslim lands. As Aḥmad Bābā's involvement in the slavery debate makes clear, discussions of slavery and mechanisms of resistance were confined not only to the Americas but were topics of wide concern in Africa as well. Most enslaved Muslims in the Americas came from relatively cosmopolitan and educated backgrounds, and frequently individuals had traveled widely within West Africa and sometimes to other parts of the Muslim world. Moreover, these were places where slavery was common and legal norms well established, if not always applied. The debate over slavery stretched back into the medieval period and the political struggle in Iberia, and it occurred in both western Europe and its overseas domains and in Muslim regions, including Morocco and parts of sub-Saharan Africa. The Atlantic world and the Islamic world of North and West Africa were to some extent isolated from each other, which is reflected in the terms of reference and nature of the discourse over slavery, which in West Africa derived from Islam and was understood in the context of ethnicity.

APPENDIX

Aḥmad Bābā and the Ethics of Slavery

In this section, the Muslim scholar from Timbuktu, Aḥmad Bābā, provides us with a legal opinion outlining the legitimate grounds for the enslavement of Africans in 1615. He argues that those who came from specific countries that had long had Muslim governments or who were identified with specific ethnic groups that were known to be Muslim could not be enslaved, and that the onus of proof in establishing the legitimacy of enslavement rested with the purchaser of slaves, not with the slaves themselves. In attempting to protect Muslims from enslavement, Aḥmad Bābā provides one of the earliest descriptions of ethnicity in the interior of West Africa. The sections here are from his Mi'raj al-su'ud, which was one of several exchanges with other Muslim scholars on the question of slavery.

The Ladder of Ascent towards Grasping the Law concerning Transported Blacks

Praise be to God, the Lord of the worlds and may His blessing and peace be upon the Lord of the Messengers.

Thereafter, Says the one in need of his Lord, Aḥmad Bābā b. *al-ḥajj* Ahmad—may God Most High inspire him with right guidance and direct him to that which pleases Him and draw him close to Him.... Three years ago, or a little more, there reached me a question from the land of Tuwāt.... Now I had the intention of writing about the matter at the time, but something prevented me from so doing until it passed into the category of things forgotten. And now there arrived at the end of this year, the year 1023 [1614–15], a request for a reply to it....

You asked: "What have you to say concerning slaves imported from lands whose people have been established to be Muslims, such as Bornu, 'Afnu, Kano, Gao and Katsina, and others among whom adherence to Islam is widely acknowledged? Is it permissible to own them or not?" [The Reply]: "Be it known—may God Most High grant us and you success—that the people of these lands are, as you have said, Muslims, except for 'Afnu whose location I do not know, nor have I heard of it. However, close to each of these is a land in which there are unbelievers (*kafara*) whom the Muslim people of these lands make raids on. Some of them, as is well known, are under their protection and pay *kharaj* [tribute paid by subject people], according to what has come to our ears. Sometimes the sultans of these lands are in a state of discord the one with the other, and the sultan of one land attacks the other and takes whatever captives he can, they being Muslims. These captives, free Muslims, are then sold—to God we belong and to Him shall we return! This is commonplace among them in their lands. The people of Katsina attack Kano, and others do likewise, though they speak one tongue and their languages are united and their way of life similar. The only thing that distinguishes them is that some are born Muslims and others are born unbelievers. This is what confuses the situation concerning those who are brought to them, so that they do not know the true situation of the one imported."

You said: "It is known that according to the *shari'a* the sole reason for being owned is unbelief (*kufr*). Thus whoever purchases an unbeliever is allowed to own him. In the contrary case he is not. Conversion to Islam subsequent to the existence of the aforementioned condition has no effect on continued ownership." The Reply is that this is so, provided he is not one with whom a pact has been made, or who possesses [a contract of] protection (*dhimma*). There is no way round that.

You asked: "Were these aforementioned lands belonging to the Muslims of the Sudan conquered and their people enslaved in a state of unbelief, while their conversion to Islam occurred subsequently, so there is no harm [in owning them], or not?" The Reply is that they converted to Islam without anyone conquering them, like the people of Kano, Katsina, Bornu and Songhay. We never heard that anyone conquered them before their conversion to Islam. Among them are some who have long been Muslims, like the people of Borno and Songhay.

You said: "One of the *qadis* [judges] of the Sudan reported
that the imam [ruler] who conquered them whilst they were
unbelievers chose to spare them [as slaves]." I say: "This is
something we have never heard of, nor has [any information
about it] reached us. So ask this Sudani *qadi* who this imam
was and at what time he conquered their land, and which land
he conquered? Let him specify all this to you. His statement
is very close to being devoid of truth. If you investigate now,
you will not find anyone who will confirm the truth of what
he said. What is based upon what he says, therefore, is not
to be given consideration. God Most High knows best.
Look at the statement of Wal'l-Din Ibn Khaldun concerning
the people of Bornu, which will be given later, if God Most
High wills. You asked if this is correct or not. The reply is
that in all probability it is incorrect."

You asked: "How could this be so in regard to the
people of Bornu, which is the abode of their sultanate, and
people are frequently brought to us from there. Are they
slaves or not?" The Reply is they are free Muslims, who
converted to Islam long ago. However, close to their borders
are unbelievers whom they raid and take hold of and sell,
as we have said before. . . .

You said: "Similarly he whose land [of origin] is unknown
and whose status is unclear, and it is not known whether
his enslavement preceded his conversion to Islam or not: is
it permissible to buy him and sell him without investigation?
Or is investigation mandatory, or is it [merely] recommended?"
The Reply is that you know that the cause of enslavement
is unbelief, and the unbelievers of the Sudan are like any
other unbelievers in this regard—Jews, Christians, Persians,
Berbers or others whose persistence in unbelief rather than
Islam has been established. . . . This is proof that there is
no difference between any unbelievers in this regard.
Whoever is enslaved in a state of unbelief may rightly be
owned, whoever he is, as opposed to those of all groups
who converted to Islam of their own free will, such as the
people of Bornu, Kano, Songhay, Katsina, Gobir and Mali
and some of [the people of] Zakzak [Zaria]. They are all

free Muslims who may not be enslaved under any circumstance. So also are the majority of the Fulani, except, so we have heard, a group living near Jenne who are said to be unbelievers. We do not know if [their unbelief] is ancestral or occurred through apostasy. Indeed, disputes occur between them and they raid one another. . . .

We will add another rule for you, that is that whoever now comes to you from the group called Mossi, or Gurma, or Busa or Borgu, or Dagomba or Kotokoli, or Yoruba, or Tombo, or Bobo or K.rmu [?]—all of these are unbelievers, remaining in their unbelief until now. Similarly Kumbe, except for a few of the people of Hombori and Da'anka, though their Islam is shallow, so there is no harm in possessing them without posing questions. This is the rule regarding these groups. God Most High knows best and is the Best Judge.

Let this be the end of what we attempt in *The Ladder of Ascent towards Grasping the Law concerning Transported Blacks*, or if you wish call it *The Exposition and Explanation concerning the Varieties of Transported Black Africans*. May God seal you and us with faith and make us among the folk of goodliness, through the grace of the lord of the sons of 'Adnan [i.e., the Prophet Muhammad]— may God bless him and his Family and his Companions, so long as day follows night, and so long as man finds joy in achieving his desire. Our last prayer is that praise be to God the Lord of the Worlds, and may God bless our master Muhammad, His Prophet, and grant him peace, likewise all those who follow him in goodliness to the Day of Judgment.

Dated Monday 10 Muharram 1024 [February 9, 1615], at the hand of the compiler Aḥmad Bābā b. Ahmad b. Ahmad b. 'Umar b. Muhammad Aqit— may God inspire in him right guidance.

John Hunwick and Fatima Harrak, *Mi'raj al-su'ud: Ahmad Baba's Replies on Slavery* (Rabat: Institut des Etudes Africaines, Université Mohamed V, 2000), 21–24, 27, 39–40.

NOTES

1. For a discussion of the changing meanings of *Mina*, see Gwendolyn
   Midlo Hall, "African Ethnicities and the Meanings of 'Mina,'" in
   Trans-Atlantic Dimensions of Ethnicity in the African Diaspora, ed. Paul E.
   Lovejoy and David V. Trotman (London: Continuum, 2003), 65–81;
   Paul E. Lovejoy, "Ethnic Designations of the Slave Trade and the
   Reconstruction of the History of Trans-Atlantic Slavery," in ibid., 9–42;
   Mary Karasch, "Guiné, Mina, Angola, and Benguela: African and
   Crioulo Nations in Central Brazil, 1780–1820," in *Enslaving
   Connections: Changing Cultures of Africa and Brazil during the Era of
   Slavery*, ed. José C. Curto and Paul E. Lovejoy (Amherst, NY:
   Humanities Books, 2004), 163–86; Olabiyi Yai, "Texts of Enslavement:
   Fon and Yoruba Vocabularies from Eighteenth- and Nineteenth-
   Century Brazil," in *Identity in the Shadow of Slavery*, ed. Paul E.
   Lovejoy (London: Continuum, 2000), 102–12.

2. This analysis is based on the voyage database of David Eltis, Stephen
   Behrendt, David Richardson, and Herbert Klein, *The Atlantic Slave
   Trade: A Database in CD-Rom* (Cambridge: Cambridge University
   Press, 1999). The database is being revised and expanded, which
   will affect the analysis here but is unlikely to alter the general
   proportions of the trade.

3. Paul E. Lovejoy, "Islam, Slavery, and Political Transformation in
   West Africa: Constraints on the Trans-Atlantic Slave Trade," *Revue
   française d'histoire d'outre mer* 89, nos. 336–37 (2002): 247–82.

4. For the writings of Aḥmad Bābā, see John Hunwick and Fatima
   Harrak, *Mi'raj al-su'ud: Ahmad Baba's Replies on Slavery* (Rabat:
   Institut des Etudes Africaines, Université Mohamed V, 2000).
   (The quotations in this chapter are taken from this work.) Also see
   Bernard and Michelle Jacobs, "The *Mi'rāj*: A Legal Treatise on
   Slavery by Aḥmad Bābā," in *Slaves and Slavery in Muslim Africa*, ed.
   John Ralph Willis (London: Frank Cass, 1985), 1:125–59. See also
   Elias N. Saad, *Social History of Timbuktu: The Role of Muslim Scholars
   and Notables, 1400–1900* (Cambridge: Cambridge University
   Press, 1983). Excerpts are also to be found in John Hunwick and
   Eve Troutt Powell, eds., *The African Diaspora in the Mediterranean
   Lands of Islam* (Princeton: Markus Wiener, 2002).

5. In addition to the *Miʿrāj al-suʿud*, Aḥmad Bābā also wrote *Nayl al-ibtihāj bi-taṭrīz al-dībāj and Tāj al-dīn fī mā yajib ʿalā al-mulūk*; see Hunwick and Harrak, *Ahmad Baba's Replies on Slavery*. For a brief biography, see John Hunwick, "A New Source for the Biography of Ahmad Baba al-Tinbukti," *Bulletin of the School of Oriental and African Studie*s 28 (1964): 569–93.

6. The attempt to unify Morocco was partially a response to the crisis in Iberia in the fifteenth century. Initially promoted by Imam al-Djazuli (d. 1465), the movement advocated no cooperation with Christians and from a dozen *zawiya* (retreats of the Sufi brotherhood) and *ribat* (frontier fortresses) resisted Portuguese encroachment after the conquest of Ceuta in 1415 and Tanger in 1437; see Michel Abitol, *Tombouctou et les Arma: De la conquête marocaine du Soudan nigérien en 1591 à l'hégémonie de l'Empire Peul du Macina en 1833* (Paris: Maisonneuve & LaRose, 1979), 35–39.

7. As sharif, they claimed to possess *baraka*, or blessing, that could only be inherited by blood from the prophet; the sharif had been invited to Dra' in Morocco in the twelfth century and were widely respected; see Abitol, *Tombouctou et les Arma*, 35.

8. Ibid., 40–46.

9. P. Berthier, *Les anciennes sucreries du Maroc et leurs réseaux hydrauliques* (Rabat: Imprimeries Françaises et Marocaines, 1966), 2:72–78, 233–39. Also see Abitol, *Tombouctou et les Arma*, 42–43. Hence one of the reasons for the invasion of sub-Saharan Africa was to acquire more enslaved workers. Also important were the gold supplies of sub-Saharan Africa, some of which passed along the trade routes of the western Sudan to Morocco.

10. On the slave estates of Songhay, see especially John Hunwick, "Notes on Slavery in the Songhay Empire," in Willis, *Slaves and Slavery in Muslim Africa*, 2:16–32; N. G. Kodjo, "Contribution à l'étude des tribus dites servile du Songai," *Bulletin de l'IFAN* 38, no. 4 (1976): 790–812. See also Paul E. Lovejoy, *Transformations in Slavery: A History of Slavery in Africa*, 2nd ed. (Cambridge: Cambridge University Press, 2000), 31–32. This work has been translated by Regina A. R. F. Bhering and Luiz Guilherme B. Chaves as *A escravidão na África: Uma história de suas transformações* (Rio de Janeiro: Civilização Brasileira, 2002).

11. The antecedents of sugar cultivation in southern Morocco are largely overlooked in the literature on the spread of sugar to the Americas.

12. John Hunwick, "Islamic Law and Polemics over Race and Slavery in North and West Africa (16th–19th Century)," in *Slavery in the Islamic Middle East*, ed. Shaun E. Marmon (Princeton: Princeton University Press, 1999), 45–46.

13. Ibid., 46.

14. As Naṣr al-Dīn, who led the Muslim revolt among the Wolof in the 1670s, wrote: "God does not allow kings to plunder, kill, or make their people captive"; quoted in Michael A. Gomez, "Muslims in Early America," *Journal of Southern History* 60, no. 4 (1994): 678.

15. P. E. H. Hair, "Sources on Early Sierra Leone: (6) Barreira on Just Enslavement, 1606," *Africana Research Bulletin* 6 (1975): 52–74.

16. Stephan Bühnen, "Ethnic Origins of Peruvian Slaves (1548–1650): Figures for Upper Guinea," *Paiduema* 39 (1993): 57–110. Bühnen's study builds on the earlier work of Frederick P. Bowser, *The African Slave in Colonial Peru, 1524–1650* (Stanford: Stanford University Press, 1974).

17. Alonso de Sandoval, *Un tratado sobre la esclavitud*, ed. Enriqueta Vila Vilar (Madrid, 1987; orig. pub. 1627).

18. For the ethnic terms used in Latin America, see especially Fernando Ortiz, *Los negros esclavos* (Havana: Editorial de Ciencias Sociales, 1975; orig. pub. 1916), 41–66; Gonzalo Aguirre Beltrán, *Obra antropológica II: La población negra de México, estudio etnohistórico* (Mexico City: Fondo de Cultura Económica, 1989; orig. pub. 1946), 99–129, and for a discussion of the "tribal" origins of the enslaved population from West Africa in Mexico, see especially pp. 114–29. Also see Rina Cáceres, ed., *Rutas de la esclavitud en África y América Latina* (San José: Editorial de la Universidad de Costa Rica, 2001); José Marcial Ramos Guédez, *Contribución a la historia de las culturas negras en Venezuela colonial* (Caracas: Instituto Municipal de Publicaciones-Alcaldía de Caracas, 2001).

19. João José Reis, *Slave Rebellion in Brazil* (Baltimore: Johns Hopkins University Press, 1993); Gwendolyn Midlo Hall, *Africans in Colonial Louisiana: The Development of Afro-Creole Culture in the Eighteenth Century* (Baton Rouge: Louisiana State University Press, 1992); Peter Caron, "The Peopling of French Colonial Louisiana: The Origins and Demographic Distributions of African Slaves, 1718–1735" (paper presented at the conference "From Slavery to Emancipation: The Atlantic World," Tulane University, 1996); idem, "'Of a nation which others do not understand': Bambara Slaves and African Ethnicity in Colonial Louisiana, 1718–60," *Slavery and Abolition* 18 (1997); Colin A. Palmer, "From Africa to the Americas: Ethnicity in the Early Black Communities of the Americas," *Journal of World History* 6, no. 2 (1995): 223–37; David Pavy, "The Provenience of Colombian Negroes," *Journal of Negro History* 52 (1967): 35–58; Walter Rodney, "Upper Guinea and the Significance of the Origins of Africans Enslaved in the New World,"

Journal of Negro History 54, no. 4 (1969): 327–45; Donald D. Wax, "Preferences for Slaves in Colonial America," *Journal of Negro History* 58, no. 4 (1973): 371–401; Jean-Pierre Tardieu, "Origines des esclaves au Perou: La region de Lima (XVIᵉ XVIIᵉ siècle)," in *La chaîne et le lien: Une vision de la traite négrière*, ed. Doudou Diène (Paris: Éditions UNESCO, 1998).

20. Ivor Wilks, "The Transmission of Islamic Learning in the Western Sudan," in *Literacy in Traditional Societies*, ed. J. Goody (Cambridge: Cambridge University Press, 1968).

21. The literature is extensive, but see 'Abdullah ibn Muḥammad dan Fodio's *Ḍiyā' al-sulṭān wa ghayrihi min al-ikhwān fī ahamm ma yuṭlab 'ilmuhu fī umūr al-zamān* (see Muhammad Sani Zahradeen, "'Abd Allah ibn Fodio's Contributions to the Fulani Jihad in Nineteenth-Century Hausaland" [Ph.D. diss., McGill University, 1976], 13–14); *Tazyīn al-Waraqāt* (Ibadan, 1963) and *Ḍiyā' al-Ḥukkām* (see Shehu Yamusa, "The Political Ideas of the Jihad Leaders: Being a Translation, Edition, and Analysis of (1) *Uṣ l al-Siyāsa* by Muhammad Bello and (2) *Ḍiyā' al-Ḥukkām* by Abdallah B. Fodio" [master's thesis, Bayero University, Kano, 1975], 270–85); 'Uthman ibn Muḥammad dan Fodio's *Al-ajwibah al-muharrarah 'an al-as'ilah al-muqarrarah fī wathiqat al-shaykh al-Ḥājj al-ma'rūf bi-laqabih Shisummas ibn Ahmad* (see Zahradeen, "'Abd Allah ibn Fodio's Contributions," 20), *Nūr al-albāb*, *Taʔlīm al-ikhwān bi-al-umūr allati kaffarnā bihā mulūk al-sūdān alladhīna kānū min ahl hadhih al-buldān*, *Sirāj al-ikhwān fī ahamm mā yuḥtāj ilayhi fī hadha al-zamān*, *Kitāb al-farq*, *Wathīqat ahl al-sūdān*, and *Tanbīh al-ikhwān*; and Muḥammad Bello's *Infāq al-maysūr fī ta'rīkh bilād al-takrūr* and *Miftāḥ al-sadād*. See also 'Abd al-Qādir b. al-Muṣṭafā (d. 1864), *Radat al-afkar*.

22. The exchange between al-Kānemī and the Sokoto leadership over the justification of the jihad in Borno produced a series of letters, not all of which have survived. See, for example, the letter from al-Kānemī to Goni Mukhtar and others, the Fulani leaders in Borno, University of Ibadan, MSS 82/237, 17 Rabī' al-Awwal 1223 (May 13, 1808). Also see Muhammad Al-Hajj and Murray Last, "Attempts at Defining a Muslim in Nineteenth Century Hausaland," *Journal of the Historical Society of Nigeria* 3, no. 2 (1965); Humphrey J. Fisher, "A Muslim William Wilberforce? The Sokoto Jihad as Anti-Slavery Crusade: An Enquiry into Historical Causes," in *De la traite à l'esclavage: Actes du Colloque international sur la traite des noirs*, ed. S. Daget (Nantes: Centre de Recherche sur l'Histoire du Monde Atlantique, 1985); Paul E. Lovejoy, "The Clapperton-Bello Exchange: The Sokoto Jihad and the Trans-Atlantic Slave Trade,

1804–1837," in *The Desert Shore: Literatures of the African Sahel*, ed. Christopher Wise (Boulder: Lynne Rienner, 2000).

23. Patrick Manning has argued convincingly that most of the enslaved population leaving the Bight of Benin in the late seventeenth and first half of the eighteenth centuries came from near the coast, and this pattern appears to have applied to all of West Africa; see *Slavery and African Life: Occidental, Oriental, and African Slave Trades* (Cambridge: Cambridge University Press, 1990).

24. Bühnen, "Ethnic Origins of Peruvian Slaves"; Paul E. Lovejoy and Renée Soulodre-La France, "Nueces de cola en Cartagena: Intercambios transatlánticos en el siglo XVII," in *Afrodescendientes en las Américas: Trayectorias sociales e identitarias*, ed. Claudia Mosquera, Mauricio Pardo, and Odile Hoffmann (Bogotá: Universidad Nacional de Colombia), 195–212; Sylviane Diouf, "Devils or Sorcerers, Muslims or Studs: Manding in the Americas," in Lovejoy and Trotman, *Trans-Atlantic Dimensions of Ethnicity in the African Diaspora*, 139–57; Gwendlyn Midlo Hall, ed., *Afro-Louisiana History and Genealogy, 1699–1860* [electronic resource] (Baton Rouge: Louisiana State University Press, 2000).

25. Robin Law, "Between the Sea and Lagoons: The Interaction of Maritime and Inland Navigation on the Precolonial Slave Coast," *Cahiers d'études africaines* 29 (1980): 209–37.

26. See Hall, "Meanings of 'Mina.'"

27. Renée Soulodre-La France, "'I, Francisco Castañeda, Negro Esclavo Caravalí': Caravalí Ethnicity in Colonial New Granada," in Lovejoy and Trotman, *Trans-Atlantic Dimensions of Ethnicity in the African Diaspora*, 96–114; Michael A. Gomez, "The Quality of Anguish: The Igbo Response to Enslavement in the Americas," in Lovejoy and Trotman, ibid., 82–95; Rina Cáceres Gómez, *Negros, mulatos, esclavos y libertos en la Costa Rica del siglo XVII* (Mexico, DF: Instituto Panamericano de Geografía e Historia, 2000).

28. See Paul E. Lovejoy, "Jihad e escravidão: As origens dos escravos muçulmanos de Bahia," *Topoi* 1 (2000): 11–44. Also see Pierre Verger, *Trade Relations between the Bight of Benin and Bahia, 17th–19th centuries* (Ibadan: Ibadan University Press, 1976).

29. P. E. H. Hair, "Ethnolinguistic Continuity on the Guinea Coast," *Journal of African History* 8, no. 2 (1967): 247–68.

30. Robin Law, "Ethnicity and the Slave Trade: 'Lucumí' and 'Nago' as Ethnonyms in West Africa," *History in Africa* 24 (1997): 205–19.

CHAPTER TWO

Boiling It Down

Slavery on the First Commercial Sugarcane Ingenios in the Americas (Hispaniola, 1530–45)

Lynne Guitar

"It's almost dawn," whispered Lemba to Coculi, one of his most trusted lieutenants. "Anbo confirms that the Spanish captain Leguizamán and half his soldiers are seeking us in Azua, and the rest in Yaguana. So there should be little resistence here. We attack in unison the very moment that the sun's rays first touch the heights of the guard tower."

"I'll spread the word, Captain," said Coculi, adding, as he looked down upon his mangled left hand, "and remember, you promised that the mill itself is mine to burn." His dark coloring helped him to blend into the tropical forest that bordered the cane sugar ingenio[1] just outside the town of San Juan de la Maguana.

Lemba patted his horse's forehead, climbed upon its broad back, placed his loaded arquebus across his legs, and made sure that his sword would slide easily out of its cowhide sheath. Ready, he peered into the darkness toward the outlying buildings that he could see silhouetted against the slowly lightening sky. In these last moments of night—the dead time—he prayed to all his ancestors who had gone before him for strength and luck on his soul's path today.

Lemba raised his arquebus in the air and rode forward as the sun's rays brushed the tall watchtower's palm-thatched roof with golden strokes. He looked *to the right and left and thought about how Spaniards always rode to battle shouting, "Santiago!" with the clanging of their steel swords and metal shields adding to the chaos. But the two hundred-plus dark-skinned warriors who accompanied him, more than half of them mounted on horses they had stolen in previous raids, poured silently out of the forest like a black tide, the soft snorting of the horses the only sound out of the ordinary. Silently, they split into five units. Lemba and his forty men headed for the bohíos, the woven huts, surrounding the watchtower, for it was here that the few Spaniards on the ingenio were likely to be sleeping with their black or indigenous mistresses. Coculi and his men headed toward the mill, a third group toward the supervisor's house, a stone mansion at the top of the hill beside the church, a fourth to the drying sheds, and the fifth group to the storage barns. Within minutes, all were set afire. A few Spaniards and several hundred indigenous and African slaves came running out of the burning buildings, crying, screaming, confused. . . .*

Lemba raised and then lowered his arquebus, a previously arranged signal, and his men fired upon the Spaniards, who never had time to load their own firearms. Lemba shot one square in the chest, then ran down another and beheaded him with his sword. He pulled up his horse, turned back to face the bohíos, and watched as the last of the seven Spaniards who had been sleeping peacefully just moments ago was dispatched by his men, who then gathered around him. "Well done," he congratulated them. "Quickly now. Collect all the horses and mules you can find, plus any weapons, clothes, salt, food, and women that you can carry . . . and head back to our encampment when I give the signal."

"Captain Lemba," said Anbo, riding up beside him a few moments later. "I found the blacksmith, just like you said I would," indicating the muscular African mounted behind him. "He was chained up in the wine cellar. He speaks a dialect of Kikongo."

"Good! We can certainly use him to make more lances and horseshoes and to teach some of the younger men his skills." Speaking to the new man in Kikongo, Lemba asked his name, then, grasping the man's right arm with both hands, said, "Welcome, Nzinga. You are no longer a slave."

Less than half an hour after the attack had begun, seeing that all of the horses and mules were loaded and most of the ingenio's buildings were aflame, Lemba gave the signal to leave. As silently as they had come, he and his men left to return to their encampment in the nearby mountains, now reinforced by more than fifty extra men, twenty-some young women, plus more horses, mules, and supplies.

Sebastián Lemba (d. 1547) is the most famous rebel African slave leader in Hispaniola's long history, for he was the very first that we know by name. He was "an extraordinarily cunning Negro and very knowledge-able about things of war, whom all obey and all fear."[2] Lemba, who was probably from the Kongo,[3] appears to have become a *cimarrón* (runaway) sometime in the late 1520s or early 1530s. He probably had been a slave on one of the island's many cane sugar ingenios, for this was the era when the first commercial cane sugar industry in the "New World" was on the rise, and Spaniards were clamoring to bring in more and more African slave laborers. Lemba and his men (up to four hundred were reported) were among the many African cimarrones who joined the rebellion of the Taíno cacique Enriquillo from 1519 to 1534. Although Enriquillo finally negotiated a peace treaty with the Spanish crown for himself and his peo-ple, Lemba refused to accept the terms, refused to stop rebelling against the Spaniards. Lemba and his men pillaged and attacked the Spaniards of Hispaniola and their allies, including Enriquillo's men, who had accepted the crown's terms, for more than a decade longer.

Lemba was stabbed with a lance in September of 1547 by an African slave who was part of a Spanish patrol led by Captain Villalpando—that slave's reward was his liberty. Lemba's head was taken back to Santo Domingo and set upon a pike at the main gate leading to the wharves along the Río Ozama as a warning to others not to rebel.[4] It did not work. Just a few months later, there was another huge rebellion on an ingenio in La Vega (perhaps incited by some of Lemba's own men who had escaped the Spanish patrol),[5] and other African slave captains such as Dieguillo de Ocampo and Juan Vaquero remained on the loose, causing havoc across the island. By 1548 African cimarrones had caused so much destruction among the island's cane sugar ingenios that only ten (out of more than thirty) were still in production.[6]

Hispaniola, the "Seasoning Ground" for Slaves in the New World

Between 1504 and 1518, fewer than two thousand African slaves were legally shipped to the island of Hispaniola,[7] most as personal servants and the others destined to labor in gold mines and construction. By the 1520s, however, the demand for African slaves mounted to a crescendo,

FIGURE 2.1: *First African Slave Rebellion in Hispaniola, on the sugar ingenio of Diego Colón, as depicted in an early 16th-century woodcut by Theodor De Bry. From:* De ontdekking van de Nieuwe Wereld *(Amsterdam: Van Hoeve, c1979), 4.*

in part because of the diminution of the indigenous population and in part because of the growth of the cane sugar industry, which Spain successfully transplanted from the Canary Islands. Hispaniola's planters shipped two thousand *arrobas* of cane sugar to Spain in 1522—by the 1530s, shipments had risen to ninety thousand arrobas annually.[8] The thousands of African slaves forced to labor in the ingenios of Hispaniola were the first of the millions who would eventually make the Middle Passage. It was on Hispaniola that many of the patterns were formed that governed relations between African slaves and their new masters, patterns that spread to the other Spanish colonies across the Americas— patterns that included rebellion.

The Spaniards who left Hispaniola to conquer and found other New World colonies took along some of their commended Indians[9] as well as slaves of indigenous, African, and mixed descent.[10] Hispaniola's royal judges complained in 1528 that this had happened repeatedly. In the settlement of Cuba, for example, they claimed that Diego Velázquez took along with him most of the populace of seven of the island's villages.[11] Peoples of all ethnic backgrounds from Hispaniola—conquerors, commended Indians, and slaves—also went to Jamaica with Juan de Esquivel and with Ponce de León, to Cubagua, "the pearl island" (today's Isla Margarita), and with Hernando Cortés to New Spain, a region that included much of today's U.S. Southwest as well as all of Mexico. They went to San Miguel de Gualdape in today's South Carolina with Lucas Vásquez de Ayllón and Fray Antonio de Montesinos. They went on the expeditions of Diego de Nicuesa, Alonso de Ojeda, Gil González, Alonso Núñez de Balboa, Francisco Pizarro, and others to settle Central and South America.[12]

All of the slaves and servant peoples who accompanied the Spaniards to their new colonies were "seasoned" by their experiences on Hispaniola. That is, on Hispaniola they became accustomed to the climate, foods, and diseases of post-1492 America, where the "weakest" among them died off. They also became accustomed to living with and working for Spaniards— thus they not only provided their labor in the newly conquered regions, they served as models for newly conquered peoples. A letter to the emperor from Hispaniola's governor, Alonso López de Cerrato, dated July 15, 1546, explained these benefits as he described how *negros bozales* were first brought to Hispaniola, where they were "instructed and then sold" as workers for the colonies of the mainland.[13]

Hispaniola's importance as a seasoning ground for the model slaves and other forced laborers of all the other Spanish American colonies makes it imperative to study just what kinds of behavior it was that they were modeling. Many of the forced laborers did not, of course, just learn acquiescent behavior on Hispaniola. They learned how to frustrate the Spaniards' efforts at control—they learned how to rebel. Despite all the problems the Spaniards encountered on Hispaniola in their attempts to control the Indians who were commended to them as well as their slaves, they needed them to build their forts, towns, cities, and roads; to grow and prepare their food; and to work the island's gold mines. As the easily mined gold began to run out—which happened before the 1520s—they also needed their commended Indians and slaves to work the island's cane sugar ingenios.

FIGURE 2.2: *Indians and Africans working together in the processing of sugar on Hispaniola. From:* De ontdekking van de Nieuwe Wereld *(Amsterdam: Van Hoeve, c1979)*, 2.

Mixed Labor Force on the First New World Cane Sugar Ingenios

Spaniards had quickly discovered that Hispaniola's soil and climate were excellent for growing sugarcane—Columbus brought some along on his second voyage in 1493, and Spaniards began milling cane sugar commercially on the island between 1505 and 1515. By 1522 Hispaniola's planters were shipping significant quantities of sugar to Spain for refining—two thousand arrobas, or fifty thousand pounds annually. By 1530 shipments had risen to more than 2 million pounds, and they continued to rise, albeit sporadically because of slave uprisings, for the next thirty years.[14] To grow and process sugarcane in those quantities required a large labor force, a slave labor force that, at least through the mid-sixteenth century, was comprised of both Africans and Indians.

The Indians, of course, were already in place when Europeans arrived in 1492, though Spaniards quickly began to supplement the postcontact population of the native Taínos of Hispaniola with Taínos brought in from today's Bahamas, which were basically depopulated by 1513.[15] The replacements were needed because of indigenous deaths in battle and because of abuses committed under the *encomienda* system (a grant giving the recipient the labor and/or tribute of commended Indians), but mostly because the Indians had no natural immunities to the diseases inadvertently brought to the Americas by the newcomers and their animals, diseases that were especially virulent in the tropics.[16] Throughout the second and third decades of the sixteenth century, Spaniards sailed all over the Caribbean and circum-Caribbean capturing indigenous "cannibals" and selling them as slaves on Hispaniola.[17] Spanish slavers also raided the coasts of Central America, Mexico, Brazil, and Florida. Except for the Taínos from the Bahamas, all of the indigenous slaves brought to the island spoke different languages, but their customs and beliefs were relatively similar to those of the Taínos, especially in comparison to the customs and beliefs of their Spanish owners. In a variety of ways, the customs and beliefs of many of the Africans who came to the island were similar to those of the Taínos, too, and both peoples were alike in their enslaved condition under the Spaniards.[18]

The First Africans on Hispaniola

The first Africans on Hispaniola were illegally imported slaves and free *ladinos*.[19] Obviously, they arrived before 1503, the year that Governor Nicolas de Ovando wrote his oft-quoted complaint to the crown asking that no more Africans be allowed in the Indies because "they run away, join up with the Indians, teach them bad customs, and cannot be recaptured."[20] Despite Ovando's plea, groups of seventeen to one hundred African slaves were shipped in to work the gold mines from 1504 on,[21] and royal licenses were issued to permit the importation of particular slaves (usually acculturated females) or small quantities of slaves by individual Spaniards to whom the crown owed favors. It wasn't until after 1519, however, that African slaves were imported in large quantities, such as the monopoly to import and sell four thousand that was granted by the Spanish crown to the governor of Bresa, Lorenzo de Gorrevod (who promptly sold his monopoly to the Genoese agents Adán de Vivaldo and

Tomás de Forne). Even then, it wasn't until 1527 or 1528 that all four thousand of those African slaves had been delivered, and only half stayed in Hispaniola.[22] The 1519 contract must have been fulfilled by early 1528, however, for the crown issued another bulk permit for four thousand African slaves on April 22 of that year, this time to German factors.[23]

Africans were the slaves of choice because they were adaptable,[24] readily available, and had proven to be good workers on the ingenios established by the Portuguese and Spaniards on the Atlantic islands off the West African coast. Some of the Africans had invaluable technical skills—many were blacksmiths and "sugar masters," the supervisors who directed the complex process of sugar's heating and crystallization. Africans were also valuable on Hispaniola because they were accustomed to a tropical climate, because they did not know the land or have established kinship networks there like the Indians did, and because they were already immune to most of the diseases to which Indians fell prey. African slaves did not, however, replace Indians on Hispaniola, at least not during the first half of the sixteenth century.

Analyzing Three Early Censuses

There are not many extant censuses from the first half of the sixteenth century on Hispaniola, but there are three that give us an idea of the ratio of indigenous and African slaves on the island's sugar ingenios. The first of the three censuses resulted from a lawsuit that was initiated on July 19, 1533, between the civil and ecclesiastical *cabildos* in Santo Domingo. The evidence that was gathered included census information taken in 1530 on nineteen of Hispaniola's ingenios, plus a scattering of small estates.[25] The total head count included 1,870 Africans, most of whom were probably slaves, and 427 Spaniards. Although the legal papers pertaining to the case say there were "some" Indians working on the ingenios, the only numerical quantity provided is for five ingenios on the River Nigua that, combined, had 200 Indians (such a round number, too, is suspect—it was probably an approximation). No quantities are provided for the category of Indians on the other ingenios, just question marks. Clearly, no one wanted to release the actual numbers of Indians connected to the estates and/or there was confusion over just how to categorize some of the workers, most likely those who were free Africans or people of mixed blood.[26] None of the censuses included categories for mestizos or mulattos until

1582, despite the fact that the first mixed-blood children were most likely born nine months after Columbus and his men came ashore in 1492.[27] In addition to the questions marks, the 1530 census lists a total of 700 unspecified "others."

In 1533 Archbishop Alonso de Avila of Santo Domingo ordered a census taken to determine the number of chapels and clergymen required to service the twenty-three cane sugar ingenios that there were then on the island of Hispaniola. He reported that there were five ingenios on the Río Nigua alone, plus several cattle ranches. Altogether, Avila wrote that there were "at least" 700 Africans, 200 Indians (note that this is the same quantity claimed in 1530), and 150 Spaniards who lived and worked in the region, which lay six leagues west of Santo Domingo. He noted that the Río Nigua was "the most populous river that there is at present on this island."[28] In total, Avila gave a specific count, including all twenty-three ingenios, of 1,880 Africans, 412 Spaniards, and 200 Indians. That is the kind of ratio that other historians have cited and, in fact, the quantities are almost exactly the same given for these categories of people in 1530. Avila, however, also accounted for 1,525 persons of unspecified category in his report, 825 more than in the 1530 count. He wrote that these unspecified persons included Spaniards, Africans, Indians, and "some" uncounted others; however, most of the latter he identified elsewhere in his report as Indians. Again, the implication is that there was confusion over categories on Hispaniola, just as there was elsewhere throughout the Spanish American colonies.

Six years after Avila's census, in a report that the island's governor Licenciado don Alonso de Fuenmayor sent to Emperor Charles, there was only one more ingenio listed on the Río Nigua, but the head count along that river alone had risen to 962 Africans from 700, and to 1,212 Indians from 200.[29] Fuenmayor reported a total of twenty-nine ingenios and *trapiches* (horse-powered mills) across the island. It is notable that Africans outnumbered the indigenous workforce on only nine of the twenty-nine ingenios in Fuenmayor's 1545 census. His total count was 8,952+ workers, 3,827+ of whom he identified as Africans (43 percent), and 5,125+ of whom he identified as Indians (57 percent). The quantities listed in Fuenmayor's report are suspect, of course, because there is such a dramatic increase in Indians over the 1530 and 1533 counts. We do not know what the criteria were that the census takers used for categorization. Unlike the other two censuses, Fuenmayor's did not mention any "others," nor use

TABLE 2.1.

Comparison of Three Censuses of Ingenios on Hispaniola

						No. of
Year	Spaniards	Indians	Africans	Others	Total	Ingenios
1530	427	200+	1,870	700	3,197+	14
1533	412	200+	1,880	1,525	4,017+	23
1545	—	5,125+	3,827+	—	8,952+	29

Sources: 1530 census data from a law suit between the civil and ecclesiastical cabildos of Santo Domingo in AGI, Justicia 12, N1, R2, as cited in Esteban Mira Caballos, *El indio Antillano: Repartimiento, encomienda y esclavitud (1492-1542)* (Seville: Ediciones ALFIL, July 1997), 155. 1533 census data from AGI, Justicia 12, 149, ff1ov-15; full text in José Luis Saez, *La iglesia y el esclavo negro en Santo Domingo: Una historia de tres siglos* (Santo Domingo: Patronato de la Ciudad Colonial de Santo Domingo, Colección Quinto Centenario, 1994), 267-72. 1545 census data cited in Luis Joseph Peguero, *Historia de la Conquista de la Isla Española de Santo Domingo trasumptada el año de 1762: Traducida de la Historia General de las Indias escrita por Antonio de Herrera coronista mayor de su Magestad, y de las Indias, y de Castilla; y de otros autores que han escrito sobre el particular* (Santo Domingo: Publicaciones del Museo de Las Casas Reales, 1975; originally published 1763), 217-21.

question marks, nor list workers of unspecified category—everybody was placed into the category of "African" or "Indian."[30] His report appears to include among the "slaves" of the nearby ingenios all of the independent small farmers that the other two reports mentioned separately. Nonetheless, the quantity of "more than 5,000 Indian slaves" on the island was repeated in a May 23, 1545, letter to the emperor from another royal official, Alonso López de Cerrato.[31] (López was president of the Audiencia Real and became governor of Hispaniola after Fuenmayor.)

Lack of standardization among categories of people throughout this era makes exact demographic studies impossible, but the important thing to note is that both indigenous and African slaves were working together on Hispaniola's ingenios throughout the first half of the sixteenth century. And the numbers of workers is astounding: seven of the ingenios in 1545 had more than 100 workers, five more than 200, eight more than 300, four more than 400, three more than 500, and Yamán, founded by the royal factor Juan de Ampíes, had 610 workers.

First African Slave Rebellion on Hispaniola, Christmas Day of 1521

Until the 1520s, the Spaniards of Hispaniola requested of the crown that all slaves sent to the region be bozales. Bozales were thought to be "more pacific" than acculturated African ladinos.[32] This changed dramatically on Christmas Day of 1521, when a group of approximately twenty bozales on the ingenio La Isabela, owned by the island's governor, Viceroy Diego Colón (Christopher Columbus's elder son), planned and executed the first major African slave rebellion in the Americas.[33]

Just thirteen days after the 1521 rebellion began, Colón promulgated a set of slave ordinances in an attempt to prevent any further rebellions. The ordinances, signed in Santo Domingo and dated January 6, 1522, are the first laws formulated for control of African slaves in the New World.[34] As Carlos Esteban Deive notes in his analysis of the 1522 slave ordinances, their promulgation so promptly after the Christmas Day rebellion is evidence of how frightened the Spaniards on Hispaniola were of more insurrections.[35] No doubt aware of their dwindling numbers in comparison to the rapidly growing non-Spanish population on the island,[36] Spaniards particularly feared the fact that there appeared to have been communication and organization not only among slaves on Colón's ingenio but among those of other ingenios as well. The new ordinances attempted to keep all future communication among slaves to a minimum; to restrict slave movement, even when the slave had the owner's or overseer's permission to leave the estate; to prohibit slaves, even loyal *criados*,[37] from bearing arms; and to eliminate all independent slave action, specifically such actions as coming and going at will and selling products or services. The new ordinances also required all ingenio supervisors, henceforth, to maintain strict slave registers.

Clearly, the Spanish authorities believed that the slaves on Hispaniola were living too well, too freely, and with too few controls. The extent to which the 1522 ordinances required slave masters to keep track of their slaves and to "control" them are the first indications of a new concept about slavery that would spread across the New World. King Alfonso the Wise's centuries'-old "just laws" for slaves in Spain (based upon Roman law) recognized slaves as human beings, though with limited rights. Not so the control-oriented slave laws that would become symbolic of the "plantation complex" that evolved in different forms across the Americas.[38] Despite all the attention to control, however, the ordinances and the various chronicles, taken together, indicate that Spaniards in 1521 were seeking some basis other than lack of control to explain the 1521 rebellion. The blame fell on the Wolof people.

Perhaps the Spaniards made the Wolofs the scapegoats for the 1521 rebellion because they were mostly Muslim; therefore, they were considered to be anti-Christian. They may also have targeted the Wolofs, despite the probability that there were relatively few of them, because many Wolofs were literate (Muslims were encouraged to read the Koran), and hence had more potential for communication than other slaves. Consider, too, that Wolofs were astute traders and merchants back in their homeland, experienced in maintaining relations with a wide variety of peoples from different regions and different backgrounds. From the moment of the 1521 rebellion, all the fears and accusations of "bad habits" that had formerly been attributed to acculturated Africans were transferred to Wolofs, who were stereotyped as having "an excitable and rebellious spirit."[39]

Laws to Protect the Indians

New royal *cédulas* (writs), ordinances, and provisions were promulgated on Hispaniola beginning in 1526, although they mainly focused on the regulation of Indians, not Africans. This was in part because Indians still outnumbered Africans on Hispaniola and in part because the most famous Taíno rebellion, led by the cacique Enriquillo, was escalating—it began in 1519 but was not officially declared a war until October 19, 1523.[40] The so-called Laws of Granada, dated November 17, 1526, were aimed at preventing insurrections like Enriquillo's and at protecting the new indigenous peoples who were being discovered in other parts of the Americas from enslavement and exploitation. Primarily, however, the 1526 laws were aimed at propitiating clergymen like Bartolomé de las Casas, whose pleas on behalf of American indigenes were gaining support, most notably in Rome.

Because of papal pressure, cédula after cédula in the 1530s attempted to stop the fraudulent trade in indigenous Caribe slaves, who were all designated as cannibals,[41] and to stop "the excesses being committed" against both free and enslaved indigenous females.[42] The pope issued a bull on June 2, 1537, declaring that *all* Indians were free and could not be coerced in any way except by preaching and good example. The Spanish crown eventually complied with the pressure from Rome by promulgating the New Laws of 1542 to regulate the encomienda system and protect Indians from being illegally enslaved. (The New Laws were not applied equally throughout the Spanish colonies, however, so that the encomienda system actually existed for several more centuries.)

African Slaves Laws

Unfortunately, the Catholic Church was not opposed to African slavery as it was to indigenous slavery; however, in the early sixteenth century, it consistently appealed to slave owners to remember the humanity of their charges. A royal cédula dated November 9, 1526, contains the church's recommendation that Africans would be more complacent if allowed to marry and to work for wages so that they could eventually buy their freedom.[43] A year later the Spanish crown itself recommended that each male African slave sent to the Indies be accompanied by his wife. In the provision, the crown recognized "the love that they have for their women and children," but this was not a recommendation arising out of compassion for the Africans. The crown clearly stated that the orders were issued in the hopes that "it would keep slaves from rebelling and from fleeing to the mountains."[44]

Spanish slave laws were far more liberal than "chattel" slave laws. The royal officials on Hispaniola (who owned the island's largest ingenios and the most slaves) begged the crown to rescind some centuries-old slave privileges. Bowing under the pressure, Emperor Charles and his mother, Queen Juana, cosigned a 1526 provision that African slaves were *not* to be set free when they married, nor were their children born free, even though this went "against the laws of our Reigns."[45] The cédula had to be reaffirmed on July 10, 1538, demonstrating that, twelve years after the modification went into effect, Africans were still pushing for their rights under the ancient Spanish laws.[46] African slave rebellions were on the rise across Hispaniola in the 1520s and 1530s as well.

Slaves consistently resisted Spanish controls, especially new ones, and the Spaniards on Hispaniola consistently tried to resolve problems of slave control with new ordinances. On October 9, 1528, a new thirty-item set of ordinances signed by four royal judges on Hispaniola was issued to replace those that Colón and his advisors had hastily put together six years earlier. The new ordinances were directed not only toward Africans but to "all the slaves, Negroes and whites, of whatever caliber they are, who are at present on this island of Hispaniola or who may come here in future."[47] (The "whites" were mostly enslaved Moors and Canarians.)

The 1528 ordinances, the same as those in 1522, required slave owners and supervisors to maintain strict records of their slaves and to know their whereabouts at all times. Repetition of the order suggests that these records were not being kept. The new ordinances appear to have been less concerned with organized rebellion than those of 1522.[48] Their focus was on keeping individual slaves from "fleeing to the mountains" and from "continually walking about this island" and making "unlicensed visits away from their homes," confirming that the Spaniards actually had little control over their slaves' comings and goings. The penalty for leaving the ingenios without permission became stronger and stronger, starting out with monetary fines (which supports the documents reporting that slaves on Hispaniola were earning money selling their technical skills, arts and crafts, and produce), escalating to whippings and the wearing of heavy metal collars, and culminating in the death penalty for repeated offenses. The new ordinances recognized that sometimes slaves rebelled or ran away because they were mistreated or because they were not given enough food or drink. In these cases (theoretically, of course), the owners would be investigated and punished if found guilty. Inspectors were appointed to travel to the ingenios to check up on how the slaves were being fed and clothed and to ensure that they were not being made to work on Sundays, were given enough time to sleep, and so on. Despite the humane-sounding wording of some of the provisions of the new slave ordinances, another provision specified an ominous new requirement—for every four African slaves owned, the *señor* (supervisor of the ingenio) was to have readily at hand one set of stocks and one chain.

The 1528 Spanish slave ordinances were modified in 1535, 1542, and 1544, with the restrictions and punishments remaining comparatively mild in relation to the chattel slave laws in Dutch, English, and French colonies, until the late eighteenth century. The modifications continued to emphasize control of the growing slave population, with special emphasis on keeping slaves from "walking about" the countryside unsupervised, and especially from joining "gangs" of slaves—the penalty for being at large more than thirty days was increased to a death sentence "regardless of whether it is their first or second offense."[49]

Thousands of Africans outside Spanish Control

It is obvious that the Spaniards on Hispaniola were losing valuable slaves who simply walked off at will. Once away from the principal Spanish population areas clustered around Santo Domingo and on the south coast, runaway slaves could join up with cimarrón groups of Africans and Indians who had established colonies in peripheral regions of the island. The Spaniards must also have been painfully aware that they were outnumbered by the people they supposedly dominated and that they could easily be overpowered as well. While only the 1521 rebellion is well documented, there are indications that African slave revolts continued to take place on Hispaniola from 1520 on, but that they were being covered up by Spanish officials. For example, three royal judges reported in 1532 that "a favored slave" at the Colón family's ingenio killed the supervisor there, which set the other slaves off on a killing spree. The report continues, "but nothing was done or said about it and the guilty were not punished . . . because no one wanted to admit that there was an uprising."[50]

Africans, whose numbers had constantly been growing since the island's initial settlement, were reported as comprising the majority of the population on Hispaniola by the 1540s. On March 26, 1542, Archdeacon Alonso de Castro reported to the crown that there were upwards of 25–30,000 Africans on the island and only 1,200 Spaniards. He complained that thousands of rebel Africans lived "in the countryside"— meaning free of Spanish control—in Cape San Nicolás, Samaná, Higüey, and other remote regions, where "they mine gold . . . and conduct a vast trade and commerce," most of which would have been the contraband sale of beef, hides, and produce to the enemies of Spain. The archdeacon also complained about the growing number of robberies committed by "well dressed and shod" Africans throughout the countryside as well as in the capital.[51] Despite Archdeacon de Castro's exaggerations of the African cimarrones' living conditions, some of his complaints had a legitimate basis, for many slaves did run away, and once outside the Spaniards' control, they were under no obligation to follow Spanish laws.

Slave Life on the Early Sugar Ingenios

What was life like for the slaves who *were* under Spanish control? A few documents exist that give behind-the-scenes glimpses of slave life on Hispaniola's early sugar ingenios. One such is the 1538 petition to the

Spanish crown by Diego Caballero de la Rosa, secretary of Hispaniola's Royal Audiencia, for more sugar land adjacent to that which he already had. Caballero owned one of the largest of the ingenios on the Río Nigua (west of Santo Domingo) where it empties into the Caribbean Sea. In his petition, Caballero stressed that he had spent more than fifteen thousand *ducados* of his own money to make improvements to the ingenio, improvements that included the construction and maintenance of a church, which he described as "very adorned with ornaments of silk and linen, with a cross and chalice, candelabra and silver wine containers." Caballero obviously chose to describe how richly appointed the church was as a demonstration to the crown of his devotion to Christianity and his efforts to convert the slaves under his care. (His responsibility was to provide an appropriate atmosphere where Christianity could be taught and practiced; it was a clerical responsibility to catechize, baptize, and the like.) Caballero also bragged that his ingenio had "more than seventy houses built of stone and straw," presumably of stone with straw-thatched roofs. Throughout the documents of the era, it is clear that Spaniards equated stone houses with progress and civilized customs, so Caballero was bragging here about how well his slaves lived. It would also appear that living quarters were ample (though we have no archaeological evidence yet at this ingenio), for he only claimed a population at that time of "more than twenty Spaniards and 150 Africans and Indians." That would mean an average of only two and a half people per house, so it could be that he was counting only workers. The actual population, including children, may have been higher.[52]

Caballero's descriptions make his ingenio and his intentions seem very pleasant for all, yet he gives us little idea of what the working conditions were like for the slaves. One indication that things weren't as rosy as Caballero portrayed them is that one of the witnesses who testified to the veracity of Caballero's statements in his petition for more land noted that it had taken Caballero five to six years to build his ingenio, that many Indians and Spaniards had died in the process (Africans were not mentioned), and that no cane had been milled in all that time.[53]

Unfortunately, archaeological evidence of slaves' conditions on Hispaniola, information that could fill gaps in the documents, is sparse, and what investigations have been made do not always focus on answering the questions that today's investigators are asking. The ingenio of Sanate on the Río Chavón in southeastern Hispaniola, for example, was investigated by a

FIGURE 2.3: *Remains of the Caballero Ingenio. Photograph by Lynne Guitar.*

team of archaeologists led by José Cruxent and Luis Chanlatte Baik in 1976. The completed analyses of Sanate focus on environmental changes from the pre-Taíno through early colonial eras, on indigenous ceramics and burials, and on general layout of the major ingenio structures, including the stone aqueduct that carried water from the nearby river to the mill. Little is said about the slaves' living and working conditions in the archaeological analyses, except that Indians and Africans both worked there together. [54]

Ingenio Santiago de la Paz, Azua

The most informative materials about the actual conditions of slavery that we have from any sixteenth-century ingenio on Hispaniola pertain to Santiago de la Paz in Azua, which belonged to Hernando Gorjón. A large variety of documents survives for Santiago de la Paz because the ingenio was auctioned off by the crown after its owner's death on January 25, 1547, to fund the Colegio Gorjón, the second university created in the Americas. [55] Gorjón received innumerable royal favors while he lived because of his promise to the crown to construct a university, hospital, and church (but the auction raised enough money only for the university).

It is difficult to determine how many slaves Gorjón actually had over the years. In 1514 he received a small encomienda of fifty Indians in Azua.[56] In 1537, in a document giving Pedro de Villanueva authority to represent him in court, Gorjón informed the crown that he had "one hundred Negros and Negras that are on and serve and reside on the said ingenio [of Santiago de la Paz]."[57] The year 1537 was also when Pope Paul III issued his brief and bull forbidding indigenous slavery, so if Gorjón did have any Indians still under his control, it behooved him not to mention them. In 1539 Gorjón was one of the *señores de ingenio* who was sued by the church for nonpayment of the tithes on his produce and profits. At that time he testified that he had "more than 150 persons, including Spaniards, Negroes and other persons" on his ingenio. In 1540 he repeated that he had "more than 150 persons [who were] Spaniards and Negroes"—note the omission of "others."[58]

Royal officials on Hispaniola seized Gorjón's ingenio immediately after his death in early 1547 and prepared to auction it off. One of the first things they did was to conduct an inventory that included a detailed list of all his lands, plantings, buildings, equipment, cattle . . . and slaves.[59] They found only seventy-three adult Africans at Santiago de la Paz and seventeen children. Their inventory also listed one female and one male "in the city" (perhaps in Gorjón's urban residence), one male "serving in the war" (by which was probably meant that he was assigned to a military patrol hunting down cimarrones), one male "in jail," one male "who has been absent for two years," and one "negra criolla" who was "attached to the estate" but not resident there—a total of ninety-six African slaves.

The entire Gorjón estate was sold in 1548 for ten annual payments of 2,360 pesos—a total of only 23,600 pesos.[60] What had happened to the estate that was "worth a lot," in Fuenmayor's words, and which was supposed to have had 254 African laborers in 1545, in addition to 170 Indians?

If, in fact, he had four and a half times more slaves in 1545 than two years later, he might have been quietly selling off his slaves. The prices of Africans were on the rise, and Gorjón would have known that he did not have long to live (he was approximately fifty-eight in 1540). Of course, either or both of the two counts may have been off, slaves may have run away, his ingenio might have been attacked by cimarrones and some of its slaves stolen, and/or there may have been fraud involved on the part of the ingenio's overseer or officials auctioning Gorjón's estate for the crown in 1547.

There are hints of fraud for personal gain in at least two documents connected to the sale of Santiago de la Paz. The first is a letter dated December 18, 1547, from Governor Alonso López de Cerrato to the emperor that contradicts the supposedly high value of the holdings in land, buildings, and equipment detailed in the ingenio's inventory: "He [Gorjón] left his ingenio very lost and pawned," wrote López, "without even one cane, nor one steer to eat, nor one tool. The Negroes, with their flesh exposed [*en carnes*], had been given neither shirt nor breeches in four years." López claimed responsibility "for having repaired everything," having bought 230 steers, planted four plots in sugarcane, built a house with defense tower, and "provided all that the ingenio needed so its laborers could mill *maquilas*"[61]—one hopes he also provided the slaves with adequate clothing and food.

On December 19, 1550, two years after the Gorjón estate was sold, a letter from the emperor to the president and royal judges of Santo Domingo and to Captain Alonso de Peña, the royal treasurer, reports that the new owners clearly demonstrated that the estate had been overvalued in earlier appraisals, which is the reason they were now losing money on it. The new owners were willing to take out a royal loan at 12 percent interest to back out of their contract for the purchase of Santiago de la Paz.[62] This, in an era when anything over 4 percent was considered usury, is a clear sign that the estate property had been manipulated so that its worth, in fact, had been highly overvalued.

Where Did Hispaniola's Earliest African Slaves Come From?

The documents connected to the inventory and sale of Gorjón's ingenio suggest how slave numbers could be manipulated for personal gain. Added to confusion over categories, this type of manipulation exacerbates the uncertainty that historians and demographers encounter when dealing with early censuses. The documents connected with Santiago de la Paz, however, are valuable tools for understanding better which African peoples were brought to Hispaniola during this early period. Many academics have written that the bozales brought directly from Africa to Hispaniola as slaves in the early sixteenth century were shipped mainly from the Cape Verde Islands. These slaves had been gathered there from all over the West African region called Upper Guinea, encompassing a multitude of different African peoples who lived between today's Senegal and Sierra Leone.[63] Although the ingenio's records do not positively prove where the African slaves on the inventory of 1547 came from, the provenance of many can be inferred from their names. This helps to confirm scholars' hypotheses, and it also shows that one of the planters' fears was correct—there were Muslims among the African slaves. The slaves on Santiago de Paz's inventory were:

- ✤ Anbo, an adult male—Ambos or Ambozi were from the Gulf of Biafra.
- ✤ Banón, adult male—perhaps a Bañol from the region of Upper Guinea between the Gambia and Cazamancia rivers.
- ✤ Barva, adult male—the Barva or Barba occupied territory to the north of Dahomey in the Central Sudan.
- ✤ Juan Bran, Gonçalo Bran, Pero Bran, Sona Bran, Cristóval Bran, and the females María Bran and Leonor Bran all appear on the inventory of adults—Brams were from the Gold Coast region between the Cazamancia and Cacheo rivers (also known as Cacheos); many were shipped from the Portuguese *feitoria* (factory) at São Jorge de Mina.
- ✤ Francisco Calauar and Domingo Carabi, two adult males— on later censuses, peoples from the region called Calabar, between the Niger Delta and Rey River; were most frequently called *carabalies* or *ibos*.
- ✤ Pedro Çape, Sebastián Çape, Juan Çape (two of them with the same name), and Francisco Çape, all adult males— most likely Sapis (Zapes) from Sierra Leon.
- ✤ Ganbu, adult male—perhaps he was from the Gambia River region.
- ✤ Cristóval Lucume, Hernando Lucume, and perhaps Ana Luque, all adults, were of the same people—the Lucumies were Yorubas.
- ✤ Perico Maga, adult male—the Magas were a Sudanese people.
- ✤ Gonçalo Mandinga and Mandinga, adult males—Mandingas were Mande speakers, mostly Muslims, from the Senegal and Niger valleys.

❖ Diego Olofe and María Olofa, adults—the Wolofs were from a region that extended from the Senegal River along the coast to Gambia (today's Senegambia); most were Muslims.

❖ Gonçalo Tierranova, adult male—Tierranova (or Porto Novo) was the capital of Dahomey; many slaves from Tierranova, who were actually Lucumies or Yorubas, were shipped from the Portuguese feitoria on the island of São Tomé.

❖ The males listed as Canguey, Coculi, Culi, Javja (Hausa?),[64] and Roque on the inventory may also have been Spanish attempts to reproduce the slaves' own names for their people, village, region, or language.

❖ One of the males was named Canpecho, which might indicate he was from Campeche in the Yucatán. Perhaps he was first a slave in the Yucatán, then brought to Hispaniola, or perhaps he was not an African at all, but an Indian or of Indo-African descent.

Further Analysis of the Santiago de la Paz Documents

The documents connected to Santiago de la Paz also shed light on working conditions on the early ingenios. Surprisingly, except for the position of overseer, which was held by a Spaniard named Francisco García, all of the other important positions on the ingenio of Santiago de la Paz appear to have been held by African slaves. This includes positions that would have permitted extensive freedom and mobility, such as shepherd and vaquero, for the ingenio's pastures were located in a different part of Azua, distant from the main ingenio lands.[65] The positions of *mandador* (in charge of the cane fields and, perhaps, some of the work in the mill), *estançiero* (in charge of all crops other than sugarcane), *purgador* (normally a literate person responsible for issuing supplies and maintaining production records), sugar master (responsible for processing and crystallizing the cane, which required extensive technical knowledge, precision, and the ability to make snap judgments), master brick maker, cartwright, and blacksmith—all positions that required highly specialized technical skills—were held by African slaves on Santiago de la Paz.[66]

Continuing with an analysis of the slave inventory at Santiago de la Paz, there were forty-seven adult males listed (one of whom was in jail, another away at war, and another listed as absent for two years), and

twenty-seven adult females (one of whom was living on another estate)—
a gender ratio of a little under two to one, which is not as uneven as might
have been expected. Eleven male children and six female children are also
listed, which is approximately the same ratio. The ages of the adult slaves
are obviously approximations, for they are nearly all given in even numbers of twenty, thirty, forty, and so on. There is only one male listed as
over age seventy, however, two females were ages eighty and ninety,
respectively, and six were in their sixties and seventies. This would suggest that males were doing the most dangerous work, the work in the mill
and with the pots and fires for crystallization, while the women no doubt
helped in the fields but were mainly given "domestic" jobs like cooking.
The slave woman named Catalina, however, was listed as a strainer, which
indicates that she worked in the crystallization process. Children appear
to have been relatively well treated, considering that males aged seventeen and even eighteen were included on the inventory of children. Two
eighteen-year-old males on the inventory of children appear to have been
apprentice cartwrights and, as such, may have had to work the same hard
and long hours as adults. Juanica, who was only seventeen, was included
on the adult list; the assumption is that she had borne a child. Unfortunately, there are no family groupings given except that one woman,
Juana, is listed as the wife of Pedro Çape, who was only a "kettle tender,"
which was not an important position. Among the five recently deceased
slaves listed, one died during childbirth, two in "war," and two of unspecified causes; one of the latter was a seven-year-old boy. The numbers of
recently dead are too few to arrive at any general conclusions.

As Robert S. Haskett notes, the fact that no slave houses were included in the inventory of Santiago de la Paz is an indication that "[t]hey
were probably huts of little regard or commercial value."[67] There is also
no mention of slaves' kitchen gardens, but they no doubt kept them to
supplement the cattle, sheep, yucca, corn, sweet potatoes, and oranges
that were raised on the estate as well as the salted fish that was stored in
one of the ingenio's stone towers.

The three fortified stone towers, which appear to have been the most
prominent buildings on the ingenio, held a wide variety of tools and
replacement parts for mill equipment. They also held two pairs of hand-
cuffs and six "Negro collars." The combination of the inventory's counts
of physical restraints and descriptions of slaves with wooden feet and legs
(cutting off a leg was a recommended punishment for running away),

missing eyes, and skin ulcers, are grim reminders of how harsh slave life could be on a sugar ingenio.

Resistance to Slavery

The slaves on Hispaniola's sugar ingenios responded to the harshness of their lives in many creative ways, some of which have not been recognized until recently as acts of resistance. Catherine C. LeGrand conducted a study of the Dominican Republic's twentieth-century cane workers and resistance that sheds light on slaves' responses on sugar ingenios in the sixteenth century. She found that workers feigned illness, worked slowly, engaged in malicious gossip, broke tools and equipment, "choked" the sugar presses by overloading them with cane (which then required several hours to clean up before processing could continue), maimed animals needed to haul or mill the cane, or lost or ruined materials and supplies.[68]

Normally, it was in the best interests of a smooth-running sugar ingenio for the supervisor to ignore daily acts of sabotage and resistance that could be attributed to accident or illness. If a slave were caught in a purposeful act of insubordination or rebellion, however, what James C. Scott calls "public breaches," the masters and overseers were forced to make a public example of the perpetrator in order to discourage others from rebelling. Scott explains that public breaches happened frequently because slaves were constantly "testing the limits" of their subjugation.[69]

One public breach that was virtually impossible for masters and overseers to ignore was when a slave ran away. Often, however, a slave's absence was only temporary—perhaps a visit to a wife, friend, or relative on another plantation. Punishment for temporary absence was often light. But when did "temporary absences" turn into insubordination? Although the legal definition was fifteen days as of 1528, the inventory from Santiago de la Paz illustrates that slave owners continued to be lenient with their slaves, stretching temporary absences into years—a male slave named Lorençillo was listed on Santiago de la Paz's inventory as "a *vaquero* who it is said has been absent for two years." Another male slave, Jorge Tuerto, is listed as "serving in the war," referring most likely to one of the many ongoing battles in the 1530s and 1540s against cimarrones. Tuerto could quite easily have changed sides, however, to join the cimarrones in their fight against the Spaniards (the same way it is supposed that Sebastián Lemba, mentioned in the beginning of this study, joined the war in Bahoruco). If Tuerto had become a cimarrón, both the ingenio's overseer and the census taker would, no doubt, have been reluctant to say so in an official document. Juan Grande and "another old Negro" were listed on the inventory as having been killed in the war, but they, too, could have simply changed sides and run away.[70] Furthermore, when slaves did desert, their owners might not even have known. There are clear hints in the documents that captains exaggerated the number of deaths in their squadrons because they were held less culpable for deaths than for desertions.[71]

Runaways and Other Rebels

The archival records of 1540s' Hispaniola are peppered with reports of African cimarrón "captains," some of whom the Spaniards claimed had "thousands of rebellious Negroes" among their ranks. Archdeacon Alonso de Castro, in a report to the crown dated March 26, 1542, claimed that there were two thousand to three thousand African cimarrones in the eastern part of the island alone, "hurting and robbing by night and by day everything that there is [to steal] in the country, including gold."[72] Two and a half years later, on September 12, 1544, Governor López de Cerrato did his best to convince the emperor that he had cleaned up the rebellions. He reported that, in place of the former thousands of African cimarrones, "there remain only fifteen" on the entire island, although two years later, he admitted to between twenty-five and thirty.[73]

Other Spaniards concurred with Archdeacon de Castro's high numerical assessment of African cimarrones, not with Governor López's lower figure. Melchor de Castro, for example, who was the royal scribe in charge of the island's mines, justified the fact that less gold had been mined than normal and that fewer Spaniards had gone in search of new mines by explaining to the crown on July 25, 1543: "[P]eople are afraid . . . of all the Negroes who have rebelled." As was the case with the Indians who had found refuge in the regions outside Spanish control, he explained to the crown, "The island is large and filled with cows, wild pigs and other food-stuffs, and in this way rebel Africans have security and food."[74]

Castro was not the only one writing this type of report. Later that year, a royal cédula dated October 31, 1543, attempted to force the island's administrators to control the "many Negroes" who had been reported running free "in the mountains of Santiago and Yacera and in all the cordillera up to Monte Cristi."[75] There were so many African cimarrones, several of the crown's administrators jointly reported on February 10, 1545, that "it is an embarrassment how the rebellious Negroes go about the roads killing and robbing Spaniards up to three leagues from the city [of Santo Domingo]." Ironically, in the same letter, they requested that the emperor send five thousand to six thousand more Negro slaves to the island.[76]

The Spaniards who remained on Hispaniola in the middle of the sixteenth century were caught in the grip of a painful conflict—on the one hand they needed more African slaves if they were to continue increasing sugar production and profits, but they did not know how to deal with the rebellions. The more slaves they imported, the more rebels there were. The slaves were increasingly willing to use violence to resist the Spaniards' efforts to control them, their lives, and their labors. In 1546 one frightened colonist informed the Spanish authorities that there were "squadrons of armed Negro slaves" running amok in Bahoruco and La Vega. "No man walks alone anymore," he wrote. "The island is in terror that the other twelve thousand Negroes . . . will rise up too."[77]

The fears that he expressed were not, of course, unique to Hispaniola. All across the Americas, first Spaniards and then Portuguese, Dutch, French, and British entrants in the race to colonize and reap financial benefit from the New World using African slave labor on the sugar, rice, tobacco, cacao, and cotton plantations, and in the gold and silver mines, would encounter the same painful conflict. Forced labor and oppression always end in rebellion—and the more force and oppression one uses, the more rebellion results. The patterns of slave control and rebellion that were set on Hispaniola were replicated in the other Caribbean islands and across both the American continents, where they multiplied a millionfold with the millions of Africans who survived the Middle Passage and were forced into slave labor in the New World.

APPENDIX

Three Hacienda Censuses

Writing colonial era history, especially history focused on those who left behind no documents of their own, like African slaves on the sixteenth-century Spanish sugarcane ingenios of Hispaniola, requires great effort. Only after gathering extensive material, comparing the information gathered, and trying to "fill in the gaps" can one begin to approach what life must have been like for these people who were torn from their homeland and forced to work in one of the most perilous of industries, an ocean away from all that they knew and cherished. Below are three rare documents, censuses of workers on Hispaniola's sugarcane ingenios in the first half of the sixteenth century. The first of the three censuses is from 1530, although it is to be found only among the files that pertain to a lawsuit initiated on July 19, 1533, between the civil and ecclesiastical councils of Santo Domingo. Its information is sparse but can be filled in by comparing it to what is revealed in the census taken three years later by Archbishop Alonso de Avila, whose goal was to determine how many clerics were needed for the island's growing number of ingenios. The third census, taken in 1545, was ordered by the island's incoming governor Alonso de Fuenmayor and sent along with a report to the Spanish emperor, according to historian Luis Joseph Peguero. Peguero published the census in 1763 in his history of Hispaniola (reprinted in 1975). Unfortunately, the document does not appear anywhere else to verify its data, which is very detailed—perhaps Peguero had access to a document that has since disintegrated or disappeared. The information about the island's ingenios at this time in Gonzalo Fernandez de Oviedo y Valdez's Historia general y natural de las Indias *is almost the same, however, so Oviedo appears to have had access to the same document or spoke to someone who did— perhaps to Avila himself.*

Hispaniola Ingenio Census of 1530
- Ingenio belonging to Juan de Villoria (probably Sanate— see item 1 in the next census), with 100 Africans, 60 Spaniards, and "some" Indians.
- Ingenio called Los Trejos (see item 2), with 80 Africans, 40 Spaniards, and "some" Indians.
- Along the River Cocaymaguay, a total of 700 people, but not broken down into any categories (see item 3).
- The ingenio Santi Spiritus (see item 4), with 90 Africans and 12 Spaniards. In lieu of a quantity of Indians there is a question mark.

❧ The ingenio of the admiral (La Isabela, see item 6), with 80 Africans, 20 Spaniards, and ? Indians.

❧ An ingenio belonging to Benito de Astorga, with 60 Africans, 15 Spaniards, and ? Indians.

❧ Diego Caballero's ingenio (see item 6), with 70 Africans, 10 Spaniards, and ? Indians.

❧ Pero Vázquez's ingenio, with 120 Africans, 20 Spaniards, and ? Indians.

❧ Francisco de Tapia's ingenio (probably item 8), with 80 Africans, 12 Spaniards, and ? Indians.

❧ Licenciado Lebrón's ingenio (see item 9), probably Arbol Gordo, with 70 Africans, 6 Spaniards, and ? Indians.

❧ The ingenios of Juan de Ampies, Esteban Pasamonte, Francisco Tostado, Diego Caballero, and the heirs of Francisco de Tapia (see item 10), with a total of 700 Africans, 150 Spaniards, and 200 Indians.

❧ The ingenios of Lope de Bardeci, Alonso de Avila, and the heirs of Miguel de Pasamonte (see item 11), with 250 Africans, 60 Spaniards, and "some" Indians.

❧ Zuazo's ingenio, with 90 Africans, 12 Spaniards, and "some" Indians.

❧ Diego Caballero's ingenio called Cipecipi (see item 12), with 80 Africans, 10 Spaniards, and "some" Indians.

Data from a lawsuit between the civil and ecclesiastical cabildos of Santo Domingo, in AGI, Justicia 12, N1, R2, as cited in Esteban Mira Caballos, *El indio antillano: Repartimiento, encomienda y esclavitud (1492–1542)* (Seville: Ediciones ALFIL, July 1997), 155.

Alonso de Avila's Census of 1533

1. On the ingenio called Sanate, which belonged to Juan de Villoria and was located five leagues from the village of Higüey, there were 100 Africans and 20 Spaniards, some of whom were married (but Avila did not specify if he meant that some of the Africans, the Spaniards, or both were married). In the general vicinity of Sanate, there were about 40 Spaniards with smaller estates, "without much abundance of Negroes and Indians."

2. The ingenio called Las Trejos, on the Río Quiabón (today called the Chavón), only two leagues away from Sanate, had 15 Spaniards and 80 Africans. The houses of another 25 workers were nearby, along the riverbank, some of whom had Africans and Indians with them (unspecified quantities).

3. On the Cocomagua and Cacay rivers, in a region about four leagues square that was fifteen leagues from Santo Domingo, "a large quantity of people lived" on small estates with cattle herds. Avila estimated that there were more than 700 people altogether, including Spaniards, Africans, and Indians.

4. The ingenio of Sancti Espíritus, on the Río Cacay, twelve leagues from Santo Domingo, had 12 Spaniards, some of whom were married, plus there were 90 Africans. There were estates "both small and large all around this ingenio, herds of cattle, and the haciendas of laborers." A clergyman already resided there.

5. The ingenio of La Isabela, which belonged to the (third) Admiral Luis Colón, was on the Río Ibuca, five leagues from Santo Domingo. It had 20 Spaniards and 80 Africans. One league away was the ingenio belonging to Benito de Astorga, which had 15 Spaniards and 70 Africans. Nearby haciendas accounted for another 200 persons.

6. The ingenio of the *contador* (royal accountant) Diego Caballero was on the Río Yuca, two leagues from Santo Domingo. It had 10 Spaniards and 70 Africans, with another 200 persons living nearby. It, too, already had a resident clergyman.

7. The ingenio belonging to Pedro Vázquez, on the Río Haina, three leagues from Santo Domingo, had 20 Spaniards and 120 Africans, with "at least" another 400 persons living along the river on their own small farms and haciendas.

8. The ingenio of de Tapia (possibly Cristóbal, for Francisco was already dead), one league from that of Vázquez, had 12 Spaniards and 80 Africans.

9. The ingenio of Arbol Gordo, which belonged to the heirs of Licenciado Lebrón and which was one and one-half leagues from the pueblo of Buenaventura, had 6 Spaniards and 70 Africans.

10. There were several ingenios and haciendas at the head of the Río Nigua, where it joined the Río Yamán, six leagues from Santo Domingo. They belonged to the royal treasurer Esteban Pasamonte, Francisco Tostado, the heirs of Francisco de Tapia, and to secretary Diego Caballero. Additionally, there were "at least" 700 Africans, 200 Indians, and 150 Spaniards living together in this region, "for it is the most populous river that there is at present on this island." Altogether, there were five ingenios on the Río Nigua, with clerics residing on the two main ones.
11. There were three other ingenios on the Río Nigua that were approximately ten leagues from Santo Domingo. They belonged to Lope de Bardecí, Alonso de Avila, and the heirs of Miguel de Pasamonte. The rivers of Paya, Baní, and Iguare were also nearby, "all of which is very heavily populated," with 70 Spaniards, 250 Africans, and "some Indians." The people there raised cattle and sheep in addition to cultivating sugarcane.
12. The ingenios called Orcia and Capecipi were both on the Río Ocoa, sixteen leagues from Santo Domingo. The first belonged to Licenciado Alonso Orcia, who was an oidor on the audiencia. It had 12 Spaniards, 90 Africans, and "some Indians." Capecipi, which belonged to Secretary Diego Caballero, had 10 Spaniards and 80 Africans. No other haciendas or populations were nearby.

Data from AGI, Justicia 12, 149, fols. 10v-15; full text in José Luis Sáez, *La iglesia y el esclavo negro en Santo Domingo: Una historia de tres siglos* (Santo Domingo: Patronato de la Ciudad Colonial de Santo Domingo, Colección Quinto Centenario, 1994), 267–72.

Alonso de Fuenmayor's Census of 1545

Sanate, founded by Juan de Villoria, twenty-four leagues east of Santo Domingo at the edge of the village of Higüey, had 27 Africans and 30 Indians. (Oviedo wrote that Sanate was owned in 1536 by Villoria's widow, doña Aldonza de Acevedo. Probably the same ingenio as item 1 in the census above.)

✤ An ingenio named Quiabón on the Río Quiabón, twenty-four leagues east of Santo Domingo in the jurisdiction of Seybo (which is quite likely the ingenio in item 2, which Avila called Las Trejos), was founded by Melchor de Castro and Hernando de Caraval. It was "well built, has good profits, and is well situated," and had "more than 200 Negroes and 200 Indians."

✤ A "powerful" ingenio named Casuy on the river of the same name, in the province of Seybo, eleven leagues north of Santo Domingo, was founded by Juan de Villoria and was now owned by his brother-in-law Gerónimo de Agüero. Casuy had "50 Negroes but more than 200 Indians." (Probably built in the region that Avila called the rivers Cocomagua and Cacay, where there were no ingenios in 1533, but a large mixed population of over 700 persons, or this is the ingenio called Sancti Espíritus in 1533—see items 3 and 4.)

✤ The ingenio Cañaboba, on the Río Hayna just three leagues from Santo Domingo, owned by Admiral Luis Colón, had 215 Africans and 300 Indians. It had been moved from a site that was four leagues from the capital, where the ingenio had been called Nueva Isabela. (In Davila's day, the admiral's ingenio was called La Isabela—item 5—and was on the Río Ibuca, five leagues from the capital. The family, therefore, kept moving it closer and closer to Santo Domingo.)

✤ The unnamed ingenio owned by the *veedor* (supervisor) Pedro Vázquez de Mella and Estevan Justinian Ginovés on the Río Hayna, four and one-half leagues from Santo Domingo, had 100 Africans and 80 Indians. (Vázquez may have taken Ginoves on as a partner after the 1533 census and may have relocated the ingenio in item 7 one and one-half leagues farther upriver.)

✤ An ingenio in Itabo, four leagues from Santo Domingo, owned by veedor Francisco de Tapia, had 93 Africans and 210 Indians. (This may be the ingenio in item 10 that belonged to the heirs of Franciso, but it is more likely to be item 8, the ingenio founded by Cristóbal de Tapia.)

✤ An ingenio on the Río Nigua, near where it emptied into the sea, four and one-half leagues from Santo Domingo, was "one of the biggest and richest on the island." It belonged to Diego Caballero de la Rosa (regidor, contador, and secretary

of the audiencia) and had 310 Africans and 50 Indians.
(Probably the ingenio in item 10.)

✢ Santa Isabel, also on the Río Nigua, upriver from Caballero's
and five leagues from Santo Domingo, was owned by the scribe
Francisco Tostado. It had 70 Africans and 130 Indians.
(Probably one of the ingenios in item 10.)

✢ Seven leagues from Santo Domingo on the Río Nigua was an
ingenio named San Cristóbal for the father of the founders, the
brothers Miguel and Esteban Pasamonte. It had 207 Africans
and 300 Indians. (Could be one of the ingenios in either item
10 or item 11.)

✢ An ingenio owned by the heirs of Miguel de Pasamonte on the
Río Nigua eight leagues from Santo Domingo, "which is one
of the best ever built on this island," had 80 Africans and
300 Indians. (Could be one of those listed in item 10 or item 11
but most likely the former.)

✢ Eight and one-half leagues from Santo Domingo on the Río
Nigua was an ingenio owned by the contador Alonso de Avila
with 200 Africans and 352 Indians. (Oviedo wrote that in 1536,
it was owned by Avila's heirs, his sister, and Esteban Davila.
Probably one of the ingenios in item 11.)

✢ Nine leagues from Santo Domingo on the Río Nigua was an
ingenio owned by Lope de Baldesia, who boxed his sugar using
a kind of balsa wood called *champanes* that grew at the river's
mouth. It had 95 Africans and 80 Indians. (Possibly the ingenio
listed in item 11 as belonging to Lope de Bardecí.)

✢ An ingenio belonging to the oidor Alonzo de Zuazo on the
Río Ocoa, sixteen leagues from Santo Domingo. He bought
it from Diego Basán. It had 150 Africans and 200 Indians.
(Oviedo wrote that in 1536 it belonged to Zuazo's heirs,
his widow doña Felipa, and his two daughters, Leonor and
Emerenciana. Possibly the ingenio in item 12 listed as
belonging to Orcia.)

✢ The ingenio Cepi Cepin on the river of the same name, twenty
leagues from Santo Domingo, belonged to Diego Caballero
de Rosas. It had "no more than" 70 Africans and 365 Indians.[78]
(The ingenio is most likely the same one in item 12 called
Capecipi by Avila.)

✻ An ingenio that was "very useful and well made," ten leagues
from Santo Domingo, was founded by the oidor don Cristóval
Lebron. Called Arbolgordo, it had 193 Africans and 208
Indians. (See item 9.)

Data from Luis Joseph Peguero, *Historia de la conquista de la Isla Española
de Santo Domingo trasumptada el año de 1762: Traducida de la historia
general de las Indias escrita por Antonio de Herrera coronista mayor de su
magestad, y de las Indias, y de Castilla; y de otros autores que han escrito sobre
el particular* (Santo Domingo: Publicaciones del Museo de Las Casas
Reales, 1975; orig. pub. 1763), 217–21.

***The following ingenios appear on the 1545 census,
but not on the 1533 census:***

✻ Eight leagues from Santo Domingo on the Río Nigua was an
ingenio founded by the royal factor Juan Ampíes called Yamán
(Oviedo said it was owned in 1536 by Ampíes's widow, doña
Florencia de Avila Yamán). It also produced cacao and had
110 Africans and 500 Indians. (Either it was right next to the
ingenio owned by the heirs of Miguel de Pasamonte, above, and
the ingenio called Pedergal, below, or the distance given from
Santo Domingo was in error—all three are listed as being eight
leagues from Santo Domingo on the Río Nigua.)

✻ Eight leagues from Santo Domingo on the Río Nigua was
an ingenio called Pedergal owned by Bachiller Antonio de
Fuenmayor. It had 114 Africans and 218 Indians.

✻ Jacomé de Castellon had an ingenio with "one of the best rents
on the island," twenty-three leagues from Santo Domingo
on the outskirts of Azua. It had 83 Africans and 98 Indians.
(Oviedo wrote that it was owned in 1536 by Castellon's widow
doña Francisca de Isásaga, and his sons.)

✻ Also in Azua, twenty-four leagues from Santo Domingo, was
an ingenio belonging to Hernando Gorjón, which was "worth
a lot." It had 214 Africans and 170 Indians, "plus 40 more"
Africans "in the capital," working in the manufacturing shop
called La casa y estudio general.

✻ The clergyman don Alonso de Peralta, a vecino of the village
of Azua who was at the Cathedral of Santo Domingo in 1545,
founded a trapiche there that was now owned by Bachiller

Gonzalo de Vellosa (the surgeon who had been in partnership with the Tapia brothers). It had 136 Africans and 28 Indians.

❧ Another trapiche in Azua was owned by Martín García, "a very honorable man and one of the richest on the island." It had 97 Africans and 110 Indians.

❧ "A powerful ingenio" forty leagues from Santo Domingo, in the village of San Juan de la Maguana, was owned by the heirs of a vecino from there named Juan de León, who had been "in the company of the Belgian Germans." It had 92 Africans and 25 Indians.

❧ Another ingenio in San Juan de la Maguana, on the Río Neiba, was called La Companía. It was founded by Pedro de Vadillo, royal secretary Pedro de Ledesma, and Bachiller Moreno, who were "rich, putting a large force of 300" Africans "and some few Indians" to work on it. La Compania also had "a herd of 3,000 cows to maintain it."

❧ An ingenio on the Río Yuca, two leagues north of Santo Domingo, was founded by the licenciados Antonio Serrano and Francisco de Prados and was now owned by contador Diego Savallo. It "paid good rents" and had 80 Africans and 40 Indians.

❧ A "large ingenio" founded by the oidor Lucas Vázquez de Ayllón and Francisco de Savallos in the city of Puerta Plata, forty-five leagues north of Santo Domingo, was "a very beautiful hacienda," with 225 Africans and 200 Indians.

❧ Another ingenio "with good rents" was founded in Puerto Plata by don Diego de Morales and Pedro de Barrionuevo. It had 114 Africans and 138 Indians.

❧ A horse-driven trapiche in Puerto Plata was founded by Francisco de Barrionuevo (who by 1545 was governor of Castilla del Oro, in today's Panama). It had 70 Africans and 300 Indians.

❧ Another trapiche in Puerto Plata, "the largest milled by horses," was "very well provided for." It was founded by Sancho Monasterio and Juan de Aguilar and had 60 Africans and 110 Indians.

❧ An ingenio in Bonao, nineteen leagues from Santo Domingo, also grew cacao. It was founded by Miguel Jover, Sebastián de Fonte, and Hernando Carrion and had 32 Africans and 183 Indians.

NOTES

1. The Spanish word *ingenio*, which literally means "ingenious," initially referred to the water-powered or animal-powered machinery that was used to press the juice from the sugarcane. By the time the processes were imported to Hispaniola, however, the phrase *ingenio azucarero*, or the word *ingenio* alone, had come to encompass not only the mill but the entire complex of lands, buildings, equipment, and workers devoted to sugar's growth, harvest, and production.

2. Letter from *oidores* (judges on the high court) Grajeda and Zorita to the Spanish Emperor, October 16, 1547, transcribed in Fray Cipriano de Utrera, *Polémica de Enriquillo* (Santo Domingo: Editora del Caribe, 1973), 483; originally from Archivo General de India (AGI), Audiencia de Santo Domingo 49.

3. Jane Landers, "Maroon Ethnicity and Identity in Ecuador, Colombia, and Hispaniola" (paper presented at the annual Latin American Studies Association conference, Miami, March 2000. <http://lasa.international.pitt.edu/Lasa2000/Landers.PDF>

4. Utrera, *Polémica de Enriquillo*, 483; originally AGI, Justicia 76.

5. José Antonio Saco, *Historia de la esclavitud de la raza africana en el nuevo mundo y en especial en los países américo-hispánicos* (Havana: Cultural, 1932), 2: 14–15.

6. Report to the Spanish Crown, March 7, 1548, from Hispaniola's governor Alonso López de Cerrato, in Roberto Marté, ed., *Santo Domingo en los manuscritos de Juan Bautista Muñoz* (Santo Domingo: Ediciones Fundación García-Arévalo, 1981), 420–21.

7. See app.5 of Esteban Mira Caballos, *El Indio Antillano: Repartimiento, encomienda y esclavitud (1492–1542)* (Seville, ALFIL, 1997), 400–401.

8. One arroba is equivalent to 25 pounds or approximately 11.5 kilograms. Lorenzo E. López and Sebastián Justo L. del Río Moreno, "Comercio y transporte en la economia del azúcar Antillano durante el siglo XVI," *Anuario de estudios hispanoamericanos* 49 (1992): 83–84.

9. As the closest approximation to the Spanish racial category of *indio*, the term *Indian* is employed here and elsewhere when appropriate. The encomienda system arose in Spain and was brought to the Americas with Christopher Columbus in the 1490s (emanating out of Hispaniola as the conquest spread), where it was first known as *repartimiento*, from the Spanish verb meaning "to divide up." Queen Isabella wrote in a royal *cédula* (writ) dated December 20, 1503, in Medina del Campo, that the

system prevented the Taíno Indians from "going about as vagabonds without wanting to be indoctrinated [into the Catholic faith] nor to work on the land nor in the mines." AGI, Indiferente General 418, L1, fols. 121v–22; full text available in Marté, *Manuscritos de Juan Bautista Muñoz*, 52–53. In theory, the encomienda system was mutually beneficial. Groups of people like the Taíno, who were considered to be too naïve to make important decisions on their own, were commended to the care of a Spanish male, their *encomendero*. In exchange for taking care of them and making sure that they learned how to live as proper Christians, the commended Indians were forced to give tribute or to labor for their encomendero in the mines, construction, agriculture, and any other work he required of them. Many scholars equate the encomienda system with slavery, but encomenderos did not purchase their Indians—the Spanish crown commended the Indians to their care—and could not sell them, though the crown could take them away and commend them to another Spaniard at will. For the initial development of the encomienda system, see Robert S. Chamberlain, *Castilian Background of the Repartimiento-Encomienda System* (Washington, DC: Carnegie Institute, 1939). See also Lewis Hanke, *The Spanish Struggle for Justice in the Conquest of America* and *The First Social Experiments in America: A Study in the Development of Spanish Indian Policy in the Sixteenth Century* (Cambridge, MA: Harvard University Press, 1935); José Antonio Saco, *Historia de la esclavitud de los indios en el nuevo mundo* (Havana: Cultural, 1932); Lesley Byrd Simpson, *The Encomienda in New Spain: The Beginning of Spanish Mexico* (Los Angeles: University of California Press, 1966); Luis Arranz Márquez, *Repartimientos y encomiendas en la isla Española (El repartimiento de Albuquerque de 1514)* (Santo Domingo: Fundación García-Arévalo, 1991); Carlos Esteban Deive, *La Española y la esclavitud del Indio* (Santo Domingo: Fundación García-Arévalo, 1995); Esteban Mira Caballos, *El indio antillano: Repartimiento, encomienda y esclavitud (1492–1542)* (Seville: Ediciones ALFIL, July 1997); Emilio Rodríguez Demorizi, *Los Dominicos y las encomiendas de indios de la Isla Española* (Santo Domingo: Editora del Caribe, 1971).

10. Archivo General de Indias, Seville (hereafter AGI), Indiferente General 421, L12, fol. 116v; Indiferente General 195, L1, fol. 9. See also Indiferente General 421, L11, fols. 300–303. Text published in *Colección de documentos inéditos relativos al descubrimiento, conquista y organización de las antiguas posesiones españoles en Ultramar (*hereafter *CDIU)* (Madrid: Establecimiento Tipográfico, 1885–1932), 5(9):248–56.

11. Marté, *Manuscritos de Juan Bautista Muñoz*, 331–32.

12. See *CDIU*, 17:23–31. This document is a long list of many of the licenses for "discovery and conquest" in the Indies that were issued by the Spanish crown through the 1560s.

13. Marté, *Manuscritos de Juan Bautista Muñoz*, 413–14.

14. López and del Río Moreno, "Comercio y transporte en la economia del azúcar Antillano durante el siglo XVI," 83–84. The best summary of the origins of the sugar industry on Hispaniola is Mervyn Ratekin, "The Early Sugar Industry in Española," *Hispanic American Historical Review* 34, no. 1 (1954): 1–19.

15. William F. Keegan estimates nearly twenty-six thousand Taínos were carried to Hispaniola from the Bahamas in 1510, which was depopulated by 1513. *The People Who Discovered Columbus: The Prehistory of the Bahamas* (Gainesville: University of Florida Press, 1992), 221–23.

16. The Spaniards labeled the Indians "weak" because of their susceptibility to disease. For more details, see Noble David Cook, "Disease and the Depopulation of Hispaniola, 1492–1518," *Colonial Latin American Review* 2, nos. 1–2 (1993): 213–45; see N. David Cook and W. George Lovell, "Unraveling the Web of Disease," in *Secret Judgements of God: Old World Disease in Colonial Spanish America*, ed. N. David Cook and W. George Lovell (Norman: University of Oklahoma Press, 1992), 213–42; Alfred W. Crosby, *Ecological Imperialism: The Biological Expansion of Europe, 900–1900* (Cambridge: Cambridge University Press, 1986) and *The Columbian Exchange: Biological and Cultural Consequences of 1492* (Westport, CT: Greenwood, 1972); William M. Denevan, ed., *Native Population of the Americas in 1492* (Madison: University of Wisconsin Press, 1976); John W. Verano and Douglas H. Ubelaker, "Health and Disease in the Pre-Columbian World," in *Seeds of Change*, ed. Herman Viola and Carolyn Margolis (Washington, DC: Smithsonian Institution Press, 1991), 209–23.

17. Indians who were designated as cannibals were subject to enslavement, which included all of those of the Lesser Antilles and most of the Central and South American coasts. Any Indians who resisted Spanish dominion were also subject to enslavement. In an attempt to appease those who opposed the enslavement of the Indians, in 1513 a new legal document and procedure called *El requerimiento* (The Requirement) was created by a committee of scholars, theologians, and jurists led by Dr. Juan López de Palacios Rubios. See Lynne Guitar, "The Requirement," in *Historical Encyclopedia of World Slavery*, ed. Junius P. Rodriguez (Santa Barbara: ABC-CLIO, 1997), 2:545; Lewis Hanke, "The 'Requerimiento' and its Interpreters," *Revista de historia de América* 1 (1938): 25–34;

Patricia Seed, "The Requirement," in *Ceremonies of Possession in Europe's Conquest of the New World, 1492–1640* (New York: Cambridge University Press, 1995). For Caribbean and circum-Caribbean permits to enslave "cannibals," see, for example, AGI, Indiferente General 418, L3, fol. 211v and fols. 213–14v, dated December 23, 1511 and December 24, 1511, respectively; AGI, Indiferente General 41, L1, fols. 131v–32, December 24, 1511. For Indian slave permits relating to Central America, see AGI, Indiferente General 420, L10, fols. 243r–v. For Mexico, see Roberto Cassá, *Historia social y económica de la República Dominicana*, 2nd ed., 2 vols. (Santo Domingo: Editora Alfa y Omega, 1992), 1:54. For Brazil, see AGI, Indiferente General 420, L8, fols. 177r–78r. For Florida, see AGI, Indiferente General 419, fols. 245r–v.

18. In the appendixes to her study of Haitian culture, the late anthropologist Maya Deren used the concept of "cultural convergence" to explain the similarities among the many different African and Indian peoples, noting that it was precisely those points of their customs and beliefs that were most alike that have survived in strong measure on the island through the present day. Maya Deren, *Divine Horsemen: The Living Gods of Haiti* (New York: McPherson, 1991; orig. pub 1953).

19. Ladinos were acculturated Africans, or people of African descent, who had been baptized, had Spanish names, and had adapted to Spanish customs. They are often indistinguishable from Spaniards in the historical records.

20. José Antonio Saco, *Historia de la esclavitud de la raza africana en el nuevo mundo y en especial en los países américo-hispánicos*, 2 vols. (Havana: Cultural, 1938), 1:97; *Colección de documentos inéditos para la historia de Ibero-América* (hereafter *CDIA*) (Madrid: Compañía Ibero-Americana de Publicaciones, 1925–37), 5:43–45. See also royal response to Ovando in Marté, *Manuscritos de Juan Bautista Muñoz*, 48–50.

21. Royal letter dated March 10, 1504, to the officials of the Casa de Contratación. Marté, *Manuscritos de Juan Bautista Muñoz*, 54. Carlos Esteban Deive found documentation indicating that the first *bozales* (slaves brought directly from Africa) who were sent to Hispaniola to work the royal gold mines arrived in early 1505. They were a group of seventeen, he says, purchased in Lisbon but brought directly there from Guinea by the Portuguese. Carlos Esteban Deive, *Los guerrilleros negros: Esclavos fugitivos y cimarrones en Santo Domingo* (Santo Domingo: Fundación Cultural Dominicana, 1997). Mira Caballos has listed information about all royal licenses issued for slaves going to Hispaniola and Puerto Rico in *El Indio antillano*, app. 5, 400–401. See also *CDIA*,

6:129–33, in which the crown suggested that the African slaves be offered the incentive of a percentage of the gold they mined, with which they could eventually purchase their freedom. There are no extant documents, however, to indicate that any slaves on Hispaniola achieved their freedom in this manner. Mira Caballos has listed all licenses for slaves that are on file in the AGI.

22. In a series of *interrogatories* in Santo Domingo in June of 1521, dozens of witnesses testified about the monopoly and how the slaves were being shipped "little by little, to gain time so as to sell them at a higher price." *CDIA*, 1:366–467, question no. 21. Evidence that the full four thousand slaves were not delivered until 1527 or 1528 is the multitude of new licenses that were issued to ship slaves contingent upon the fulfillment of the earlier contract. See cédulas dated February 10, 1526—AGI, Indiferente General 420, L10, fols. 260r–v for one hundred slaves, fols. 260v–61r for fifty, and fols. 261r–v for one hundred; also fols. 290r–v dated March 24, 1526, for one hundred slaves; fols. 297r–98r dated April 12, 1526, for one hundred; fols. 323r–v dated May 5, 1526 (this license is for a woman, María de Vilda, royal seamstress, who was permitted to bring twenty slaves to Hispaniola after Bresa fulfilled his contract); and Indiferente General 421, L11, fols. 5v–6v dated May 16, 1526, for fifty slaves, and fols. 63v–64r dated June 20, 1526, for one thousand slaves.

23. AGI, Indiferente General 421, L13, fols. 98r–100v.

24. Jane Landers noted that even before African slaves left Africa, most had already experienced extensive cultural and ethnic "intermingling." Jane Landers, *"Cimarrón* Ethnicity and Cultural Adaptation in the Spanish Domains of the Circum-Caribbean, 1503–1763," in *Identity in the Shadow of Slavery*, ed. Paul E. Lovejoy (London and New York: Continuum, 2000), 30.

25. Information from AGI, Justicia 12, N1, R2, as cited in Mira Caballos, *El indio antillano*, 155.

26. An excellent exploration of how differently "ethnicity" was conceptualized in the sixteenth century than it is today is David Eltis, "Ethnicity in the Early Modern Atlantic World," chapter 9 of *The Rise of African Slavery in the Americas* (Cambridge: Cambridge University Press, 2000), 224–306.

27. The first census in America with a category for "mestizos" was in Cuba in 1582—ninety years after the Europeans' arrival. Franklin W. Knight, *The Caribbean: The Genesis of a Fragmented Nationalism* (New York: Oxford University Press, 1990), 44–45.

28. AGI, Justicia 12, 149, fols. 10v–15; full text of the census available in José Luis Sáez, ed., *La iglesia y el esclavo negro en Santo Domingo* (Santo Domingo: Patronato de la Ciudad Colonial de Santo Domingo, Colección Quinto Centenario, 1994), 267–72.

29. The data is from Luis Joseph Peguero, *Historia de la conquista de la Isla Española de Santo Domingo Herrera coronista mayor de su magestad, y de las Indias, y de Castilla; y de otros autores que han escrito sobre el particular* (Santo Domingo: Publicaciones del Museo de Las Casas Reales, 1975; orig. pub. 1763), 217–21. Peguero claims to have had access to the document written by Fuenmayor, who began compiling the information when he arrived on Hispaniola for his second term in office on August 3, 1545; but Peguero does not say how or where he encountered the document, which may have been in a private collection. I have not been able to locate it, nor a copy, in the AGI in Seville, Archivo General de la Nación in Santo Domingo, nor in other collections or published sources. Peguero noted that Fuenmayor's report took the ingenios' locations and their owners from the 1536 description in Gonzalo Fernández de Oviedo y Valdez's *Historia general y natural de las Indias* (originally published in 1535), book 4, chap. 8. Oviedo, however, did not list quantities of workers and he had one additional ingenio listed, called Yaguate, owned by Francisco de Tapia, that Peguero/Fuenmayor did not mention.

30. Fuenmayor, who came to his office directly from Spain, may have been counting everyone on Hispaniola with the least bit of Indian heritage as "Indian," a precursor of the distinctions that would later be made in all the Spanish American possessions between *peninsulares*, Spaniards born in the Iberian Peninsula, and *criollos*, Spaniards born in the Americas. The implication was that peninsulars were superior because they were "pure" Spanish, whereas all criollos were suspected of having some Indian blood.

31. López, who was in charge of enforcing compliance to the New Laws, informed the emperor that "of the more than five thousand Indian slaves" on the island, none were "the original natives . . . all were brought from elsewhere." The letter has been cited by other historians as evidence that the native Taínos were extinct by then, but López more likely meant that, to the best of his knowledge, none of the Taínos (who were protected by the New Laws) were among the island's documented slaves, only those who had been taken legally, in which case the letter was an indication to the crown that López was doing his job. AGI, Audiencia de Santo Domingo 49, R16, N101; cited in Mira Caballos, *El indio antillano*, 290.

32. See, for example, AGI, Patronato 174, R6 (January 18, 1518) and Patronato 177, N1, R2 (1518, unspecified date).

33. For more details on the 1521 rebellion, see Roberto Cassá and Genaro Rodríguez Morel, "Consideraciones alternativas acerca de las rebeliones de esclavos en Santo Domingo," *Anuario de estudios hispanoamericanos* 51 (1993): 101–31; Deive, *Los guerrilleros negros*, 31–36; Gonzalo Fernández de Oviedo y Valdéz, *Historia general y natural de las Indias* (Madrid: Gráfica Orbe, 1959; orig. pub. 1535), Biblioteca de Autores Españoles, vols. 117–21, book 6, chap. 51.

34. AGI, Patronato 295, no. 104; full text of the ordinances, which were for both the island of Hispaniola and the island of Puerto Rico, where the Colón family also had property and held slaves, can be found in Deive, *Los guerrilleros negros*, 281–89. Note that many historians cite 1528 as the year that the first slave laws were promulgated in the Americas, but Deive has proven them wrong.

35. Deive, "Las ordenanzas sobre esclavos cimarrones de 1522," *Boletín Museo del Hombre Dominicano* 19, no. 25 (1992): 135.

36. See Fray Cipriano de Utrera, "La condición social de los negros en la época colonial," *Eme Eme: Estudios dominicanos* 3, no. 17 (1975): 50–51.

37. Criados were "trusted men," who were frequently servants or slaves of the Spaniard they served. Henceforth, it would take special royal permission, such as the cédula issued in 1536 to Gonzalo Fernández de Oviedo y Valdéz, *alcalde* of the fortress in Santo Domingo, "to carry with him two Negroes armed with offensive and defensive weapons to accompany him and to go on foot and by horse . . . to guard and to defend his person." AGI, Audiencia de Santo Domingo 868, L1, fol. 14v.

38. See Philip D. Curtin, *The Rise and Fall of the Plantation Complex: Essays in Atlantic History* (Cambridge: Cambridge University Press, 1990).

39. On September 28, 1532, the crown issued a general prohibition "that no one can bring to the Indies slaves from the island of Gelofe [*sic*] because of their excitable and rebellious spirit." AGI, Indiferente General 1961, L2, fols. 223r–v. The royal order was reinforced April 18, 1534 (L3, fol. 138v), wherein the Casa de Contratación was reminded to enforce compliance to the 1532 cédula prohibiting the passage of Wolofs to the Indies.

40. Carlos Esteban Deive, *La Española y la esclavitud del indio* (Santo Domingo: Fundación García-Arévalo, 1995), 290. Enrique's rebellion lasted until 1534, when the Spanish crown negotiated a treaty with him and his followers. Meanwhile, however, he served as a model for others—many African slaves ran away and joined him, and by 1526, the Taínos had also risen up on Cuba (see AGI, Indiferente General 421, L11, fols. 304v–5r),

and the Spaniards were at full-blown war on and around Puerto Rico with both Caribes and Taínos, who had formed an alliance (AGI, Indiferente General 421, L13, fols. 31v–32v).

41. See *CDIU*, 5(9):368–71 and 386–99; 10:55–56, 38–43, and 72–73; AGI, Patronato 231, N4, R2; AGI, Indiferente General 422, L16, fols. 61v–66v (text in *CDIU*,10:192–203); Ricardo Konetzke, ed. *Colección de documentos para la historia de la formación social de Hispanoamérica, 1493–1910* (hereafter *CDHFS*) (Madrid: Consejo Superior de Investigaciones Científicas, 1953–62), 138–39.

42. AGI, Indiferente General 1962, L4, fols. 27r–v.

43. Neither idea was original. The recommendations appear over and over in the sixteenth-century documents, but there is little evidence that they were acted upon.

44. Sáez, *La iglesia y el negro esclavo en Santo Domingo*, 230–31.

45. AGI, Indiferente General 420, L10, fol. 350; text in *CDHFS*, 1:81–82; *CDIU*, 5(9):239–42.

46. *CDIU*, 10:430–31.

47. The 1528 slave ordinances are detailed in Sáez, *La iglesia y el esclavo negro en Santo Domingo*, 236–49; initially from Archivo Nacional de Cuba, doc. 243, file 3, no. 97a, fols. 24–33. See also Franklin J. Franco, *Los negros, los mulatos y la nación dominicana* (Santo Domingo: Editora Valle, 1989), 20–21; Javier Malagón Barceló, *El código negro o código negro español (Santo Domingo, 1784)* (Santo Domingo: Ediciones de Taller, 1974), 128–37.

48. This despite the fact that in 1526 a joint uprising of native Guales and African slaves imported from Santo Domingo destroyed the Spaniards' first settlement in what would later become the United States of America, San Miguel de Gualdape. Only 150 of the original 500–600 settlers who had left Hispaniola returned, no doubt with horror stories of the Indo-African rebellion. See Paul E. Hoffman, *A New Andalucia and a Way to the Orient: The American Southeast during the Sixteenth Century* (Baton Rouge: University of Louisiana Press, 1990), 76–83.

49. Franco, *Los negros, los mulatos y la nación dominicana*, 19.

50. Fray Cipriano de Utrera, *Historia militar de Santo Domingo (documento y noticias)* (Ciudad Trujillo: n.p., 1950), 1:138.

51. Archdeacon de Castro noted in his report that he had traveled all over the island in his religious capacity, visiting Indians, Spaniards and, presumably, Africans. Marté, *Manuscritos de Juan Bautista Muñoz*, 396–97.

52. Diego Caballero de la Rosato to the Crown, December 5, 1538, in César Cabral Herrera, *Colección César Herrera*, vol. 1, *Junta de procuradores, 1518–1545* (Santo Domingo: Patronato de la Ceudad de Santo Domingo, Talles Isabell la Católica, 1995), 105–28.

53. Ibid.

54. See *Boletín del Museo del Hombre Dominicano* 7, no. 10 (1978). Most of the first 160 pages are dedicated to the 1976 excavation at Sanate, which was the first of a planned series to locate and catalog sugar ingenios that were established on Hispaniola through the mid-sixteenth century. The project was organized by the Museo del Hombre Dominicano and funded by the Gulf and Western Americas Corporation; however, funding ran out before the end of the first year. Archaeological investigations were begun at Caballero's ingenio on the Río Nigua, too, investigations that might have shed more light on the living and working conditions there, had there been enough funding. Neither the supervisor's mansion nor the workers' housing area has been studied except to trace some of the foundations. What is even more unfortunate is that the skeletons and other material remains uncovered during the ingenio's brief period of excavation were marked and bagged, but never cataloged nor even sorted, and have since "disappeared," as one of the leading investigators explained in a private interview, March 2000. During a recent visit to the ruins of Caballero's ingenio (June 2001), I photographed evidence that some funding has now been made available—the mill, crystallization buildings, and aqueducts have been partially reconstructed.

55. The oldest university is today's Universidad Autónoma de Santo Domingo, founded by Dominican friars in 1538 as the Universidad de Santo Tomás de Aquino. Note that many other historians have used the Santiago de la Paz documents over the years. See Robert S. Haskett, "Santiago de la Paz: Anatomy of a Sixteenth-Century Caribbean Sugar Estate," *UCLA Historical Journal* 1 (1980): 51–79—this article contains translations of several of the most important documents related to African slaves on the ingenio; Ursula Lamb, *"Cristóbal de Tapia vs, Nicolás de Ovando": Un fragmento de residencia de 1509*, trans. Eduardo Villanueva, which is included in Emilio Rodríguez Demorizi, *El Pleito Ovando-Tapia: Comienzos de la vida urbana en América* (Santo Domingo: Editora de Caribe, 1978), 20–30; Genaro Rodríguez Morel, "Cartas privadas de Hernando Gorjón," *Anuario de estudios americanos* 52 (1995): 203–33.

56. *CDIA*, 1:156.

57. AGI, Patronato 173, N1, R8; text in J. Marino Incháustegui, *Reales cédulas y correspondencia de gobernadores de Santo Domingo de la regencia del Cardenal Cisneros en adelante* (Madrid: Colección Histórico-Documental Trujilloniana, 1958), 1:225.

58. AGI, Audiencia de Santo Domingo 868, L1, fol. 246v, cédula dated June 18, 1540.

59. Incháustegui, *Reales cédulas y correspondencia*, 1:233–58.

60. Marté, *Manuscritos de Juan Bautista Muñoz*, 420–21.

61. Ibid., 418. A *maquila* is a measure of weight (about 125 pounds), used today for corn.

62. Incháustegui, *Reales cédulas y correspondencia*, 1:258–60.

63. For more detail on the "nations" of Africans who were brought to Hispaniola, see Philip D. Curtin, *The Atlantic Slave Trade: A Census* and *Economic Change in Precolonial Africa: Senegambia in the Era of the Slave Trade* (Madison: University of Wisconsin Press, 1975); Carlos Esteban Deive, *Vodú y Magia en Santo Domingo* (Santo Domingo: Fundación Cultural Dominicana, 1972), 88–101; Herbert S. Klein, *African Slavery in Latin America and the Caribbean* (New York: Oxford University Press, 1986); Martin A. Klein, ed., *Peasants in Africa: Historical and Contemporary Perspectives* (Beverley Hills, CA: Sage, 1980); Martin A. Klein and G. Wesley Johnson, eds., *Perspectives of the African Past* (Boston: Little, Brown, 1972); Carlos Larrazabal Blanco, *Los negros y la esclavitud en Santo Domingo* (Santo Domingo: Julio D. Postigo e Hijos, 1967); Walter Rodney, "Upper Guinea and the Significance of the Origins of Africans Enslaved in the New World," *Journal of Negro History* 54, no. 4 (1969): 327–45 (particularly 328–34); John Thornton, *Africa and Africans in the Making of the Atlantic World, 1400–1680* (Cambridge: Cambridge University Press, 1992).

64. Thanks to Jonathan Reynolds, who suggested that the name Javja may have referred to the Hausa language. Open discussion, July 31, 1997, at the SSHRC/UNESCO Identifying Enslaved Africans workshop, York University.

65. Lolita Gutiérrez Brockington found Africans in similar positions of authority on the ranches of New Spain in the 1580s. See her chapter on "Hacienda Slave Labor," in *The Leverage of Labor: Managing the Cortés Hacienda in Tehauntepac, 1588–1688* (Durham, NC: Duke University Press, 1989), 126–42.

66. For more detail, see Haskett, "Santiago de la Paz," 64–68. Stuart B. Schwartz found that in Brazil, African slaves also held most of the positions requiring skill and technical ability, whereas the Indians did mainly fieldwork. He notes this was due, in part, "to Portuguese perceptions of the relative abilities of Africans and Indians." See his "Indian Labor and New World Plantations: European Demands and Indian Responses in Northeastern Brazil," *American Historical Review* 83, no. 1 (1978): 58.

67. Haskett, "Santiago de la Paz," 61.

68. See Catherine C. LeGrand, "Informal Resistance on a Dominican Sugar Plantation during the Trujillo Dictatorship," *ECOS—Organo del Instituto de Historia de la Universidad Autónoma de Santo Domingo* 4, no. 5 (1996): 141–98.

69. James C. Scott, *Domination and the Arts of Resistance: Hidden Transcripts* (New Haven, CT: Yale University Press, 1990), 49–50, 197.

70. Santiago de la Paz inventory, AGI, Patronato Real 173, no. 1, R8; also in Incháustegui, *Reales cédulas y correspondencia*, 1:233–58.

71. In a similar way, supervisors of sugar ingenios overstated the ages of their slaves so that more deaths could be attributed to natural causes, not abuse or mismanagement. Haskett, "Santiago de la Paz," 70.

72. Marté, *Manuscritos de Juan Bautista Muñoz*, 396–98.

73. AGI, Audiencia de Santo Domingo 868, L2, fols. 246–47; letter dated November 16, 1546, Marté, *Manuscritos de Juan Bautista Muñoz*, 416–17.

74. Marté, *Manuscritos de Juan Bautista Muñoz*, 401–4; also in Herrera, *Colección César Herrera, Junta de Procuradores*, 129–32. The quantities of gold that Castro reported were 5,087 pesos and three tomines in 1537; 3,568 pesos and two tomines in 1538; 5,425 pesos and one tomin in 1539; 3,943 pesos and four tomines in 1540; 4,947 pesos and six tomines in 1541; and 3,046 pesos in 1542. He also reported that 110,000 arrobas of sugar had been shipped in 1542 and "a small quantity" of *cañafístola*.

75. AGI, Audiencia de Santo Domingo 868, L2, fol. 204.

76. Marté, *Manuscritos de Juan Bautista Muñoz*, 406–7; also in Utrera, *Historia militar*, 1:384. See also the letter of March 26, 1542, in Marté, *Manuscritos de Juan Bautista Muñoz*, 396–98.

77. July 17, 1546. Marté, *Manuscritos de Juan Bautista Muñoz*, 301.

78. Peguero/Fuenmayor identified these 365 Indians as *indígenas* using the feminine form of the noun, whereas in all the other instances he used the masculine or neutral form. The feminine ending may have been a printing error.

CHAPTER THREE

Central Africa in the
Era of the Slave Trade

JOHN K. THORNTON

☙IN 1604 THE KONGOLESE DIPLOMAT ANTONIO MANUEL STOPPED IN BRAZIL
on his way to represent Kongo before the Holy See in Rome. He was a
man steeped in European culture: literate, deeply Christian (though he
had studied and worshipped for his whole life in Kongo), a diplomat and
formerly the head of a church, secretary to various officials, and most
recently Marquis of Funta. When he stopped in Spain he would corre-
spond with a wide range of Europeans, Spanish, and Belgian priests,
Portuguese nuns, the pope and various kings, all of whom were impressed
by him. Although we do not know for sure, he almost certainly crossed
the Atlantic on the first leg of his journey on a slave ship. He must have
appreciated the horrors of slavery, for among his personal papers is the
certificate of freedom of Dom Pedro Manibala, a Kongolese noble whose
freedom from slavery he probably arranged while in Brazil. It is quite
likely that Dom Pedro was someone much like him, educated in the
European sense, probably literate, and perhaps as comfortable as Antonio
Manuel in upper-class European society. Both men represent what made
Central Africa an unusual contributor to the culture and history of Latin

83

America, the coexistence of an African variant of European Christianity and civility with the degradations of the slave trade.[1]

The Central African contribution to Latin America is different from that of other parts of Africa primarily because the region possessed a much higher degree of homogeneity than other regions did, and because no other African region had such a deep engagement in European culture. Central Africans, beginning in the fifteenth century, were quick to adapt elements of European culture, including religion and aspects of material culture. Beyond this propensity, Portugal founded a large colony in Angola and governed hundreds of thousands of Africans, with the inevitable cultural consequences. As a result, by the mid-seventeenth century Angola resembled Latin American countries in ways that no other part of Africa did.[2]

The people who were enslaved and exported from West Central Africa came from a vast and geographically varied region. In the north, the coast of the Kingdom of Loango was forested and low, though mostly uninhabited mountains lay behind it. Farther south, the Kingdom of Kongo dominated the lands south of the Congo River. The country was flat and dry along the coast, but inland the terrain moved from hilly to mountainous as one reached the eastern end of the country around the Inkisi River. To the south of Kongo lay a rough and broken plateau, home of the Dembos, a group of small states whose mountainous terrain protected them from domination by their more powerful neighbors.[3] South of this the coast became even more arid, although rivers arriving at the sea made them more habitable. Luanda, the capital of Angola, was located next to a beautiful natural harbor in land that was otherwise marginal. The city had to be constantly supplied from inland, either along the Bengo River to its north or the Kwanza to the south. The interior behind Luanda belonged to the Kingdom of Ndongo on a fine high plateau between the Kwanza and Lukala rivers. As the Portuguese invaded Angola after 1575 their principal aim was the domination of this plateau, which they only partially achieved during their seventeenth-century campaigns.

The Kwango River, flowing north and south, formed the eastern limit of the great coastal kingdoms. A deep depression, the Baixa de Cassange, lying roughly due east of the plateau that Ndongo controlled, through which the Kwango ran, was the home of Matamba, an ancient state conquered by Queen Njinga when her dynasty was forced eastward by Portuguese expansion, and south of that the kingdom established by the

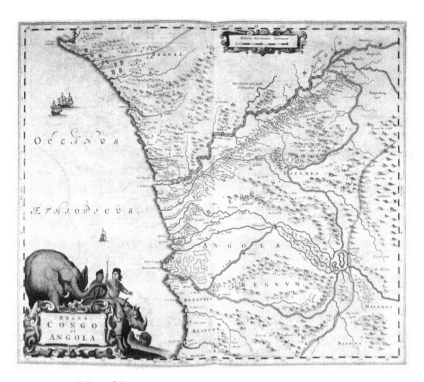

FIGURE 3.1: *Map of Congo and Angola, 1662. From: Joan Blaeu's*
Geographia, quae est Cosmographia Blaviana,
(A 1662 .B53). Reproduced courtesy of the Tracy W. McGregor
Library, Special Collections, University of Virginia Library.

army of Kasanje advancing in the 1630s from the wars over Ndongo.
Beyond the Kwango to the east the land was flatter, though probably never
very densely inhabited. People were not enslaved in this region for export
before the conquests of the Lunda Empire, whose capital was much farther
east in the heart of the continent in the mid-eighteenth century.

  South of the Kwanza River the land rose abruptly to the great central highlands. Although the margins of the central highlands were sharp
and broken, the plateau itself was relatively flat, with a temperate climate
created by its elevation. Although its history is the least well known of the
lands that furnished America with enslaved laborers, it probably had the
largest population.

Origins and Direction of the Central African Slave Trade

Although the Portuguese first contacted Central Africa in 1483 when Diogo
Cão's exploration stopped and exchanged hostages in Kongo, there were
very few substantial contacts until almost a decade later. In 1490 the king
of Portugal was still sufficiently uninformed about the situation in Kongo
that he sent an exile from São Tomé there to spy the country out and be
retrieved by "any ship [*nao*] that might go there."[4] The slave trade from
Central Africa probably did not begin in the 1490s—it seems likely that the
military-diplomatic mission to Kongo in 1491 that baptized that ruler as
João I was compensated by slaves captured in its military expedition against
rebels.[5] A map legend of 1502 confirms that slaves were prominent among
Kongo's exports, even though a 1506 account cites them as being "a few."[6]

In any case, the slave trade from Kongo soon boomed, so that there
were thousands of slaves carried annually to São Tomé by 1516,[7] and by
1548 there were three or four thousand a year, according to a Kongolese
royal investigation of the trade. That investigation revealed that Kongo's
southern neighbor, Ndongo, had joined in the Central African slave trade
as well, for the merchants that were interviewed complained that competition from Portuguese doing business in Angola (as that region was
already called) was drawing away shipping from their coast. Although the
inquest cited specific incidents only from 1542, a Ndongo slave trade
probably dated from the 1520s when São Tomé-based merchants founded
an unofficial trading base there.[8]

The rapid development of the slave trade had many causes, not the
least the fact that Kongolese law (and probably the law of its less well-
documented neighbors) in the early sixteenth century recognized slavery
and slave trading as legitimate activities, for which there were functioning
markets within Kongo. The existence of a slave market is first revealed in
a letter written by King Afonso I of Kongo (1509–42) in 1514, where he
noted that some priests and Portuguese officials bought slaves with
money he gave them, something that would have been impossible had
there not been a market in slaves where money was employed already in
existence for local use.[9] Most slaves seem to have been captives taken in
war, for the same letter gives an account of one such war, conducted
against a southern region, in which hundreds of captives are mentioned
but probably thousands were taken. Some were distributed to soldiers (of
which Afonso only mentions those given to Portuguese), and others were
returned to the capital.[10]

In fact, the Atlantic slave trade was in some ways an outgrowth of a well-established Central African system of slavery and slave trading.[11] Central Africa was very sparsely populated in the sixteenth century; it probably had fewer people than in the seventeenth when we can establish that the average population density in Kongo was somewhere around three people per square kilometer.[12] While other areas may have had higher densities, such as the favored highlands around Ndongo or the Angolan central plateau farther south still, few probably had average densities over ten per square kilometer.

Not only was the population sparse, it was remarkably mobile. Central Africans did not recognize ownership of land, and therefore had little stake in remaining in one place. Building techniques stressed temporary structures, often rebuilt or replaced, and agriculture rarely involved long-term capital investments. Therefore, it was very easy for whole villages to move should circumstances require it or opportunities favor it. Central Africans were inclined to move their villages to avoid taxation or other circumstances they regarded as onerous.[13]

Building kingdoms with such small and scattered populations required creating local centers of population, especially as can be seen in Kongo, given that the rural population could literally hide itself away from roads and supervision in the woods and bush. Kings overcame the problem of the sparse rural population by building very densely settled capital districts, which may not have had very large cities but did have large agricultural districts, where population densities might exceed fifty per square kilometer. This seems to have been the case in the district around Kongo's capital of Mbanza Kongo (later São Salvador) as early as 1548.[14] Such a strategy produced a population that probably numbered one hundred thousand within a few kilometers' radius of São Salvador by the 1620s.[15]

While the process is best illustrated in Kongo, where quantitative data is available, one gets the same impression from other major states of Central Africa. Ndongo, Loango, which dominated the coast north of the Congo River, and even Lunda, the great empire of the deep interior that rose to prominence in the mid-eighteenth century, all had densely populated capital regions, even if they did not have extraordinarily large or even stable capitals.[16] In Loango the towns of the various strong nobles and potential successors to the throne were all located within a few miles of the king's capital, while in Lunda the royal capital was rebuilt in each reign, but always in the same small region.[17] It was probably even true of the shadowy early kingdoms of the central highlands; certainly the pattern of demographic concentration is visible from the late eighteenth century onward.[18] Rulers who could maintain a densely populated capital region ensured that they could concentrate surplus production without paying high transport costs, support large armies to protect the monarchy, and entice the nobility to regard the region as home (or actually to reside there), which discouraged rebellions.[19]

While all these centers were in ecologically favored locations, the high population densities cannot be explained by environment alone—rather, the concentrations were created by force. Wars, like that of Afonso in 1514, were probably instrumental in shaping Kongo in its early years, even before the possibility of selling captives in the Atlantic slave trade, in which people were captured and returned to the capital to be integrated into life there as a servile class. That the class had the legal characteristics of slaves, including the right of owners to sell them, is clear enough in Kongo, and is probably just as true in the less well-documented other regions as well.

While in Central Africa the development of the external slave trade followed the development of states and their wars to some degree, as in West Africa, Europeans played an independent role in it as well. In the earliest years, Portuguese served as mercenaries in Kongo's armies and received shares of the spoils for their efforts. During much of the sixteenth century, in Kongo and probably in Ndongo as well, where there was no formal relationship with the two crowns, Portuguese mercenaries were firmly under the control of African rulers. This relationship changed gradually with the arrival of Paulo Dias de Novais in Angola in 1575. Initially Dias de Novais served as a mercenary as well, but when the ruler of Ndongo suddenly attacked his force, he was required to fight independently. Although he probably could not have survived without support from Kongo, by 1580 he had built an independent colony around Luanda and the valley of the Kwanza.

The colony of Angola was not unlike the neighboring African states politically, and Luanda and the related river valleys, especially the Bengo River, formed the sort of slave-based population center that characterized Kongo or Ndongo. But Angola was far more committed to developing the slave trade as forcefully as it could, and more so than any of its African neighbors. Slaves did remain in Luanda and its vicinity to labor and serve, but more than anything else the city and even its settler-run estates were established to support a large slave trade, and politics were frequently oriented around the capture of people to export.

The Central African slave trade was originally directed primarily to São Tomé rather than America. The vast majority of the slaves delivered to the Spanish Indies during most of the sixteenth century came from Senegambia and Sierra Leone. In a surviving sugar estate inventory from Hispaniola in 1549, for example, only 2 percent of the slaves were of Central African origin, and only 5 percent in an inventory of Cortés's slaves in Mexico of the same time.[20] Their numbers had risen to only 10 percent of the population recorded in notarial documents in Peru from 1549 to 1560.[21]

After 1575, when Paulo Dias de Novais arrived in Angola, and then in the wars after 1579, the number of Central Africans rose sharply in the Atlantic trade to America, thus increasing the ability of the Portuguese to obtain slaves directly. Portuguese slave traders with a base in Angola obtained the *asiento* (permission to carry slaves to Spanish possessions in the New World) in the 1590s, but the real breakthrough came during the governorship of Luis Mendes de Vasconcelos in Angola from 1617 to 1621. Mendes de Vasconcelos had excellent contacts in Madrid, and his associates held the asiento. He succeeded in recruiting the Imbangala, rootless mercenary soldiers who had been terrorizing the region south of the Kwanza River for many years, to come and fight for the Portuguese. With their help, he and his successors were very successful against their African opponents, enslaving thousands. Mendes de Vasconcelos may have enslaved as many as fifty thousand people in his three-year term.[22] For the next twenty years Angolans made up as much as 75 percent of the slaves brought to the Spanish Indies under the asiento trade, and they were probably an even higher percentage of those going to Brazil. The Dutch West India Company, formed to assist the emerging Dutch Republic wage naval war on the Iberian possessions in 1621, captured Bahia in 1623–24 and then, after losing that, took Pernambuco in 1629 and held it until 1654. The Dutch noted that virtually all the slaves brought to Pernambuco in the years just prior to the capture of the district in 1623 were from Angola.[23]

These years of near-complete dominance of the slave trade to Latin America by Angolans ended with the Dutch seizure of Luanda in 1641, which they had done as an extension of their operations against Brazil and to deprive the Iberian monarchies of the revenues of the slave trade and related American industries that relied on Angolan slaves. The Spanish reorganized the asiento system following the recapture of Luanda by Portuguese forces from Brazil in 1648, granting it to a number of non-Portuguese, first Dutch and then English, suppliers who drew on different sources. Nevertheless, the Dutch and English both had Central African contacts, primarily in Loango and the northern parts of Kongo, and these in turn were taken to Loango as well as Portuguese ports.[24] The English South Sea Company, which held the asiento in the early eighteenth century, drew on much different sources of slaves than its predecessors, but still brought in around 15 percent of its slaves from Central Africa.[25]

In the period after the expulsion of the Dutch, the whole system of slave procurement changed. The Portuguese found themselves increasingly fought to a standstill by the African powers that surrounded their colony in Angola. In 1656 they signed a treaty with Queen Njinga, who had led Ndongo since 1624 and had now managed to build a military force that could challenge them. Meanwhile, many of the Imbangala bands had settled down, some in Portuguese service and others, most notably the powerful army of Kasanje, as independent rulers on their own. Costly victories, such as the siege of Pungo Andongo in 1671–72, defeats such as the loss at the battle of Kitombo against Soyo (a province of Kongo) in 1670, and the ending of aggressive interventions along the Kwango in the 1680s gradually brought Portuguese direct procurement of slaves to a halt.[26]

In the period that followed, people were enslaved by military campaigns waged by African powers as well as some smaller-scale and low-keyed raiding within and around Portuguese territory.[27] Portuguese armies that launched punitive campaigns against the Kisama region south of the Kwanza on a fairly regular basis through the eighteenth century were typical of these military events.[28] Most operations were much smaller, involving few troops and few captives, such as the series of raids and counterraids between Portuguese settlers in Ambaca (eastern Angola) and their African neighbors in 1755, or a similar engagement in 1773 near Cahenda in the Dembos region that lay between Kongo and Angola.[29] Local complaints make it clear that Portuguese soldiers also occasionally raided people near their jurisdiction, even those nominally at peace with Portugal.[30] Portuguese settlers joined this pattern when they illegally enslaved their neighbors or those subject to the Portuguese crown using their own private armies, as we learn from a denunciation of the 1770s.[31]

While relatively few people were enslaved in any of these events, the area from which they were drawn was quite large, and we can only guess what percentage they represented of those exported to the New World.

The Portuguese conducted major wars on only a few occasions. Certainly the most significant was the war against Matamba in 1744, which netted thousands of slaves, if it did not result in much change in the balance of power.[32] The Portuguese also launched a much more substantial series of wars into the central highlands from their south coastal colony of Benguela and its outlying fortress of Caconda during much of the first half of the eighteenth century, again in 1755, and especially in the long wars of 1773–75.[33]

If Portuguese aggression declined as a source of enslavement, African wars continued to result in people being enslaved and deported. The civil war that ravaged Kongo for much of the late seventeenth and eighteenth century was responsible for many people losing their freedom and probably compensated for the decrease in numbers of people captured with the end of Portugal's campaigns in Angola. In 1665 a Portuguese army defeated the army of Kongo's King António I at the battle of Mbwila. Though it was an inconclusive victory, quickly offset by the Portuguese defeat at Kitombo, the war plunged Kongo into a civil war in which rival kings contested for the throne. For most of the rest of the seventeenth century, rival pretenders, fortified in different parts of the country, waged war on each other, enslaving people as a part of the larger program of military aggression.[34] Although a peace was patched together in the early eighteenth century, Kongo witnessed a number of new episodes of civil war throughout the eighteenth century, often at a considerable human cost.[35]

The remaining growth of the slave trade in the eighteenth century can be accounted for by the expansion of states and regions engaged in the export trade to the east. Toward the middle of the eighteenth century, the armies of the emerging Lunda empire smashed into the lands east of the Kwango River. Lunda campaigns, like those of the Portuguese in the seventeenth century, often had enslavement as one of their primary objectives. As their wars expanded their empire, merchants from Kongo (especially the Zombo region in the far east)[36] and from independent African states like Kasanje or the kingdoms of the central highlands purchased these captives and transported them to the coast for sale. By the nineteenth century, as many as one-third of all the slaves carried from Angola had been enslaved in Lunda or its environs.[37]

Some of the victims of this new pattern of enslavement found themselves in Spanish territories. Thus, Aguirre Beltrán's study of slave origins
in Mexico at the end of the seventeenth century still showed Central
Africans making up three quarters of the total, as does a smaller study of
Cuzco for the same period.[38] The Portuguese of Luanda, no longer involved to the same degree in the trade with Spanish America, thus focused
on Brazil, and in the late seventeenth century Angolans dominated that
trade as before the Dutch episode.

In the eighteenth century the Portuguese gradually shifted some of
their efforts from Angola to West Africa, marked symbolically by the
founding of the Portuguese factory at Whydah on the so-called Slave
Coast in 1718. For much of the eighteenth century slaves arriving in
Brazil came from just two general areas: Angola and the Lower Guinea
Coast (which the Portuguese called the Costa da Mina). From around
1700 to 1730, Angolans made up a bit less than half of the imports into
Brazil, but after 1730 the percentage of Angolans rose past half the total,
from nearly 70 percent in the 1740s to nearly 90 percent by the 1780s.[39]

The Culture of Central Africa

Central Africans coming to Brazil and the Spanish Indies brought with
them a distinctive regional culture, notable not only for its original elements but for having absorbed a significant amount of European culture.
Some of this absorption was in the highly creative process under African
control that began in Kongo in the late fifteenth century, and some of it
came from the presence of the Portuguese colony at Luanda, Benguela,
and along the Kwanza and Lucala rivers. The growth and development of
this element of Central African culture can be traced in documents, and
it played a critical role in the easy integration of Central Africans into the
culture of Latin America. However, there were also substantial elements
in this culture of more purely African origin that had joined with, com-
peted with, or operated alongside the European elements.

These African elements are harder to distinguish in West Central
Africa, especially since more recent events have made ethnographic reconstruction of more ancient culture difficult. This is because in the mid-
nineteenth century West Central Africa went through a huge economic
change. The Industrial Revolution in Europe, with the resulting trade and
transport revolution, led Central Africans to divert their energies from a

local to a world market. Local industry producing textiles and metal goods declined in the face of imports, while the increasing volume of imported products was paid for by exports of ivory, wax and other gathered products, peanuts, and wild rubber, among others. Hundreds of thousands of porters carrying rubber, peanuts, or ivory would trek hundreds of miles to move these goods to the coast and to buy manufactured goods from Europe. [40] Thus, even without a single factory being built, the Industrial Revolution arrived in Central Africa, with social changes that rivaled those that transformed western Europe or America. Settlement patterns changed, family structure was altered in important ways, individualism became rampant, powerful states were shaken to their cores as formerly dependent commoners asserted their rights, and novel forms of local government emerged.[41] These changes place a veil over the preceding period, for most of what anthropologists were able to document as "traditional society" in the late nineteenth and early twentieth centuries was in fact configured only in the half century preceding. Consequently, what we can reconstruct of the pre-nineteenth century culture of West Central Africa must come from a painstaking study of its contemporary, usually European-authored, documentation, with careful and controlled study of more modern ethnographic materials.

Most West Central Africans in the sixteenth through early nineteenth centuries lived in small, scattered villages that rarely exceeded populations of two hundred, interspersed with larger regional capitals of perhaps a thousand people. But a significant minority lived in much larger capital-area agglomerations, as we have already noted. These agglomerations accounted for as much as 20 percent of the population in Kongo and probably elsewhere as well, even though the levels of density were less than what most geographers would describe as urban in all but a small part of the area.[42] Wars were often focused on these capital regions, and thus their residents were somewhat more likely to be enslaved than those residing among the scattered populations of rural areas. This is particularly visible in Kongo, where eighteenth-century military strategy and resulting enslavement focused on the attempt to establish large and loyal populations at São Salvador.[43]

Economically, villages were substantially self-sufficient, and although there was a vigorous local market system, the markets primarily connected relatively close neighbors to each other, though a certain amount of long-distance trade brought quite exotic goods to markets as well. Still, the economy probably did not cause many people to go far from home, a fact that was to change dramatically with the nineteenth-century trade revolution.

It was military activity, not trade, that broke the parochialism of the village economy and created larger loyalties and identities in Central Africa. Although seventeenth-century armies throughout Central Africa often had a core of professional soldiers that might not number more than a few thousand and might reside in fairly restricted areas, they were supported by vast numbers of porters and camp followers, who might mobilize a significant portion of the population and bring them together. In the eighteenth century, military changes often led to larger armies that were recruited by mass levy.[44] Such armies would draw a significant number of people from a large area into their ranks, and given the frequent hostilities and disturbances of the time, many people would have served more than once in a military campaign.[45]

While most armies were led by state political authorities, there were also military forces like the Imbangala whose mode of mobilization was different. The Imbangala recruited their members by violent capture, focusing especially on adolescent boys. They were held in military service for the rest of their lives through participation in what amounted to an enforced witchcraft ritual involving cannibalism that they were required to repeat from time to time. These armies were also characterized by high levels of alcohol consumption, which probably helped to keep members dependent, much as such types of organizations work in modern Africa with child soldiers.[46] These military forces lived by virtually permanent rapine until by military action or treaty they settled down, like the celebrated armies of the Imbangala leader Kasanje, who carved out a state along the Kwango in the 1630s. Imbangala were regarded by most people in Angola as evil, and their radical model of forced recruitment was not favored by any state system, although some rulers, like Queen Njinga, reluctantly used Imbangala units and sometimes even reorganized their own armies along Imbangala lines. It is for this reason also that Imbangala bands were unlikely to become the model for runaway settlements, like Palmares in Brazil.[47]

Military service not only led people to travel, it also united them with people from disparate parts of the country and shaped identity. Facing hardship and danger together in the name of the political entity that mobilized them had a significant impact on the people who were recruited to serve, whether as combatant or supporter. Furthermore, as should be obvious, it was through military service that people were most often enslaved; most Africans brought as slaves to Latin America were likely to have had military experience and organization as their last African experience. At the very least, this background would have an impact on their propensity to revolt as well as the effectiveness of their rebellions.[48]

West Central Africa was quite homogenous culturally, at least by comparison with West Africa. Virtually all the people in the zone spoke closely related languages of the Bantu family. Kikongo, spoken in the north, was the language of virtually the whole population of the Kingdom of Kongo and Kingdom of Loango. It gradually yielded to the Teke language around the Maleba Pool region and to Kimbundu in the Dembos area to the south. An early visitor described Kikongo and Kimbundu as being as similar to each other as Spanish and Portuguese, not an unfair comparison.[49] The two languages are remarkably similar in grammar and idiom as well as vocabulary.

In the seventeenth century the two languages were even more similar than they are today. For example, in those days Kikongo still used a *ku-* prefix for the infinitive form of verbs, which it has since lost but Kimbundu has retained. Likewise, the evolution of the sixteenth-century Kikongo "l" into seventeenth-century "r" and then to the modern "d" has distanced the two languages phonetically.[50] A good many people on the borderlands between the two countries were bilingual, and in any case, the linguistic similarities made it fairly easy for Kimbundu speakers to learn Kikongo or vice versa.

Umbundu, the language of the central plateau, was less similar, forming a different subgroup, although certainly there are strong convergences between it and its northern neighbors in both vocabulary and grammar. The eastern languages beyond the Kwango River are different again, though the total range of difference in all the languages of the region is limited, and the whole group might accurately be described as being no more diverse than the Latin family of languages in Europe.

Portuguese was introduced into West Central Africa soon after the conversion of Kongo in 1491. The Kongolese used Portuguese for written communication, which promoted widespread use of the language by the elite even before the establishment of the colony of Angola spread the language to the south and brought thousands of native speakers into Africa. Although Portuguese did not displace Kimbundu even in Angola, it did serve as a lingua franca over a much wider area than the region that Portugal conquered. Even as early as 1700 one might have occasionally heard Portuguese spoken all along the Kwango, and it was frequently the language of traders going to Lunda in the mid-eighteenth century.[51]

Cultural similarities were perhaps greater than those of language. The general principles of religion were quite uniform. For example, all the religious traditions maintained that ancestors, members of people's families who had died recently, could exercise considerable power over their descendants from beyond the grave. This resulted in a good deal of family-oriented religious activity, often centered at the graves of ancestors, seeking their protection and support.

In addition to ancestors, Central Africans recognized a number of local deities, who might reside in water courses, mountains, or uninhabited wild areas, but who were propitiated most often in either large shrines, like the *kitekes* of the Mbundu areas or the *nkisis* of the Kongo area, or in smaller, often portable charms. Many times the deities had specific names and jurisdictions, ranging from kingdoms and provinces to fields and villages, and were typically territorial rather than having control over general natural phenomena. One would not expect, for example, a god of rain or fire in Central Africa. The only general deity was known as Nzambi in Kikongo and Kimbundu, though he might go under other names as well, who was credited with creation and the general oversight of the world. But Nzambi was nowhere the subject of a general cult, and religious activity was focused more on shrines of local deities.

Central African religions had neither authoritative clergy nor dogma, but they did have priests whose primary role was to communicate with the other world. Some did this through various means of divination, others through spirit possession. The messages they received or delivered were not under their control, and they served simply in an advisory role. The most important qualification for a priest, generally called *nganga* in the languages of the area, was the capacity to contact and communicate with the other world, a capacity that was proved by the efficacy of their messages.

In Central Africa, evil was seen as arising from the intentions of people rather than any external source, such as a devil or evil spirits. There were evil spirits, to be sure—the souls of those who had been evil in life or other angry spirits, such as those who had been killed in wars, eaten by wild animals, or not properly buried. While they were considered nuisances, real evil came from people who used the other world's power to advance their own selfish goals. Such people were witches, *ndoki* in Kikongo, from the word *loka* (to curse), who had the power to cause harm supernaturally through curses, or *muloji* in Kimbundu, who had similar powers to work destruction from poison. A witch worked his or her power by enlisting the assistance of amoral spirits from the other world. Witches could be controlled by ngangas, who might learn their intentions and stop them, but ngangas themselves could be witches if they chose to use their unusual access to the other world to work harm. Likewise, public officials had a responsibility to use their own powers to eliminate witchcraft, and ultimately all rulers or others holding power might be considered witches if their actions seemed to be self-serving and greedy.

Few rulers, no matter how cruel and wicked they might actually be, acknowledged witchcraft, with the notable exception of the Imbangala groups. Cannibalism, a characteristic of witches, deriving in part from the wide semantic field of the verb *dia* (to eat, but also to destroy, capture, kill), was the symbol of adherence to the Imbangala cult. By making their members eat their captives and fallen enemies, leaders of the Imbangala forced them to engage in a fundamentally antisocial and wicked practice as a way of enforcing their continued membership in the group.[52]

Nowhere in precolonial Africa did European culture make a greater penetration than in Central Africa, a phenomenon that has interested many observers. Its clearest manifestation was in the conversion of Kongo in 1491 and the subsequent development of the country as a Catholic state complete with a state-financed and institutional church. Christian penetration was deepest in Kongo of any region. By 1600 most Kongolese proudly reported themselves to be Christian, a fact that impressed visitors. But the Kongolese took the religion and shaped it to their own culture as well, being both enthusiastic borrowers and diligent transformers of European culture. Missionaries complained of the Kongolese propensity to continue to follow practices of their old religion and to see no essential distinction between them and Christianity. They took the creation story, probably from Christian sources, and made God create Kongo ahead of all other countries. They transformed the territorial deities into saints through the process of corevelation, whereby saints might reveal themselves in a place appropriate for the revelation of a precontact deity. They made All Saints' Day a celebration of the cult of ancestors by practicing it at their family tombs and combining it with Mass.[53]

FIGURE 3.2: *King Dom Garcia II of Kongo Receiving Capuchin Missionaries,*
1648. From Giovanni Antonio Cavazzi's Istorica descrittione
de' tre regni Congo, Matamba, et Angola, *(Milan, 1690)*
p. 269. Reproduced courtesy of the John Carter Brown Library,
Brown University.

   Christianity did not penetrate nearly as deeply elsewhere in Central
Africa, but it was influential nevertheless. There was little in the way of
Christian conversion in the Kikongo-speaking lands north of the Congo
River, like Loango and Ngoyo or Kakongo, even though the rulers of these
states frequently requested missionaries and occasionally they made converts. South of Kongo the faith fared better, but still fell short of the standard of Kongo. It had made substantial inroads in the Dembos region by the
1560s, and continued to grow irregularly there through the seventeenth and
eighteenth centuries, without, however, becoming an official state church
as in Kongo.

In Angola the Portuguese built a colony and required that those local rulers who submitted to them accept baptism and provide for the religious instruction of their flocks. As in Kongo, the Mbundu-speaking areas where missionaries worked had corevelations, and crosses were erected, sometimes spontaneously, in the places where there had formerly been shrines to territorial deities. For all this, however, Mbundus were conscious of Christianity as a religion of conquerors, and they were more inclined to argue with it or reject it than in Kongo or even in Loango. Still, notable figures of African resistance, like Queen Njinga, were baptized (as were a number of her successors in the seventeenth and eighteenth centuries), and if we are to believe the priests who lived with her at the end of her life, she was a committed Christian for her last ten years.[54]

Even Portuguese residents and their descendents absorbed the syncretic religion of Angola, as did Antonio Dias Pilarte, a white solider resident in the presidio of Muxima in 1715, when he participated in making a *mandinga*, a protective charm that included both the sort of ingredients typical of charms in Central Africa and Catholic religious paraphernalia.[55] Indeed, even in Luanda, the Portuguese settlers and their offspring participated in African-influenced funerals (*tambos*), took oaths, and even spoke Kimbundu.[56]

At times the religion, or organizations created by religion like the lay fraternities, connected Africans directly to other Christians in Portugal and Brazil and provided possible links to other Catholic countries. Thus lay fraternities, especially that of Our Lady of the Rosary, had branches in Angola, Brazil, and Portugal as well as in the independent African country of Kongo.[57]

European culture mixed in West Central Africa beyond religion. We have already noted the use of Portuguese as a lingua franca in regions far away from Kongo or the colony of Angola. In addition, Portuguese food items, items of dress, and occasionally other elements of culture might be found in independent states. These elements were particularly noticeable in the regions where Portuguese had settled, in Luanda, their inland posts, and Massangano and Ambaca, and where the local population was creole in a sense that was more typically American than African. These people, like those of the farther interior, found their way into the slave trade though military operations or other forms of enslavement such as the harassing of local population by Portuguese garrisons in the interior.

Thus the people living around this center of intense creolization also shared to a greater or lesser degree an absorption of European culture. Heywood has envisioned this as a series of bands of influence of varying degrees of creolization radiating from centers of more intense cultural exchange.[58] This situation is well illustrated by the meal that the ruler of Mbwila, a Dembo state, served to the visiting priest Marcellino d'Atri in 1698, in which the preparation of the table and the menu made him think that he was in "some European country" rather than in the unconquered interior of Central Africa.[59] While much of this penetration affected the elite more than ordinary people, it helped create a distinctly Central African cultural flavor that had a hint of European influence.[60]

This cultural background may help to explain why Central Africans did not always appear so distinctive when coming to Latin America. Some conceived themselves as "missionaries" spreading Christianity to the non-Christian West Africans, as did Pedro Congo in Itaubira (Minas Gerais), Brazil, who held unofficial and certainly unsanctioned Catholic religious services in 1754 for women, mostly Minas from the region around Dahomey.[61] Many others were, as some writers noted, *ladino*, and still others, though less knowledgeable of European culture, might acquire the mixed culture of African America quickly by mixing with the Kongos or those from Angola. Yet in this no Central Africans completely lost the distinctly African elements of their culture, which regularly showed up in denunciations of their behavior to the Inquisition. The same sort of oracles, ordeals, and religious symbols that were denounced in Africa as being perversions of religion appear in Brazil.[62] Beyond this, the slave trade brought Central Africans in substantial numbers through-out the Latin American world and especially to Brazil, where they were well placed to have a tremendous influence on its culture.

APPENDIX

The King of Kongo Writes to the King of Portugal

Garcia II, the King of Kongo, sent this letter to the rector of the Jesuit college in Luanda, Angola in 1643, at a time when the Dutch occupied Luanda. The king's mention of his own religious faith, his outrage at the Portuguese, complaint about the slave trade, and familiarity with other parts of the world provide a rarely seen African perspective on the international relations of the period.

The bearer of this letter is my servant Dom Bernardo de Menezes, very well known to Reverend Father João de Paiua. He goes to the city of Luanda to deal with certain matters with the Dutch general. Your Reverence has advised me of your health and other news and that of the fathers of the Company of Jesus and those of Saint Francis, which I have received with infinite pleasure; mine is good, God be forever praised, along with the spirit to serve, honor, and embrace all ecclesiastical people, especially those of the Holy College, who have always been favorable to matters of this kingdom. And they were seized and exiled for preaching the truth to the people and residents of Loanda, for very little cause, until it pleased God to give punishment, which he did not fail to do, and it was not a mystery of heaven that the punishment was prolonged, because one could easily see that last year God has punished them with the fall of the city, if my letters arrive at a time before the Sobas and most people are aggrieved and scandalized, they cannot do but what they do, from which is born a thousand evils.

Nothing is more damaging to people than ambition and pride. This reigns in the city of Luanda. And as long as this remains there can never be peace with this kingdom, because in place of gold, silver, and other things that serve as money in other places, the trade and money are pieces, which are not gold nor cloth, but creatures. Our disgrace, and that of my ancestors, is that in our simplicity we gave place to that from which grows all the evils in our kingdoms, and above all that there are people who affirm that we were never lords of Angola and Matamba. The inequality of arms has caused us to lose all, as where there is force, right is lost.

In closing this chapter or prologue, nothing would
have taken place as it has taken place if it were not for
ambition. And Your Reverence knows that if they and we
do not ask God for mercy and refrain from hate and
vengeance, it seems to me that his punishment will
doubtless come in time.

I have ordered Father Miguel Afonso to return to
Congo because he cannot continue here for so long. Because
of his age I excuse him. It is my determination to send to
your fathers to inform them of everything, so that it will
match the arrival of Anrrique Cornelio, who is the comissioner
that the general sent, and the governor is not yet in Loanda,
whom they hope for, I have certified that he is at Bengo.

You fathers will see that we are served in Congo with
more fathers to cultivate the vine of God. And I believe, with
the Lord that we believe in and confess, that my soul is not
anything except that which they take from me of my lands
and this is my firm intent and proposal, that even if rays fall
I will die to liberate my own. And this . . . to not be as much
a Catholic as King Dom João, Dom Felipe, and [the king
of] France.

Will Your Paternity send me more news of the clergy,
as I have heard that the Reverend Bishop D. Francisco Soveral
has died, to whom I have also written; God will remember
him and wish to give him Paradise, the inconviences which
were also placed before, or would be born from him or the
enemies of this kingdom, were the cause of all the evils that
as it happened did not take place as has been said. And I
suppose that he called us hypocrites and bad Christians,
there are good and bad people in all parts of the world,
and no one can judge them, only God knows to judge
them, as he knows our interior intentions; but quickly
it was well accepted that they called us stupid and beasts,
since he has more confidence is us than what others
call us.

I will conclude by asking Your Paternity to be attentive to
this Christianity, as I am ready to receive with open arms all
who are ecclesiastics. Will Our Lord protect you and give you

health that you wish. I kiss the habit and hands of Reverend
Father João de Pauia. The same to Your Paternity and the
minister of Saint Joseph.

On the 23 of February of 1643
King dom Garcia

Garcia II to Jesuit rector, February 23, 1643, Arquivo Histórico
Ultramarino, Lisbon, box 4, doc. 23, published in António Brásio,
Monumenta missionaria africana, 1st series, 15 vols. (Lisbon: Agência
Geral do Ultramar, 1952–88), 9:17–19 (autograph is illustrated in text).

NOTES

1. Antonio Manuel's personal papers, some seventy letters and documents
   ranging from 1591 to shortly before his death in 1608, allow his African
   career as diplomat, secretary, and church official to be revealed as well as
   his comfort in European culture: see Archivio Segreto Vaticano, Armadio
   II, vol. 91, fols. 125–254v; see also Teobaldo Filesi, *Roma e Congo all'inizio
   del 1600: Nuove testimonianze* (Como, 1968); another summary and details
   is found in Graziano Saccardo, *Congo e Angola con la storia dell'antica
   missione dei capuccini*, 3 vols. (Venice, 1982–3) 1:122–25, for treatments
   of his mission written without knowledge of his papers.

2. Modern visitors to Angola with experience in Latin America might
   also observe this convergence in such diverse areas as architecture or
   attitudes of the independent ruling elite.

3. The term *Dembos*, which occasionally turns up in inventories as an ethnic
   name in Latin America, derives from the title *ndembu* borne by many of
   the leaders in this area; see Ilídio do Amaral, *O reino do Congo os Mbundu
   (ou Ambundos) o reino dos "Ngola" (ou de Angola) e a presença Portuguesa,
   de finasi do século XV a meados do século XVI* (Lisbon, 1996), 42–44.

4. Letter of Commutation of Exile to Manuel de Vila Maior, August 9,
   1490, in Maria Luísa Oliveira Esteves, ed., *Portugaliae monmenta
   africana* (Lisbon, 1994–95), 2:56.

5. The best primary account of the first contact with Kongo and of this
   mission was written by Rui da Pina shortly after the mission's return
   in 1491. This account is no longer extant, but an Italian translation

is preserved in an untitled account found in the Codex Riccardiano 1910 (Biblioteca Riccardiana, Florence), which served as the basis for his better-known account in his chronicle of King João II (1515). The Italian and Portuguese versions have been published in Carmen Radulet, *O cronista Rui de Pina e a "Relação do Reino do Congo": Manuscrfito inédito do "Códice Riccardiano 1910"* (Lisbon, 1992). The military campaign is described at fols. 97v–98r, but no specific mention of slaves is made. On the other hand, instructions given to Gonçalo Rodrigues, leader of the second mission to Kongo in 1509, specify how he is to dispose of profits that might come from the king of Kongo "from captures and seizures that he might make in the war" that Rodrigues was to help with against "the blacks of the islands [in the Congo River] who are in rebellion against the Manycongo," in "Despacho de Go Roiz pera se lhe fazer seu cõtrauto por que sy o despachou elRey noso senho" in António Brásio, ed. *Monumenta missionaria africana*, 1st ser., 15 vol. (Lisbon, 1952–88) 4:61.

6. For the 1502 map, see Armando Cortesão and Avelino Teixeira da Mota, eds., *Portugaliae monumenta cartographica* (Lisbon: Comissão Executiva das Comemorações do V Centenário da Morte do Infante D. Henrique, 1960), 1:12 (plates 4–5). The 1506 account is found in Duarte Pacheco Pereira, *Esmeraldo de situ orbis*, ed. Epiphânio da Silva Dias (Lisbon: Typ. Universal, 1905), vol. 3, chap. 2, p.134.

7. Bernardo de Segura to King, March 15, 1516, Brásio, *Monumenta*, 1:378. Segura inspected customs books and found 4,072 slaves had entered in that year. Though not all were from Central Africa, it is fairly sure that the majority were.

8. Inquiry of Simão de Mota, November 12, 1548, Brásio, *Monumenta*, 2:197–205. Da Mota held judicial appointments from both the king of Portugal and Kongo. This inquest seems to have been initiated by Diogo I of Kongo. For the earliest period and contacts, see do Amaral, *Reino de Congo*, 75–85.

9. Afonso to Manuel, October 5, 1514, Brásio, *Monumenta*, 1:300–301 and 317.

10. Ibid., 1:312–14.

11. The description that follows is similar in some respects to that given in Joseph C. Miller, *Way of Death: Merchant Capitalism and the Angolan Slave Trade, 1726–1826* (Madison: University of Wisconsin Press, 1988), 3–70, though it differs in many particulars.

12. For demographic information on Kongo, based on baptismal records, see John Thornton, "Demography and History in the Kingdom of Kongo, 1550–1750," *Journal of African History* 18 (1977): 507–30.

13. For general evidence, mostly from Kongo, see John K. Thornton, "Mbanza Congo/São Salvador: Kongo's Holy City," in *Africa's Urban Past*, ed. David Anderson and Richard Rathbone (Portsmouth, NH: Heinemann, 1999), 70–72.

14. Thornton, "Demography and History."

15. This population estimate is based on the assumption that the statement made by a Kongo-based, probably Jesuit priest at the time that the annual baptisms in the parish of São Salvador, which included the city and its immediate hinterland, numbered some 4,500, which when multiplied by a ratio that assumes a birth rate of forty-seven per thousand suggests a population of 94,000; see Instituto Histórico e Geográfico Brasileiro (Rio de Janeiro), DL 848, doc. 16, "Descrição das necessidades do reino do Congo sobre assuntos religiosos . . . ," fol. 2 (undated, but probably late 1620s).

16. On Lunda, see Jean Luc Vellut, "Notes sur le Lunda et la frontière luso-africaine (ca. 1750–1810)," *Études d'histoire africaine* 3 (1972): 61–166 at 67–75.

17. Loango's capital region in the mid-seventeenth century is revealed in the geography of Olfert Dapper, *Naukeurige Beschrijvinge van Africa gewesten*, 2nd ed. (Amsterdam: J. van Meurs, 1676; orig. pub. 1668), 143–45. Ndongo's capital region with its dense population is described in John Thornton, "The African Experience of the '20 and Odd Negroes' arriving in Virginia in 1619," *William & Mary Quarterly* 55, no. 3 (1998): 421–39.

18. Linda Heywood and John Thornton, "African Fiscal Systems and Demographic History: The Case of Central Angola, 1799–1920," *Journal of African History* 29, no. 2 (1988): 213–28.

19. For this interpretation of the role of the capital region in the history of Kongo, see John Thornton, *The Kingdom of Kongo: Civil War and Transition, 1641–1718* (Madison: University of Wisconsin Press, 1983).

20. Gonzalo Aguirre Beltrán, *La población negra de México, 1521–1810* (Mexico, DF: Ediciones Fuente Cultural, 1946), 242–43.

21. James Lockhart, *Spanish Peru, 1532–60: A Colonial Society* (Madison: University of Wisconsin Press, 1968), 173.

22. For a full picture from the Angolan side, see Beatrix Heintze, "Das Ende des unabhängigen Staates Ndongo (1617–1630)," in *Studien zur Geschichte Angolas im 16. und 17. Jahrhundert. Ein Lesebuch*, ed. Beatrix Heintze (Cologne, 1996), 111–68. (This is a revised article. Fuller bibliographic references are found in the original version in *Paideuma* 27 [1981]: 197–273).

23. Johannes de Laet, *Iaerlijke verhael van de Verrichtigen der Geoctroyeerde West-Indische Compagnie*, 4 vols., ed. S. P. L'Honoré Naber and J. M. C. Warsinck (The Hague, 1937; orig. pub. 1644).

24. For a study of the slave trade from Loango, see Phyllis Martin, *The External Trade of the Loango Coast, 1576–1870* (Oxford: Clarendon, 1972).

25. See records published by Elizabeth Donnan, *Documents Illustrative of the Slave Trade to America*, 4 vols. (Washington, DC: Carnegie Institution, 1930–35) 2:308–9.

26. A summary of this period's events is found in David Brimingham, *Trade and Conflict in Angola* (Oxford: Oxford University Press, 1966), and Graziano Maria Saccardo da Leguzzano, *Congo e Angola con la storia del missione dei' Cappuccini*, 3 vols. (Venice, 1982–84).

27. For an overview, but somewhat different interpretation, see Miller, *Way of Death*, 105–39.

28. Alexandre Elias da Silva Corrêa, *História de Angola*, 2 vols., ed. Manuel Múrias (Lisbon, 1937; orig. pub. c. 1789), 2:223–26, 311, 335–36, 361, 365–66.

29. Arquivo Histórico Ultramarino, Lisbon (henceforth AHU), box 40, doc. 32, António Alvares da Cunha to Crown, March 23, 1755; doc. 73, António Alvares da Cunha to Crown, January 22, 1756; António Lancastro to Dembo Paulo of Cahenda, 1773, archives of Cahenda, summarized in António de Almeida, "Relações com os Dembos das cartas do Dembado de Kakulu-Kahenda, *I congresso da história da expansão portuguesa nu mundo* (Lisbon, 1938)," 41–42 (this document was not in the collection edited by Ana Paula Tavares and Catarina Madeira Santos, *Africae monumenta: A apropriação da escrita pelos africanos*) (Lisbon: Instituto de Investigação Cientítica Tropical, 2002), 377.

30. Archivio de Propaganda Fide (Rome): Scritture Originale nelli Congressi Generali, vol. 552, fols. 62–62v, Bernardo da Firenze to Propaganda Fide, June 22, 1705.

31. AHU, box 55, doc. 1, Bando of Sousa Coutinho, January 2, 1771.

32. Silva Corrêa, *História* 1:363–66.

33. For the wars of the first half of the eighteenth century, see Silva Corrêa, *História*, 2:328–29, 338–39, 348–56. For the 1775 wars, see AHU, box 40, doc. 73, António Alvares da Cunha, June 22, 1756; Instituto Histórico e Geografico Brasileiro, box 106, doc. 15, "Relação que faço cormanamente assem da viagem como das Marchas, Sitios e Provincia donde passou o Exercito, que ele mandou ao Reyno de Beng[uel]a castigar aos Souvass Cabundas e seus aliaddos, por ordem do M[uit]o Ex[celentissi]mo Gov[overnador] o S[en]n[ho]r Dom Antonio Al[avre]z da Cunha no anno de 1755 . . . "; a brief notice in Silva Corrêa, *História*, 2:11–12. For the 1773–75 wars, see AHU, box 61, doc. 18, António de Lencastro, July 1, 1776; Silva Corrêa, *História*, 2:48–66.

34. On the civil wars, see John Thornton, *Kingdom of Kongo* and Thornton, *The Kongolese Saint Anthony: Dona Beatriz Kimpa Vita and the Antonian Movement, 1684–1706* (Cambridge: Cambridge University Press, 1998).

35. For estimates of the human cost of a late-eighteenth-century war in Kongo, see John Thornton, "As guerras civis no Congo e o tráfico de escravos: a história e demografia de 1718 a 1844 revisitadas," *Estudos afro-asiaticos* 32 (1997): 55–74.

36. Cherubino da Savona, "Breve ragguaglio . . . ," in "Relazioni inedite di P. Cherubino Cassinis da Savona sul 'Congo e sue Missioni,'" ed. Carlo Toso, *L'Italia francescana* 45 (1975): 136–214.

37. On Lunda expansion and its role in the slave trade, see John Thornton, "The Causes and Consequences of Lunda Expansion to the West, 1750–1852," *Zambia Journal of History* 1 (1981): 1–16.

38. Aguirre Beltrán, *Población negra*, 244–45; Jean-Pierre Tardieu, *El negro en el Cusco: Los caminos de la alienación en la segunda mitad del siglo XVII* (Lima, 1998), 20 (a small sample of only fifty-two bozales).

39. This general information is calculated from tables in Philip Curtin, *The Atlantic Slave Trade: A Census* (Madison: University of Wisconsin Press, 1969), 207. There has been a great deal of local work in notarial archives in recent years that can modify these figures for local areas, which are based on import figures. In general Bahia and northern regions got more of the Costa da Mina slaves, while the southern ports received a greater share of the Central Africans.

40. On the impact of the trade revolution, see John Thornton, "Mbanza Kongo," in *Contested Power in Angola: 1840s to the Present*, ed. Linda Heywood (Rochester: University of Rochester Press, 2000), 1–30 (for the central highlands), among others.

41. A good example of a trade-induced novel local government is found in John Jantzen, *Lemba: 1650–1930: A Drum of Affliction in Africa and the New World* (New York, 1982).

42. The 20 percent estimate for Kongo assumes that the capital region held 100,000 people in 1650, out of a total Kongo population of about 500,000 as calculated from baptismal records in Thornton, "Demography and History." One should note that the Jesuit note of the 1620s (Instituto Histórico e Geografico Brasileiro, DL 848, doc. 12, fol. 2) suggested that there were some 4,500 baptisms in the capital of Kongo, and also that there were an estimated 40,000 babies baptized in the rest of the country (suggesting only a 10 percent share in the capital, but an overall Kongo population of nearly 850,000). We believe that the estimate was exaggerated for effect (a plea for priests to fill empty parishes) and was not based on actual records of baptisms, as those for the capital region would be.

43. John Thornton, "As guerras civis no Congo e o tráfico de escravos: A história e a demografia de 1718 a 1844 revisitadas." *Estudos afro-asiáticos* (Rio de Janeiro) 32 (1997): 55–74.

44. John Thornton, *Warfare in Atlantic Africa, 1500–1800* (London, 1999), 99–125. For the earlier periods see also John Thornton, "The Art of War in Angola, 1575–1680," *Comparative Studies in Society and History* 30 (1988): 360–78.

45. Thornton, *Kongolese Saint Anthony*.

46. John Thornton, "African Background to American Colonization." In *Cambridge Economic History of the United States*, vol. 1, *The Colonial Era*, ed. Stanley Engerman and Robert Gallman (New York: Cambridge University Press, 1996), 53–94.

47. Scholars have looked to the Imbangala as a model for Palmares mostly because of the belief that the term *kilombo*, used only in the late seventeenth century to describe the Palmares runaways, was connected to the term in use in Angola (since the early seventeenth century). It seems likely that the term, perhaps originally applied to Imbangala armies, entered colonial Portuguese as a term for any hostile settlement.

48. Thornton, *Warfare*, 127–47.

49. Filipo Pigafetta, *Relatione del reame di Congo et delle circonvincine contrade . . .*, ed. Giorgio Raimondo Cardona (Bologna, 1978; orig. pub. 1591). Pigafetta based his account on both written documents and oral testimony of Duarte Lopes, a Portuguese New Christian who was serving as Kongo's ambassador to Rome in 1588 and had lived in both areas.

50. See Kikongo usage in the catechism of 1624, *Doutrina christãa composta pelo P. Marcos Iorge . . . traduzida na lingua do Reyno do Congo*, ed. François Bontinck and D Ndembe Nsasi (Brussels, 1978; orig. pub. 1624) in comparison to the Kimbundu catechism of 1642 (but composed around 1626), [Diogo de Couto], *Gentio de Angola sufficimente instruido*, ed. António do Couto (Lisbon, 1642).

51. Jean-Luc Vellut, "Relations internationales du Moyen-Kwango et de l'Angola dans la deuxième moitié du XVIIIe siècle," *Etudes d'histoire africaine* 1 (1970): 75–135.

52. John Thornton, "Religion and Cultural Life in Kongo and Mbundu Areas, 1500–1800," in *Central Africans and Cultural Transformations in the American Diaspora*, ed. Linda M. Heywood (Cambridge: Cambridge University Press, 2002), 71–90.

53. John Thornton, "Perspectives on African Christianity," in *Race, Discourse, and the Origin of the Americas*, ed. Vera Hyatt and Rex Nettleford (Washington, DC, 1994), 169–98.

54. John Thornton, "Afro-Christian Syncretism in Central Africa," *Plantation Societies* (forthcoming).

55. Anquivo Nacional de Torre do Tombo, Inquisição de Lisboa, processo 5477 (no foliation). Two other soldiers tested the protective charm by fixing it to a dog and shooting the animal twice; when it was unwounded, they declared it a true charm.

56. Linda Heywood, "Portuguese into African: The Eighteenth Century Central African Background to Atlantic Creole Cultures," in Heywood, *Central Africans*, 91–113.

57. Linda Heywood, "The Angolan-Afro-Brazilian Cultural Connections," in *From Slavery to Emancipation in the Atlantic World*, ed. Sylvia Frey and Betty Wood (London: Frank Cass, 1999), 9–23; idem, "Portuguese into African."

58. Linda Heywood, "Portuguese into African: The Eighteenth Century Central African Background to Atlantic Creole Cultures," in Heywood, *Central Africans*, 91–116.

59. Marcellino d'Atri, "Gionate Apostoliche . . ." in *L'anarchia congolese nel secolo XVII: La relazione inedita di Marcellino d'Atri*, ed. Carlo Toso (Genoa, 1984; orig. written c. 1702), 427.

60. Heywood, "Portuguese into African."

61. Arquivo Nacional de Torre do Tombo, Inquisação de Lisboa, Processos, no. 16001, fols. 2–2v.

62. James Sweet, *Recreating Africa: Culture, Kinship, and Religion in the Portuguese World, 1441–1770* (Chapel Hill, 2003), esp. 119–89, gives some fascinating examples drawn from the Inquisition archives of the sort of religious syncretism stretching to both sides of the Atlantic that was possible.

CHAPTER FOUR

Cimarrón and Citizen

African Ethnicity, Corporate Identity, and the Evolution of Free Black Towns in the Spanish Circum-Caribbean

JANE G. LANDERS

❧ IN 1609 A TROOP OF AFRICANS PLAYING DRUMS AND COWBELLS PROCESSED down a mountain in the rugged Orizaba countryside of New Spain. The musicians were part of a royal procession escorting their aged king, Yanga, to the spot where a Spanish captive awaited the worst. The African monarch reassured the trembling Spaniard that, solely by having seen his face, he was assured life. After ordering the man fed, Yanga released him to deliver a rude challenge to the Spanish forces that were bent on destroying his settlement. Spaniards who wrote about this event were shocked by the "arrogance" of Yanga's missive. Recounting his many victories against the Spaniards, Yanga condemned them as cruel, treacherous, and cowardly—ironically, deploying many of the same stereotypical insults Spaniards levied against the maroons. He challenged the Spanish troops to follow the bearer of the letter, who would guide them back to the maroon stronghold. Finally, Yanga warned the messenger not to return with the Spanish forces if he did not wish to die with them.[1] This vignette reveals glimpses of ritual acts, warfare, courtly displays, hospitality, and diplomacy that might have taken

place on the West African coast. Yanga's claims to magical as well as political power also demonstrate that African religious and social systems persisted in the Americas despite the traumas of enslavement and dislocation.

Over twenty years ago Richard Price noted that in their earliest and
most vulnerable stages, maroon communities created virtual monarchies in
the wild, with power and authority concentrated into the hands of powerful warrior-kings. By the eighteenth century, however, surviving maroon
settlements had developed new social and political institutions that dispersed authority and vested leadership in acculturated American-born creoles better equipped, argued Price, to deal with Europeans and negotiate
the best interests of their people.[2] This chapter traces that historical evolution of maroon communities in seventeenth-century Mexico and supports
the main contours of Price's argument. In the viceroyalty of New Spain
African-born kings gave way to creole governors and captains who shared
power with African-born war captains. And Christian churches eventually
operated alongside and shared religious authority with African religious systems. However, because documentation was scare when Price wrote, he had
not discerned an intermediate stage in this evolutionary process that only
strengthens his claims for the dynamism and adaptability of Africans in the
Americas. For a brief historical moment in the seventeenth century, in the
viceroyalty of New Spain, blacks represented themselves as a republic analogous to that of Spaniards and Indios, and the viceroy and Spain recognized
them as such. This political development came at a time when the imprac-
ticability of the so-called Dual Republic of Indios and Spaniards was becoming more obvious daily, and so the timing could not have been worse.
However truncated this republican moment, however, the fact that blacks
had laid successful claim to the civic values associated with a *república y
común* facilitated their transition into free black towns. But free black towns,
unless they were very remote, were also short-lived. Treaty provisions
notwithstanding, by the late eighteenth century in-migration by whites and
mestizos had transformed black towns into pueblos almost indistinguishable
from others of different origin.

Africans in the Spanish American Historical Record

Africans, free and enslaved, had formed sizeable populations in southern
Iberia for centuries preceding Spanish colonization of the "New World,"
and the medieval Spanish pattern of incorporating the converted other

(although never fully) shaped early modern Spanish society as it was transplanted to the Americas. While retaining much of their "national" culture, African subjects and slaves living in Spain were able to claim several different corporate identities—as *vecinos* and as members of parishes and religious brotherhoods called *cofradías*. Isabel and Ferdinand appointed a royal servant, Juan de Valladolid, "of noble lineage among Blacks," to regulate Seville's large black population and serve as its "Chief and Judge." The monarchs thus formalized an administrative model of ruling African "others" through their own leaders.[3] After several centuries, Afro-Iberian identities and institutions were so well established that they were transplanted to Spanish America without question.[4] Because Spain was the first European power to introduce free and enslaved Africans into the Americas, and because its records are the oldest and most extensive on Africans in the Americas, all other studies must build on these Spanish precedents.

Free and acculturated Africans, or *ladinos*, from Spain joined in the first "wars of pacification" against indigenous populations in the Antilles and circum-Caribbean, and some of these war-tested veterans also participated in the conquests of the great Aztec and Incan empires, gaining yet another corporate identity as part of the military establishment. The free West African Juan Garrido, for example, who was a Spanish-speaking Catholic, fought alongside Spaniards in Hispaniola, Puerto Rico, and Florida before he helped defeat the Aztecs at Tenochtitlan. His services won him land, a minor government post in New Spain, and a place in the Spanish documentary record.[5]

Because they were still "other" and of military, economic, political, and social significance, Spanish bureaucrats created a rich documentary record of the Africans living throughout their empire, capturing moments of their lives in censuses, military rosters, civil and criminal proceedings, land grants, and correspondence.[6] Although the primary outreach of the Catholic Church was to the vast new indigenous populations of the Americas, it also worked to convert Africans and, in the process, generated some of the oldest extant records (and ethnohistories) of Africans in the Americas—dating to the mid-sixteenth century. Catholic baptismal, marriage, and burial registers recorded not only the names, races, and legal statuses of the individuals presenting themselves but, most important for modern scholarship, their African "nations." In rare cases the sacramental records also yield birthplaces in Africa. The choices Africans made of marriage sponsors and godparents allow the reconstitution of family and fictive kin networks among some populations. Serial church records can also be used to explore a range of important questions including mortality and fertility rates, miscegenation and naming patterns, and even rates of manumissions. And, as will be noted later in Matt Childs's chapter 7 in this collection, Africans established cofradías (*irmandades* in Portuguese) and ethnic associations that were organized by African nations and authorized by church and government officials throughout the Americas. Members elected their own kings, queens, and officers and devoted themselves to Catholic saints who had some symbolic association with their own favored deities, or *orishas*. Brothers recorded the rules by which they operated, lists of their officers and members, and the charitable deeds they undertook, including establishing hospitals, caring for the poor, and burying their dead brothers and their families.[7]

While the secular church[8] generated those rich records, missionary friars also left valuable records of their encounters with Africans living beyond the pale, in *cimarrón* (maroon) communities outside Spanish dominion. Jesuit and Franciscan fathers did their utmost to bring the "lost souls" to God and back into the Spanish fold. The accounts of priests sent out to reduce the maroons, and even those of military forces sent to eradicate them, can offer useful clues about the physical layout, demographics, and civil, religious, and military leadership of the fugitive communities, known most commonly as *palenques*, *manieles*, and *cumbes* in the Spanish colonies. Spanish records also give scattered information on subsistence patterns and trade networks with Europeans, Indians, and other Africans, free and enslaved. When unconquerable palenques were legitimated, a new level of documentation was generated through town charters, parish registers, militia records, notarial accounts, and many of the same materials available for other Spanish towns. In most cases these rich sources have yet to be fully mined.

Most important, perhaps, both free and enslaved Africans generated their own historical record in Spanish colonies. Depending on their individual histories, Africans were sometimes literate in several languages and, just as indigenous groups did, they quickly learned and adapted to the Spanish legal culture. They wrote petitions and correspondence to royal officials and to the king, made proclamations of fealty, initiated legal suits and property transactions, and left wills. Their verbatim testimonies also come to us through civil and criminal proceedings, which Spanish notaries recorded and read back to the sworn witnesses for verification, alteration, or amendment. If Africans could not speak Spanish, court officials used translators, just as they did for non-Spanish speaking witnesses of other ethnicities. This may have added new layers of linguistic filters, but was, nonetheless, an effort to understand and record the voice of Africans.[9]

Historical archaeology is also offering important new insights into the material life of Africans, but with the exception of some work in the Dominican Republic (Hispaniola), Cuba, and Florida, little has been done on Hispanic areas of settlement. In the Dominican Republic archaeologists investigating cave shelters and the Maniel (another term for maroon community) José Leta have discovered copper bracelets, metal arrow tips, and a variety of iron objects, including tongs and a lance point. Iron slag deposits show that maroon smiths were manufacturing objects on site. Other finds include triton shell trumpets and pottery crafted by maroons.[10] Cuban archaeologists are beginning to excavate nineteenth-century plantation sites, where Africans of the Lucumí, Gangá, Mandinga, Carabalí, and Kongo nations were enslaved. And in Florida, Kathleen A. Deagan has excavated the oldest free black town in what became the United States, Gracia Real de Santa Teresa de Mose, where Africans of the same nations as those found in Cuba lived, along with some Indian wives. Material unearthed there included clay pipes and pottery, military artifacts such as gunflints and strikers, broken coins, and religious items such as rosary beads and a handcrafted St. Christopher's medal.[11] Most of the archaeology projects related to Africans in the Americas, however, have so far focused on enslaved populations in English-speaking areas.[12] On Barbados Jerome Handler and Frederick Lange excavated the burial of an adult male wearing copper bracelets and rings, a necklace of cowrie shells, dog canines, glass beads, fish vertebrae, and an agate bead. Beside the buried man lay a seventeenth-century pipe from Ghana. From the slave cabins at Andrew Jackson's Hermitage plantation in Tennessee, Larry McKee excavated familiar items such as pierced coins, cowrie shells, and gaming pieces, but also more unusual finds such as a raccoon baculum (penis) and three tiny copper amulets in the shape of a hand gripping a circle.[13] Through such material items as pottery, pipes, baskets, and iron implements, architectural features and spatial patterning, plant and faunal remains, skeletal evidence from bones and teeth, some of which are filed or mutilated, grave goods, and items of seemingly socioreligious significance such as beads (63 percent of which are blue), buttons, pierced or broken coins, gaming pieces, and amulets, to name a few, archaeologists attempt to "recover meaning" and posit African origins and American cultural adaptations.[14]

While such finds are exciting, the noted archaeologist of sub-Saharan Africa Merrick Posnansky has urged colleagues working on African sites in the Americas, and historians as well, to reject the fallacy of a common African culture and to pay more attention to the regional and temporal developments in African histories while searching for ethnic and cultural connections.[15] Historians of sub-Saharan Africa such as Robin Law, Joseph Miller, and Paul Lovejoy and John Thornton (whose essays appear in this volume), offer similar cautions. Scholars of specific African and American diasporic sites are now joining in exciting and fruitful collaborations and getting much closer to understanding the lived experience of Africans on both sides of the Atlantic.[16]

Further historical and archaeological research of palenques and their derivative free black towns is still needed, for it is in such sites, where Africans were more free to shape their lives as they would, that scholars may begin to answer important questions about the ethnicities of Africans in particular places and times, the variety of their free and enslaved experiences, distinct forms of resistance, the nature of family structures, the impact of Christianity and religious syncretism, cultural adaptation, the process of creolization, and the formation of an African American culture.[17] As collaborative historical and archaeological research on the eighteenth-century free black town of Gracia Real de Santa Teresa de Mose in Spanish Florida showed, it is possible to recover significant portions of the history of a group too long thought to be without one. It is also possible to know about the lives of specific individuals, not just anonymous masses. Such studies will not only enrich but improve our understanding of American colonial societies.

Patterns of Resistance and Incorporation

After successfully concluding their long religious and territorial wars against the Muslims, Spaniards came to the Americas convinced that they had a divine mission to convert and civilize the newly discovered worlds they entered. In order to promote conversion to Christianity and righteous living, the conquerors established towns wherever they went. Attaching a special value to living a *vida política*, Spaniards believed people of reason lived in stable urban situations, while "barbarians" lived in the wild countryside beyond city walls, or worse, as nomads. Royal legis-lation reflected a continuing obsession with reforming and settling so-called vagabonds of all races, and while Indians (*indios* or *naturales*) were the primary focus of reduction efforts, Spaniards also tried to assimilate persons of African descent into their "civilized" urban model.[18]

Although some Africans, like Juan Garrido, who served as a military ally to the Spaniards in Florida, Mexico, and elsewhere, chose assimilation, many more did not, and one of the central dilemmas Spaniards faced in the Americas was how to eliminate, subjugate, or incorporate blacks who sub-verted their colonial order. No sooner had the American wars of conquest subsided than Spaniards began importing slaves directly from Africa, to do the hard work of building new settlements and to labor on livestock ranches, mines, and sugar plantations. Lynne Guitar's chapter 2 in this collection documents the extensive size of African labor forces working in sixteenth-century sugar plantations on Hispaniola and the grueling nature of their work. Unable to speak Spanish and to access the corporate privileges their free ladino compatriots enjoyed, unacculturated Africans tried to escape slavery as soon as possible and created independent communities in remote hinterlands all over the Americas. As early as 1503 Hispaniola's new gover-nor, Nicolás de Ovando, complained to the crown that slave runaways could not be recovered from Taíno hideouts in the mountains and that they were teaching the Indians "bad customs." Spain had only recently concluded the war to reconquer Granada and had just expelled all Muslims who failed to convert to Catholicism. Hispaniola's governor feared the potential religious "contamination" of the Indians and also that the Africans, reputed for their bellicose natures (rather than for the military training some had), might influence and assist indigenous resistance, and so he recommended against introducing any more slaves. Governor Ovando's concern was not un-founded. In 1521 Wolof slaves from Senegambia led the first major slave revolt on Hispaniola, leading Spain temporarily to forbid the importation of Africans from areas of Muslim influence.[19] Survivors of the slave revolt headed for the Bahoruco Mountains to join forces with insurgent Taínos, and by mid-sixteenth century approximately seven thousand other slaves had followed suit. Not content to simply escape, maroon leaders like the famed Lemba led daring assaults on Spanish towns like San Juan de la Maguna and Azua where the maroons once had been held as slaves. Outnumbered and beleaguered Spanish settlers were largely restricted to the capital of Santo Domingo during the "maroon wars" of the 1540s.[20]

Despite the obvious danger, because indigenous populations had succumbed in great numbers to brutal warfare, disease, and overwork, Spanish
colonists throughout the Caribbean hungrily demanded more slaves, and
the region rapidly became even more African. Pedro Menéndez de Avilés,
captain general and governor of both Cuba and Florida, reported to King
Philip II in the 1560s that a dangerous racial disparity had developed
throughout the circum-Caribbean. In alarmist tones, he warned that because
neither England nor France permitted slavery, with a few thousand men,
either power could seize all Spain's possessions by freeing and arming the
grateful slaves, whom he alleged would then slay their Spanish masters.[21]

Spanish administrators of the viceroyalty of New Spain faced the same
dilemma as their Caribbean counterparts. They were fearful of slave rebellion but dependent upon slaves. According to some captured maroons and
to official Spanish chroniclers, runaway slaves established formidable palenques in New Spain even as Spaniards were concluding the conquest of
the Aztec empire.[22] Establishing control over the colony's vast indigenous
populations was the primary Spanish objective, but before long, Africans
were a significant, and often a majority, population in the cities of New
Spain, and Spanish officials began to worry about the potential for slave
revolts. The colony's first viceroy, Antonio de Mendoza, owner of one of
the region's largest sugar mills, the Orizaba, and more than one hundred
African slaves, summarily executed and quartered the alleged leaders of
Mexico City's first known slave conspiracy in 1537. Repeating the warnings
of his Caribbean counterparts, viceroy Mendoza recommended halting
slave imports, but local demand for slave labor trumped security concerns
and importation continued.[23]

By 1553 New Spain's second viceroy, Luis de Velasco, estimated the
colony's black population at more than twenty thousand (which included
approximately two thousand maroons) and he, too, urged the crown to forbid further African importation—to no avail. By 1570 the port city of
Veracruz was home to six hundred slaves and only two hundred Spaniards,
while the population of the mining center of Taxco was even more racially
skewed, with seven hundred slaves and only a hundred Spaniards. Africans
also outnumbered Europeans almost four to one in the bishopric of Mexico
and surpassed European populations in the colony at large from the sixteenth through the eighteenth centuries.[24]

West Africans from Cabo Verde and the Senegambian region predominated in the early slave shipments to the Americas and constituted

approximately 90 percent of all slaves entering Mexico in the mid-six-teenth century, but Central Africans were also present from at least the 1540s. When Spain claimed the Portuguese throne in 1580 and gained access to Portuguese merchants and factories in Central Africa, Africans from Kongo and Angola quickly became more numerous.[25] Thus Africans from many disparate locations and cultures learned to live together, and some found common cause in their mutual oppression. It was such cross-cultural accommodations that made both resistance and incorporation into the Spanish world possible.

Acculturated Africans and their descendants drew on customary and legal privileges to replicate institutions and social patterns in Mexico City that their counterparts had earlier established in Spain and the Caribbean.[26] Spanish and foreign visitors alike remarked upon the virtual free rein the black population seemed to enjoy in the capital city and on the elaborate clothing free and enslaved blacks wore when attending dances, weddings, funerals, and brotherhood functions. When black confraternity brothers processed during Easter season from the Santo Domingo church, they were followed by many more of their community in ritual displays of penance and observation. A company of armed brothers accompanied the proces-sion, shouldering devotional images and the sepulcher of Christ.[27] Such social gatherings were important to the black communities that devoted hard-earned resources to support them, and they were more than mere entertainments. In these relatively private functions persons of African descent communicated and exchanged political information as well as gos-sip. The organization of these events promoted social cohesion, reinforced fictive and kin networks, and recognized leadership that was generated from within the black community. Public displays of religiosity and of civic organization also confirmed black claims to Christian brotherhood and membership in the corporate community.[28]

But even institutions authorized by the church and community could be turned to subversion. In 1611, convinced that their deceased sister had been beaten to death, more than fifteen hundred members of the broth-erhood of Nuestra Señora de la Merced angrily marched her body through the streets of Mexico City to display it at the palaces of the arch-bishop, the Inquisition, and finally at the home of her owner, where they threw rocks and shouted insults until dispersed. As a result of that distur-bance, worried officials deported the brotherhood's elderly steward. With that, the brothers began to plot in serious, electing an Angolan king and queen to lead a Christmastime revolt. The newly elected but elderly King Pablo, however, died unexpectedly. Instead of a revolt, his brotherhood staged an elaborate funeral at which mourners sang African songs and danced before covering Pablo's body and casket in wine and oils. The Catholic friars who were to conduct the burial at the monastery remonstrated to no avail, and one distraught African was said to have jumped into Pablo's casket. Covering himself with wine and earth and then jumping back out with a weapon in his raised hand, he cried that this was how war was launched. The following year, in 1612, Portuguese merchants in Mexico City reported overhearing plotters discussing that war in "la lengua Angola." Arrested and tortured slaves began to give up details, such as that a witch named Sebastian would cast spells and poison Mexico City's water and food supplies. Officials were shocked to find that many of the implicated slaves belonged to the city's most influential residents and that some of the plotters were free. Convinced the threat was real, they reacted swiftly and harshly, publicly hanging thirty-five people (seven of whom were women). The Spaniards then nailed their heads to the gallows, quartered six of the bodies, buried the rest, and sold the surviving plotters into exile. They also disbanded all black brotherhoods, forbade black gatherings, tried to enforce sumptuary laws and prohibitions against blacks carrying weapons, and established new police patrols to monitor the city.[29]

Officials in New Spain, as elsewhere in the Americas, also worried about the possibility of a coordinated black and indigenous rebellion, but repeated legislative attempts to separate these populations were largely ineffectual, as were other sorts of social restrictions. Administrators and churchmen alike complained about what they considered the inappropriate dominion blacks exercised over natives and their abuses of the allegedly "weaker" peoples.[30] But from the earliest days of conquest, Spaniards actually helped create animosity between the groups by employing blacks as supervisors of Indians. This was true in Veracruz. In 1592 the magistrate of Veracruz sent a mulatto armed with an official Spanish staff to collect tribute from the native inhabitants of Atucpa, where townspeople complained to the viceroy that the man also demanded food and personal services. Such "public and notorious" misbehaviors required a response. Viceroy Luis de Velasco II promptly reprimanded the magistrate for appointing the mulatto to the position and ordered him not to reappoint him.[31]

Few Spaniards, however, chose to live in Veracruz. The port city was described as hot and humid, plagued by mosquitoes and gnats, and generally unhealthy. Flocks of colorful parrots roosted in the lush tropical landscape, and crocodiles and alligators sunned themselves in the surrounding marshes and bogs. It was a landscape that might have reminded some of the African inhabitants of their own coasts, but it was alien to Spaniards, who preferred other locales. Thus officials in Veracruz often had to rely on the more numerous persons of color to fill roles normally held by Spaniards.[32]

From Maroon Palenque to Free Black Republic: Yanga and the Town of San Lorenzo

More critical to the viceroy than such breaches in caste and class protocols was the ongoing *marronage* (slave flight) that plagued his and earlier administrations. None had been able to staunch the flow of runaways, and maroon communities had only multiplied since the conquest. Spanish concerns about the maroons intensified as European wars spilled over into the Americas. King Philip II was preoccupied waging wars of Counter-Reformation in Europe, and French, English, and later, Dutch corsairs began trolling for treasure fleets and raiding Spanish and Portuguese coastal settlements in the Americas and Africa. French Huguenots also challenged Spanish territorial claims by launching settlements in Brazil and in Florida.[33] Because the wealth of the Indies and of the Orient flowed back to Spain through Veracruz, and because so many foreign merchants and African bozales also passed through, the Spanish Inquisition established a tribunal in Veracruz that investigated and condemned Jews and Protestants alike but did little to eliminate foreign threats. The 1568 attempt by English slave trader and corsair John Hawkins to take the island fortress of San Juan de Ulúa in the Veracruz harbor failed, but for the next two decades Hawkins and his kinsman Francis Drake (El Draque) became Spain's nemeses. Drake raided Cartagena, Santo Domingo, and St. Augustine, and with the help of maroon allies in Panama stole a fortune in Spanish silver as mule trains carted it across the isthmus.[34]

In this turbulent era Yanga (or Ñanga), an enslaved West African of the Bran nation and (reputedly of royal lineage) escaped near Veracruz and with a group of followers formed a long-lived palenque at Cofre de Perote in the mountainous terrain inland from that port.[35] Yanga's maroons soon were plundering the cargos of goods being transported along the Camino Real from Veracruz to Mexico City, and they were also

FIGURE 4.1: *Armed Maroon, Suriname, 1770s. From John Gabriel Stedman,* Voyage a Surinam et dans l'intérieur de la Guiane, contenant la relation de cinq années de courses et d'observationes faites dans cette contrée intéressante et peu connue; avec des details sur les Indiens de la Guiane et les Nègres, *(Paris, F. Buisson, 1799) plate 53.*

accused of kidnapping indigenous men and women, and even some Spaniards. The archbishop of Tlaxcala described the aftermath of one attack in 1608 during which raiders stopped a convoy, broke open a money box and stole one hundred pesos, absconded with two married indigenous women, and killed a twelve-year-old Spanish boy, cutting his throat and disemboweling him.[36] The abduction of the women and the ritual violence against the young boy is reminiscent of the practices of contemporary multiethnic Imbangala mercenaries, who lived much like maroons on the fringes of the Portuguese settlements in Central Africa.[37]

Spanish officials throughout the empire echoed similar complaints about maroons. They charged that the maroons enticed or stole away other slaves and carried on contraband trade with corsairs. Maroon palenques also challenged Spanish notions of civilized living and appropriate racial and social order, but repeated military efforts to eradicate them were, more often than not, unsuccessful. Located on the peripheries of European cities, and also on the fringes of indigenous worlds, maroon communities borrowed elements they found useful from both the dominant and native cultures. They drew as well on a variety of African cultural models—especially in the areas that reinforced authority so necessary for the communities' survival. Africans built remote strongholds protected by wooden palisades and camouflaged pits concealing sharpened stakes. They laid false trails to deceive the enemy and established sentry systems to patrol their settlements. Moreover, when discovered, the maroons had the disconcerting habit of melting away into the jungles, mountains, and swamps, only to coalesce again and form new encampments. If left in peace, many became stable communities based on agriculture, rather than on theft as the Spaniards alleged.[38]

Spanish officials developed a fairly standard pattern of interaction with maroon settlements. When the communities became large enough to be threatening, Spaniards first tried to eradicate them. If they were repeatedly unsuccessful, Spaniards used church intermediaries to negotiate peace and "reduce" the communities to legitimate towns. The policy of *reducción* was initially used to congregate indigenous populations into "human polity," meaning into Christian settlements, and Christian Indian towns became the model for later free black towns.[39]

The viceroys of New Spain commissioned local elites to lead military expeditions to search for and destroy the palenques that directly threatened their own economic interests. These men received the title of

captain and the corresponding military status and privileges. Captain
Pedro de Yebra held the commission for Veracruz in the late sixteenth
century. Yebra was succeeded in 1602 by Captains Antón de la Parada and
Alvaro de Baena (commissioned again in 1607), followed by Captain
Pedro González de Herrera, a wealthy landowner from Puebla, in 1608.[40]
González de Herrera's charge was to finally destroy the notorious
palenque ruled by King Yanga.[41]

Yanga's initial source of authority probably rested on his having
founded the settlement. His claim to royal lineage may have also been
accepted by his followers. Moreover, Yanga had assumed the role of religious leader of his community—the sort of "sacred chieftainship" or
"divine kingship" noted in other African societies. As a military leader,
he successfully defended his well-ordered community for many years,
thereby maintaining another claim on the loyalty of his adherents/sub-
jects, and the bravery and haughtiness with which he faced the final attack
are illustrative.

Yanga's community existed as a palenque for over thirty years, during which time it occupied multiple sites. Although its residents did,
indeed, raid Spanish convoys along the Camino Real and nearby haciendas for items they could not produce themselves, like manufactured goods
and luxury clothing, plunder alone did not sustain the community. For
that the maroons developed diversified agriculture and raised chickens
and herds of cattle and horses, which gave them added range and speed
for raiding.[42]

Because it seemed impossible to defeat Yanga, in 1608 Spanish officials sent the Franciscan friar Alonso de Benavides to try to reduce the
maroons, and he lived among them for almost five months. In that time
one couple asked to be married, but the mulatto mother of the bride
objected to her daughter marrying the black who had kidnapped her. A
debate ensued among the maroons, with Francisco Angola supporting the
position that no wedding could take place, given the mother's objections.
Francisco Mozambique (whose name proves that at least some slaves from
East Africa also lived in the settlement) argued that "mountain marriages"
were different. In the end the friar conducted the wedding but confessed
voluntarily to the Inquisition when he returned to Mexico City that he
did not know if the ceremony was valid. The friar reported other concerns he had about the salvation of the maroons, primary being that
despite his admonitions, they persisted in eating meat on Fridays, even

though the nearby rivers held abundant fish and they had eggs and vegetables to eat. Benavides also reported that another resident named Antonio Bolador chastised his fellow maroons for having allowed the priest to live there and that Bolador angrily rejected the Mass the friar offered to perform, adding that the priest was a deceiver.[43]

Whether the friar's strategic knowledge of Yanga's settlement was utilized by its attackers is unknown, but in 1609 Viceroy Luis de Velasco II commissioned Pedro González de Herrera to lead a major expedition against the settlement.[44] One of the Jesuit priests accompanying the force, Padre Juan Laurencio, left an account of the events that followed. In it he cast the expedition against Yanga almost as a crusade, describing González as a "Christian prince" and the expedition against Yanga as a "pious work" and "a service to God and for the public good." The Jesuit also made much of the need to save the souls of the maroons who, although raiders, included baptized Christians.[45]

Spanish officials attempted to keep the expedition secret, but Yanga's sympathizers made sure he knew what was afoot. The maroons, perhaps led by Francisco Angola, made an audacious and preemptive attack against a nearby hacienda and killed a Spaniard who claimed not to know the expedition's whereabouts. In what may have been an act of psychological warfare, the maroons allegedly split the unlucky captive's head with a broadsword, drank cupped handfuls of his blood, and rode back to their settlement with the man's scalp as their banner. The raiders took six indigenous women and another Spaniard back to their mountain settlement.

The Spaniards could hardly ignore such a challenge, and in February 1609 the Spanish captive, whom Yanga had released, guided Captain González's troops, which included 150 indigenous archers, 100 royal troops, and some Spanish mercenaries, back to the maroon's town. Pausing in the foothills, the Spaniards built a storehouse for their supplies and munitions and gathered additional troops of local hacendados and cowboys, including blacks, mulattos, and mestizos. After Father Laurencio confessed the multiracial force, they set off. Almost immediately, the Spaniards surprised a squadron of black horsemen raiding a sugar ingenio and managed to collect some of the horses and arms they abandoned as they raced home to warn their families.[46]

Three squads of Spaniards followed the maroons along the single trail that led to their mountaintop town, coming to their main spring and a large planted clearing. Farther up the mountain the Spaniards encountered a

defensive wall formed of large boulders behind which many men could hide
and fire down on attackers. Beyond that advance position the Spaniards
came to a clearing filled with brambles and rattan, meant to entrap advancing enemies. The Spaniards had no choice but to enter, and as they did, the
maroons attacked with scythes and a shower of iron-tipped arrows, rocks,
and boulders. During the engagement, which became known as the battle
of El Peñol, the defenders concentrated their fire on Captain González,
who barely escaped being crushed by a large rock. Another large slab hurled
at him carried González downhill and badly wounded his page. Although
his men feared him dead, González pulled himself up and, calling on
Santiago, the patron saint of the Spanish reconquest, urged his men forward. The Spanish forces advanced only to find a more dangerous situation—a single large log bridging a pass that could only be crossed single
file. Once they made it over the bridge they had to make it through a series
of three narrow passageways formed by log palisades and blocked by rattan
doorways. All the while, Yanga's men fired arrows at them from above.[47]

Yanga, the old Bran chieftain, had once led his own war parties, but
by this time he was aged, and at this battle his war captain, the Angolan
Francisco de la Matosa, commanded the maroons.[48] This would suggest
that Yanga's camp included a number of Angolan men in addition to the
Bran component. Slave trade records document a rise in the number of
Angolans entering the colony in this period.[49]

As Francisco and his men fought back against the Spaniards, Yanga
gathered the women in the community's small church and prayed before an
altar covered in lighted candles and in front of which they had planted
arrows in the ground. Like their counterparts in contemporary maroon settlements in Colombia, the Mexican maroons seem to have syncretized
Christian and indigenous African elements in their worship.[50] At nightfall,
the maroons received word that the Spaniards were almost upon them, and
Yanga led the women to the safety of another nearby palisaded fort. The
Spaniards finally entered the emptied town, extinguished the still-burning
candles, uprooted the arrows before the altar, rang the church bells, and
raised their own standard.[51]

The following morning, the victorious troops reconnoitered and
reported on the prospering settlement. Although the maroons had been
at this site for only nine months, Yanga had assigned half the population
to agriculture, and the Spaniards found fields planted with cotton, sweet
potatoes, chiles, tobacco, squashes, corn, beans, sugarcane, and other

vegetables. As some of the maroons had prepared and tilled fields, others had built the impressive fortifications as well as sixty houses, indicating that a population of several hundred may have lived at that single site.[52] In the homes the Spaniards found a wide variety of clothing, swords, hatchets, a few arquebuses, some salt, corn, and money. Yanga's larger house was located in the center of the town and was filled with benches for seating, which led the Spaniards to assume it also served as a town meeting place. The building sat at the foot of a large tree topped with a sentinel's watchtower from which the maroons had confidently watched the five-day Spanish advance. Knowing full well the number and strength of the forces arrayed against them, they still did not evacuate their town until the last possible moment.[53]

From their nearby fort, Yanga's people saw the Spaniards torch their homes, but the maroons were far from defeated. Father Laurencio said that instead, they sent the Spaniards insulting letters threatening to make jerked meat out of the hearts of the captain, soldiers, and priests. The maroons ridiculed their attackers in a constant barrage of shouted insults and noisily danced beneath lighted lanterns in a show of unconcern. They also ignored Captain González's white flag and repeated requests for negotiations.[54]

During one of the many battles that followed, Yanga's Angolan war captain, Francisco, was killed. Finally, after nine years of battling on the run and in a starving state, Yanga sent the Spaniards a list of eleven conditions (see appendix) that the Spaniards must meet in order to secure a peace. These included freedom for all those living in his town before 1608, formal recognition as a legitimate town of which Yanga and his heirs would become governors, the exclusion of Spaniards from that town (except on market days), and a church ministered to by Franciscans. In turn, Yanga and his people vowed to pay required tributes and to serve their monarch at arms when required. The fact that the maroons offered to track and return future runaways to their owners, and demanded to be paid for the service, has been frequently commented on by scholars, who debate whether or not the maroons really meant it. Studies of the institution of slavery in Africa would suggest that the Mexican maroons would have had no qualms about enslaving non-kin. However, scholars have ignored a significant clause in the controversial pledge, which is that the maroons would supply the owners with some of their own (slaves or dependents) until such time as they captured the runaways, and should they be unable to do so they would pay the owners the slaves' value. This arrangement is basically an American variant on the pawning institution African slave traders used in Old Calabar and other parts of Africa.[55] The tone of these demands is confident and authoritative and was surely taken by the Spaniards as another example of arrogance. The maroons stated that they would designate the place for their town and that should the monarch not confirm their charter within a year and a half, they would return to their previous state—of war.[56]

The free black town that Yanga's subjects, now also those of the Spanish crown, created was carved out of lands belonging to the wealthy family of Riva de Neyra. The landowner, like others before and after, would claim the crown's gratitude for having assisted in the pacification of the maroons and also for having formed a town, another commendable act given the premium Spaniards placed on living a "vida politica." In a ceremony witnessed by Spaniards, the "reduced" maroons, and the natives from whom both had now taken hereditary lands, the town of San Lorenzo de los Negros (also called San Lorenzo de Cerralvo and commonly called Yanga today) was established on six hundred varas of land, measured in the direction of the four winds, as were indigenous towns.[57] Spanish authorities did not formally recognize the free black town of San Lorenzo until 1618, possibly because of ongoing resistance from nearby landowners and anxieties produced by the major slave conspiracy in the capital in 1612.[58] Founding San Lorenzo did little to squelch marronage, and finally Spaniards decided, ironically, that the best solution would be to create a Spanish town in the midst of maroon territory. In 1624 thirty Spanish vecinos petitioned for and were granted a license to establish the town of Córdoba near San Lorenzo "to provide vigilance over the abuses of the blacks."[59]

Thereafter, the town of San Lorenzo appears periodically in the records, allowing scholars to track its fortunes. In 1643 its elected officials and its *cabildo* swore to obey Spanish regulations, care for the well-being of the townspeople, plant their fields, follow the rules of the church, and avoid drunkenness, unmarried sex, and other sins.[60] Despite the appropriate behavior of the townspeople, however, Spaniards continued to complain about runaways in the area. In 1641 they also lodged a complaint against Captain Gaspar Ñanga, charging that he sheltered and aided the runaways rather than returning them as required by his town's charter.[61] Gaspar was presumably hereditary heir to the leadership of the town and perhaps a son of Yanga, but he also had the given name of the contemporary heir of the Riva de Neyra family, suggesting that he or someone else in that family with that name may have served as godfather to the black leader. Fictive kinships with important Spaniards would have been a source of protection for the black townspeople and a form of noblesse oblige for the Spaniards, whose social status was enhanced by assuming responsibility for added dependents. A further sign of the partial evolution of the maroons into Spanish subjects is that their leader was now styled a captain rather than an African king.

Perhaps in an effort to refute the charges against Captain Gaspar Ñanga, the following year San Lorenzo's *alcaldes* Cristobal Valgoniz and Juan Pasqual reported that they had chased a runaway band of slaves for over a month and a half, had killed the maroon captain, and returned seven others at their own costs, and to the detriment of their own untended *milpas*, or corn fields. Claiming to be the only ones skilled enough to track runaway slaves in such rugged territory, they asked the viceroy to pay them one hundred pesos for any slaves captured across the Rio Blanco (their own former hideout) and fifty pesos for those captured on the same side.[62]

By 1695 the townspeople of San Lorenzo had accumulated large herds of horses that they claimed to need for military service and tracking runaways. Don Gaspar Carlos de Riva de Neyra argued that because the population of San Lorenzo by that time numbered only about one hundred persons, there was no need for so many mounts. He complained that the horses strayed onto his land and devoured his pastures, causing him to lose more than two thousand head of cattle to starvation. The irate hacendado asked for and received permission to shoot down with arrows any wandering or untended horses.[63] Two years later, Italian traveler Gemelli Carreri and his black guide stopped for dinner at San Lorenzo. After repeating throughout his account many of the most commonplace stereotypes of blacks, Gemelli Carreri commented that San Lorenzo "would make anyone think they were in Guinea." He commented favorably, however, on the residents' talent for agriculture and ate the food they prepared for him.[64]

Mexican historian Adriana Naveda Chávez-Hita has documented the campaign of harassment local hacendados waged against San Lorenzo and other black towns in the region in the subsequent decades, the many complaints the black townspeople lodged with the viceroy, and his consistent support of their rights.[65] Viceroys supported black towns out of pragmatism, not altruism. They had found it was cheaper to "reduce" maroons than to conquer them, and so in 1670 the crown authorized establishment of another black town, San Miguel de Soyaltepeque, also on lands owned by the Riva De Neyra family. Its residents soon experienced many of the same difficulties as those of San Lorenzo. In 1695 the black governor and alcaldes of San Miguel de Soyaltepeque complained to the viceroy that a mestizo captain and the alcalde mayor of Antigua Veracruz were harassing them in the collection of tribute.[66] They charged that when Juan de la Cruz was absent from San Miguel the Spaniards had burned his home and that on another occasion Juan de Córdoba, the mulatto standard bearer of Veracruz's black militia, had destroyed Manuel de Olandeta's milpas. The officials of San Miguel asked the viceroy to order Spanish officials in Veracruz to treat them with the respect due to governors and alcaldes. They referred to their community as a "República de Negros" and reminded the viceroy that they had always defended his coasts and had loyally paid tribute as required.[67] Flipping a cultural and racial stereotype on its head, they charged that local Spaniards were interfering with the good government of their republic, and they asked for justice and for damages. The viceroy ordered the former and ignored the latter, but in replying to these men as leaders of a black republic, he proved that their use of the title was no mere presumption.[68] Rather, it seems that as in so many other ways, Spanish officials consciously modeled free black towns after indigenous towns, and that despite what all scholarly texts commonly hold, Spanish officials in the most important viceroyalty in the empire administered three, not two, republics: a República de Españoles, a República de Indios, and a República de Negros.

Although their herds may have been proliferating and their crops growing well, those economic activities were apparently not sufficient to sustain the former maroons, and their towns began to lose population to nearby Veracruz. Veracruz officials tried to force a group of free black women to return to San Lorenzo de Cerralvo at the beginning of the eighteenth century, but the women protested their expulsion to the viceroy, arguing that they would have no way to support themselves or their church in San Lorenzo. They claimed to have been living peacefully in Veracruz for more than twelve years, engaged in domestic service, and added that although they no longer lived in San Lorenzo they paid the tribute originally assessed them as residents. The viceroy rescinded the expulsion order and gave the women permission to remain in Veracruz.[69]

In the mid-eighteenth century, San Lorenzo's black alcaldes Joseph de Panama and Domingo Ramos and the rest of the officials of their *república*

FIGURE 4.2: *Militia of Veracruz, 1767. The order in this illustration mirrors the status accorded each of the various groups of militiamen in Spanish units with higher ranked persons, units, and colors listed before those of lower status. Top row, left to right: Official of the Granaderos, Official of the Fusileros, Soldier of the Granaderos, Soldier of the Fusileros. Lower row, left to right: Official of the Free Pardos, Official of the Free Morenos, Soldier of the Free Pardos, Soldier of the Free Morenos. Archivo General de Indias, Mapas y Planos, Uniformes, 95. Reproduced courtesy of the Florida Museum of Natural History, Fort Mose Exhibition.*

y común were still defending the town's six hundred varas of land against the encroachment of Spanish hacendados. They complained directly to the viceroy that the officials of Córdoba were alienating their lands and harassing them incessantly. Once again, the viceroy ordered the Spanish officials to respect the sovereignty of the black towns or face charges, but the distant support of the viceroy (or even more distant, of the Spanish crown) did not impede the locals, whose opposition to the free black towns in their midst was implacable.[70] Eventually, many of the townspeople of San Lorenzo left for better employment opportunities in the town of New Veracruz, and as residents continued to trickle away, driven either by threat or poverty, Spanish hacendados acquired their lands.

The maroons of New Spain managed to survive repeated Spanish assaults and were able to manipulate Spanish medieval constructs and refashion themselves and their settlements from "illegal" kingdoms led by "pagan" Africans to ordered black republics and townships composed of Christian, tribute-paying subjects. Free black towns like San Lorenzo de Cerralvo, San Miguel de Soyaltepeque (1670), Mandinga (1735), and Nuestra Señora de Guadalupe de los Morenos de Amapa (1769) represented a successful adaptation by maroons to changing conditions such as the growth and hostility of nearby Spanish populations.[71] Although coexistence with fellow Spanish subjects proved contentious, black officials and town leaders saw it as an accommodation worth making. The former maroons gained some autonomy and peace for their families. Despite chronic complaints from its Spanish subjects, the crown also found utility in recognizing the black towns. One advantage was that it was relieved of the continuous outlay for military expeditions. The crown could also claim to have fulfilled its humanitarian and religious duty in converting the maroons and reducing them to an orderly urban life. Black towns also served Spanish goals of populating contested or inhospitable reaches of the empire with loyal vassals and military reserves, and so the metropolitan officials, at least, continued to support them. Viceroy Francisco de Croix once again defended Amapa in 1771 and Viceroy Bucarelli defended Amapa and Soyaltepeque again in 1778 against local officials who decried the decadence of these towns and the failure of their elected officials to honor their obligations. In the latter case, the viceroy's counselor warned that "extinguishing towns is a serious business," and that were the towns eliminated the blacks might return to the mountains.[72]

APPENDIX

The Maroons' Conditions for Peace

In 1608, after Spaniards had tried for more than thirty years to extinguish Yanga's palenques, Viceroy Luis de Velasco II commissioned the Franciscan friar Alonso de Benavides and Manuel Carrillo, a councilman of Veracruz (who with that commission earned the title of captain), to solicit a peace treaty. The maroons dictated the following conditions under which they would accept peace and become loyal vassals, tribute payers, and defenders of the crown of Spain. They also agreed to become Christians. Terms such as these became the pattern for later peace treaties with maroons and legitimation of their free black towns.

R/da en 24 de marzo 1608　　　del comis de la an/a Veracruz
Con
Copia de los conciertos que
Piden los negros cimarrones

Acabado de cerrar este pliego llego un regidor desta ciudad llamado manuel carrillo a quien su ex/a cometio los conciertos con los negros simarrones que estan por esta comarca y da la rason de lo con ellos le passo conforme vera V.S/a por este papel y porque el correo se va a prisa nom prospec el ciclo el estado del S/a Vera+

8 de marzo
Fr Balthasar de Morales

Las condiciones que piden los Negros simarrones desta comarca

1. a Que sean libres todos los que se an huido hasta el mes de septiembre proximo passado y los de entonces aca se bolveran a sus dueños
2. que an de tener just/a mayor que no sea mestizo ni criollo ni letrado sino de capa y espada
3. que no ha de aver casa ni morada de español dentro del pueblo sino fuere a fueren a los tianques lunes y jueves que le haran en su pueblo
4. que an de tener los regidores y forma de cabildo

5. que el capitan Ñaga que es el mayoral dellos ha de ser
    governador y despues del sus hijo y descendientes

6. que los negros que hujeren de los puertos aca se obligen
    atraerlos asus dueños co tal que por el trabaxo les den
    dose pesos a los negros que los fueren a buscar y mientras
    no los bolbieron asus dueñosles daran otros de los
    suyos que les sirvan y quasi no los bolbieren que pagaran
    lo que valen

7. que dentro de un año y medio se les an de dar estas
    capitulaciones confirmadas por su mag/d y sino que se
    bolberan a su primer estado

8. que an de fundar su pueblo enter Rio Blanco y las hasiendas
    de Ribadeneira a donde ellos señalaren

9. que pagaran los tributos a su magestad como todos los
    demas negros y mulatos horros de las indias

10. la ultima condicion que piden es que los administre frailes
    franciscanos y no otros ningunos y que los ornam/tos se an
    de haser a costa de su mag/d p/a la iglesia

11. que asistiran a sus armas todos los negros que su mag/
    d tuviese necess/r destas para defender la trra

[The conditions that the black maroons of this region ask for:

1. That all those who fled before last September will be free
    and those who flee after that [time] will be returned to
    their owners

2. That they must have a chief judge who shall not be a
    mestizo nor criollo nor a letrado but rather be [?] a warrior

3. That no Spaniard will have a house in or stay within the
    town excepting during the markets they will have in their
    town on Mondays and Thursdays

4. That they must have councilmen and a town council

5. That the Captain Ñanga, who is their leader, must be
    governor and after him his sons and descendants

6. That they obligate themselves to return to their owners the
    blacks who flee to them from the ports, and for their work
    the blacks who track and return the runaways will be paid
    twelve pesos, and until they return the runaways, they
    will provide [the owners] with others of their own who will

serve them, and if they do not return them they will pay
[the owners] their value

7. And within a year and a half they must be given a charter
   confirmed by Your Majesty and if not they will return to
   their original state

8. That their town must be founded between the Rio Blanco
   and the estates of Ribadeneira where they indicate

9. That they will pay tribute to Your Majesty like all the rest
   of the free blacks and mulattos of the Indies

10. The last condition they request is that Franciscan friars
    and no others minister to them and that the costs of the
    ornaments for the church be paid for by Your Majesty

11. They will present themselves with their arms every time
    Your Majesty has need of them to defend the land]

Archivo General de la Nación, Mexico, Inquisición 1608, vol. 283,
file 26, fol. 186–87.

NOTES

1. Andrés Pérez de Ribas, *Corónica y historia religiosa de la Provincia de la
   Compañía de Jesus de Mexico en Nueva España*, 2 vols. (Mexico City, 1896),
   "Relación de la misión á que fué enviado el P. Juan Laurencio,
   acompañando a una escuadra de soldados que salía á la reducción de
   negros foragidos y salteadores," 282–94.

2. Ganga Zumba of Palmares, Domingo Bioho of San Basilio, Yanga of
   Cofre del Perote, and Bayano of Panama claimed to have been kings
   in their own countries. Richard Price, *Maroon Societies: Rebel Slave
   Communities in the Americas* (Baltimore: Johns Hopkins University
   Press, 1973), 16–22.

3. William D. Phillips, Jr., *Slavery from Roman Times to the Early Atlantic
   Trade* (Minneapolis: University of Minnesota Press, 1985), 162–63;
   Ruth Pike, *Aristocrats and Traders: Sevillian Society in the Sixteenth
   Century* (Ithaca, NY: Cornell University Press, 1972), 173, 180, 186–89.

4. José Luis Cortés López, *Los orígenes de la esclavitud negra en España* (Madrid: Ediciones Universidad de Salamanca, 1986), 151–76; Pike, *Aristocrats and Traders*, 170–92.

5. Ricardo E. Alegría, *Juan Garrido, el conquistador negro en las Antilles, Florida, México y California, c. 1503–1540* (San Juan de Puerto Rico: Centro de Estudios Avanzados de Puerto Rico y el Caribe, 1990); Peter Gerhard, "A Black Conquistador in Mexico," *Hispanic American Historical Review* 58 (1978): 451–59. For other examples of blacks involved in circum-Caribbean explorations and conquests, see Jane Landers, *Black Society in Spanish Florida* (Urbana: University of Illinois Press, 1999), chap. 1; Matthew Restall, "Black Conquistadores: Armed Africans in Early Spanish America," *Americas* 57, no. 2 (2000): 171–205.

6. For examples of the variety of records see Landers, *Black Society*; Gwendolyn Midlo Hall, *Africans in Colonial Louisiana: The Development of Afro-Creole Culture in the Eighteenth Century* (Baton Rouge: Louisiana State University Press, 1992); Kimberly S. Hanger, *Bounded Lives, Bounded Places: Free Black Society in Colonial New Orleans, 1769–1803* (Durham, NC: Duke University Press, 1997).

7. The Biafara and Mandinga nations formed the brotherhood of Nuestra Señora de la Candelaria in Santo Domingo in the late sixteenth century. José Luis Sáez, *La iglesia y el negro esclavo en Santo Domingo: Una historia de tres siglos* (Santo Domingo: Editora Amigo del Hogar, 1994). Although he does not state the national origins, Colin Palmer notes the existence of a black brotherhood in Mexico City as early as 1572, and of hospitals serving free and enslaved blacks in Mexico City and Vera Cruz in the same period. Colin A. Palmer, *Slaves of the White God: Blacks in Mexico, 1570–1650* (Cambridge, MA: Cambridge University Press, 1976), 54. Because it affected his conversion efforts, the Jesuit Alonso de Sandoval paid particular attention to the bewildering array of ethnicities and languages of the Africans to whom he ministered in seventeenth-century Cartagena, detailing which groups spoke mutually intelligible languages. Alonso de Sandoval, *Un tratado sobre la esclavitud* (Madrid: Alianza Editorial, 1987).

8. The secular church was an arm of the Spanish state and ministered to urban parishioners, while members of the missionary or regular orders were responsible for the conversion and spiritual care of indigenous peoples.

9. Spanish concepts of *buen gobierno* or just government extended access to groups often excluded by other systems, including women and slaves. See Charles Cutter, *The Legal Culture of Northern New Spain, 1700–1810*

(Albuquerque: University of New Mexico Press, 1994). On indigenous use of Spanish law, see Susan Kellogg, *Law and the Transformation of Aztec Culture, 1500–1700* (Norman: University of Oklahoma Press, 1995). On Africans' use of Spanish law, see Landers, *Black Society*; idem, "Felipe Edimboro Sues for Manumission," in *Colonial Lives: Documents on Latin American History, 1550–1850*, ed. Geoffrey Spurling and Richard Boyer (Oxford: Oxford University Press, 1999), 249–68; idem, "African and African American Women and Their Pursuit of Rights through Eighteenth-Century Spanish Texts," in *Haunted Bodies: Gender and Southern Texts*, ed. Anne Goodwyn Jones and Susan V. Donaldson (Charlottesville: University of Virginia Press, 1998), 56–76; "In Consideration of Her Enormous Crime: Rape and Infanticide in Spanish St. Augustine," in *The Devil's Lane: Sex and Race in the Early South*, ed. Catherine Clinton and Michele Gillespie (New York: Oxford University Press, 1997), 205–17. Also see Hanger, *Bounded Lives*.

Peter Caron argues that contemporary French interrogatories are suspect and without any reference to French legal culture or practice asserts that the "preliminary questions as to name and 'nation' of origin were not asked." Peter Caron, "'Of a nation which others do not Understand': Bambara Slaves and African Ethnicity in Colonial Louisiana, 1718–60," *Slavery and Abolition* 18 (1997): 108. This is not the case with Spanish interrogatories, which often include idiomatic answers to such questions. Laura Lewis has found the same attention to accuracy and to the voice of the informants in Spanish Inquisition records. Laura A. Lewis, *Hall of Mirrors: Power, Witchcraft, and Caste in Colonial Mexico* (Durham, NC: Duke University Press, 2003), 43–45.

10. On Hispaniola, see José Juan Arrom and Manuel A. García Arévalo, *Cimarrón* (Santo Domingo: Fundación García Arevalo, 1986).

11. St. Christopher was the Catholic patron saint of travelers. The reverse side of the medal features a compass rose. Both images are associated with European symbolism, but this object could also refer to African beliefs about water passage and return to Africa. Landers, *Black Society*; Kathleen A. Deagan and Darcie MacMahon, *Fort Mose: Colonial America's Black Fortress of Freedom* (Gainesville: University Press of Florida, 1995).

12. Among the most well-known projects are excavations of the slave quarters of the various plantations of U.S. presidents Washington, Jefferson, and Jackson in Virginia and Tennessee, a series of projects in low-country South Carolina and Georgia plantations, plantation slave villages and burial grounds in Jamaica and Barbados, and the African burial ground in New York City.

13. Many of the U.S. sites are discussed in Theresa A. Singleton, ed., *"I, Too Am America": Archaeological Studies of African-American Life* (Charlottesville: University of Virginia Press, 1999) and in her earlier volume, *The Archaeology of Slavery and Plantation Life* (San Diego: Academic Press, 1985). Also see Douglas V. Armstrong, *The Old Village and the Great House: An Archaeological and Historical Examination of Drax Hall Plantation, St. Ann's Bay, Jamaica* (Urbana: University of Illinois Press, 1990); Jerome S. Handler and Frederick W. Lange, *Plantation Slavery in Barbados: An Archaeological and Historical Investigation* (Cambridge: Harvard University Press, 1978); Jerome S. Handler, "An African-Type Healer/Diviner and His Grave Goods: A Burial from a Plantation Slave Cemetery in Barbados, West Indies," *International Journal of Historical Archaeology* 1 (1997): 89–128; Larry McKee, "Summary Report on the 1991 Hermitage Field Quarter Excavation," *Tennessean Anthropological Association Newsletter* 18 (1993):1–17. For periodic updates on New York's African burial ground, see Jerome S. Handler, "Updates # 1, 2, 3, and 4," *African-American Archeology* (Spring 1992, Spring 1993, Winter 1993, and Winter 1994); Spencer P. M. Harrington, "Bones and Bureaucrats: New York's Great Cemetery Imbroglio," *Archaeology* 46 (1993): 28–38.

14. Leland Ferguson, *Uncommon Ground: Archaeology and Early African America, 1650–1800* (Washington, DC: Smithsonian Institution Press, 1992); Linda France Stine, Melanie A. Cabak, and Mark D. Groover, "Blue Beads as African-American Cultural Symbols," *Historical Archaeology* 30 (1996): 49–75; Jerome S. Handler, "Determining African Birth from Skeletal Remains: A Note on Tooth Mutilation," *Historical Archaeology* 28 (1994): 113–19; Ross W. Jamieson, "Material Culture and Social Death: African-American Burial Practices," *Historical Archaeology* 29 (1995): 39–58.

15. Posnansky argues that recycling, functional substitution, innovation, and adaptation are constants in West African material production and that searching for exact duplication of African patterns and techniques in the Americas is a fool's game. Merrick Posnansky, "West African Reflections on African American Archaeology," in Singleton, *I, Too, Am American*; Christopher DeCorse, "Culture Contact, Continuity, and Change on the Gold Coast, A.D. 1400–1900," *African Archaeological Review* 10 (1992): 163–96, "The Danes on the Gold Coast: Culture Change and the European Presence," *African Archaeological Review* 11 (1993): 149–73, and *An Archaeology of El Mina* (Washington, DC, 2001).

16. For example, see the essays in Paul Lovejoy, ed., *Identity in the Shadow of Slavery* (London: Continuum, 2000) and Linda M. Heywood, ed., *Central Africans and Cultural Transformations in the American Diaspora* (Cambridge: Cambridge University Press, 2002). Case studies are now also tracking individual Africans across the Atlantic. See Paul E. Lovejoy, "Background to Rebellion: The Origins of Muslim Slaves in Bahia," *Slavery and Abolition* 15 (1994): 151–80 and Lovejoy and Robin Law, eds. *The Biography of Muhammad Gardo Baquaqua* (Princeton, NJ, 2001); Randy Sparks, *The Two Princes of Calabar: An Eighteenth-Century Atlantic Odyssey* (Cambridge, MA: Marcus Wiener, 2004); James Walvin, *An African's Life: The Life and Times of Olaudah Equiano, 1745–1797* (Washington, DC: Cassell, 1998).

17. There is a wealth of information on material culture in Spanish documents. See Jane Landers, "La cultura material de los cimarrones: los casos de Ecuador, La Española, México y Colombia," in *Rutas de la esclavitud en África y América Latina*, ed. Rina Cáceres (San José: Editorial de la Universidad de Costa Rica, 2001), 145–56.

18. Richard Morse analyzed the concept of the *ciudad perfecta* and Spanish efforts to reproduce it in the New World. Richard Morse, "A Framework for Latin American Urban History," in *Urbanization in Latin America: Approaches and Issues*, ed. Jorge Hardoy (Garden City, NJ: Anchor, 1975), 57–107.

19. Royal Cédula Replying to Governor Nicolás de Ovando, March 29, 1503, Archivo General de Indias, Seville, Spain (hereafter cited as AGI), Indiferente General; Slave Codes, Santo Domingo (hereafter cited as SD), January 6, 1522, AGI, Patronato 295. The most important work on slavery and marronage in Hispaniola is that of Carlos Estéban Deive, *Los guerrilleros negros: Esclavos fugitivos y cimarrones en Santo Domingo* (Santo Domingo: Fundación Cultural Dominicana, 1989).

20. Deive, *Los guerrilleros negros*; Jane Landers, "Cimarrón Ethnicity and Cultural Adaptation in the Spanish Domains of the Circum-Caribbean, 1503–1763," in Lovejoy, *Identity in the Shadow of Slavery*, 30–54; Landers, "The Central African Presence in Spanish Maroon Communities," in Heywood, *Central Africans and Cultural*, 227–41.

21. Menéndez informed the king that Hispaniola was populated by thirty thousand blacks and fewer than two thousand Spaniards, while Puerto Rico held fifteen thousand blacks and only five hundred Spaniards. He also warned that Veracruz had a similar racial profile. Memorial of Pedro Menéndez de Avilés, undated (1561–62), in E. Ruidíaz y Caravia, *La Florida* (Madrid: Imprenta de los Hijos de J. A. Garcia, 1893), 2:322,

cited in Woodbury Lowery, *The Spanish Settlements in the Present Day Limits of the United States* (New York: Russell & Russell, 1959), 14–15, 96. This document also appears in the collection of the St. Augustine Historical Collection and is identified as being from the Archivo del Instituto de Valencia de Don Juan Madrid, Envio 25–H, no. 162, Council of the Indies, n.d.

22. Gonzalo Aguirre Beltrán, *La población negra de México: Estudios etnohistórico* (Mexico City: Ediciones Fuente Cultural, 1946), 208. Aguirre Beltrán collaborated with the famed anthropologist of Africa Melville Herskovits and was a pioneer in analyzing African ethnicities in Mexico. See also *Obra antropológica XVI, El negro en Nueva España, La formación colonial, La medicina popular y otros ensayos* (Veracruz, Mexico: Universidad Veracruzana Instituto Nacional Indigenista, 1994).

23. David M. Davidson, "Negro Slave Control and Resistance in Colonial Mexico, 1519–1650," *Hispanic American Historical Review* 46 (1966): 235–53. Patrick Carroll credits blacks with playing a critical role in the economic takeoff of New Spain. Patrick J. Carroll, *Blacks in Colonial Veracruz: Race, Ethnicity, and Economic Development* (Austin: University of Texas Press, 1991), 63.

24. Aguirre Beltrán, *La población negra*, 200, 209, 213. Herman Bennett reminds his readers that New Spain held the second-largest slave and largest free black population in the Americas in the late seventeenth century. Herman L. Bennett, *Africans in Colonial Mexico* (Bloomington: Indiana University Press, 2003).

25. Carroll, *Blacks in Colonial Veracruz*, 29 and table 3 (32–33).

26. On the complexity and ambiguities of racial categories and racial dynamics in colonial Mexico City, see R. Douglas Cope, *The Limits of Racial Domination: Plebeian Society in Colonial Mexico City, 1660–1720* (Madison: University of Wisconsin Press, 1994); also see Bennett, *Africans in Colonial Mexico*; Lewis, *Hall of Mirrors*.

27. *Las cosas más considerables vistas en la Nueva España por el Doctor Don Juan Francisco Gemelli Carreri*, trans. José María de Agreda y Sánchez (Mexico City, 1946).

28. Ibid. In 1608, during Velasco's second term as viceroy, he discovered a Christmas season plot allegedly conceived in the homes of free blacks who were hosting banquets and dances for their elected king and queen and their court. Thomas Gage also commented on the luxurious dress and attractiveness of mulatto women in Mexico City after his 1625 visit. Thomas Gage, *Thomas Gage's Travels in the New World*,

ed. J. Eric S. Thompson (Norman: University of Oklahoma Press, 1958), 69–70. In 1697 Italian traveler Gemelli Carreri commented on the same phenomenon. Giovanni Francesco Gemelli Carreri, *Voyage du tour du monde,* 6 vols. (Paris, 1727).

29. "Relación del alzamiento que negros y mulatos, libres y cautivos de la ciudad de Méjico de la Nueva España, pretendieron hacer contra los españoles por cuaresma del año 1612 y del castigo que se hizo de las cabezas y culpados," MS 2,010, fols. 236–41, no. 168, Biblioteca Nacional de Madrid, Sección de Manuscritos, transcribed by Luis Querol y Roso, "Negros y mulatos de Nueva España (Historia de su alzamiento en Méjico en 1612)," *Anales de la Universidad de Valencia* 90 (1931–32): 141–53. For examples of similar Spanish treatment of slave rebels in Colombia, see Jane Landers, "Conspiradores esclavizados en Colombia en el siglo XVII," in *Afrodescendientes en las américas: Trayectorias sociales e identitarias: 150 años de la abolición de la esclavitud en Colombia,* ed. Claudia Mosquera, Mauricio Pardo, and Odile Hoffman (Bogotá: Universidad Nacional de Colombia, 2002), 181–93.

30. Laura Lewis discusses Spaniards' early use of the charge that aggressive blacks abused Indians and shows how Spaniards used this stereotype for their own advantage. Lewis, *Hall of Mirrors,* 68–74.

31. Don Luis de Velasco to the governor of Veracruz, January 15, 1592, Indios 6, second part, fol. 89, file 396, Archivo General de la Nación, Mexico City (hereafter cited as AGN). A classic study of racial politics in Mexico in this time period is J. I. Israel, *Race, Class, and Politics in Colonial Mexico, 1610–1670* (London: Oxford University Press, 1975).

32. Irving B. Leonard, *Baroque Times in Old Mexico* (Ann Arbor: University of Michigan Press, 1959), 3.

33. Captain General Menéndez de Avilés brutally eradicated the Florida settlement in 1565. Eugene Lyon, *The Enterprise of Florida: Pedro Menéndez de Avilés and the Spanish Conquest of 1565–1568* (Gainesville: University of Florida, 1974).

34. On Caribbean piracy, see Kenneth R. Andrews, *The Spanish Caribbean: Trade and Plunder, 1530–1630* (New Haven, CT: Yale University Press, 1978); Kris E. Lane, *Pillaging the Empire: Piracy in the Americas, 1500–1700* (Armonk, NY: M. E. Sharpe, 1998).

35. On maroon leadership and claims to royalty, see Jane Landers, "Leadership and Authority in Maroon Settlements in Spanish America and Brazil," in *Africa and the Americas: Interconnections during the Slave Trade,* ed. José C. Curto and Renée Soulodre-La France (Trenton, NJ: Africa World Press, 2005).

36. Octaviano Corro, *Los cimarrones en Veracruz y la fundación de Amapa* (Jalapa, Mexico, 1951). Patrick Carroll comments on this incident and on maroon aggression toward native women and explains it partially by the uneven sex ratios of the period and place. Carroll, *Blacks in Colonial Veracruz*, 90–91.

37. Angolans formed an important component of the slave and maroon populations in New Spain in this period. Joseph Miller, "Central Africa during the Era of the Slave Trade, c. 1490s–1850s," in Heywood, *Central Africans and Cultural Transformations*, 46–47, and *Way of Death: Merchant Capitalism and the Angolan Save Trade, 1730–1830* (Madison: University of Wisconsin Press, 1988), 142–43. On the Imbangala, see also David Birmingham, *Central Africa to 1870: Zambezia, Zaire, and the South Atlantic* (Cambridge: Cambridge University Press, 1981), 232–34.

38. Price, *Maroon Societies*.

39. Declaration of Emperor Charles, 1538, cited in Lyle N. McAlister, *Spain and Portugal in the New World, 1492–1700* (Minneapolis: University of Minnesota Press, 1984), 172.

40. Commission of Alvaro de Baena, March 21, 1602, AGN, General de Partes, 6 (1601–9), file 83, fol. 42v and file 302, fol. 115v. The commission of don Matheo de Garay of Córdoba over a century later specified that he should "pursue and apprehend" the blacks of the palenque known as Matta de Caña. Garay took sixty-two of his own slaves along on this expedition. Commission of don Matheo de Garay, August 24, 1709, AGN, General de Partes, 19 (1708–10), file 217, fol. 166v.

41. Gonzalo Aguirre Beltrán argues that it was actually a rancher from nearby Tlaliscoyan, Pedro Gómez de Herrera, who went after Yanga. Aguirre Beltrán, *Obra antropológica*, 185–86.

42. African cowboys were ubiquitous throughout the circum-Caribbean. For New Spain, see Lolita Gutierrez Brockington, *The Leverage of Labor: Managing the Cortés Haciendas in Tehuantepec, 1588–1688* (Durham, NC: Duke University Press, 1989); Landers, *Black Society*. In a common complaint, the chief constable of Veracruz reported in 1632 that after almost fifty years of cattle ranching in the region, many "negros, mulatos, y mestizos" were living in nearby Indian towns such as Tlaliscoya and Albora, and were abusing the inhabitants. Juan de Zabala, April 10, 1632, AGN, General de Partes, 7 (1631–33), file 84.

43. Declaration of Fray Alonso de Benavides to Fray Báltazar de Morales, March 24, 1609, Inquisición, 1609, file 284, fol. 77, cited in Gonzalo Aguirre Beltrán, *Obra antropológica*, 183–84.

44. Davidson, "Negro Slave Control and Resistance in Colonial Mexico"; Palmer, *Slaves of the White God*, 126–30.

45. Pérez de Ribas, *Corónica*.

46. Ibid.

47. Ibid. The maroons of the famed quilombo of Palmares in seventeenth-century Brazil, many of whom were Central Africans, built impressive palisaded fortresses and utilized many of the same defensive techniques. Landers, "Leadership and Authority in Maroon Settlements."

48. Landers, "Leadership and Authority in Maroon Settlements." John Thornton has analyzed Kongo/Angolan war strategies and tactics in several works including *Warfare in Atlantic Africa, 1500–1800* (London: University College London Press, 1999), *The Kingdom of Kongo: Civil War and Transition* (Madison: University of Wisconsin Press, 1983), "African Dimensions of the Stono Rebellion," *American Historical Review* 96 (October 1991): 1101–11, and "African Soldiers in the Haitian Revolution," *Journal of Caribbean History* 25 (1991): 58–80.

49. Contemporary Colombian palenques such as San Basilio and Matudere also divided military responsibilities along ethnic lines, with war captains commanding squadrons of their own nation. See Landers, "Conspiradores esclavizados en Colombia en el siglo XVII."

50. Ibid.

51. Pérez de Ribas, *Corónica*.

52. For further discussion of the material life in maroon settlements, see Jane Landers, "Maroon Women in Spanish America," in *Beyond Bondage: Free Women of Color in the Slave Societies of the Americas*, ed. David Barry Gaspar and Darlene C. Hine (Bloomington: Indiana University Press, 2004), 3–18.

53. Pérez de Ribas, *Corónica*.

54. Ibid.

55. Ibid.; Paul E. Lovejoy and David Richardson, "Trust, Pawnship, and Atlantic History: The Institutional Foundations of the Old Calabar Slave Trade, *American Historical Review* 104 (April 1999): 333–55. See also Paul E. Lovejoy and Toyin Falola, eds., *Pawnship, Slavery, and Colonialism in Africa* (Trenton, NJ: Africa World Press, 2003).

56. "Conditions That the Black Maroons of the Region Request," AGN, Inquisition, vol. 283, file 26, fols. 186–87.

57. Memorial of don Gaspar Carlos de Riva de Neyra, August 23, 1695, AGN, Mercedes, vol. 63 (1688–93), fol. 108 and vol. 64–66 (1694–1707), fols. 8–9v.

58. "Relación del alzamiento."

59. Adriana Naveda Chávez-Hita, *Esclavos negros en las haciendas azucareras de Córdoba, Veracruz, 1690–1830* (Xalapa: Universidad Veracruzana Centro de Investigaciones Históricas, 1987). Other regional studies of black populations in Mexico include Mónica Leticia Gálvez Jiménez, *Celaya: Sus raíces africanas* (Guanajuato: Ediciones La Rana, 1995) and María Guadalupe Chávez Carbajal, *Propietarios y esclavos negros en Valladolid de Michoacan (1600–1650)* (Morelia: Universidad Michoacana de San Nicolás de Hidalgo Instituto de Investigaciones Históricas, 1994).

60. Chávez-Hita, *Esclavos negros.* In 1643 the black officials of San Lorenzo Cerralvo included *alcaldes* (magistrates) Cristobal Gomez and Gaspar Hernandez, *regidores* (councilmen) Miguel Jacinto and Domingo de Rivadeneira (named after the great landowner), *alguacil mayor* (chief constable) Tomas de Santiago and *alguaciles* (constables) Juan Primo and Simon de la Cruz. The *mayordomo* (manager) of the cabildo was Cristobal Rios. February 21, 1643, 100 Reales Cédulas, AGN, vol. 49, file 328, fol. 263.

61. Archivo Notarial de Orizaba, 1641, file 1, fol. 8, cited in Chávez-Hita, *Esclavos negros,* 128.

62. Relación de Xpto Valgoniz y Juan Pasqual, April 3, 1642, Reales Cédulas, AGN, Duplicados (1642), vol. 49, file 10, fols. 112–112v.

63. Memorial of don Gaspar Carlos de Riva de Neyra, August 23, 1695, AGN, Mercedes, vol. 63 (1688–93), fol. 108 and vol. 64–66 (1694–1707), fols. 8–9v.

64. *Las cosas más considerables vistas,* 166.

65. Chávez-Hita, *Esclavos negros,* 129–30.

66. Free black militias were established in the circum-Caribbean as early as the sixteenth century. See Jane Landers, "Transforming Bondsmen into Vassals: Arming the Slaves in Colonial Spanish America," in *Arming Slaves in World History,* ed. Philip Morgan and Christopher Brown (New Haven, CT: Yale University Press, 2006). On eighteenth-century militias in Veracruz, see "El reglamento para las milicias de Veracruz," AGN, Indiferente de Guerra (1767–69), vol. 40b. Also see Ben Vinson, III, *Bearing Arms for His Majesty: The Free-Colored Militia in Colonial Mexico* (Stanford: Stanford University Press, 2001); Jackie R. Booker, "Needed

but Unwanted: Black Militiamen in Veracruz, Mexico," *Historian* 55, no. 2 (1993): 259–76; Juan M. De la Serna H., "Integración e identidad, pardos y morenos en las milicias y cuerpo de lanceros de Veracruz en el S. XVIII," in *Fuerzas militares en Iberoamérica*, ed. Juan Ortiz (in press).

67. The men of San Miguel served alongside the free black militia of Veracruz so this may have been a personal quarrel. See the appointment of Diego Hernández as Infantry Captain of the Compañía del Batallón de Morenos y Negros Libres de la Ciudad de Nueva Veracruz and Francisco de Torres as Alféres, July 28, 1643, AGN, 100 Reales Cédulas, file 390 (Hernández) and file 391 (Torres).

68. Manuel de Olandete Governador y Antonio Moreno alcalde ordinario del Pueblo de San Miguel . . . y demas officiales de su República al Conde de Galve (Viceroy Gaspar de Sandoval Cerda Silva y Mendoza), and his reply, July 23, 1695, AGN, Indios, vol. 32, on microfilm reel 12, file 303.

69. Representación de Nicolasa Martínez y demas compañeras, August 31, 1708, AGN, General de Partes, vol. 19 (1708–10).

70. Don Pedro Cebrian por parte de Jph de Panama y Domingo Ramos, December 20, 1742, AGN, Indios 1741, file 97.

71. Amapa was formed by residents of various palenques near the Rio Amapa, including Palacios, Breve Cozina, and Mandinga. Spanish documents on the foundation of Nuestra Señora de Guadalupe de los Morenos de Amapa are found in AGN, Tierras, vol. 3543 (1769–78), file 1 and have been published by Fernando Winfield Capitaine as *Los cimarrones de Mazateopan* (Xalapa: Universidad Veracruzana, 1992). Scholars who have written about this town include Corro, *Los cimarrones*; William B. Taylor, "The Foundation of Nuestra Señora de Guadalupe de los Morenos de Amapa," *Americas* 26 (1970): 439–46 and in William B. Taylor and Kenneth Mills, "The Foundation of Nuestra Señora de Guadalupe de los Morenos de Amapa, Mexico (1769)," in *Colonial Spanish America: A Documentary History* (Delaware, MD: Scholarly Resources, 1998), 274–81; Adriana Naveda Chávez-Hita, "De San Lorenzo de los negros a Los Morenos de Amapa: Cimarrones veracruzanos, 1609–1735," in Cáceres, *Rutas de la esclavitud*, 157–74. On Mandinga, see Patrick J. Carroll, "Mandinga: The Evolution of a Mexican Runaway Slave Community, 1735–1827," *Comparative Studies in Society and History* 19, no. 4 (October 1977): 488–505.

72. Viceroy Carlos Francisco de Croix, responding to complaints of Governor Juan Fernando de Palacio, governor of Veracruz, April 10, 1771, AGN, Tierras, vol, 3543 (1769–78), file 1, fol. 117, and Viceroy Bucareli's February 13, 1778 approval of the recommendation of Licenciado Martin de Aramburu, November 20, 1777, ibid.

CHAPTER FIVE

Manuel's Worlds

Black Yucatan and the Colonial Caribbean

MATTHEW RESTALL

✣ IN FEBRUARY OF 1778 A FREE BLACK MAN NAMED FELIS MANUEL BOLIO, also known as Manuel Bolio and Manuel de Lara, was arrested by the Inquisition under suspicion of having committed the crime of double matrimony. The arrest took place in the city of Cartagena, on the Caribbean coast of what is today Colombia. Interrogated by church officials, Manuel explained how the course of his life had led him into bigamy.[1] In this chapter I will seek to explain how Manuel's life illustrates the existence and nature of a black Caribbean world that crossed the boundaries between colonies and empires, and included within it the circum-Caribbean colony where Manuel spent most of his adult life—the Spanish province of Yucatan.

Middle Passages

Manuel's life began in Africa, but all we know of his years before he arrived in the Americas is what he told the Inquisitors, confirmed in the record of his first marriage—that he was *negro adulto natural de Congo*, "a black adult native of Congo." In Spanish America, "Congo" tended to refer to

FIGURE 5.1: *View of colonial Campeche from the sea. This would have
been Manuel Bolio's first view of Yucatan. From Arnoldus
Montanus*, Beschryving van America *(Amsterdam, 1671),
258–59 inter. Reproduced courtesy of the John Carter Brown
Library, Brown University.*

the Kingdom of Kongo in West Central Africa; as a result of the civil wars
that wracked the kingdom from 1655 through the eighteenth century,
millions of men and women from the region were sold into slavery and
shipped across the Atlantic, among them the Congolese African who became Manuel Bolio.[2]

Based on the larger patterns of the slave trade, we can reasonably speculate that Manuel was enslaved in his late teens as a result of the wars in
West Central Africa that fed—and were stimulated by—trans-Atlantic slavery. He would probably have crossed the ocean, the terrible journey known
as the Middle Passage, in a British, Dutch, or French ship, not a Spanish

FIGURE 5.2: *Manuel's worlds: Yucatan and the Caribbean, showing places featured in this chapter. Map by Matthew Restall.*

one, and only in the Americas would he have been sold into Spanish hands.[3] The Africans that ended up in Yucatan typically came through the Caribbean, purchased by Spanish merchants in Jamaica, Havana, or Santo Domingo, and then were resold most commonly in Campeche—where Manuel Bolio spent the earliest of his years in Yucatan.

In colonial times traveling overland into Yucatan was arduous, even dangerous, rendering the peninsula effectively an island and the port town of Campeche its main gateway (as we shall see later, there was also a backdoor into the colony, through Bacalar and Belize; see figure 5.2). African slaves and servants had been coming into Campeche since the decades of the Spanish conquest in the mid-sixteenth century. Some became conquistadors themselves; one example is Sebastián Toral, who fought the Mayas during the Montejo-led invasions of the 1530s and was freed as a reward for his services. In the 1540s he settled in the colonial capital of Mérida as one of its unheralded founders. There Toral raised a family and lived into old age.[4]

Toral was hardly the only African to participate in the "pacification" of the Mayas or to leave descendants to contribute to the development of multiracial communities in the colony. Don Francisco de Montejo the elder had been granted a royal license to bring up to one hundred black

TABLE 5.1. The Afro-Yucatecan Population, 1570–1805

Year	Africans or Negros	Mulattos and Pardos	Both
1570	265	20	—
1574	—	—	500
1600	500	—	—
1605	—	350	—
1618	—	—	2,000
1646	497	15,770	—
1742	274	35,712	—
1779	1,490	17,605	—
1790	2,800	43,426	—
1791	—	—	45,201
1805	—	—	28,100

Sources: Aguirre Beltrán, Población negra, 197–222 (for 1570, 1646, 1742); García Bernal, Yucatán, 154–58 (for 1574, 1600, 1618); Sherburne F. Cook and Woodrow Borah, Essays in Population History: Mexico and the Caribbean (Berkeley: University of California Press, 1974), 2:79, 95 (for 1605, 1805); Robert W. Patch, Maya and Spaniard in Yucatán, 1648–1812 (Stanford: Stanford University Press, 1993), 234 (for 1779); Nancy M. Farriss, Maya Society under Colonial Rule: The Collective Enterprise of Survival (Princeton: Princeton University Press, 1984), 65 (for 1790); J. Ignacio Rubio Mañé, Archivo de la historia de Yucatán, Campeche, y Tabasco (Mexico City: Imprenta Aldina, Robredo y Rosell, 1942), 1:250 (for 1791).

slaves on his conquest campaigns. It is not known whether that license was filled, but there is detailed evidence of black slaves playing important auxiliary roles in the early decades of colonization in Yucatan. One of these, for example, an African baptized in Mexico as Marcos, was a slave of Francisco de Montejo the younger. Marcos was so successful at rounding up village Mayas to work as construction workers and domestic servants in Mérida that he prompted written protest by Mayas and by Spanish settlers not allied to the Montejo faction.[5] The Montejos and their allies were not the only Spaniards to bring in black slaves; by 1570 there were several hundred Africans in Yucatan (see table 5.1)—almost as many as the number of Spaniards.[6]

Over the succeeding centuries, African slaves were introduced into the colony in steady but small numbers. The *Nuestra Señora del Pilar*, a merchant vessel that dropped anchor off Campeche in 1791, en route from Cuba to Veracruz, was typical of the pattern. When the ship was detained by colonial Yucatec authorities on suspicion of smuggling, its cargo was inventoried; its holds contained dozens of different trade items, with a human cargo of a few paying European passengers and fourteen black slaves. In this case, only one of the slaves was disembarked and sold in Campeche, but a delivery of fourteen slaves from one ship would have been the norm. The annual arrival rate of Africans to the colony ranged from a handful to some 150—the number from "Guinea" on board a ship that reached Campeche, via Veracruz, in the summer of 1599.[7] Two British traders were given a license to bring 199 slaves into Campeche in the early 1730s, although Spanish records show that the total legal importation of enslaved Africans into the port in 1731–33 was 167—an average rate of three ships a year and just over 18 slaves per ship.[8] Most sales in the slave markets of Campeche and Mérida had Africans changing hands in ones, twos, or threes, and going to work in similar numbers for priests, merchants, military officers, and those able to support well-staffed households. For a Spaniard in Yucatan to own more than four black slaves, as did Captain Diego de Acevedo in the 1690s, was unusual; in eighteenth-century Mérida, Spanish slave-owners held an average of one to two black slaves each, and only 5 percent of slave owners had ten or more slaves.[9]

Thus as the Spanish population of Yucatan slowly grew, and the Maya population—always the majority—began to recover from the impact of early colonial epidemics, African-born slaves and servants became more of a minority. But at the same time the mixed-race population grew dramatically in size. In Yucatan this meant mestizos of mixed Spanish-Maya descent, mulattos of mixed Spanish-African descent, and *pardos*, a term applied in this colony both to those of Spanish-African and Maya-African descent (and thus inclusive of mulattos). As table 5.1 shows, by the early nineteenth century the combined total of all people of African descent in the province numbered nearly 30,000—again, almost as many as Spaniards.[10]

As an Afro-Yucatecan (a person of African descent living in Yucatan) Manuel Bolio was thus a member of a demographically significant minority in the late colony. As was the case in many other regions of Spanish America, the province's local native population met most colonial labor demands. But African slaves from the outset comprised a permanent labor force that was more directly and closely tied to the colonists.[11] Before long, African slaves—and later free pardos—were participating in all areas of colony building as auxiliaries to Spaniards and often as overseers of Maya workers. Many became personal slaves or servants in the urban homes of Spanish settlers, as did Manuel Bolio. With the possible exception of slave laborers on the few sugar plantations that were set up later in the colonial period, Afro-Yucatecans were not anonymous members of a mass labor force; they were individuals.[12]

This meant that they were more likely to be treated in a somewhat humane manner than were the African slaves put to work on plantations or in mines. But this fact should not be misread as meaning that slavery was without brutality in a colony such as Yucatan, or that Afro-Yucatecans of all kinds were not viewed with suspicion and disdain. The question of "race" and "racism" in Spanish America is a complex one, largely because evidence on colonial Spanish conceptions of race is inconclusive; in other words, Spanish ethnocentrism and prejudice cannot be equated with modern racism. This was certainly true of Yucatan, where categories like "pardo" and "mulatto" and "mestizo" were used loosely and inconsistently, and where there was a fair amount of "passing" from one category to another. Furthermore, Yucatan was not a slave society but a society with slaves, where for most of the colonial period black slaves were significantly outnumbered by free coloreds (see table 5.1).[13] Yet there was clearly also considerable prejudice against people of African descent. In Yucatan, as elsewhere in the empire, African slaves were treated as pieces of property, branded (usually on the face), and exploited as a source of labor.[14] Likewise, blacks and mulattos were scapegoats for whatever social problems colonial officials believed were afflicting the colony (in Campeche and Mérida, Afro-Yucatecans were accused and convicted of criminal activities out of all proportion to their numbers).[15]

Spaniards, of course, seldom thought that Afro-Yucatecans had anything to complain about. Like Spaniards elsewhere, Yucatan's colonists believed that a life of slavery in their empire was preferable to life in Africa; according to a 1766 report on Yucatan's economy, blacks there were fortunate to have been given "happier lives" than the barbarous existence to which their compatriots in Africa were condemned.[16] By this date, Manuel Bolio had left Yucatan. Perhaps his restlessness had something to do with Spanish attitudes toward Africans and their descendants.

Settling Down

By 1757 three important developments had taken place in Manuel Bolio's life. He had acquired or been granted his freedom. He had moved—or more likely he had been moved—from Campeche to the city of Mérida, where he lived in the predominantly Afro-Yucatecan parish of Jesús María. And he had married. The marriage had taken place in the Jesús parish church, a modest building no longer in existence but in colonial times located just a block and a half from the city plaza—Spaniards had settled their black and mulatto slaves and servants in small neighborhoods between the Spanish homes at the city center and the five Maya neighborhoods that encircled the city.[17] But Spanish efforts to keep Mayas and Africans apart were halfhearted and fruitless, as symbolized by Manuel's marriage. For his wife, Josepha Chan, was Maya.

Manuel did not state to Inquisition officials how he acquired his freedom, but there is no suggestion in the record that it was acquired other than through legal means. Under Spanish law, slaves had the right to petition for manumission, either for services rendered (ranging from formal military service to informal sexual services), or as a grant, or as self-purchase (*coartación*, with the slave permitted to seek adjudication of the price in the colonial courts).[18] As we saw above, by Manuel's time, the vast majority of Afro-Yucatecans were pardos or mulattos, most of them free, either by birth or through manumission. As was the case elsewhere in the Americas, slaves in Yucatan also sought that most direct means of emancipation—escape. But records of slave escapes in Yucatan are few in number and are only for individuals subsequently recaptured, not for groups of escapees at large.[19] Indeed, there were no significant maroon communities in the colony, partly because after the early seventeenth century most Afro-Yucatecans were free and partly because Guatemala and Belize offered a refuge of sorts (more on Belize's role in a moment).[20]

The details of Manuel's Campeche years are murky, but after that things become clearer. He was owned by a Spaniard named Bolio, who must have had business dealings in Hunucmá, as it was there that the slave was baptized as Felis Manuel Bolio. Hunucmá was a large Maya town a little to the east of Mérida, where Spaniards had become heavily involved in cattle ranching and which consequently had a minority population of Spaniards and Afro-Yucatecans by Manuel's day. There were four Bolio cousins, one of whom was named Manuel, who owned haciendas devoted to cattle and other enterprises all around Mérida in the late eighteenth century; don Manuel or one of his cousins probably owned "our" Manuel Bolio.[21]

Manuel was then sold to a prominent Spaniard in Mérida named don Julián de Lara, and it is by the name of Manuel de Lara that witnesses to his life later remembered him.[22] Although an acquaintance of Manuel from his Mérida years later told the Inquisition that Manuel had married in Campeche, marriage records confirm that he was married in Mérida, in 1757. Either before or at the time of his marriage, don Julián had granted or sold to Manuel his freedom, for he appears in the marriage records as a "black adult," not a slave.

His bride was Josepha Chan, *Yndia*, a Maya woman from Dzithas, a village out in the Maya countryside. From the earliest days of colonial rule, young Maya men and women were drafted or migrated into the capital city to work as domestic servants.[23] By the late colonial period, as both Mérida's labor needs and the rural Maya population grew, increasing numbers of migrants came to work in Spanish homes, in part to avoid tax and tribute obligations in their own villages—among them Josepha Chan, who was in her teens when she left behind her parents, Matheo Chan and Martha Dzul, for the Yucatec metropolis. She found work as a nun's servant, acquiring the nickname Chepa La Monja ("because before getting married she had served a nun").[24] She may have later worked for a member of the Solís family, as she was also known as Josepha Solís.[25] By 1757 she was working for doña Petrona Argaïs, who was married to the same don Julián de Lara for whom Manuel worked. Josepha seems to have spent part of her time selling in the Mérida market fish brought by Spanish *tratantes* (petty merchants) from the port of Sisal, and part of her time doing domestic chores. It was thus in the Lara-Argaïs household that Manuel and Josepha met, worked together, presumably fell in love, and married.[26]

As early as the sixteenth century, Spanish officials had complained that Mayas and Africans were illegally cohabiting in native villages.[27] In view of Spanish attempts, albeit more in word than deed, to segregate these two subordinate populations, it is ironic that it was Spanish settlers who provided the urban environment in which intense contact between Africans and Mayas led most effectively to miscegenation and the growth of a mixed-race underclass. Nor did laws against interracial marriage prevent numerous, technically illegal, formal unions. This fact is symbolized by the experience of Manuel and Josepha, a Congo-born African and a Maya, working for the same Spanish household, marrying in church, and having a child.

TABLE 5.2.

Marriage Choices by Afro-Yucatecan Men in Mérida, 1751–97

Marriages between Afro-Yucatecan men[a] and Maya or mestiza women:		435	(44%)
Marriages between Afro-Yucatecan men and Afro-Yucatecan women:		547	(56%)
	Total:	985[b]	(100%)
Included within the above are:			
Marriages between African men (*negros*) and Maya or mestiza women:		53	(34%)
Marriages between African men (*negros*) and Afro-Yucatecan women:		105	(66%)
	Total:	58	(100%)

Sources: AGAY-*Jesús*, *Libros de matrimonios*; Repetto and Sierra, *Una población perdida*, 28, 31, 32, 35.

[a]My categories of Afro-Yucatecan men and women comprise the colonial categories of *negro/negra*, *mulato/mulata*, *pardo/parda*, and *moreno/morena*.

[b]This total includes 3 entries (an insignificant percentage) that do not fit the two groupings above.

Most Mayas and Afro-Yucatecans married endogamously, that is, they married others of the same racial classification. But a significant minority in the major towns married across racial lines, by far the most common such union being between a man of African descent and a Maya or mestiza woman. This seems to have been true among the Mayas of highland Guatemala as well as among Yucatec Mayas.[28] Again, the pattern is illustrated by Manuel and Josepha. In fact, as table 5.2 shows, in the period and place of their marriage—Mérida in the late eighteenth century—parish records show that a third of all marrying African men (*negros*) chose Maya (26 percent) or mestiza (7 percent) wives (the remainder marrying Afro-Yucatecan women).

We might imagine that for the first three years of their marriage, Manuel and Josepha were happy together, but not happy with their jobs. For during those few years they moved from one household to another, three in total, but always finding work together. They also had a child, but the baby died when just a few months old, and that seems to have been a turning point in the marriage.

On the Move

Apparently disenchanted with his life as a married domestic servant in Mérida, in 1759 Manuel left Josepha behind and went south to Bacalar to find work—a journey of a week or two across the colonial border and through unconquered Maya lands on a forest path described by an English traveler in 1765 as "swampy," "serpentine," and "troublesome."[29] Only at the end of this arduous journey did one reenter colonial territory near the grim little port of Bacalar (see figure 5.2)

It is not clear whether the death of his child or marital problems brought on this move, or whether problems at work led to the separation, which in turn produced the couple's estrangement. Either way, at first Manuel made regular trips back to Mérida, returning for as long as three months at a stretch. But as the months turned to years the visits became less frequent and then stopped. Eventually, he moved on to Havana, and then sometime in the 1760s he lived in the Venezuelan port of La Guayra before reaching Cartagena, where he remarried—committing the sin and crime of "double matrimony"—and settled down among the port city's black community.

Manuel's mobility did not make him unique among those people of African descent who spent part of their lives in late colonial Yucatan—as demonstrated by table 5.3, which places Manuel in the context of seven other African men who passed through the peninsula.

One significant pattern suggested by table 5.3 is the apparent movement of Africans between British and Spanish colonies. In fact, while Manuel Bolio's life serves usefully as an exemplar of most major aspects of the Afro-Yucatecan experience, his apparent avoidance of any time spent in the British Empire makes him unrepresentative of many of the blacks and mulattos who resided in Yucatan. There was in general a surprising level of movement by slaves and free blacks between Spanish and British possessions in the Caribbean, with Yucatan receiving more Africans from British colonies than perhaps any other Spanish province in the circum-Caribbean—or indeed the Spanish Empire. One example of evidence of such movement comes from the lists of captured escapees published in the Jamaican newspaper the *Royal Gazette* in 1825. Among these unfortunate captives was a "John Philips [aka Juan Felipe?], says he is a native of Carthagena, 5 feet 6 inches, marked LH on right, and ICD on left shoulder" and "William Aikman, a Creole Negro man, 5 feet 8 inches … says that he was sold by the late Mr. Jonas Hart, when about ten years of age,

TABLE 5.3. Patterns of Mobility of Eight Africans
Temporarily Resident in Yucatan, 1757–1832

NAME, SPANISH RACIAL CATEGORY, STATUS	PLACES OF RESIDENCE IN CHRONOLOGICAL SEQUENCE	TIME PERIOD OF RECORDED MOBILITY*
Melchor de la Torre, free *negro criollo*	Cartagena, Spain, Mérida	c. 1740–63
Manuel Bolio, *negro* slave, later free	Congo, Campeche, Mérida, Bacalar, Havana, La Guayra, Cartagena	c. 1750–78
Juan Josef Sanchez, free *negro*	Jamaica, Havana, Sancti Espiritu Is., Belize, Bacalar, Mérida, Sancti Espiritu Is.	c. 1780–1802
Julian Rechet, *negro* slave	Jamaica, Belize, Bacalar, Mérida, Havana	c. 1790–1802
Christopher Hill (aka Cristobal Gil, aka Kingston), *negro* slave	Jamaica, Belize, Mérida, Belize, Bacalar, Mérida, Havana	1790s–1802
Richard Dobson (aka Ricardo Dopson), *negro* slave	Jamaica, Belize, Bacalar, Mérida, Havana	c. 1800–1802
Francisco Aznar, *negro* slave (freed 1829)	Havana, Sisal, Mérida	c. 1810–29
Juan Martín, free *moreno*	Santo Domingo, Veracruz, Campeche	1829–32

Sources: AGI-*Contratación* 5506, 2, 7, 1, fol. 13; AGN-*Inquisición* 1131, 2, fols. 80–110; AGN-*Marina* 156, 5, fols. 171–211; AGEY-*Justicia* (Poder Ejecutivo), 2, 20, fols. 4–5; AGN-*Bienes nacionales* 28, 65.

*The initial years are the earliest dates the individuals are recorded as living in the first place listed, and the terminal years are the latest dates they are recorded as living in the last place listed; they therefore could have been mobile before and after these time periods. Some of the migrations recorded here were voluntary, others forced by slave traders or colonial authorities.

to a Spaniard named don Antonio Gutteres [Gutiérrez], then living in West-street [in Kingston], and who afterwards went off and resided at the Havanna, where he lived with him until he died, ordering by his will, that he should be made free." Aikman told the British authorities that he had never liked Cuba and had missed Jamaica. Thus, when manumitted by the death of Gutiérrez, Aikman had returned to the British colony to work as a free man, only to be arrested as a runaway.[30]

Aikman's brief biography evokes three aspects of the parallel experience of Africans in Yucatan. One is the existence of both formal and informal slave markets and sales in Campeche and Mérida, involving the British as well as local Spaniards—and Africans enslaved by both. For example, Peter Williams (aka don Pedro de los Guillermos) was one of a number of Englishmen who held licenses in the seventeenth and eighteenth centuries to auction slaves in Yucatan. Williams lived in Mérida, the provincial capital, but as Campeche was the gateway to the colony it was therefore there, in the mid-seventeenth century, that English merchants established a slave trading office under license from the Spanish crown. Although this office was not technically a fully fledged "factory" (permanent trading post) and was thus second in importance in New Spain to Veracruz, for a while Campeche had crown permission to import and sell more Africans than any English trading post in the viceroyalty.[31] The often-licensed domination of this import trade by the English contributed to the creation of an Afro-Yucatecan world that included the British as well as the Spanish Caribbean.

The second Afro-Yucatecan connection to the British Caribbean is that of forced movements. Just as Aikman was obliged by his sale to move from Kingston to Havana, so were the slaves of British loggers in Belize forced to live in Yucatan or other Spanish colonies as a result of Spanish raids along the Yucatan-Belize border in the eighteenth century. Spanish sources complain—and English sources confirm—that by the late seventeenth century, Yucatan had become part of the informal orbit of the English in the Caribbean. Not only did English loggers establish permanent settlements at the southeast (Belize) and southwest (Tabasco) corners of the peninsula after 1655, but English vessels regularly worked the entire Yucatec coastline, logging, fishing, hunting inland, and on occasion raiding local communities. The English navigator William Dampier made two such voyages in the 1670s, and he describes these activities in detail, including tales of Englishmen captured by Spanish and pardo militias.[32]

By the eighteenth century free mulattos crossing temporarily into British settlements as militiamen were increasingly outnumbered by slaves being taken as booty or by slaves escaping one colony for the promise of anonymity and freedom in the other. Beginning in 1722, the Yucatan-Belize border became increasingly violent. Spanish expeditions from Mérida raided the British settlements with regularity, stealing African slaves and on several occasions forcing the loggers to temporarily abandon Belize.[33]

Between major assaults on Belize organized by the Yucatec authorities were numerous private expeditions. For example, in 1759, the very year that Manuel Bolio first traveled south from Mérida to Bacalar, a Spaniard named don Juan de Sosa made the same trip, accompanied by fourteen other armed Spaniards, with a mandate from the crown to halt British commercial expansion in northern Belize. The mandate was effectively a pirate's license, as Sosa simply raided the riverside ranches of English loggers, looting them of all movable property—including five African slaves. The slaves were taken by Sosa back to Mérida and four of them put up for sale; the fate of the fifth, who was blind and declared to be of no value, was not recorded. A five-hundred-peso offer by Canon Mendicute of Mérida cathedral was bettered by Captain don Lorenzo Villaelriego, whose payment of six hundred pesos was divided between Sosa and the crown.[34]

Although the 1760s brought war between Spain and Britain throughout the Caribbean, the result was actually a relative peace on the Yucatec-Belizean border, with small-scale raids like Sosa's less frequent for a couple of decades. Then in 1779 the Yucatec governor, ordered by the crown to attack British settlements, organized a series of autumn raids deep into Belize. The resulting booty included dozens of African slaves. During Christmas week of that year, for example, fifteen Africans were branded YR (for Yucatan and Rey—the king), and then auctioned off in the courtyard of Mérida's city hall. The governor ordered that the new owners rename the slaves, as they were recorded at auction with their English and African names.[35]

None of the Spanish border raids of the final two decades of the century were as large as that of 1779, but if Africans were less often stolen as booty, they were more often traded as commercial property; after all, the majority of the Belizean population was African by 1760, and three-quarters was by 1800.[36] Furthermore, in addition to arriving in Yucatan by force and by trade, Africans in Belize also crossed the colonial border voluntarily.

Thus the third dimension of this British-Spanish world in which many Africans moved was that of voluntary attempts by blacks and mulattos, free and enslaved, to move between Spanish and British colonies—just as Aikman had traveled from Cuba back to Jamaica.

Many escapees from slavery in Belize believed that Spaniards in Yucatan would honor crown laws offering freedom to Africans fleeing British colonies. Unfortunately, such laws were not always in effect, and when they were, local Spaniards tended to ignore them. An African named Richard Dobson, for example, fled an abusive owner in Belize in 1800, living for five months in Bacalar as a free man named Ricardo Dopson (see table 5.3). When questions were raised about Dobson's identity, he appealed to Spanish laws guaranteeing refuge to slaves of the English, adding that he reviled their heretical religion and sought salvation as a "true Christian"—showing that he not only knew about refuge laws but understood that they were technically laws of religious sanctuary.[37]

Dobson was sent to Mérida, where the authorities wrote to Mexico City for clarification on the laws of refuge, reflecting an uncertainty going back to at least 1795, when the Yucatec governor had written to the king asking what should be done with the growing number of Afro-Belizean refugees in the province. Eventually, Dobson was told that the law had been revoked, and that it had been decided that he would best serve the Spanish king as a slave in the Havana arsenal.[38] The Afro-Jamaican Julian Rechet suffered the same fate. He insisted he had been a free man in Jamaica, but when he went to Belize to join the militias, the British there tried to enslave him; escaping to Yucatan, he ended up enslaved by Spaniards.[39]

As a result of these various ways in which Africans passed from the British colonies to Yucatan, in the second half of the eighteenth century roughly half of the adult slaves coming into the colony had originated in the British Atlantic world. Table 5.4 draws on baptism records from eighteenth-century Mérida to tabulate the native origins of black adults, both free and enslaved, coming into the colony. The table illustrates not only the extent to which Africans in the province were part of a Spanish-British orbit but also a rich pattern of growing variation—both the increased variety of locations throughout the Atlantic world from which Africans in Yucatan had come and the variety of locations within the British Empire where such Africans were born. The majority came from the two colonies that were geographically closest to Yucatan, Belize and Jamaica, but England and North America were also represented.

TABLE 5.4. Native Origins of Free and Enslaved
Black Adults Baptized in Mérida, Yucatan, 1710–89

	1710–49	1750–89		1710–49	1750–89
AFRICA			**BRITISH EMPIRE**		
Anaco	0	1	Barbados	0	1
Angola	2	2	Belize	1	28
Arara	8	1	Bermuda	0	1
Berbara	1	0	Cay Kitchen, Belize	0	54
Burgu	0	1	England	0	5
Caboverde	1	0	Grenada	0	1
Canca	9	7	Jamaica	11	78
Carabal	0	5	Kingston	0	1
Caramanti	3	5	London	1	3
Congo	26	30	Mosquito Coast	0	1
Congo Mangola	2	1	New England	0	1
Craban	1	0	Philadelphia	0	2
Danguira	1	0	Providence	0	1
Diangla	1	0	**Subtotal**	**13**	**167**
Guavere	1	0			
Guinea	6	43	**ELSEWHERE**		
Mamona	0	2	Catalonia	0	1
Manda	1	0	Cuba	0	1
Mandinga	12	19	France	0	1
Mina	19	24	The Hague	0	1
Mingo	1	0	Havana	1	1
Mocó	1	6	Holland	1	1
Nanga	1	0	Lisbon	0	1
Papá	1	1	Lujat	0	1
El Puh [Po]	0	1	Portugal	0	2
Samsi	0	1	**Subtotal**	**2**	**10**
Vazmacontre	1	0			
Vron	0	1	Origin unclear	0	3
Ybo	8	17	Origin not given	79	12
Yola	1	0	**Subtotal**	**79**	**15**
Zamba	0	1			
Subtotal	**108**	**169**	**TOTAL**	**202**	**361**

Source: AGAY-*Jesús*, *Libros de bautismos*, vols. 1–6.

Endings

We left Manuel Bolio in Cartagena, where he seems to have settled down more permanently than in any of the places he lived during the peregrinations of his youth. Perhaps he felt more comfortable living in a city where people of African descent were more numerous than Spaniards or natives, which was true of Cartagena but not of anywhere in Yucatan.[40] His second wife was, like Manuel, classified by Spaniards as "black," and when she died, he proposed to another African woman. In the autumn of 1776, he received her consent.

Couples seeking formal union in Spanish America were required to request permission to marry; this was granted, usually within a matter of days, once the priest was satisfied that neither bride nor groom were already married (and, in late colonial times, that the union did not violate laws against interracial marriage).[41] Not surprisingly, the procedure was not always followed with due thoroughness; Manuel was able to marry for the second time, roughly a decade after his first marriage, without being arrested for bigamy, because the priest in Cartagena who performed the ceremony apparently could not be bothered to confirm Manuel's claim that he was a bachelor.

Unfortunately for Manuel, the priest whom Manuel asked to perform the marriage ceremony in 1776 was not prepared to take him at his word. Because Manuel stated that he had been baptized near Mérida, Yucatan, it was to that city that the priest sent a letter. Toward the end of the year it reached the old priest who had been responsible for the sacraments in Jesús parish back in the 1750s. He remembered that in those days there lived in the parish a black servant of don Julián de Lara's, commonly called Manuel de Lara but baptized Manuel Bolio. The old priest also seemed to remember that Manuel had married an "Indian" servant of don Julián's wife's. The Inquisition was now involved, and a request for formal confirmation of Manuel's first marriage was sent from Cartagena via Mexico City to Mérida (see the document in the appendix). The entry for the marriage was eventually found in the Jesús parish records, copied, and sent to Cartagena in January of 1778. The marriage record was accompanied by a stack of incriminating testimony compiled by Inquisition officials in Mérida, including a statement from Josepha herself and corroborating testimony from those who had known the couple in the 1750s.[42]

When these documents reached Cartagena, they sealed Manuel's fate; not only had he committed bigamy in marrying a second time, but

FIGURE 5.3: *Colonial Cartagena. This map of the port city was first
published in 1588; by the time that Manuel Bolio settled there
in the late 1760s, the city had grown considerably, as had the
number of enslaved and free black residents (who were greater
in number than the Afro-Yucatecan population of Mérida).
Map by Baptista Boazio, first published in Leiden as one of
four illustrating Sir Francis Drake's 1585 campaign against
Spanish Caribbean ports. Reproduced courtesy of the John
Carter Brown Library, Brown University.*

he had sought to commit the crime again with a third marriage. His sentence is missing from the records, but bigamists typically had their property seized and were often sentenced to be given two hundred lashes in
public before serving five to seven years in the galleys.[43] If the condemned
man survived all this, he was to return to his legal wife—which would
have sent Manuel back to Mérida. But the whipping alone could kill a
man. If Manuel survived a whipping or was spared one, as a former slave

he would either have been condemned back into slavery or treated like one on His Majesty's galleys. His life in the Americas began as a slave on board a ship; it probably ended likewise.

Manuel Bolio's biography illustrates the ways in which Africans in the Americas moved between victimhood and agency, between suffering at the hands of European individuals and institutions, and successfully seeking opportunity "in the spirit of finding a better fortune" (in the words of one African slave escaping Belize for Yucatan).[44] Africans could also meet with the kinds of triumphs and tragedies that awaited all those who moved within (or in and out of) the Spanish colonial world—an improved working environment, the joy of a new marriage, the death of a child, condemnation by the Inquisition simply because divorce did not exist.[45]

Finally, Manuel's life sheds light on the way in which Yucatan (especially the city of Mérida and towns of Campeche and Bacalar) was not only a meeting place for Spaniards, Africans, and Mayas, but also a place where three different worlds overlapped—worlds that were social, racial (as defined by Spaniards), and geographical (see figure 5.2). The Maya world was a landlocked one, restricted mostly to the peninsula but in some ways extending south to the Maya regions of Guatemala. The Spanish world was obviously and primarily a global one centered on Spain, but Yucatan's Spaniards tended to be connected in terms of political and commercial networks of patronage mostly with Havana and Mexico City. The latter was accessible only by sea, through Campeche and Veracruz, so that Cuba, Yucatan, and Mexico functioned effectively as an archipelago of islands for Spanish Yucatecans.[46]

During the course of his life, Manuel lived not in one world, but in many—the Congolese world of his birth, black Yucatan and the Spanish colonial world to which it was attached, the part of the Maya world that extended into multiracial Mérida, and a Caribbean world that was African, Spanish, and British. The Afro-Yucatecan world was thus a circum-Caribbean one, linking the colony to Belize and Jamaica as well as to Havana and Cartagena.

APPENDIX

An Inquisitor Investigates a Black Bigamist

The Inquisition investigated the alleged crime and sin of bigamy committed by Manuel Bolio. The document below comes relatively early in the investigation, more than a year before the information it requests provided the Inquisitor in Cartagena with sufficient evidence to arrest and imprison Manuel.

As was often the case with Inquisition investigations, this letter is not an entirely accurate summary of Manuel's past; it merely reflects what the Cartagena Inquisitor knew of him as of the date of the letter. For example, Manuel was not a native of Bacalar; he had lived there for a time, but he was born in Africa and had lived more of his life in Campeche and Mérida than in Bacalar. While Manuel became de Lara in Mérida, he was known as Bolio during his youth in Campeche, a detail not yet revealed to Cartagena officials. In addition, the Inquisitor has been told that Manuel's second marriage took place in the Venezuelan port of La Guayra and that his third wife came from Campaya (there were towns of that name in Peru and Bolivia); these details are contradicted by later testimony stating that both women were Africans whom Manuel met in Cartagena. It is also clear that the Inquisitor is not personally familiar with Yucatan; he misspells Campeche and La Mejorada (a neighborhood in Mérida) and wrongly places the colonial Spanish town of Bacalar in English hands.

Although these facts illustrate how important it is to place a document in the larger context of a whole case (let alone the even larger contexts of colonial Latin American history), this single brief letter evokes a number of themes explored further in my chapter. These include relations between Africans and native peoples in the Spanish colonies; the mobility of Africans in the colonies; Afro-Yucatan's position in the Caribbean world; and the way in which the cogs of Spanish colonial bureaucracy, as slow as they turned, could eventually crush the less privileged denizens of the empire.

En este santto off. Ay denunsia contra Manuel de Lara
(color negro) natural de Bacalar de los dominios Yngleses, de
que ciendo casado en Carmpeche [*sic*] con una Yndia llamada
Jossepha conocida Bulgarmente por la Monxa, viviendo esta
en la cuidad de Mérida en casa de dª Jossepha Zerbera Plazuela
de la Mexorana [*sic*], se bolvio ã casar en el Puerto de la Guayra
con Rosalia de Lara, del mismo color negro, de la qual haviendo
inviudado, intenta casarse con otra negra que ha traydo de

Campaya; Y para verificar el primer Matrimonio contrahido
con la d̶h̶ã Yndia nonbrada la Monxa Recidente en la Ciudad
de Mérida; suplicamos a Vs se sirva de dar las ordenes
correspondientes ã su car^a y actuadas las diligencias en la forma
de estilo esperamos nos las remita, y nos mande quanto fuere de
su satisfaccion, quedando al tanto para servir ã V.s. cuia Vida
Gu^a Dios m.^a a.^a Inq^or de Cartagena y Noviembre 16 de 1776

[In this Holy Office [the Inquisition's Cartagena branch], there is
a denunciation against Manuel de Lara (black in color), native of
Bacalar, in English territory, who was married in Campeche to an
Indian woman named Josepha, known commonly as La Monja
[the Nun]; she now lives in the city of Mérida in the house of
doña Josepha Cervera, off the La Mejorada plaza; he [Manuel]
remarried in the port of La Guayra with Rosalia de Lara, also
colored black, by whom he was widowed, [and now] intends to
marry another black woman whom he brought from Campaya;
and in order to verify the first marriage contracted with the said
Indian named La Monja, resident in the city of Mérida, we
request that you carry out the orders corresponding to your
responsibility, and we await your remittance of the appropriate
records, sent to us according to your satisfaction, remaining
entirely at the service of Your Lordship whose life is guided by
God, the Inquisitor of Cartagena, November 16th, 1776]

AGN, Inquisición 1131, 2, fol. 93.

NOTES

1. Archivo General de la Nación, Mexico City (hereafter AGN), Inquisición
1131, 2, fols. 80–110.

2. When not referring specifically to the Kingdom of Kongo, *Congo* refers
to the region of the Congo River basin. See Roland Oliver and Anthony
Atmore, *Medieval Africa, 1250–1800* (Cambridge: Cambridge University
Press, 2001), 166–79; John Thornton, "Africa: The Source," in *Captive*

Passage: The Transatlantic Slave Trade and the Making of the Americas,
ed. Beverly C. McMillan (Washington, DC: Smithsonian Institution
Press, 2002), 49.

3. On the Atlantic crossings of African slaves, see Colin A. Palmer, "The
Middle Passage," in McMillan, *Captive Passage*, 53–75. Throughout the
Spanish American colonial period there were Spanish traders taking slaves
across the Atlantic, but they remained outnumbered by the Portuguese in
the early period, then by Dutch, French, and English (later British) traders
in the seventeenth and eighteenth centuries. On the granting of the *real
asiento* in the early colonial period, see Palmer, *Slaves of the White God:
Blacks in Mexico, 1570–1650* (Cambridge: Harvard University Press, 1976),
7–13 and Gonzalo Aguirre Beltrán, *La población negra de México: Estudios
etnohistórico* (Mexico City: Ediciones Fuente Cultural, 1946), 33–80. On
the slave-import licenses granted to English and Dutch merchants by the
Spanish crown in the seventeenth and eighteenth centuries, see Palmer,
Human Cargoes: The British Slave Trade to Spanish America (Urbana:
University of Illinois Press, 1981) and the facsimile edition of original
licenses published as *Reales asientos y licencias para la introducción de esclavos
negros a la América Española (1676–1789)* (Windsor: Rolston-Bain, 1985).
Many licenses were published at the time of their signing; for example,
one published in Seville in 1682 allowed Captain don Juan de Villalobos
to resell in Spanish America two thousand slaves per annum (1683–1690)
brought to Cumaná by the Dutch (John Carter Brown Library,
Providence, Rhode Island [JCBL], Rare Book B682V714m). Although
the monopoly *asiento*, or slave license, held by the British ended in 1750,
around the time that Manuel Bolio was brought to the Americas, some
seventy-five thousand Africans had been shipped by British traders to
Spanish America and sold there as slaves in the early eighteenth century,
and British traders continued to supply the Spanish colonies in the
century's second half (Palmer, *Human Cargoes*, 108, 142). Thus our
reasonable speculation on Manuel's early years might extend to
imagining him sold in Campeche by an English trader in exchange
for logwood (ibid., 127; also see British Library [BL], Mss. Add. 38,391,
Mss. Eg. 2395, and various other documents relating to the British
logging trade in southern Yucatan).

4. Archivo General de Indias (AGI), México 2999, 2, fol. 180. For a fuller
biography of Toral, including details of his voyage to Spain and back as
an old man, see Matthew Restall, *The Black Middle: Slavery, Society, and
African-Maya Relations in Colonial Yucatan* (Stanford: Stanford University
Press, forthcoming), chap. 1.

5. AGI, Justicia 300, various folios between 380 and 442.

6. On Montejo's license, see Antonio de Herrera, *Historia general de los hechos de los Castellanos en las Islas y Tierra Firme del Mar Oceano*, 8 decadas (Madrid: Juan de la Cuesta, 1601–15), 8:10, 23; Aguirre Beltrán, *Población negra*, 19–20, 22. On the role of Africans in the Spanish conquest, see Matthew Restall, "Black Conquistadors: Armed Africans in Early Spanish America," *Americas* 57, no. 2 (2000): 171–205 and *Seven Myths of the Spanish Conquest* (New York: Oxford University Press, 2003), 52–63.

7. AGN, Marina 36, 5, fols. 167–212; Aguirre Beltrán, *Población negra*, 40; also see AGN, Alcabalas 427, 10, fols. 183–88.

8. Palmer, *Human Cargoes*, 77, 78; evidence of the British traders' license is in BL, Mss. Add. 25,553, fols. 10–11, while the Spanish evidence is in AGI, Contaduría 267, 8, both of which are cited by Palmer.

9. Archivo General del Arzobispado de Yucatán (AGAY), Jesús, Libro de Bautismos, vols. 1–6; Restall, *The Black Middle*, chap. 2; Marta Espejo-Ponce Hunt, "Colonial Yucatán: Town and Region in the Seventeenth Century" (PhD diss., University of California, Los Angeles, 1974), 93–94.

10. This demographic fact makes it surprising that Afro-Yucatecans have been so little studied. For examples of brief discussions in works whose focus is primarily Spaniards and/or Mayas in the colony, see Manuela Cristina García Bernal, *La sociedad de Yucatán, 1700–1750* (Seville: Escuela de Estudios Hispano-Americanos, 1972) and *Yucatán: Población y encomienda bajo los Austrias* (Seville: Escuela de Estudios Hispano-Americanos, 1978); Hunt, "Colonial Yucatán"; Philip C. Thompson, *Tekanto: A Maya Town in Colonial Yucatán* (New Orleans: MARI, Tulane University, 1999); Patch, *Maya and Spaniard* ; Matthew Restall, *Maya Conquistador* (Boston: Beacon, 1998). Yucatecans themselves have shown more interest in the topic than non-Yucatecans, although local studies remain brief and preliminary in their analysis: see, for example, Rodolfo Ruz Menéndez, *La emancipación de los esclavos de Yucatán* (Mérida: Universidad de Yucatán, 1970); Genny Negroe Sierra, "Procedencia y situación social de la población negra de Yucatán," *Boletín de la Escuela de Ciencias Antropológicas de la Universidad de Yucatán.* 106–7 (1991): 3–20; Brígido Redondo, *Negritud en Campeche* (Campeche: Ediciones del Congreso del Estado, 1994); Francisco Fernández Repetto and Genny Negroe Sierra, *Una población perdida en la memoria: Los negros de Yucatán* (Mérida: Universidad Autónoma de Yucatán, 1995).

11. See, for example, the cases of Morelos (Cheryl English Martin, *Rural Society in Colonial Morelos* [Albuquerque: University of New Mexico Press, 1985], 13–14, 38, 121–53); Veracruz (Patrick J. Carroll, *Blacks in Colonial Veracruz: Race, Ethnicity, and Regional Development*, 2nd ed. [Austin: University of Texas Press, 2001; orig. pub. 1991], 29–39, 61–65); central Mexico (Brígida von Mentz, *Trabajo, sujeción y libertad en el centro de la Nueva España* [Mexico City: CIESAS y Porrúa, 1999]); Guatemala (Oakah L. Jones, Jr., *Guatemala in the Spanish Colonial Period* [Norman: University of Oklahoma Press, 1994], 109–17; Christopher H. Lutz, *Santiago de Guatemala, 1541–1773: City, Caste, and the Colonial Experience* [Norman: University of Oklahoma Press, 1994], 83–99; Robinson Herrera, "The People of Santiago: Early Colonial Guatemala, 1538–1587" [PhD diss., University of California, Los Angeles, 1997]); and Peru (Frederick P. Bowser, *The African Slave in Colonial Peru, 1524–1650* [Stanford: Stanford University Press, 1974]; James Lockhart, *Spanish Peru, 1532–1560: A Social History*, 2nd ed. [Madison: University of Wisconsin Press, 1994; orig. pub. 1968], 193–224).

12. As Lockhart comments with respect to Afro-Peruvians (*Spanish Peru*, 224). Maya workers were the overwhelming majority of the labor force on sugar estates in Yucatan (Restall, *The Black Middle*, chap. 4).

13. For a detailed discussion of these terms and issues, see Restall, *The Black Middle*, chap. 3.

14. Patch, *Maya and Spaniard*, 95. Slaves were typically branded on the African coast and then again upon resale in the Americas; Philip D. Morgan, "Life in the New World," in McMillan, *Captive Passage*, 127. For example (and as mentioned below), Yucatan's royal treasurer stated in 1779 that African slaves captured from the British were to be branded with a Y (for Yucatan) and R (for rey, "king") (Archivo Notarial del Estado de Yucatán [ANEY], vol. 1778–81, n.f.).

15. This comment is based on an analysis of twenty-four criminal cases from the last colonial decade (1811–21), in the Archivo General del Estado de Yucatán (AGEY), Colonial, Criminal; see Christopher Lutz and Matthew Restall, "Wolves and Sheep? Black-Maya Relations in Colonial Guatemala and Yucatan," in *Black and Red: African-Native Relations in Colonial Latin America*, ed. Matthew Restall (Albuquerque: University of New Mexico Press, 2005), 186, 204–13; and Restall, *The Black Middle*, chap. 6.

16. *Discurso sobre la constitución de las Provincias de Yucatán y Campeche*, Biblioteca Nacional de México (BNM), Fondo Franciscano, A1150, fols. 25–26.

17. On colonial Mérida's settlement patterns, see Matthew Restall, *The Maya World: Yucatec Culture and Society, 1550–1850* (Stanford: Stanford University Press, 1997), 31–37. On the Jesús parishes in Mérida and Campeche, see Restall, *The Black Middle*, chap. 6.

18. Two late colonial examples of disputes over coartación cases in Yucatan are in AGEY, Colonial, Varios, 1, 27 (1816), and Reales Cédulas, 1, 45 (1795). Also see Fernández Repetto and Negroe Sierra, *Una población perdida*, pp. 37–45. On Spanish manumission law, see Jane Landers, *Black Society in Spanish Florida* (Urbana: University of Illinois Press, 1999), 2, 139–40. For numerous sample manumission cases from Florida and Peru, respectively, see ibid. and Christine Hünefeldt, *Paying the Price of Freedom: Family and Labor among Lima's Slaves, 1800–1854* (Berkeley: University of California Press, 1994).

19. Examples are AGEY, Criminal 1, 11a; *Reales* Cédulas, 1, 45; and AGN, Marina 156, 5, fols. 172–82.

20. There are records of slaves from Yucatan *sold* in Guatemala (Archivo General de Centroamerica [AGCA], A1.20, 1489, sale of 1608), but I have seen no good evidence that Afro-Yucatecans made the journey into Guatemala's palenques (described by Thomas Gage in *The English-American* [London, 1648], 130), although I suspect some did; for example, Yucatec slave owners in Villa del Carmen, which was closer to Guatemala than most Yucatec towns, claimed in an 1831 petition protesting the abolition of slavery that freed slaves might run off to Guatemala, although they do not specifically mention palenques (AGEY, Poder Ejecutivo, Gobernación, 2, 58). In the final three decades of colonial rule, it is possible that a small number of runaways were absorbed into the African population of San Fernando de los Negros, which was not a palenque but a legal town in northeast Yucatan set up by colonial authorities for black soldiers who had fought for Spanish forces in Haiti and Santo Domingo in the early 1790s; summaries are in Matthew Restall, "Black Slaves, Red Paint," introduction to Restall, *Black and Red*, 1–4, and in Ben Vinson, III, *Bearing Arms for His Majesty: The Free-Colored Militia in Colonial Mexico* (Stanford: Stanford University Press, 2001), 216–19. Another late colonial legal Afro-Yucatecan village that may have harbored small numbers of escaped slaves was San Francisco de Paula, located a few miles south of the port of Sisal (Anthony P. Andrews, "Archaeological Reconnaissance of Northwest Yucatán, Mexico," unpublished field reports, 2001 and 2002; Restall, *The Black Middle*, chap. 6).

21. Patch, *Maya and Spaniard*, 116, 145–47; Restall, *Maya World*, 15. By
1779 11.5 percent of all Afro-Yucatecans lived in Hunucmá and its
surrounding district (by this time there was a pardo militia company
stationed there). Put another way, the district was 10.5 percent Afro-
Yucatecan, 1 percent Spanish, 8.5 percent mestizo, and 80 percent
Maya; Patch, *Maya and Spaniard*, 233–35. On the prominence of the
Bolios in the colony, beginning with Manuel's namesake, the colonel of
Yucatan's militias, Maestre de Campo don Manuel Bolio Ojeda y Guzmán,
who married his way into the Yucatec aristocracy, see ibid., 84, 126, 191,
217–18; García Bernal, *Yucatán*, 388, 472; Ana Isabel Martínez Ortega,
Estructura y configuración de los cabildos de Yucatán en el siglo XVIII (Seville:
Diputación Provincial de Sevilla, 1993), 137–38, 290–91, 301. The mar-
riage records of the Maestre de Campo don Manuel and of his father,
Santiago de Bollio, a Genoese merchant who settled in Yucatan and
married almost as well as his son later did, are in AGAY, Sagrario,
Libros de matrimonios—e.g., book 3, fol. 59v (Santiago's, 1660) and
book 5, fol. 132r (Manuel's second, 1710).

22. The de Lara family was prominent in the colony going back at least to
the early seventeenth century, holding *encomiendas* (grants of native labor
and tribute) generations before the Bolios, and owning haciendas around
Mérida as the Bolios did; see García Bernal, *Yucatán*, 391–93, 513, 518, 532;
Martínez Ortega, *Estructura*, 137–38, 291–92; Patch, *Maya and Spaniard*,
191. The records of Lara marriages in AGAY, Sagrario, Libros de
matrimonios illustrate well the endogamy of Yucatan's Spanish élite.

23. See, for example, Manuela Cristina García Bernal, "Los servicios
personales en el Yucatán durante el siglo XVI," in *Papers of the Simposio
Hispanoamericano de Indígenismo Histórico* (Valladolid, Spain: Terceras
Jornadas Americanistas de la Universidad de Valladolid, 1976).

24. AGN, Inquisición 1131, 2, fol. 94 ("Chepa" is an abbreviation of
"Josepha" and "monja" means "nun").

25. As Manuel's possible onetime owner, don Manuel Bolio y Helguera,
married a doña Rafaela del Castillo y Solís in 1755 (Martínez Ortega,
Estructura, 302), one might speculate that Josepha and Manuel met
through work *before* ending up together in the Lara-Argaïs household.

26. AGN, Inquisición 1131, 2, fols. 80–81. The Argaïs or Argaíz family was
another Yucatec Spanish dynasty with an early colonial pedigree, and was
prominent in both Mérida and Valladolid in the eighteenth century; see
Victoria González Muñoz, *Cabildos y grupos de poder en Yucatán (siglo XVII)*
(Seville: Diputación Provincial de Sevilla, 1994), 299; Martínez Ortega,
Estructura, 54, 137–38, 198, 250, 292.

27. Patch, *Maya and Spaniard*, 94.

28. See Lutz and Restall, "Wolves and Sheep?"

29. Lieutenant James Cook made the journey from Bacalar to Mérida and back in February–March, 1765 (the same decade that Manuel Bolio repeatedly made the journey) as a British diplomat and spy; see Lieutenant Cook, *Remarks on a Passage from the River Balise, in the Bay of Honduras, to Mérida: The Capital of the Province of Jucatan in the Spanish West Indies; A Facsimile of the Original with Perspective by Muriel Haas* (New Orleans: Midameres Press, 1935); Matthew Restall, "Cook's Passage: An Englishman's Journey into Yucatan in 1765" (paper presented at the JCBL, June 2002).

30. "Extracts from the Royal Gazette," JCBL, Codex Eng 205. Of course there were also direct movements of Africans, both forced and voluntary, between Cuba and Yucatan; note that six of the eight cases presented in table 5.3 include periods of residence in Havana. One of these, Francisco Aznar, was more fortunate than William Aikman; sold by his Cuban owner to a Yucatec Spaniard in 1817, Aznar was freed when slavery was abolished in the Republic of Mexico in 1829, while it remained legal in colonial Cuba for decades more (AGEY, Justicia (Poder Ejecutivo), 2, 20, fols. 1v, 4–5).

31. AGN, Reales Cédulas, 44, fol. 122, and 54, fol. 30 (cited by Aguirre Beltrán, *Población negra*, 76); Patch, *Maya and Spaniard*, 95; Hunt, "Colonial Yucatán," 134; Palmer, *Human Cargoes*, 77, 78, 89, 91, 104.

32. William Dampier, *Voyages and Descriptions*, vol. 2, part 2, *Two Voyages to Campeachy* (London: James Knapton, 1699), gives accounts of captured Englishmen on 15–16, 19.

33. Cook, *Remarks*, 8, 10; Restall, "Cook's Passage."

34. Within two years, one of those Africans, an elderly woman, was dead (AGI, México 3050, fols. 94–184); there is no record of the fate of the others beyond baptismal records showing that a year later one was baptized María de la Luz and gave birth to a boy, baptized Joseph Dario (AGAY, Jesús, Libro de bautismos, vol. 4, fols. 140r, 142v).

35. ANEY 1778–81; Luís López Rivas, "Venta de negros en Mérida a fines del siglo XVIII," *Revista de la Universidad de Yucatán* 99–100 (1975): 118–22. The following February (1780), more than a dozen additional captives from the war were auctioned off in Mérida (ANEY 1782–84).

36. Restall, "Cook's Passage"; O. Nigel Bolland, *Struggles for Freedom: Essays on Slavery, Colonialism, and Culture in the Caribbean and Central America* (Belize City: Angelus Press, 1997), 55.

37. The first such law, applicable empirewide, was issued by a 1693 proclamation of Charles II and remained in effect until 1790, with variations between colonies and its recognition by local authorities uneven; on its history in Spanish Florida, whose developments were central to the law's promulgation and abrogation, see Landers, *Black Society*, 25, 28, 76, 79.

38. AGN, Marina 156, 5, fols. 172–95.

39. Ibid., fols. 196–210.

40. On Cartagena's demography, see María del Carmen Borrego Pla, *Palenques de negros en Cartagena de Indias a fines del siglo XVIII* (Seville: Escuela de Estudios Hispano-Americanos, 1973), 11–28.

41. There are examples of these requests throughout the Spanish American archives; most of those in Mexico City's AGN, for example, are in the Bienes nacionales section; an example from the local Yucatec archives is AGEY, Colonial, Militar, 1, 24.

42. AGN, Inquisición 1131, 2, fols. 97–98 (Josepha's statement) and 99–108. Josepha had not bigamously remarried and in 1777 was working for a doña Josepha Zerbera in the open market in the plaza of La Mejorada, a Maya suburb of Mérida (fol. 93).

43. As Richard Boyer shows with respect to Mexico: *Lives of the Bigamists: Marriage, Family, and Community in Colonial Mexico*, abr. ed. (Albuquerque: University of New Mexico Press, 2001), 158–59.

44. AGN, Marina 156, 5, fol. 186.

45. In other words, high bigamy rates in Spanish America were a product of the ban on divorce and of the high levels of mobility in the colonies. Manuel's journey into bigamy had nothing to do with his African origins; Africans appear in the records of bigamy because they were a part of the Hispanic world and its culture, not because they had brought from Africa a different set of marriage practices. In fact, because of high levels of *informal* unions among blacks and mulattos, they appear far less often than Spaniards and mestizos in bigamy records. Of the thirty-two Yucatec bigamy cases I have located in the archives to date, only two feature bigamists of African descent. For Mexico, see Boyer, *Lives*, 163–70; for Yucatan, see AGN, Inquisición (twenty-six cases), Bienes nacionales (four cases), and AGEY, Criminal (two cases).

46. Yucatan had been discovered by Spaniards searching for the larger political and demographic center that turned out to be the Mexica empire; it was then conquered by the Montejos and other Spaniards

who had survived the conquest of the Mexicas, and who brought with them Nahua warriors from central Mexico. This history, and what was deemed to be its relative proximity to Mexico, determined the 1548 decision to place the new colony in Yucatan within the jurisdiction of Mexico City, to whose high court and viceroy the provincial governor in Mérida was to answer (Herrera, *Historia general*, 8:129–30). Thus both in terms of administrative structure and settlement patterns, Yucatan was within the orbit of central Mexico (a relationship that persists to this day).

CHAPTER SIX

Los esclavos de su Magestad

Slave Protest and Politics in Late Colonial New Granada

Renée Soulodre-La France

⚡ "We, Your Majesty's slaves from the hacienda Villavieja . . ."[1] This preamble to a representation made by eighteenth-century enslaved workers on a former Jesuit estate in Nueva Granada (present-day Colombia) carried with it myriad elements of trust, expectations, and hope that shaped the political philosophy and the corporate sense of identity of the enslaved groups that issued it. Through it they made claims to a status that would protect them and ensure them a certain standard of living, and they pursued those claims through the courts in the viceregal capital of Santafé. In those trial records we can hear again the concerns that preoccupied the enslaved in eighteenth-century Nueva Granada, and we can excavate the political ideas that were embedded in the petitions they made. Of course, caveats must be placed upon the language of those documents. These sources are what James C. Scott would call the "public transcript" that describes the relations between the enslaved and slave owners in colonial Spanish America.[2] However, that public transcript was molded by the unusual status of the enslaved who spoke it. Despite all of the documents' limitations and the fact that there is much left unsaid about the relations of power experienced in this society, in the end, these sources do reveal something about the worldviews and millennial hopes harbored by these people whose history has long remained hidden to us. Furthermore, the nature of these court cases also provides us with a glimpse into the slaves' use of Spanish legal institutions and the manner in which these institutions functioned.

Collective Action

The actions of the enslaved in Nueva Granada can be analyzed through the paradigm of resistance, a theoretical framework that has been usefully applied to various slave societies in the African diaspora and within Africa itself.[3] However, the case of "His Majesty's slaves" as seen through the records of two former Jesuit estates, Villavieja and El Trapiche, enables us to expand that framework to incorporate the collective action of groups of enslaved Africans who invoked their special status and unusual circumstance within the Spanish legal system so as to preserve particular privileges and traditional rights. They based these claims squarely within a framework of corporate identity that was smoothly shifted from the context of Jesuit haciendas to that of crown-owned slaves. This occurred, though, within a dangerous reality where many former Jesuit slaves were sold off in various lots as the crown sought to cash in on the capital locked into the Jesuit properties. When the enslaved rebelled, they might suffer a worse fate if captured: deportation and sale in Havana.[4] The unusual nature of these cases unveils yet another dimension of what is known about the creation of identities among the enslaved and the political philosophy that undergirded their choices as they resisted a deepening of their subjection to slavery. They demonstrate to us how profoundly the enslaved understood the colonial society that subjected them and the tools they could expropriate from that colonial system in order to advance their interests.

There are special moments that stand out in history as crucial, potential watersheds when shifts in the course of events are realized, sometimes quite unintentionally. As Seth Meisel discusses in his study of emancipation, military service, and emergent Argentine nationalism in chapter 9, moments like the Independence era provided spaces in the colonial world that subaltern groups could seize as their own, claiming the language of freedom and liberation, of equality and fraternity, and using those words and concepts to wedge open the cracks appearing in the social structures of the former colonies.[5] These were moments when messianic hopes could rise and when collective identities could be reinforced.[6] In uncertain times new and different possibilities were created, and enslaved individuals could and did act upon changing circumstances to seek their freedom or to improve their situations even while remaining enslaved. The reaction of the enslaved to the Independence wars were as varied as the reactions of the free, but the possibilities presented by those times did not go unrecognized.

The expulsion of the Jesuits from Nueva Granada on August 1, 1767 was another such moment—as the secret command to round up the priests in the middle of the night and spirit them out of the Spanish colonies was carried out.[7] While these events proved devastating for the religious of the order and the colonial society they taught and proselytized, they also had resounding ramifications for those people left behind: the enslaved who had labored on the Jesuit estates. Africans and their descendants had been bought by the priests to work on their cacao plantations, to herd the animals on their cattle haciendas, to serve as the instrumentalists at their masses, and as cooks in their kitchens. They had worked on their tile-making haciendas and dug out the ore in their mines. The wealth of the order confiscated by the crown was concentrated in the Jesuit colleges and haciendas, and the enslaved workers were confiscated themselves as part of that wealth.[8] These laboring men, women, and children would experience the expulsion of their owners in a variety of ways. Some chose to use the opportunity provided to flee into anonymity and freedom, while others sought to reaffirm the more positive elements of their lives on the estates. Within their actions and the records they generated, we can uncover a sense of their political ideology and culture, of their mentalities, and of the interests closest to their hearts.

Literally overnight the enslaved went from being the property of a vastly wealthy and powerful religious order to belonging to the crown, eventually supervised by appointed administrators for the committees (*Junta de Temporalidades*) that were created to oversee the estates. This sudden shift provoked a number of immediate and long-term reactions by the enslaved, and it is upon those instances that we will focus in this work as we seek to understand how the enslaved perceived the changes that were occurring in their circumstances during and after 1767, and how they acted within those new constraints. What did it mean to be His Majesty's slaves? This chapter will focus upon cases that encapsulate the heterogeneity and fluidity of identity manifested by enslaved individuals and the manner in which the Jesuit expulsion was experienced by them. Then two examples of collective action, one by the enslaved on the cattle hacienda Villavieja in the province of Neiva and the other by the enslaved on the cacao hacienda of El Trapiche in the region of Pamplona, Santander, will be analyzed to determine how their sense of corporate identity affected their actions in this period.

The Jesuits

The religious order of the Company of Jesus, known as the Jesuits, probably never set out to become the biggest slaveholder in the Americas, but that is precisely what happened.[9] The original followers of St. Ignatius Loyola had thought that lay brothers would provide all of the labor the order would require, but it quickly became evident that the order would need to find another source of workers as it rapidly expanded into Africa, Asia, and the Americas. In Brazil, for example, the Jesuits originally hired salaried indigenous workers, but this practice soon gave way to dependency upon the labor of enslaved Africans.[10] Unsurprisingly, given the context of the day, even those individuals who spent their lives working to alleviate the suffering of the enslaved did not necessarily challenge the existence of the slave trade or the enslavement of Africans. For example, Father Alonso de Sandoval, who spent most of his life in Cartagena catechizing the Africans arriving in that port in the early seventeenth century, accepted slavery as a natural phenomenon. He wrote one of the most important treatises on the Africans arriving in the Americas from the period, but in that work, "*De Instauranda Aethiopum Salute,* [he] is concerned with the justification of the ministry to the Negro slaves, not with dramatizing the horrors of slavery and the slave trade."[11] There were some members of the order who raised moral objections to the use of slave labor and the slave trade, but their voices were silenced, and the status quo was maintained.[12]

Though Jesuit holdings in the viceroyalty of Nueva Granada and the *audiencia* of Quito were not as impressively valuable as the properties they owned in Peru or Mexico, they still far exceeded any private fortunes in this area.[13] One of the reasons for this was the integrated nature of the Jesuits' economic activities. They devoted themselves almost exclusively to agricultural production, and essentially their urban colleges (*colegios*) and their few mines in Popayán and Antioquia provided the markets for the hacienda

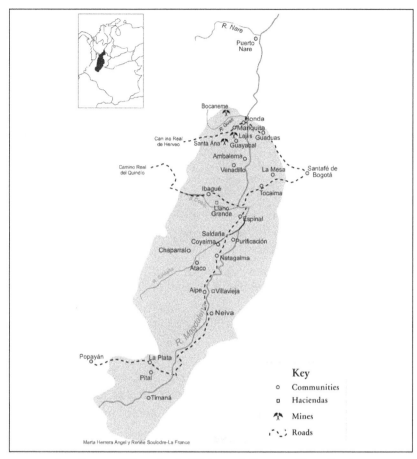

FIGURE 6.1: *Greater Tolima in the Eighteenth Century. From Renée
Soulodre-La France,* Región e imperio. El Tolima Grande
y las Reformas Borbónicas en el siglo XVIII. *Instituto
Colombiano de Antropologia e Historia, (Bogotá: 2004) p. 20.*

products so they could benefit from this advantage over their private competitors.[14] Though the order began acquiring property in Santafé de
Bogotá in 1569, it truly became established only in the early seventeenth
century, arriving in Cartagena de Indias in 1604. The priests rapidly expanded their operations through most of the territory and quickly became
powerful landholders through the inheritance of endowments from wealthy

patrons and through the judicious purchase of diverse operations. In this way, they became the proprietors of several haciendas that produced bricks for construction just outside of Cartagena in Tierrabomba.[15] They also developed huge cattle haciendas in the provinces of Mariquita and Neiva in the central valley that transected the colony. These haciendas, such as Villavieja and San Juan de la Vega, controlled vast territories.[16]

Choices

The expulsion of the Jesuits generated a range of possible reactions among the enslaved. Unsurprisingly, one of the first and probably most predictable acts that some of the enslaved chose was simply to flee the haciendas when they realized that the priests had been removed. This may have been what happened in the case of the mulatto Joseph Antonio de los Reyes Prieto and his grandmother Josepha.[17] Joseph Antonio was denounced as a runaway slave from the former Jesuit sugar hacienda Tena and made to appear before the courts to dispute this charge in 1777. He claimed he had been born free and that his parents were also free, but it was charged that they had all belonged to the hacienda Tena, which was associated with the Jesuit Colegio Máximo in Bogotá. In 1777 Joseph Antonio was only fifteen or sixteen years old, so he would have been five or six at the time of the expulsion. He claimed that he was too young to remember the expulsion and that he had always lived in Santafé with his grandmother Josepha.

Further testimony suggested, though, that the family had indeed belonged to the Jesuits. However, at the time of the expulsion they had been absent and so had sought refuge in the priest's house in the town of Tocausipa. They had stayed there for a year before coming to Santafé.[18] This story was disputed by Joseph Antonio's testimony. He claimed that they had always been free and had always lived as such. Part of the logic of his argument was that if they were slaves, why had nobody come looking for them long ago? However, there were contradictory elements in Joseph's testimony since at another point he stated that his mother had been sold away to somebody in Cali. Of course, his interrogators seized upon this and demanded to know how she could have been sold if she and her husband were both free. In this case, the courts judged against Joseph Antonio, concluding that he was indeed a runaway. This bid for freedom was ultimately unsuccessful; however, the expulsion of the Jesuits had made the escape possible and had enabled Joseph Antonio and his grand-mother to live as though they were free for several years.

As we go through this case and others we get a sense of the chaotic state of affairs that must have prevailed after the expulsion. For example, in a case brought before the courts in 1783 we see another indication of how individuals could fall between the cracks during this transitional period. This unusual case, involving three enslaved men who had belonged to the Jesuits, began with a pardon. On July 22 1783, an enslaved black named Miguel Phelix de los Reyes pardoned Pablo Caycedo, another slave who belonged to the same estate, for the murder, some twenty years before, of his enslaved uncle, Diego Villalobos. These men now belonged to don Juan Felix Ramirez de Arellano and worked on his hacienda San Juan de la Vega, another of the properties that had once belonged to the Jesuits. Miguel had his owner's support in this effort to pardon Caycedo and may, in fact, have been urged or forced to do so by his owner. Notwithstanding this, Miguel did provide a logical reason for his decision to pardon the accused murderer when he explained that he was now married to Caycedo's daughter. Furthermore, Miguel claimed that this pardon was also effective on behalf of his mother, Maria Hypolita Villalobos, sister of the murdered Diego Villalobos and of Francisca Reyes, who was the murdered man's niece.[19]

The slave owner, don Juan Felix Ramirez de Arellano, added his own plea to the court in favor of issuing a formal pardon to the enslaved murderer. In his statement he explained that he had bought the hacienda San Juan de la Vega from the crown in 1773. At that time Pablo Caycedo appeared in the inventories but was listed as absent. After some investigation he determined that in 1757 Caycedo had struck another slave with his machete, unintentionally killing him. Either in order to save him or to punish him, the Jesuits had quickly sent him off to the Choco, where he had lived ever since, notwithstanding the fact that a general pardon for all crimes had been issued with the coronation of Charles III in 1759. Ramirez de Arellano claimed that he was seeking Caycedo's pardon because the fugitive was married to an enslaved woman named Josepha Barrera who also belonged to him, and it seemed only just that they should no longer be separated. Beyond this, the enslaved man was more than fifty-six years old but still served his master well as the captain of the slave gang (*cuadrilla*) and the majordomo of the hacienda. Ramirez also claimed that Caycedo had never contested his enslavement and had voluntarily come back to the hacienda to work without raising any objections, an attitude that counted in his favor in his master's view.

According to the declaration by Ramirez de Arellano, the Jesuits were notorious for their efficiency, so he found it quite surprising that they had not taken advantage of the pardon to bring Caceydo back to the hacienda. One of the prosecutors did explain that it was very likely that the Jesuits either had not received the notice of the pardon, which they surely would have applied for, or that the pardon itself had been issued and then lost in the chaos and upheaval of the expulsion when the order's documents were seized. Notwithstanding all of these obstacles, Pablo Caycedo was granted the pardon for the 1757 murder in August 1783.[20]

This case provides glimpses into the interplay of power between the Jesuits, the state and its judiciary, and the enslaved under their control. It had been in the Jesuits' interest to protect their property by sending Caycedo off to the Choco in order to save him from a murder conviction. However, being sent to the Choco, a notoriously difficult mining region where a brutal labor regime was imposed upon the enslaved, was not usually considered a favor. It was far more often used as a punishment for intransigent slaves. The details of this case provide further evidence about the nature of family life on Jesuit haciendas. We know that Pablo's wife and daughter were still alive and enslaved on the same property over twenty years after the murder occurred. We also know that the murdered man, Diego Villalobos, had an extensive family on the same estate and that the integrity of these families was maintained over long periods of time and through the traumatic shifts that occurred with the expulsion of the order and the sale of the property.

Sorting out which enslaved individuals and families belonged to which estate was the work of many long sessions, as inventories of the Jesuit properties were taken after the expulsion. Still, in some instances, the unwary could be mistaken as former Jesuit-owned slaves, even if they were free. That these were uncertain times when an individual's status could be easily confused is obvious from the case of Pasqual de Zúñiga, who in 1768 was imprisoned in Santafé. His wife, Dominga, pleaded his defense, saying that he was a free man (*pardo libre*) and had been sent to the city as a messenger (*chasquis*) for the governor, where he was unjustly imprisoned. It seems that he had been mistaken for a slave from the Jesuit hacienda Villavieja. A group of enslaved men from the hacienda had made its way to the viceregal capital to complain about their members' treatment at the hands of the state administrators in June 1768. According to Dominga's testimony, the slaves met her husband on the journey and they traveled together. When the slaves were imprisoned, he was taken for one of their group and also incarcerated.[21] These events demonstrate the precarious nature of the "freedom" that descendants of Africans could expect in colonial Colombia.[22]

Villavieja

The fate of the enslaved on the hacienda Villavieja, associated with the Colegio Máximo in the province of Santafé, one of the largest of the former Jesuit properties in the viceroyalty, would be a difficult one, as they used every means at their disposal to lever as much autonomy and flexibility, within enslavement, as possible during these turbulent times.[23] The historical record of the events on the hacienda subsequent to the expulsion was initiated by a group of enslaved men that made its way to Santafé to complain about the hacienda administrator, don Joseph Antonio Lagos, in 1773.[24] However, as mentioned above in the case dealing with Pasqual de Zúñiga, the Villavieja workers had petitioned the courts about the change from Jesuit management to administration by the crown as early as 1768, within a year of the expulsion. Lagos also made reference to earlier issues between a former administrator and the enslaved on the hacienda in his statement to the court in 1773. These documents reveal much about the ongoing antagonisms that existed on the hacienda, about the strategies of the enslaved and their practical application of their political culture. They also hint at the tinge of messianic fervor that could color the beliefs and actions of the enslaved and the delicate balance of power that was maintained on the estate.

The first hint of trouble between Lagos and the enslaved workers on the hacienda reached the audiencia in June 1773, when one of the slaves, Pedro Cabrera, made a plea to the court to protect him and his fellows from the depredations they were suffering at the administrator's hands. This initial statement is signed Pedro Cabrera, as is a subsequent document signed by Cabrera and a group of his companions, but it is not known if he actually wrote it. Typically, such cases would be written up and argued on behalf of the enslaved by the procurador de pobres, or public defender.[25] Cabrera argued that when he tried to complain about the administrator's excesses, he had been threatened with physical punishment, including a whipping and being placed in the stocks. His only recourse had been to flee to the royal court in the company of a group of his fellows and ask for protection.[26] His proposed solution to this problem was that Lagos should be removed from his position and another administrator be appointed.[27] The issues that Cabrera raised in his complaint were echoed in the formal collective petition that was made by a group of his companions from the hacienda Villavieja in July 1773 (see the first document in the appendix).

There were several areas of contention between the enslaved laborers of the hacienda Villavieja and the royal administrator. The first of these was that the traditional and customary rights that the enslaved had enjoyed on the Jesuit hacienda, and all other properties like it, were being undermined. These included the right to feast days off, the right that each slave had to a plot of land to grow his or her own crops, and the right to sufficient clothing, salt, and meat allowances.[28] The petitioners, Ygnacio de los Rios, Francisco de los Rios, Pedro Cabrera, and Baltasar de la Oiola, accused don Joseph Lagos of depriving them of these age-old privileges, and further, of verbally abusing them. The enslaved men suggested that all of these outrages were building up to a situation where severe damage might be done to the hacienda, and this was "what we do not want," and so they asked that Lagos be removed and another administrator be appointed.[29]

In a further undated petition signed by the men, they unequivocally stated that the administrator was despoiling the hacienda by stealing cattle and branding it with his own iron. In a fascinating bit of political rhetoric, the enslaved claimed that Lagos was mistreating them and the hacienda to the point that finally, in a bid to defend the crown's property, both the estate—and themselves as crown property—they had decided to appear before the courts. Such political logic is even more interesting when we consider that in this period there was a real tension developing between personal liberty, the protection of the enslaved, and the defense of private property.[30] In their quest for justice or for an improvement in their situation, the enslaved were often caught in the contradiction between their protection and the protection of their owners' property rights. In this case, as in many others to be found in various colonial courts, the enslaved aligned themselves firmly within the boundaries of the crown's mercy as they sought the king's "charitable and pious succor."[31] Since these particular slaves were owned by the crown, though, that tension should have been negated. What benefited the enslaved should have been good for crown property in this case.

In their petition to the viceroy the enslaved also made a further significant accusation. Apparently Lagos had sent one of the hacienda's slaves away to Popayán and was trying to sell her. They said, "[W]e do not know if he sold her or not," but the fear that they would be separated and that some of them would be sold away was a real one.³² For all of these reasons they turned to the courts so that they might be rid of him. If only Lagos were dismissed, they protested, they would serve the hacienda as loyal slaves.

There are numerous themes that can be drawn out of this early petition and the defenses and counteraccusations that were generated throughout this case. An important point of contention was the enslaved workers' autonomy, the fact that they insisted on maintaining their days off and the plots of land they cultivated as well as their own property—the crops they had planted and the animals they raised. These practical considerations were intimately linked to their notions of traditions and a version of a moral economy. They used their collective status as the crown's slaves to pursue an autonomy that they claimed they had traditionally held when they belonged to the Jesuits.³³ Another factor that further legitimized their claims regarding access to the plots of land was their notion that as royal slaves they had the right to provision themselves on royal land.³⁴

Furthermore, and ironically, it was the enslaved on the hacienda who had a history on the property and who provided the continuity between the era of the Jesuits and the new administration. These circumstances permitted them to make certain claims about the traditions and customs on Jesuit properties, and the enslaved may very well have harbored the hope that the new regime was a temporary situation. Indeed, the enslaved women on Villavieja told the priest that their only masters were the Jesuits, and that they would come and put things right, even if they "had to come from hell" to do it.³⁵

One of the more striking details of this case is that the enslaved made a collective demand, opening their petition with the words "We Your Majesty's slaves" and signing their complaint "Your Majesty's slaves." The petition was written in the first person plural, so the wording of the documents leaves no doubt that these were collective concerns.³⁶ The fact that these enslaved individuals could act as a group, in the name of the others on the hacienda, was perhaps directly linked to their understanding of the fact that they were "His Majesty's slaves" and the sense of identity that they developed because of this fact.[37] That collective identity may have been strongly fostered on the Jesuit haciendas prior to the expulsion and developed within the stronghold of slave families on those properties. For example, historian Robert Slenes argues that despite the vulnerable conditions of slave families they emerged as a viable social institution in the plantations of southeast Brazil. In Brazil and elsewhere, the family was a space in which the identity of the enslaved could prosper, even while it also provided the masters effective tools for social control.[38] Given the information we have of the nature of family formation on Jesuit haciendas in Nueva Granada and the demographic profiles of the properties to be found in the works of historians such as Chandler, Colmenares, and Cushner, it seems that the enslaved populations on these Jesuit estates were relatively stable, and that "the highest percent of married slaves was among those on the old Jesuit estates."[39] Although there is evidence that the Jesuits were important slave traders in Ecuador, and thus sold away their surplus workers, this does not seem to have been the case in Colombia.[40] The Jesuits in Nueva Granada did not sell away the enslaved, while the demographic information we have for the Jesuit properties there indicates that neither did the population depend on importations for its growth by the second half of the eighteenth century.[41]

There is evidence that the Jesuits sought to maintain a hierarchical structure among the enslaved themselves, but they also sought to preserve family structures, so that families were rarely divided.[42] For example, by the mid-eighteenth century, the number of adults living in coresidential unions had increased significantly compared to a century earlier on Brazilian Jesuit estates.[43] In Nueva Granada, of 476 enslaved individuals who labored on four Jesuit estates (three in Cartagena and one in Tolima), there were 223 males, or 47 percent, and 253 females (53 percent).[44] Of these, 232 (48 percent) were between the ages of twelve and fifty. Of the 145 females above the age of twelve in the data set, 46, or nearly 32 percent, were defined as the "wife of" someone, whereas 42 of the 143 (29 percent) males were "husband of" someone.[45] There were then 244 children (51 percent) under the age of twelve on the properties. These demographic profiles differed substantially from those of the sugar plantations owned by the Jesuits in Peru, for example.[46] This type of quantifiable data is not as complete as we might like, but when coupled with qualitative information it lends itself to an image of enslaved family formation on these estates as a relatively robust institution. Still, it is difficult to gauge whether or not the Jesuits provided a more favorable environment for their enslaved laborers than did private slaveholders. In the case of Brazil, Alden straightforwardly states that "slaves who toiled for the fathers were no better off than those who served other owners."[47]

His Majesty's Slaves

Collective action of the sort evident in the cases under discussion was relatively rare among the enslaved in Nueva Granada by the end of the eighteenth century, though there are many instances of individual petitions.[48] While corporate identities were an accepted form within colonial societies at large, this type of action had usually been reserved to the enslaved within their *cabildos de nación* and maroon communities that sought to legitimize their existence within colonial society.[49] The choice to opt for collective petition may have had to do with the hierarchical nature of the social structures that had been fostered on the Jesuit haciendas, where a small and select group of elders were treated as natural leaders by the priests, and where that hierarchy of elders was intimately entwined with the rest of the enslaved population through kinship ties.[50] Beyond all of the practical reasons behind their collective action, when they equated their well-being with the idea that they were protecting the king's property they were displaying the same type of group solidarity as those enslaved miners in colonial Cuba's El Cobre copper mine who somehow held a special status, since they were also "His Majesty's slaves."[51]

That sense of identity may also have been directly related to the mystique of the cult of the king as protector of the weak against powerful oppressors, a popular belief that prevailed in many parts of colonial Spanish America, especially among subaltern groups. Such a belief was prevalent in Brazil as well as in the Caribbean and was translated into the idea that the king would be the source of emancipation.[52] In Nueva Granada this was also manifested in the persistence of the legend or myth of the "Secret *Cédula Real*," a mythical law that had been issued by the king to liberate the enslaved but that had been suppressed by white slave owners. This was no doubt part of the political culture that led to the equation of the person of the monarch with the notion of justice in the popular mentality and fed rumors about the supposed emancipation decree that had been suppressed, or the story of the evil imposter who had taken over as king, a plot that was popularized in Europe by Alexandre Dumas' story of the Man with the Iron Mask.[53]

That kind of political and ideological climate could have provided the context for the events of 1766 in Cartagena, for example, when an indigenous man, José Luis Reyes, claimed to be Luis I, the son of Felipe V, a monarch who had the authority to relieve the indigenous population of its tribute burden.[54] Similarly, just as the indigenous communities of Independence Mexico discussed by Eric Van Young sought the king's protection directly by leapfrogging over local authority, the enslaved men and women in Nueva Granada who now belonged to His Majesty had an even more secure connection to the figure of the king.[55] These notions were juxtaposed against the contrary assertions that in some instances belonging to the king could be particularly onerous, since those slaves might be made to suffer arbitrary treatment, being shifted from one place to the next, working on fortifications or crown properties.[56]

As mentioned above, another factor that may have helped shape the identity of the enslaved was the longevity and integrity of slave families on Jesuit haciendas. On Jesuit haciendas such as Villavieja or El Trapiche we get an image of groups of enslaved people who really had a sense of belonging to the property, heightened, of course, by the fact that they had invested their labor in the plots. Indeed, in discussing these cases, historian Anthony McFarlane suggests that the enslaved on Villavieja and on El Trapiche behaved more like peasants, trying to protect their traditional rights, rather than enslaved men and women seeking more freedom from their masters.[57] In fact, part of the rationale for giving the enslaved plots of land to work, aside from relieving the owner of the responsibility of maintaining them, was that they would be less likely to flee if they had invested their time and labor on the property.

For example, David Chandler suggested that in 1767 the captain of the slave gang on El Trapiche, Francisco Borja, owned a grove of more than six thousand cacao trees and could easily have bought his own freedom and that of his family, but the land upon which his trees were planted belonged to the hacienda, so he would have forfeited his cacao groves if he had followed the path of freedom.[58] We get a reflexive image of how important a sense of belonging the enslaved developed on properties when we examine the ways in which administrators sought to punish the enslaved who caused problems. In the case of Villavieja, Lagos stated that

he had tried to deal with the leaders of this resistance by mollifying them
since they had caused tremendous problems for the former administrator.
By 1773, however, he was determined to sell them and their families away
from the hacienda. He suggested that this was the only way he would ever
regain control of the rest of the labor force, but he also considered the
fact of selling them as a form of punishment for their intransigence. This
was a drastic move since he sought to sell thirty-six of the hacienda's
eighty-nine slaves (40 percent).[59] The terms through which both the
enslaved and the administrator and his witnesses manipulated these possibilities indicate that the slaves' sense of identity was inextricably bound
to the properties and to each other.[60]

In his statement Lagos made it clear that earlier, when the hacienda
had been given over to the administration of don Fernando de Guzman,
the slaves had risen against him, without any motivation, and that it had
been necessary to send troops to imprison the instigators in Santafé, and
these were then sent to work on the haciendas Tena and Espinal as punishment. They then fled those properties and returned to Villavieja,
where they tried to murder the administrator. When Lagos had taken
over the hacienda, he sought to pacify the slaves and diffuse the situation
by pardoning the disobedient who had fled and trying to win over especially the leaders, because that was the only way he could subjugate the
rest of the work gangs, giving them pastures that they could use for themselves, and, in his words, treating them with love. They continued their
unreasonable customs and demands, especially drinking and making trips
to Santafé to complain before the courts. In light of this he was asking
permission to sell away the leaders, their wives, and their children so that
he might be able to regain control of the hacienda. "These are pernicious
and useless slaves that cost a lot in food and clothing and are useless for
work because of their injuries, illnesses and advanced age, and others
because of their drunkenness." He stated that they might be useful for
plantation labor in sugar or cacao production, but for cattle they were
useless, especially the women, since in order to work with the cattle one
needed intelligence and strength and thus women were unsuitable. To
round out the logic of his request to sell the lot of them, then, he laid out
the reasons why they were useless for a cattle hacienda, but how they
might be put to better use on a different type of property.[61]

The course of events developed rapidly after the enslaved made their
first complaint. The next documents that appeared in the case were letters

sent to the administrator, don Joseph Antonio Lagos, from various people, warning him about the nefarious intentions of the enslaved on Villavieja. On June 29, 1773 a chaplain (*capellán*), Baltesar Barreino, wrote that one of their neighbors in the town of Retiro had heard that the blacks of Villavieja were intending to murder Lagos and that they were simply awaiting the best opportunity to do so.[62] In another missive that he forwarded to the royal court, Lagos was again warned, this time by another priest, the chaplain on the hacienda, Father Joseph Francisco Lomez, who wrote him from Villavieja on July 24, 1773. It is in this letter that there is a hint of what may have been a messianic fervor among the enslaved, associated with the need and desire to overturn the order of things on the hacienda, harkening back to the days when the Jesuits were the masters. Such movements were relatively rare among the enslaved, according to historian Alida Metcalf, although they did exist. She analyzes the example of the Santidade de Jaguaripe movement in sixteenth-century Bahia and shows how both indigenous and enslaved believed in the movement.[63]

Some elements of the case suggest the enslaved on the hacienda believed that they could overturn the existing order, but that evidence is presented through the voices of the dominant. The priest wrote that "the people are awaiting the Messiah, like Jews, for since the Pharisees have gone, they are like Moors without a lord."[64] It seems that the women especially taunted him with the information that their leader, Juan Fortunato, had gone to the royal court and that their masters, even if they were in hell, were going to come and liberate them. Speaking of the expatriate priests (the Jesuits), they said that they had no other masters than them, and that they would return. The priest claimed the women were the worst offenders, one saying that "her grandfather Fortunato," and the other that her "uncle Fortunato," would come back as the new administrator and those who were giving the orders now would be giving them in hell.[65] Beyond this, the unruly behavior of the enslaved was imitated by the free mulattos who banded together with the enslaved to challenge the authority of the estate's managers, again suggesting the possibility of the coming of a new order. Such statements and actions appear to have been a public expression of the "private" transcripts the enslaved and free workers of color on the estates shared and were now using to intimidate the managers. This exchange between the enslaved and the authority figures on the estate also again demonstrates the kinship ties between enslaved leaders and their followers.

The religious aspect of the language of the enslaved is subtle and embedded in the recounting of events, but this was also reinforced by the priest's complaint that some of the enslaved were no longer attending Mass, something that was expected and demanded of the enslaved within colonial society. Certainly, the use of Christian imagery and concepts such as "hell" were not unlikely for the enslaved who had labored for the Jesuits, but when we couple this with their assertions that they were "His Majesty's slaves" and that as such, they held a special status, it seems likely that they believed they could turn the world "upside down" and that Fortunato, their leader, would return triumphantly to take over the position of administrator. This language, repeated by a priest, also might reflect an instance of textual hybridization, as the subaltern, in this case the enslaved, used the language of hegemony, that of the Catholic Church and colonial society, in order to threaten that very system. This form of hybridity was also evident in the actions of the enslaved, since they had become "maroons" by taking up the journey to Santafé to bring their case before the judges in the capital.[66]

Through the course of this case and the documentation it generated, it is evident that Lagos had to contend with a group of enslaved men and women who were deeply and affectively attached to the property, and to each other, through many kinship ties. In his report about the enslaved men and their families who were causing him the most problems, he traced out the close ties that existed—between parents, children, in-laws, and extended family members.[67] Lagos also informed the courts that the enslaved acted in concert with the free laborers who rented land on the hacienda. Such a dangerous precedent was particularly damaging for the smooth functioning of the property—Lagos claimed that the free renters were indispensable because they cost so little and because they should have been active in helping to control the enslaved. This provided him further justification for seeking to rid himself of the troublemakers on the estate. He suggested that the enslaved men he had had imprisoned in Santafé had corrupted the free workers and had to be removed to regain control of the property.[68]

On February 19 1774, the imprisoned slaves from Villavieja wrote yet another letter to the viceroy (the second document in the appendix). In this document they admitted defeat and simply begged to be allowed to return to the hacienda, since two of the small children had died and many of the group were quite ill, especially their leader, Juan Fortunato. Having

suffered eight months of incarceration, they continued to assert that everything they had said was true, and that they knew the administrator was the
cause of their imprisonment, but they had had enough and simply wanted
to be allowed to go home.[69] Even in this letter, at the end of their ability to
withstand Lagos's power, they sought to distance themselves from the
administrator and to draw upon their closeness to the king, through his
viceroy, when they signed themselves "your most humble slaves."

In the end, some of their worst fears were realized while they were
imprisoned. They lost their children and then two of the young women
from the hacienda were sold away to don Juan Felix Arellano, the owner
of the hacienda San Juan de la Vega. That slave owner explained to the
court that when he had bought the former Jesuit estate there were several
single enslaved men on the property and this had caused him some problems. He needed to buy some females to round out the slave gang and so
offered 250 pesos for Thereza and Ygnacia, who were fourteen and sixteen years old, from the group of imprisoned Villavieja slaves. That sale
was finalized on May 11, 1774.[70] But then in September 1774 Arellano
also tried to buy the rest of the prisoners.[71] So it looked like the integrity
of the enslaved group would be maintained and that they would all be
reunited, albeit on a different estate. This was not to be, though, since at
the end of the documentary trail we find that it was another buyer, from
the town of Tocayma, who won the bidding. By December 24, 1774,
another of the group's women had died—from typhus, according to the
purchaser's complaint.[72] Aside from those few, the ultimate fate of the rest
of "His Majesty's slaves" remains unknown.

El Trapiche

The events of 1773 were largely repeated on December 15, 1780 by
another group of enslaved men from yet another former Jesuit estate, the
hacienda Trapiche de Cucuta in the province of Santander. This property
had been sold on credit for twenty-eight thousand pesos in 1771 to don
Juan Gregorio Almeyda. Before finally purchasing the property he had
administered it on behalf of the Junta de Temporalidades, and the enslaved knew that Almeyda had obtained a mortgage for the total value of
the estate from the Temporalidades. The complaint brought against
Almeyda in the 1780s was not the first challenge he had received from his
enslaved workers.[73] In 1780 the enslaved Luis Nicacio Dias appeared

before the royal courts again in the name of his fellow slaves to make a complaint against the owner of the cacao hacienda.[74] Dias stated that it was an ancient custom in this hacienda and others like it that the slave master would give the enslaved a plot of land where they could produce their crops as well as give them Saturdays to work on the plots. This was a custom that the Jesuit fathers as well as the later administrators had followed.[75] Many of the concerns raised by Dias reflected the areas of contention that had existed on Villavieja, but Dias also complained that their owner was forcing the enslaved to sell him the product of their labor on their plots, their cacao, and that he was either paying them only half of its value or not paying them at all. To make matters worse, he did not give them the rations of food and clothing that were their due, and he punished them harshly.

Mirroring the actions by the enslaved group from Villavieja, one of the significant details of this petition to the royal court is that Dias brought his complaint "por mi, y a nombre de otros compañeros" (for myself and in the name of other companions). He had traveled to the viceregal capital of Santafé de Bogotá to make a collective petition and stated this fact twice. Sent by his fellows as the captain (*mandador*) of the enslaved on the hacienda, he explained that he had turned to the support of the courts for help in "the name of all of them" (*a nombre de todos*). Again, then, in this case, the enslaved from former Jesuit haciendas used collective action and a corporate identity to protect their traditional rights and to try to undermine the authority of their new owner. As noted above, the image of a group of enslaved workers undertaking the long trip to the savannah of Bogotá to be heard in the royal court is a relatively rare one in the colonial documents. Indigenous groups more often behaved this way, something that is not surprising given their strong sense of corporate identity and interest. It is possible that the very fact that these were enslaved individuals who had belonged to the Jesuits and who now belonged to the crown shaped their political notions and allowed for the development of this corporate ideology.

Within all of the issues involved in this long case are a few details that stand out in the documentation. The first of these is the way in which the enslaved sought to challenge Almeyda's ownership and his right to treat them as his property. Their very detailed understanding of their owner's financial dealings with the crown was impressive. In the original petition that Dias made on behalf of his fellow slaves, he explained to the judges of the royal court that "Almeyda was no more than a mere servant [*servitario*] of the royal treasury, and thus could not act as though he had bought the hacienda with cash."[76] Such a statement indicates that the enslaved knew perfectly well the terms under which Almeyda had obtained the property, and since he had not put any down payment on it at all, and the entire value was mortgaged, then surely he did not really own it. Dias finished his petition by indicating that if things did not change, the enslaved would start fleeing, the hacienda would them be ruined, and the royal treasury would never get its money. As they undermined the administrator, the enslaved exposed the contradiction between his interests and that of the crown, and the workers who were crown property.

A fascinating aspect of this case is how seriously indeed the audiencia took the complaint made by the enslaved. By February 1781, an order had been issued that Almeyda should not mistreat the enslaved and that the local justices should inquire into the allegations. Thus a *careo* was organized, a face-to-face confrontation between the master and his slaves, before witnesses and a scribe who would take down the testimony as part of a formal institution in the Spanish legal system. The meeting took place on the hacienda. The enslaved were called before the witnesses and Almeyda, their complaint was read to them, one by one, and they were asked whether or not they agreed with what was in the petition. This judicial process produced intriguing details about the lives of the enslaved on the hacienda. For example, when Norato Torres claimed that Almeyda had made him work on Saturdays instead of allowing him to work on his plot, Almeyda countered that Torres had only been a child of about eleven or twelve years old when he had bought the hacienda, so how could he have owned a plot of land? When challenged again with this information, the enslaved man calmly explained that sure enough, he had been too young to own a plot and tend the crops, but he had subsequently inherited the plot from his grandmother when she had died eighteen months before.[77]

This process also brought the relationships that predominated on the hacienda into sharp focus. One would imagine that, challenged by the justices with their owner standing by, the enslaved may very well have been completely intimidated. However, it is surprising how many of them stuck to their accusations, even when Almeyda denied the validity of their statements. One of the ways in which he contradicted the complaints that he did not pay them for their cacao was by producing an account book in which he listed the exchanges he claimed had occurred on the property.[78]

As an interesting testimony to the power of the written word, his accounts proved very convincing for the witnesses. How could the enslaved deny the records—here was hard evidence that attested to his virtue as a slave master, and nobody dared suggest that the accounts might have been falsified.

In the end, Almeyda had many upstanding witnesses who testified to his virtue and fairness as a slave master and to the duplicity, vices, and deviance of the enslaved. Thus he determined that he could no longer trust this group of slaves and he sought permission to sell them away, even though he had not actually paid for them and they were all heavily mortgaged. His reaction to the challenge to his authority by the enslaved was very similar to the way that the administrator Lagos had behaved. In this case, though, the judges admonished the enslaved and their owner that they should strive to get along. The verdict was that Almeyda should adhere to the traditional arrangements that had existed on the hacienda and that the enslaved should be obedient, submissive, and virtuous.

The expulsion of the Jesuits in 1767 developed into a moment when the enslaved who had belonged to them could express their attachment to the land that their labor rendered productive. The new status as crown-owned slaves that came with the expulsion provided the enslaved an opportunity to manifest their political culture through the act of collectively petitioning the courts, boldly claiming redress. Their sense of collective identity had developed while under Jesuit rule through their historical circumstances, and now they sought to apply their understanding of what it meant to be "His Majesty's slaves" to their situations. The cases of collective action when the enslaved tried to gain flexibility and autonomy within the slave system by identifying their interests with the crown's are relatively few, but they reveal a dimension of the spectrum of resistance that highlights their ties to the land and to each other. Taking advantage of existing legal institutions, they employed a popular political culture that imagined the king as a protector, and they used the fact that they belonged to the most powerful figure in colonial society to dare to try to overturn the social, political, and economic order of life on the former Jesuit estates.

APPENDIX

Petitions of the Slaves of the Hacienda Villavieja

The following petitions demonstrate the conflict resulting from the Jesuit expulsion and the subsequent social strife on the confiscated estates. In the first document, slaves from the hacienda of Villavieja protest to the viceroy the perceived abuses of the new hacienda administrator, don Joseph Antonio Lagos. Speaking with a collective voice, they respectfully request that Lagos be removed from his position. The second document shows how circumstances forced the Villavieja slaves to revise their aims. After losing their struggle with Lagos, who arranged for them to be imprisoned in Santafé de Bogotá, the petitioners ask simply to be allowed to return to Villavieja.

The Slaves of Villavieja Complain
against the New Administrator

Esmo Senor Virey,
Los esclabos de su magestad de la hasienda de BillaBieja puestos a
los pies de VA con la mas rependida umildad que nos es possible
y desimos que sea de serbir en meritos de justisia de admitirnos
estar umilde suplica que Vsasemos cuyo refugio y amparo emos
benido a solisitar para nuestro alibio por el maltrato que nos dan
el administrador dicha asienda Jose Antonio Lagos y a demas
desto los mismos cabos que abido en lasienda desde que el dentro
a ella cuyo motibo asido causa por defender la nosotros nos
adegado a pereser pues asta unas cortas labransas que abiamos
echo paramantenernos las mando remoler qitandonos nuestros
animalitos que criabamos para nuestro bistuario y de nuestras
mugeres tambien ase mas presente Vs que en la primera partda
tres balsas de carne a onda y para estas balsas mato siento
cuarenta y ocho reses de la asienda desto no a gastado nada en
la asienda mas otros dies nobillas que le bendio a?andeolaya, y de
beynte y siete caballos mansos que a bendido y tres yeguas con
mas nuebe mulas y un macho que era de la asienda le bonaron el
fiero pegandole otro ensima tambien todos los arendatarios de las
tierras an pagado el ano en toros y estos los a erado? Con su fiero
no con el de la asienda y ajuntamente se nos deben dosrasiones
vustuarios de dos anos como tambien mando una esclaba de la

asienda y la de uno de los que estamos aqui presos a popayan con
el pretesto de benderla y no sabemos si la bendio o no por lo que
bendidamente Ocuerimos al caritatibo y piadoso amparo de VeA.
Que mirando nos en caridad como nuestro amo que es senos
consedila grasia de que el mensionado Jose Antonio Lagos salga
de administrado de dicha asienda que protestamos serba como
fieles esclabos en a quellos que VA fuere serbido como tnabien
protestamos justifica lo que en este llebamos espresado—fabor y
mersed que esperamos de la gran piedad de VA y a llamediante
pedimos y suplicamos se nos consede segun y como llebamos
pedido que protestamos no ser demalisia y juramos lo nesesario
puestos alos pies de VA esclabos de su magestad.

Ynasio de Los Rios y Pedro Cabrera,
Fransisco de Los Rios Baltasar de la Oyola

[Your Excellency the Viceroy,
We, Your Majesty's slaves from the hacienda of Villavieja,
at Your Highness' feet with the most devoted humility that is
possible, and we say that merit and justice would be served if
our humble supplication is admitted by yourself, who is our
refuge and sanctuary. We have come to solicit for our relief
from the mistreatment of the administrator of the hacienda,
Jose Antonio Lagos, and moreover for the same that he has
committed to the hacienda since entering as administrator. It
is this motivation that has caused us to defend the hacienda—
he has left us to perish, even up to the small cultivated plots that
we had made to maintain ourselves he has ordered that they be
taken from us bit by bit, taking also the little animals that we
raised to clothe ourselves and our wives. We say to you, sir,
that in the first *partida* three raft-loads of meat were sent to
Honda, and for those loads he killed 148 heads of cattle from
this hacienda, but he has not spent anything on the hacienda.
Furthermore, he sold 10 young bulls to Andre Olaya and
27 horses that had been broken, and 3 mares, as well as
9 mules and one male that belonged to the hacienda, but they
put another brand on top of the hacienda's brand. Also all of
the renters on the land have paid their rent in bulls and he
branded these with his iron, not with that of the hacienda.

Furthermore, he owes us two rations of clothing for two years,
and also he sent a slave who belonged to the hacienda and one
who belongs to one of us here, as a prisoner to Popayan under
the pretext of selling her, and we do not know if he sold her or
not. For these reasons, we prayerfully have resorted to your
charitable and pious succor, that you seeing us with charity like
our master who concedes his grace so that the aforementioned
Jose Antonio Lagos will leave the administration of this
hacienda. We protest that we serve as faithful slaves in all that
you should be served, and we also protest the justice of what we
have expressed—we hope for favor and mercy from your great
piety and we ask and supplicate that our request be granted as
we have asked. We protest that this is not out of malice and we
swear, necessarily prostate, at your feet as Your Majesty's slaves.

Signed,

Ynasio de los Rios y Pedro Cabrera,

Fransisco de los Rios, Baltasar de la Oyola.]

Archivo General de la Nación, Negros y esclavos del Tolima, vol. 3, fols.
999r–v. (This document is undated.)

The Slaves of Villavieja Petition to
Return to the Hacienda

19 febrero de 1774
[on the margin it states Santa Fe
19 de febrero de 1774].
Pase esta representacion a la junta
de temporalidades de deonde
dimano la providencia de prision de estos esclavos.

Exelentisimo Señor Birey por el rey nuestro senor y magestad
Nosotros los esclabos de su magestad postrados a los pies de
vuestra altesa con la mas rendida umildad que debemos y
podemos y desimos que a el tiempo de ocho meses que estamos
padesiendo en esta Real Carcel en justamente porque nos parese
que por vosotros no abido distruido ninguno en la asienda
pues antes nosotros por contener los menos cabas que en dicha
asienda abido por el administrador de ella es causa de nuestra

prision lo que protestamos-justificar debajo de la religion del
juramento todo lo que tenemos dedusido por ser sierto y que a
nosotros no nos a de justificar la menor cosa el mensionado
administrador, tambien asemos presente a vuestra exelencia
de que se an muerto dos de los chiquitos y estan los mas bien
enfermos asi mugeres como hombres y en particular nuestro
capitan Juan fortunate por lo que rendidamente pedimos y
suplicamos a la alta piedad vuestra exelensia nos mire en caridad
y probea la que major conbiniesre y fuere serbido y nos debuelba
a la asienda a onde desensia fuere serbido porque aunque emos
mandado dos escritos con el Alcayde esta carcel para vesensensia
y no emos tenido rrespuesta ninguna fabor y mersed que
esperamos resibir con justisia y a ella mediante,

A Usted Senor Pedimos y suplicamos se nos consede segun
y como llebamos pedido que protestamos no ser demalisia y
juramos en debida forma y esperamos su felis respuesta, los
mas umildes esclabos de Usted. Que a sus pies estan postrados.

[February 19, 1774 (written in the margin).
This representation was sent to the committee
for the Jesuit Trust, from which came
the order to imprison the slaves.

Your Excellency the Viceroy for our king, lord, and majesty:
We, Your Majesty's slaves, prostrate at Your Highness' feet with
the most devoted humility that we can, and should, offer you,
state that it has been eight months that we have been suffering
unjustly in this royal prison, because it seems to us that nothing
on the hacienda was destroyed and for us that the end was never
to do the least damage. It is the administrator who has caused
our imprisonment and we protest—and swear justly in religion
everything we have deduced to be true and that we do not have
to justify the least thing to the aforementioned administrator.
We also present to Your Excellency that two of the small ones
have died and the others are very sick, both the women and the
men, and particularly our captain, Juan Fortunato. For these
reasons we devotedly ask and supplicate, that in your deep piety,
Your Excellency, you look upon us with charity and determine in

the most convenient and best way that justice be served,
and return us to the hacienda where Your Excellency will be
served because, although we have sent three messages to the
administrator of the prison for Your Excellency, and we have
not received any response, nor favor, nor mercy, but we hope
to receive justice through this measure.

To you sir, we ask and supplicate you concede to us as
we have begged, and we protest that it is not out of malice. We
swear in the proper form and hope for a happy response, your
most humble slaves, who are prostrated at your feet.]

Archivo General de la Nación, Colombia, Colonia, Negros y esclavos
del Tolima, vol. 3, fols. 1023r-v.

NOTES

1. Archivo General de la Nación, Colombia, Colonia, Negros y esclavos
   del Tolima, vol. 3, fol. 999r, no date.

2. James C. Scott, *Domination and the Arts of Resistance: Hidden Transcripts*
   (New Haven and London: Yale University Press, 1990), 3 and passim. See
   also the discussions about the caution with which court records should be
   approached in Peter Blanchard, "The Language of Liberation: Slave
   Voices in the Wars of Independence," *Hispanic American Historical Review*.
   82, no. 3 (2002): 499–523; Maria Elena Díaz, *The Virgin, the King, and
   the Royal Slaves of El Cobre: Negotiating Freedom in Colonial Cuba,
   1670–1780* (Stanford: Stanford University Press, 2000); Bernard
   Lavallé, *Amor y opresión en los Andes coloniales* (Lima: Instituto de
   Estudios Peruanos, 1999), 235.

3. For example, the carryover of this framework into Africa is highlighted
   in events such as the conference "Fighting Back: Resistance to
   Enslavement and the Slave Trade in Africa," which took place at Rutgers
   University in February 2001. Such analysis is also evident in the works
   of Joseph Miller for West Central Africa, João José Reis for Brazil, and
   the voluminous historiography that deals with quilombos or palenques
   and marronage. See Joseph C. Miller, *Way of Death: Merchant Capitalism
   and the Angolan Slave Trade, 1726–1826* (Madison: University of Wisconsin

Press, 1988); Jane Landers, "Leadership and Authority in Maroon Settlements in Spanish America and Brazil," in *Africa and the Americas: Interconnections during the Slave Trade*, ed. José C. Curto and Renée Soulodre-La France (Trenton, NJ: Africa World Press, 2005); and all the work that has been done on brotherhoods, such as Elizabeth Kiddy, *Blacks of the Rosary: Memory and History in Minas Gerais, Brazil* (University Park: Pennsylvania State University Press, 2006) and Mariza C. Soares, *Devotos da cor: Identidade étnica, religiosidade e escravidão no Rio de Janeiro, século XVIII* (Rio de Janeiro: Civilização Brasileira, 2000) in Brazil and Nina S. de Friedemann, *La saga del negro: Presencia africana en Colombia* (Santafé de Bogotá: Instituto de Genetica Humana/Pontificia Universidad Janeriana, 1993) in Colombia.

4. See the cases discussed by Hermes Tovar Pinzón, *Grandes empresas agricolas y ganaderas: Su desarrolo en el siglo XVIII* (Bogotá: Ediciones CIEC, 1980), 183–84.

5. See, for example, the discussion by Blanchard in "The Language of Liberation," 499–523. Along the same lines, Maria Eugenia Cháves analyzes the way in which women could appropriate the concept of "honor" in late colonial Guayaquil in order to use it as a weapon to gain their freedom. See *Honor y libertad: Discursos y recursos en la estrategia de libertad de una mujer esclava (Guayaquil a fines del periodo colonial)* (Gotemborgo: Avhandilingar fran Historiska Institutionen I Goteborg, 2001), 147–81.

6. Eric Van Young argues that this defense of community and collective identity was often blended with messianic and millennial aspirations that usually looked to the king as a source of succor for many indigenous groups in Independence era Mexico. See "Los sectores populares en el movimiento mexicano de independencia, 1810–1821: Una perspectiva comparada," in *Naciones, gentes y territorios: Ensayos de historia e historiografía comparada de América Latina y el Caribe*, ed. Luis Javier Ortiz Mesa and Victor Manuel Uribe Urán (Medellín: Editorial Universidad de Antioquia, 2000), 151–56.

7. Roberto Velandia, *La Villa de San Bartolome de Honda: Epocas de la conquista y la colonia*, (Bogotá: Editorial Kelly, 1989), 1:208.

8. Pinzón, *Grandes empresas agrícolas y Ganaderas*, 160. For a history of the Jesuits in Cartagena, see Tulio Aristizabal Giraldo, S.J. *Retrazo de historia: Los Jesuitas en Cartagena de Indias* (Cartagena: Ediciones Antropos, 1995), and for a study of their economic activity, see Germán Colmenares, *Haciendas de los Jesuitas en el Nuevo Reino de Granada, siglo XVIII*, 2nd ed. (Cali: Tercer Mundo Editores, Universidad del Valle, Banco de la República, Colciencias, Santafé de Bogotá, 1998; orig. pub. 1969).

9. Colmenares suggests that in Peru the Jesuits owned 5,224 slaves and in New Granada, including Mérida and the Audiencia of Quito, they owned only about 1,722 (*Haciendas de los Jesuitas*, 71). His estimates are that there were 89 slaves on Villavieja between 1767 and 1772 and 129 on El Trapiche and El Salado (72).

10. Dauril Alden, *The Making of an Enterprise: The Society of Jesus in Portugal, Its Empire, and Beyond, 1540–1750* (Stanford: Stanford University Press, 1996), 505; Rosario Coronel Feijoo, *El Valle Sangriento: De los Indígenas de la Coca y el Algodón a la Hacienda Cañera Jesuita, 1580–1700* (Quito: FLACSO and ABYA-YALA, 1991), 86.

11. Vincent P. Franklin, "Bibliographical Essay: Alonso de Sandoval and the Jesuit Conception of the Negro," *Journal of Negro History.* 58, no. 3 (1973): 358–59.

12. Alden, *Making of an Enterprise*, 525, 527; Nicholas P. Cushner, "Slave Mortality and Reproduction on Jesuit Haciendas in Colonial Peru," *Hispanic American Historical Review*, 55, no. 2 (1975): 179.

13. Colmenares, *Haciendas de los Jesuitas*, xvi; Feijoo, *El Valle Sangriento*, 105–32.

14. Colmenares, *Haciendas de los Jesuitas*, xvii, 4. In this work the author lists over 130 properties owned and controlled by the various Jesuit colleges in the Nuevo Reino de Granada and Audiencia of Quito (xvii–xxii). See also Tovar Pinzón, *Grandes empresas agrícolas y ganaderas*, 160–61.

15. See Colmenares, *Haciendas de los Jesuitas*, 38; Aristizabal Giraldo, *Retrazo de historia*, 125–26.

16. Tovar Pinzón, *Grandes empresas agrícolas y ganaderas*, 178.

17. This case can be found in Archivo General de la Nación, Colombia (hereafter AGN), Colonia, Negros y esclavos de Bolivar, vol. 10, fols. 985–1004.

18. For a similar situation, see Lavallé, *Amor y opresión*, 210. This is a case from 1788 about a family of three enslaved runaways that the administrator of the former Jesuit property, Cuenca, claimed had been hidden and then secretly sold.

19. See AGN, Colonia, Negros y esclavos de Cundinamarca, vol. 6, fols. 829–34.

20. Ibid., fol. 833r.

21. See AGN, Colonia, Negros y esclavos del Tolima, vol. 3, fols. 658–60.

22. This case also leads us to reflect upon the way in which individuals could be enslaved in colonial Spanish America. We should note that it was only imported Africans and the children of enslaved women who could be enslaved in the colonies. Individuals who had been born free could not be sold into slavery, although they could be mistaken for or fraudulently denounced as slaves.

23. Colmenares, *Haciendas de los Jesuitas*, 32. This was a property that the Jesuits had obtained through their missionary work with the indigenous groups the Neivas and the Natagaimas, land they had acquired through their efforts to occupy these territories.

24. These documents are in AGN, Colonia, Negros y esclavos del Tolima, vol. 3, fols. 996–1048.

25. Ibid., fols. 997r–v.

26. The obstacles the enslaved faced when they sought to complain about their treatment were sometimes almost insurmountable, and they often needed to bring their cases to the royal justices of the audiencia to make sure that they were heard, given the fact that local justices generally were well known by or often related to their owners. See Lavallé, *Amor y opresión*, 224–25.

27. One of the witnesses of events on the hacienda, the priest Gomez Soriane, disingenuously claimed that when the Jesuits had owned and managed the estate, the enslaved had easily removed and replaced administrators if one of them did not please the Jesuits because Soriane prevented them from indulging in drinking binges and other excesses. See AGN, Colonia, Negros y esclavos del Tolima, vol. 3, fol. 1005v.

28. The traditional rights described in this case were similar to the demands made by the enslaved who had escaped from the former Jesuit Engenho Santana of Ilhéus in Brazil. That case is discussed by Stuart B. Schwartz, "Resistance and Accommodation in Eighteenth-Century Brazil: The Slaves' View of Slavery," *Hispanic American Historical Review* 57, no. 1 (1977): 69–81.

29. AGN, Colonia, Negros y esclavos del Tolima, vol. 3, fols. 998r–v. In a similar case from the Chota-Mira valley in Ecuador, a group of enslaved men from the Hacienda La Concepcion complained about their poor treatment by their new owner in 1788. See Lavallé, *Amor y opresión*, 245–46.

30. Silvia C. Mallo, "La libertad en el discurso del estado de amos y esclavos, 1780–1830," *Revista de historia de America*, 112 (July–December 1991): 122. See also Hermes Tovar Pinzón, "De una chispa se forma una hoguera: Esclavitud, insubordinación y liberación (1780–1821),"*Nuevas lecturas de historia*, 17 (1992): 18. There were recurring instances when the enslaved in various parts of the Americas chose to believe in the idea of a distant ruler who had emancipated them, but whose decree had been intercepted by unethical slave owners. See, for example, David Geggus, "Slavery, War, and Revolution in the Greater Caribbean," in *A Turbulent Time: The French Revolution and the Greater Caribbean*, ed. David Barry Gaspar and David Patrick Geggus (Bloomington: Indiana University Press, 1997), 9.

31. See the language used by the enslaved from Villavieja in the first document in the appendix. This was also a strategy used by many of the enslaved in cases from the Audiencia of Quito, as traced out by Sherwyn K. Bryant, "Enslaved Rebels, Fugitives, and Litigants: The Resistance Continuum in Colonial Quito," *Colonial Latin American Review* 13, no. 1 (2004): 11.

32. Lavallé, *Amor y opresión*, 249–51. In 1768 in Santa Marta, in another example, a group of runaways agreed to come back to their owner's property only if he swore on the Holy Sacrament that if he wanted to sell one of them, he would sell them all together, men women, and children, so that they would not be separated. See Anthony McFarlane, "Cimarrones and Palenques: Runaways and Resistance in Colonial Colombia," in "Out of the House of Bondage: Runaways, Resistance, and Marronage in Africa and the New World," ed. Gad Heuman, special issue, *Slavery and Abolition* 6, no. 3 (1985): 138–39.

33. This contradicts Nicholas Cushner's assessment that the enslaved on Jesuit estates in Peru may have enjoyed a slightly better material existence, although this was at the expense of experiencing a more regimented life. See "Slave Mortality and Reproduction on Jesuit Haciendas in Colonial Peru," 187.

34. Díaz, *The Virgin, the King, and the Royal Slaves of El Cobre*, 62.

35. AGN, Colonia, Negros y esclavos del Tolima, vol. 3, fols. 1004r–v.

36. The same type of phenomenon occurred when a group of representatives of the enslaved on the former Jesuit hacienda of La Concepcion in Ecuador made a complaint about their new owner's attempt to sell some of them away. See Lavallé, *Amor y opresión*, 242. "Lucumin y sus acompanantes insistieron en que se hacia *en conjunta de todos los morenos de la hazienda*."

37. For another case in which the enslaved on former Jesuit properties sought to preserve their group's integrity, see Bryant, "Enslaved Rebels, Fugitives, and Litigants," 19. This occurred in 1783 when workers on the sugar plantation Quejara threatened to kill the indigenous workers and flee to the mountains if their community was disrupted.

38. See Robert W. Slenes, *Na Senzala, uma Flor: Esperanças e recordaçoes na formação da família escrava-Brazil Sudeste, século XIX* (Rio de Janerio: Editora Nova Fronteira, Coleção Histórias do Brasil, 1999), 13.

39. David L. Chandler, "Family Bonds and the Bondsman: The Slave Family in Colonial Colombia," *Latin American Research Review* 16, no. 2 (1981): 113. Chandler states that on the former Jesuit properties some 60 percent of adult slaves had been or were married (112). See also Colmenares, *Haciendas de los Jesuitas*, 69; Cushner, "Slave Mortality and Reproduction on Jesuit Haciendas in Colonial Peru," 189.

40. Rosario Coronel Feijoo, "Indios y eslcavos negros en el Valle del Chota colonial," in *Actas del Primer Congreso de Historia del Negro en el Ecuador y Sur de Colombia: Esmeraldas, 14–16 de Octubre, 1988*, ed. P. Rafael Savoia (Quito: Centro Cultural Afro-Ecuatoriano, 1988), 182–84.

41. Colmenares, *Haciendas de los Jesuitas*, 69.

42. Cushner, "Slave Mortality and Reproduction on Jesuit Haciendas in Colonial Peru," 189. We should note that there is evidence from Argentina that the Jesuits resorted to the sale of individuals in order to deal with recalcitrant slaves. See Jorge Troisi Melean, "Catholic Ethics and Labor: The Slavery Policy of the Jesuits in Colonial Argentina (Second Half of the Eighteenth Century)," in *Confiscations of the Estates of the Regular Clergy and Capitalistic Accumulation in Early Modern Europe and the American Continent*, ed. F. Landi (Milan: F. Angeli, 2003), 6.

43. Alden, *Making of an Enterprise*, 523.

44. These figures are taken from a data set based on the inventories of four former Jesuit haciendas: Egypciaca in Tolima from 1794, the Texars of Alcivia, el Preceptor, and Tierra Bomba in Cartagena dating from 1770.

45. These discrepancies might be caused by the way in which individuals were described in the inventories and might not accurately reflect the realities of life on the haciendas.

46. Colmenares, *Haciendas de los Jesuitas*, 70.

47. Alden, *Making of an Enterprise*, 518.

48. Díaz makes the argument that collective petitions were a very unusual act since the enslaved had fewer opportunities to develop corporate groups or associations than, say, indigenous communities, and she attributes it to the collective identity that was created through the status of royal slave and place of birth, since she discusses a creole enslaved population, natives of the mines. *The Virgin, the King, and the Royal Slaves of El Cobre*, 77.

49. See the beautiful example of Gracia Real de Santa Teresa de Mose in Jane Landers, *Black Society in Spanish Florida* (Urbana and Chicago: University of Illinois Press, 1999), 29–61; and for the case of Nueva Granada, María Cristina Navarrete, *Historia social del negro en la colonia, Cartagena siglo XVII* (Cali: Universidad del Valle, 1995). For the cabildo de nación as a space for African cultures, see Nina S. de Friedemann, "Cabildos negros: Refugios de africanía en Colombia," *Caribbean Studies*, 23, nos. 1–2 (1990): 83–97.

50. Cushner, "Slave Mortality and Reproduction on Jesuit Haciendas in Colonial Peru," 189; McFarlane, "Cimarrones and Palenques," 146. This becomes evident when we look at the list of the imprisoned slaves from Villavieja published in Gerardo Andrade González, "Aprecio económico y desprecio social del negro," in Savoia, *Actas*, 193–226, and which can be found in AGN, Colonia, Negros y esclavos del Tolima, vol. 3, fols. 1017v–18v.

51. See Díaz, *The Virgin, the King, and the Royal Slaves of El Cobre*, 15. In this work Díaz studies "how the royal slaves ideologically portrayed their relation to an abstract master who was also the monarch."

52. See, for example, A. J. R. Russell-Wood, "'Acts of Grace': Portuguese Monarchs and Their Subjects of African Descent in Eighteenth-Century Brazil," *Journal of Latin American Studies*. 32 (May 2000): 332.

53. See, for example, the discussion in Mario Aguilera Peña and Renan Vega Cantor, *Ideal democratico y revuelta popular: Bosquejo histórico de la mentalidad política popular en Colombia, 1781–1948* (Santafé de Bogotá: Edciones Antropos, 1991), 72–76. See also the case of Josef Luciano Guambo in early nineteenth-century Tolima, who told the enslaved workers in Chaparral that the king had freed them and they were fools for continuing to work, in Renée Soulodre-La France, "Socially Not So Dead! Slave Identities in Bourbon Nueva Granada," *Colonial Latin American Review* 10, no. 1 (2001): 94.

54. This case is cited in Aguilera Peña and Vega Cantor, *Ideal democratico y revuelta popular*, 76.

55. For the case of Mexico, see Van Young, "Los sectores populares," 151.

56. See Mallo, "La libertad en el discurso del estado de amos y esclavos," 129.

57. See McFarlane, "Cimarrones and Palenques,"146.

58. David L. Chandler, "Slave over Master in Colonial Colombia and Ecuador," *Americas* 38, no. 3 (1982): 318.

59. See Colmenares, *Haciendas de los Jesuitas*, 72 for the number of enslaved workers on the haciendas.

60. See Díaz, *The Virgin, the King, and the Royal Slaves of El Cobre*, 88.

61. AGN, Colonia, Negros y esclavos del Tolima, vol. 3, fols. 1007r–8v.

62. Ibid., fol. 1000r.

63. Alida Metcalf, "Millenarian Slaves? The Santidade de Jaguaripe and Slave Resistance in the Americas," American Historical Review Forum, *American Historical Review* 104, no. 5 (1999): 1531–59.

64. AGN, Colonia, Negros y esclavos del Tolima, vol. 3, fol. 1002r: "la gente esta esperando al mesias, como los judios, por que desde que los fariseos se fueron estan como moros sin sinor."

65. Ibid., fols. 1002r and 1002v: "que los que estan mandando aora ira a mandar a los Ynfiernos."

66. For a discussion of colonial texts and marronage, see Margaret M. Olsen, "Africans and Textual *Marronage* in Colonial Latin America," *Revista de estudios hispánicos* 37 (2003): 238.

67. AGN, Colonia, Negros y esclavos del Tolima, vol. 3, fols. 1006r–v.

68. Ibid., fols. 1011r–v.

69. Ibid., fols. 1023r–v.

70. Ibid., fol. 1031r.

71. Ibid., fol. 1036r.

72. Ibid., fols. 1048r–v.

73. Juan Gregorio Almeyda had been named the administrator of the hacienda after the priests' expulsion and he soon became embroiled in a legal battle with the enslaved widow of the hacienda's slave gang, Captain Francisco Borja. When Borja died in 1768, he controlled two large cacao groves, from which he must have earned a fair living, but he did not buy his freedom or that of his wife and children. Disputes and subsequent legal battles between Almeyda and Isabel Borja lasted for years, and she ended up being despoiled of her inheritance. See the discussion of this case in Chandler, "Slave over Master in Colonial Colombia and Ecuador," 318–21. This author suggests that Borja had never bought his family's freedom because they were so comfortable living as slaves on the Jesuit hacienda: "life on the Jesuit estates was easily bearable" (318). See also Colmenares, *Haciendas de los Jesuitas*, 113.

74. AGN, Negros y esclavos de Santander, vol. 3, fols. 880–935. This case is also discussed in McFarlane, "Cimarrones and Palenques," 147.

75. The original *informe*, or statement, is in fols. 88or and 88ov. The custom of allowing the enslaved the right to sow crops on plots of land was also prevalent on Jesuit haciendas in the Audiencia of Quito (present-day Ecuador), and this custom was continued by the administrators of the properties after the expulsion. See Feijoo, *El Valle Sangriento*, 110. The author does caution, however, that on many counts Jesuit estates were not run in a homogeneous manner throughout Hispanic America (104).

76. AGN, Colonial, Negros y esclavos de Santander, vol. 3, fols. 88or–v: "pues no siendo mas que un mero servitario de la Real Hacienda, no debe proceder a todo aquello que pudiera executar si hubiera comprado la Hacienda en contado."

77. Ibid., fol. 897r.

78. See, for example, ibid., fol. 899v.

CHAPTER SEVEN

"The Defects of Being a Black Creole"

The Degrees of African Identity in the Cuban
Cabildos de Nación, 1790–1820

MATT D. CHILDS

❧ IN THE 1790S SPANISH COLONIAL AUTHORITIES IN CUBA INVESTIGATED A
financial dispute between the free black man Salvador Ternero and several
of his associates who shared a common African ethnicity. Ternero served
as the leader of the Mina Guagni fraternal and mutual-aid society in
Havana that based its membership on a shared cultural and geographic
heritage rooted in the Gold Coast of West Africa.[1] Prevalent in colonial
society, these collective organizations became known as *cabildos de nación* to
reflect the voluntary grouping by common ethnic identity of the numerous African "nations" forcibly imported to Cuba. Contemporaries of the
early modern Atlantic world, both European and African, used the term
nation for Congos, Lucumies, Minas, and so on to connote African ethnicity.[2] The Spanish term *cabildo* represents the equivalent of a town council or a town government. Consequently, the labeling of these societies as
cabildos de nación provides some indication of how they functioned as
representative bodies for African nations by providing political and administrative services.[3]

On three separate occasions in the 1790s, several members of the
cabildo Mina Guagni challenged Ternero's authority as *capatáz* (steward or

leader but also used for an overseer or foreman) to direct the financial affairs of the society. Unnamed members complained to the captain general in 1794 that "capatáz Salvador Ternero ... had sold the cabildo" house where the society regularly held reunions and bought a new house without consulting the nation.[4] Three years later members of the Mina Guagni nation discovered that Ternero had purchased their new house in what amounted to a silent partnership with free mulatta Juana de Mesa, who demanded to be paid the money the cabildo generated by renting out rooms. The judge investigating the case ruled that Salvador Ternero as capatáz of the Mina Guagni nation would have to pay seven hundred pesos to Juana de Mesa.[5] After selling the old cabildo house, purchasing a new one, and then being forced to pay seven hundred pesos, several members of the Mina Guagni nation petitioned to have Salvador Ternero removed as capatáz.[6]

Some members believed Ternero's actions recklessly jeopardized the existence of the cabildo Mina Guagni. The ownership of a house uniting slaves and free people of color by a common African ethnicity provided a sacred space for solidarity in a society increasingly divided along racial lines between slavery and freedom at the end of the eighteenth century. The cabildo house served numerous functions vital to the Mina Guagni nation: a home that rented rooms; a conference center for holding meetings and reunions; a school for education and training in the artisan trades; a bank that collected membership dues, offered loans, and even purchased freedom for slaves; a restaurant with food services such as the "plate of the day"; a theater for dances; and even a funeral parlor. The official investigation prevented the cabildo house from carrying out its regular functions. Catarina Barrera, along with eight other members of the nation, pleaded with the captain general of Cuba to reopen the cabildo house "because it has been more than a year and a half since there has been amusement on the festival days."[7]

Responding to the challenge to his authority, Ternero defended his position as capatáz of the cabildo on the basis of what he described as his legitimate Mina Guagni ethnicity. According to Ternero, "the intention of some black creoles that endeavor to destroy" the cabildo caused the division in the society.[8] He dismissed the complaints as irrelevant because they were made by "creoles who are not members of the national body." Ternero further argued that "the creoles and slaves do not have a voice or a vote in cabildo" functions.[9] Ternero explained that slaves of Mina Guagni ethnicity could be members and participate in the society but could not vote because the "touch of slavery" prevented them from always "attending cabildo" meetings. Only upon becoming free did they become entitled to full membership rights. As for free creoles, Ternero argued that "according to the constitution of the cabildo, and according to general custom they are prohibited representation . . . even if they are the children of black members of the nation." The loudest voice calling for Ternero's removal as capatáz belonged to free creole Manuel Vásquez. "Ultimately," Ternero reasoned, "the defects (speaking with reservation) of being a black creole" rendered Manuel Vásquez's complaints illegitimate since he was not born in Africa of the Mina Guagni nation.[10] Ternero reversed the standard explanation of colonial society that structured hierarchical privileges by place of birth, from the white Spaniard on top of the hierarchy, followed by the white Cuban, mulatto Cuban, black Cuban, and then the "pure-blooded" African on the bottom. Puzzled as to how to respond to Ternero's argument of pure ethnic identity and full membership in the Mina Guagni nation, Captain General Luis de Las Casas ordered officials to investigate other cabildos to determine if creoles participated and received voting rights.[11]

After receiving the order, Francisco Faveda and notary José Díaz Velásquez visited several cabildo houses to inquire if they had creole members. According to Juan de la Torre and José de Jesús, the leaders of the Congo Masinga nation, creoles "were not represented in the cabildo." Upon inquiring at the cabildos Congo and Carabalí Osso, Faveda and Velásquez learned that creoles were members but "did not have votes" for deciding the nations' functions.[12] Believing that nations drew their membership from only the African-born sectors of Cuba's population, the presence of creoles in cabildos perplexed authorities and revealed how little they knew about the societies.

Ternero, keenly aware that Cuban officials disapproved of creole participation in cabildos, had emphasized creole participation in the Mina Guagni nation to discredit their challenge to his leadership. Ternero acknowledged that "it is true [creoles] dance and amuse themselves in the cabildos, but it is not by a right that they have, but by permission."[13] For Cuban authorities, cabildo dances represented the clearest indication of the cultural differences between Africans and Europeans. Black creoles who voluntarily participated in the ethnic-based cabildos contradicted the ideological justification for slavery that supposedly saved Africans from "heathenism" and "backwardness" with the benefits of Western culture. It further called into question the comforting belief of masters that the

African-born and Cuban-born population remained culturally distinct and would not make common cause. Despite evidence of financial mismanagement, the captain general allowed Ternero to retain the title of capatáz and ruled that "black creoles should not vote . . . as a consequence of the custom of such communities."[14]

The dispute between the creole and African members of the Mina Guagni nation provides crucial insights into the process of both identifying others and self-identification in early-nineteenth-century Cuba. Spanish authorities sought to separate the African- and Cuban-born populations from making common cause and, therefore, discouraged creole participation in cabildos. As a strategy to prevent a unifying racial identity, government officials encouraged the formation of cabildos because they emphasized distinct African ethnicities. Despite official discouragement and even limited political rights, some creoles joined cabildos and continued to identify with the nation of their parents and ancestors. Although Cuban society at large tended to privilege Cuban-born blacks over Africans, within cabildos, African-born *bozales* exerted more authority by claiming "legitimate" ethnicity as members of the nation. Examining the membership and activities of the cabildos demonstrates that social identity for individuals of African ancestry in Cuba displayed an incredible degree of diversity. The population of African descent continued to identify with their geographic and cultural origins in West and Central Africa by joining national ethnic associations. At the same time, a common, albeit tenuous, racial identity developed among slaves and free people of color forged by their experience in the New World. This chapter explores the tensions created within cabildo societies among members who had an identity linked in part to their specific cultural and geographic origins in Africa (labeled for clarity African ethnicity) and also to their racial identity formed in Cuba as a consequence of living in a slave society.

"Joining Together with a True National Spirit"
African Nations in Cuba

The formation of ethnic organizations based upon African nations represented a common feature of slave societies in the Americas. Masters throughout the New World recognized that Africans did not represent an undifferentiated mass of laborers but brought with them forms of social organization and cultural differences that they perpetuated and refashioned in the Americas as survival strategies. Robert Jameson, a British observer in Cuba, recognized how both master and slaves identified Africans by nations in the early nineteenth century: "The different nations to which the negroes belonged in Africa are marked out in the colonies both by the master and the slaves; the former considering them variously characterized in the desired qualities, and the latter joining together with a true national spirit in such union as their lords allow."[15] Masters often stereotyped certain nations for possessing distinguishing characteristics that some historians regard as offering a few "glitters of truth" about African cultural traits.[16] Regardless of what masters' stereotypes reveal specifically about African identity in the New World, it is clear that profits depended on an awareness of cultural differences. Historian David Eltis has soundly observed, "While the planters' basic requirement was slave labor from anywhere in Africa, no one can read the transatlantic correspondence of the early modern slave systems without recognizing the importance of African nationhood in the shaping of the plantation regimes."[17]

In Spain and Spanish America the earliest practices of recognizing national differences among Africans occurred through religious lay brotherhoods. At least a century before the conquest of the New World, slavery had been firmly established in Seville. Municipal authorities appointed a steward to settle disputes between slaves and masters and allowed the African population the right to gather on feast days and perform their own dances and songs. In addition, black congregationalists established religious brotherhoods.[18] These practices were then carried to the Americas and expanded when introduced to a larger African slave population. By 1560 over half the population of Lima, Peru could claim African ancestry. Unsurprisingly, sodalities in Lima often reflected African ethnicity, such as the Dominican brotherhood for the "negros Congos," and the brotherhood of Nuestra Señora del Socorro for Angolans.[19] Catholic brotherhoods that catered to the specific needs of African members could be found throughout Spanish America.[20] In addition, organizations formed along lines of African ethnicity expressed the desire to separate from church control. In Buenos Aires, for example, Africans in the nineteenth century regularly petitioned the police department to form societies based upon their common national backgrounds to better serve their spiritual, cultural, and financial needs.[21] Whether through the church or by state-sanctioned societies, Africans in Latin America grouped themselves along lines of African ethnicity and culture.

In Cuba the presence of Catholic brotherhoods that included the participation of people of African ancestry dates back to the sixteenth century.
In 1573 the town council of Havana reported that Africans took part in the
procession of Corpus Christi, and several wills indicate they regularly made
donations to sodalities.[22] Historian Jane Landers found that the Mandinga,
Carabalí, Lucumí, Arara, Ganga, and Congo nations proliferated in Havana
and organized important brotherhoods. Most of the brotherhoods selected
a patron saint that they honored on his or her feast day with elaborate festivals and ceremonies.[23] Surprisingly, if there was an institutional association
between Catholic lay brotherhoods and the African nations for the late eighteenth and early nineteenth century, court records do not mention any religious official called upon to testify on the activities and practices of the
cabildos. According to a report issued by Bishop Morell de Santa Cruz in
1755, during the span of the sixteenth and seventeenth centuries several
brotherhoods no longer supervised all of the cabildos' activities.[24] By the late
1700s, if not earlier, it appears cabildos and Catholic brotherhoods had taken
on different social functions that had earlier overlapped in Cuba's history.[25]

Various scholars have traced the origins of the cabildos to religious
holidays and Catholic brotherhoods of Spanish origin, but historian Philip
Howard has pointed out that analogous societies were common to West
and Central Africa.[26] Associations, organizations, and secret societies in
West and Central Africa provided an institutional framework that enslaved
and free Africans molded to their New World surroundings.[27] These societies performed charitable, recreational, political, and economic functions
for members, who often shared the same language, ethnicity, and national-
ity.[28] Spanish colonial administrators and Catholic priests regarded African
cabildos in Cuba as an extension of religious sodalities with their origins in
Europe. The organizations for Africans, however, surely did not represent
something entirely of Spanish or Cuban origin but an Old World African
institution modified in a New World Caribbean setting.

"Those from Ethiopia That Want to Join Today"
The Africanization of Cuba and the Increase in Cabildos

In the last decade of the eighteenth century the African population in Cuba
rose dramatically as a result of two related events. First, after a decade of
incessant fighting, the slaves of Saint Domingue freed themselves by revolution and gave birth to the independent black republic of Haiti. The

destruction of Saint Domingue provided the structural opening for Cuba to expand sugar and coffee production across the island. The second cause for the rapid increase of the African population was the Spanish crown's 1789 declaration of free trade in trans-Atlantic slavery.[29] Once the slave trade became open to all nations, Cuban slaveholders regularly petitioned the crown to ensure the policy would not be reversed. After the two-year trial period of free trade in slaves ended in 1791, Francisco Arango y Parreño, the most influential spokesman of the planter class, wrote to have the policy extended, stating "with all frankness . . . the free introduction [of slaves] has allowed the island to prosper."[30] In the span of fifteen years from 1789 to 1804 the crown issued altogether eleven decrees aimed at expanding the slave trade.[31] Although the Cuban slave trade dates to the first decades of the sixteenth century and stands out as the longest in the history of New World slavery, only during the period from 1789 until its final abolition in 1867 did it fundamentally alter the social, racial, and ethnic composition of the island. While no consensus has emerged over exact figures, most scholars would agree that from 1790 to 1820 as many as three hundred thousand slaves, or more, entered Cuba.[32] The massive importation of slaves and the radical transformations for Cuban society are all the more dramatic given that in the previous 280 years only one hundred thousand slaves had been imported to the island. In the span of thirty years the overall volume of the entire history of the Atlantic slave trade to Cuba had increased threefold.[33]

The radical increase in the volume of the trans-Atlantic slave trade resulted in the rapid growth of the African population across the island. Consequently, the total number of cabildos also increased markedly. Charting the detailed growth of the number of cabildos and the membership in each nation, however, proves difficult because no single governmental institution supervised the associations for the early nineteenth century. As a result, a concentrated corpus of records on the societies has yet to be found. While quantifying the growth of cabildos remains difficult, qualitative sources indicate a clear increase in these societies from 1750 to 1820. In 1753 the bishop of Cuba wrote to the king of Spain complaining of the "noisy shouting of males mixed with females amusing themselves in extremely clumsy and provocative dances . . . of the Ethiopians of both sexes that sanctify the festivals in this city." The bishop counted "twenty-one houses that have served the devil": the Carabalies owned five, the Minas three. the Lucumies two, the Araras two, the Congos two, the Mondongos two, the Gangas two, the Mandingas one, the Luangos one, and the

Suangos one.[34] Scattered references to more than thirty cabildos found in
civil disputes for the years 1790 to 1820, along with frequent mentions of
associations in official correspondence and criminal proceedings, suggest
the number of societies increased to at least fifty by 1820.[35]

A qualitative indication of the growth of cabildos as a result of what
Mina Guagni leader Salvador Ternero described in the 1790s as the "arrival
of those from Ethiopia that want to join today," is reflected by the division
of several nations. In the 1780s a dispute surfaced within the Lucumí cabildo
between the diverse ethnicities that claimed membership. By the seventeenth century Yoruba culture and language had become a lingua franca
along the western African coast, promoting what Africanist John Thornton
has described as "cultural intercommunication."[36] In Cuba this process
apparently expanded the cultural boundaries of inclusion that facilitated the
collaboration of several nations under a broad Lucumí identity. One member recalled that "the cabildo was erected by the Lucumí nations, specifically
the Nangas and the Barbaes."[37] In addition, Chabas and Bambaras such as
free black Pedro José could join as well, despite not sharing the ethnicity of
the founders.[38] Near the end of the eighteenth century, however, with the
increase of slaves from the Yoruba region, the society divided into separate
cabildos represented by the Nangas and Barbaes in one house and the
Chabas and Bambaras in another. A similar division emerged in the cabildo
Congo Musolongo in 1806, indicated by their request to separate into two
different societies.[39] Likewise, as a result of a contested election, Juan
Gavilan and a group identifying itself as the Carabalí Osso desired to separate from the Carabalí Umugini cabildo despite "fourteen years more or less
of unity."[40] The division of cabildos as membership increased indicates how
the Atlantic slave trade fundamentally shaped African ethnicity in Cuba.
Further, the ability to incorporate members from different nations at one
moment and then at another draw lines of exclusion demonstrates the flexibility of African ethnicity and culture in the New World.

"Children of the Same Nation"
The Diversity of Cabildo Membership

Cabildo membership served to strengthen networks and resources weakened by a slave society that showed little hesitation about destroying
kin relations. Members who often described each other with familial con-
notations reveal the example of how cabildos served as a surrogate for an

incomplete family structure. Francisco Alas, the "emperor" of a Mina and Mandinga cabildo in Bayamo, mentioned a meeting attended by his *parientes* [relatives], free Blas Tamayo, slave Mateo and his wife, and the slave Candelaria Dolores."[41] One member of a cabildo reported that while he "was sick, all of his relatives had come to visit him."[42] José Caridad Perera, a free black of Carabalí ethnicity, ate dinner during festival days in "the house of Antonio José Barraga the Captain General" of the cabildo together with "other various relatives."[43] Other cabildos simply referred to members as part of one family. Cristóbal Govín, the second captain of the cabildo Carabalí Oquella, complained of the new discord caused by an election "between a family that has always carried on with the utmost peace and harmony."[44] Still others described their fellow cabildo members with the more general *compañero* (companion), which conveyed a sense of shared camaraderie from being part of a community.[45] Whether described as "family" members, "relatives," or "companions," cabildos provided a widened network of associations that fostered collective solidarity.

Salvador Ternero's dispute with the Cuban-born creoles in the Mina Guagni cabildo indicates that within a nation, the rights and benefits accorded to "family" members, "relatives," or "companions" could vary widely. While African ethnic identification tended to define who could be counted on cabildo membership lists, evidence from various nations suggests the treatment of mulattos, Cuban-born creoles, and slaves depended on the regulations and customs of each society. Contemporary documents indicate little mulatto participation in cabildos. Given that nations in Cuba based their membership on a shared African ethnicity, cabildos may have excluded mulattos. Cuban officials may have also prevented them from joining cabildos as they sought to separate blacks and mulattos from making a common cause, further revealing the precarious position of a mixed-race population in a society largely divided between people of European and African ancestry. Nonetheless, some mulattos may have participated in the nations or attended cabildo houses during festival days. On February 25, 1811, authorities arrested José Montero, Felipe Santiago, and Rafael Rodríguez, all soldiers in the free mulatto militia, for attending a meeting at a "cabildo of blacks."[46] Other than this brief reference, there is no evidence to conclude that mulattos regularly participated in cabildo functions, just as there is no evidence to argue that the nations specified their exclusion.

There are few references of mulatto participation in cabildos, yet ample evidence suggests that Cuban-born blacks regularly participated in the nations. For example, free creole Juan Bautista Valiente, known as "el Cubano," served in the Mina cabildo.[47] Some cabildos accepted creole children of members. The cabildo Musolongo included creoles and recognized Juan Ruíz as a member, "even though he is a creole, son of a father and a mother of the nation, and married to a free black of the nation."[48] Regardless of Salvador Ternero's bitter dispute with Manuel Vásquez over creoles' voting rights, he recognized their membership as "children of the same" nation and never proposed their expulsion.[49] While the differences between African-born and Cuban-born members sometimes led to rivalries within cabildos, colonial officials acted more alarmed than the nations that the two groups fraternized. Judicial authorities chastised free black Clemente Chacón's parenting skills for allowing his son Juan Bautista, "a free black Creole, to play the drums with the Congo nation."[50]

Numerous creoles actively participated in the nations as membership increased, providing a heightened significance to African ethnicity in Cuba. Others, however, began to separate themselves from the African-born population. Leaders of the Lucumí cabildo complained of the formation of a creole group that opposed the interest of the bozales. As Cuban authorities settled divisions within cabildos and became cognizant of creole participation in the associations, they came to suspect that "there had formed a cabildo of black creoles." Free black José Herrera denied any association with the society, insisting that he had no knowledge that his "sister-in-law Manuela González had been elected queen of the creole cabildo." Herrera, further, elaborated that "should one [cabildo] form, he would not join, because he was not a man of cabildos . . . and could not make the movements of the bozales." Rather, Herrera emphasized, he was somebody who "danced the minuet, as is the custom of creoles."[51] Herrera's contrast between the minuet and cabildo dances drew a clear distinction between creole and African dances cultures. He also revealed the degree to which some creoles defined themselves in contradistinction to bozales and the complexity of racial and ethnic identity in Cuba.

Slaves and creoles alike had limited rights and privileges in cabildos. Salvador Ternero explained that slaves of the Mina Guagni nation participated in cabildo functions not by "a right that they have, but by voluntary permission."[52] The cabildo Carabalí prevented slaves from voting for leaders, as evidenced by the organization's electoral roster, which listed only free members.[53] Likewise, other societies barred slaves from voting in elections and deciding the financial expenditures of the nations.[54] Given both that the distinction between free and slave represented the primary division of Cuban society and the prevalence of slavery in Africa, it should not be surprising that cabildos defined membership rights based upon legal status.

Afro-Cuban historian Pedro Deschamps-Chapeaux has identified numerous people of African ancestry who owned slaves, representing what he describes as the interests of the "bourgeoisie of color."[55] A few cabildo members even owned slaves. In 1807 Antonio Ribero of the Lucumí Llane nation purchased a slave for five hundred pesos. The transaction caught the attention of the cabildo not because the members opposed the purchase on moral grounds, but because they suspected Ribero had bought the slave with money stolen from the nation.[56] In 1804 Cristóbal Govín, capatáz of the Carabalí Oquella nation, opposed remodeling several dilapidated rooms of the cabildo house, including his own. Govín protested that "I would have to transfer my habitation during the construction" to the one of "Rafaela, slave of Teresa Barreto, who lives in another room of the same house."[57] When Salvador Ternero assumed the title of capatáz of the Mina Guagni cabildo, the nation authorized him to administer "whatever quantities of maravedíes, gold pesos, silver pesos, jewelry, slaves, merchandise, agricultural products, and other goods."[58] Although nations fostered ethnic identification and a community beyond the immediate supervision of white masters, the ownership of slaves by some cabildo members and the limited voting rights extended to human chattel illustrate how slavery pervaded every aspect of Cuban society.

Some nations limited the participation of slaves in cabildo functions because of their servile condition, yet others attempted to overcome the barriers that blocked active participation. Festival days represented crucial events that allowed for a collective solidarity to be expressed through ceremony and dance. Numerous masters granted slaves permission to participate in cabildos as a reward, but some also financially benefited from slave participation.[59] The nation Carabalí Osso recognized the important value of slaves in cabildo functions. In 1803 their account book recorded the entry "payment for slaves' daily wages of our nation" to masters in order to secure their participation at cabildo events.[60] The Carabalí Osso nation, in effect, hired the attendance of its enslaved members by paying wages to their masters. As slavery presented obstacles to full participation, generated additional expenses by paying wages to masters, and undermined collective strength, cabildos often provided loans to emancipate members.[61] The cabildo Congo, for example, reported that Cayetano García owed "eighty pesos of the two hundred that he was given for his freedom."[62] Free members could participate more actively in cabildos than slaves, and as the rightful owners of their own labor they could contribute more generously to the nation's financial resources.

Some societies accepted members from different nations. Authorities assumed that free black Antonio from Bayamo was Carabalí because he participated in the nation's festival days and "lived among them," but he described his ethnicity as Congo.[63] Although the Mina and Mandinga could trace their nations to the distinct geographic areas of the Gold Coast and the Upper Niger Valley, respectively, they formed a joint cabildo that extended membership to both groups.[64] Members of different nations occasionally gained considerable authority within a cabildo with which they did not share a common ethnicity. On July 17, 1803, the cabildo Carabalí Induri elected Juan Echevarría to the position of second capatáz by an overwhelming majority. Jesús Sollazo, the leader of the cabildo, immediately declared Echevarría's election "null . . . because he is not of the nation Induri . . . for which he should not be admitted." The captain general of Cuba decided to uphold the election because "the majority of the individuals of the cabildo Carabalí Induri agreed upon" Juan Echevarría for the position of second capatáz.[65] Echevarría's election reveals both the flexibility and rigidity of African ethnicity in Cuba. Although not an African-born member of the Carabalí Induri nation, he apparently had enough supporters within the cabildo who did not define leadership qualities exclusively by ethnicity. For the leader of the nation, however, it was precisely his lack of African ethnicity that made him unsuitable to serve as an elected officer.

The captain general sided with Echevarría because he had won the election outright and because of "the fact that he had been admitted to the cabildo" long before the election took place.[66] Cabildos occasionally extended membership to people of diverse ethnicities but, as with creoles and slaves, tended to restrict their voting rights. The Carabalí Apapa, like other nations, did not limit membership to one ethnicity. When a dispute over buying a new house divided the cabildo, only those members of Carabalí Apapa ethnicity and those who had been extended voting rights were allowed to debate the purchase. The cabildo leaders explained that members of different ethnicities "do not have representation in the cabildo according to the resolutions of this government, *without obtaining the right and permission of us*, and the others who make up the nation."[67] Voting rights appear to have been universally granted to free African-born members who represented the ethnicity of the cabildo. For creoles, slaves, and cabildo members of ethnicities distinct from that of the dominant group, generalizations prove elusive because the practices and custom of each nation tended to differ, illustrating the diverse experiences of people of African ancestry in Cuba.

Although cabildos often restricted participation in their associations along ethnic lines, they also recognized commonalties with larger cultural groups common to areas of the slave trade. Manuel Blanco of the Lucumí cabildo explained to authorities that the division of the Lucumies into separate nations reflected the different homelands of the members while recognizing their common Yoruba culture. According to Blanco, "the truth is that among the blacks who call themselves Lucumies, some are Chabes, others Barbaes, Bambaras, and Nangas...all of them take the name Lucumí, but some are from one homeland and the others from another." The same recognition of a larger shared culture can be observed among the different Congo groups in Cuba. Blanco observed that "there are many blacks who call themselves members of the Congo nation, but as they are from diverse homelands, they have in this city diverse cabildos." Blanco recognized the common culture of the Congo, yet pointed out that the "Congos Luangos" and the "Congos Mondongos" had their own cabildos.[68] The Carabalí also identified themselves as part of a larger cultural group but divided their cabildos ethnically to a specific homeland. In addition to choosing leaders for each Carabalí cabildo, they also elected "José Aróstegui as the capatáz of the five Carabalí nations" to coordinate activities among the organizations.[69] The Lucumies, Congos, and Carabalies formed associations based upon a broad shared cultural identity rooted in Africa. They then limited cabildo membership to reflect the same nation and homeland of those they described as their *paisanos* (countrymen).[70] The ability of Africans in Cuba to narrow their fraternal societies to reflect both a common nation and homeland supports John Thornton's argument that "slaves would typically have no trouble finding members of their own nation with whom to communicate."[71]

"Who Moves All of These Machinations?"
The Leadership of Cabildos

Within each cabildo, several members held administrative positions that strengthened the capatáz's leadership. The cabildo Carabalí, in Matanzas, elected Rafael its new leader in 1814. The members then decided upon a general staff that resembled a king's court. They agreed that Rafael's wife would serves as queen mother, María Rosario Domínguez as princess, Diego as first minister, Nicario as second minister, Bernardo as first captain, Miguel de la Cruz as second lieutenant, Manuel del Portillo and Felipe as musicians, and Francisco as treasurer.[72] In addition to these titles, other cabildos created positions such as governor, emperor, sergeant of arms, queen of war, and captain of war.[73] Although denied voting rights within cabildos, slaves often attained leadership roles. The slave Patricio served as "captain of the Carabalí slaves" and Alonzo Santa Cruz held the position of "king of the Congo slaves."[74] The captain general of Cuba attempted to prevent the establishment of an elaborate leadership structure and recommended that "there should not be positions other than first, second, and third capatáz."[75] Despite the limited influence of cabildos beyond their own nation, the captain general realized the possible dangers of allowing slaves and free people of color to create their own hierarchical structures and select their own leaders.

Cabildo leaders tended to be influential members of the free colored community tied to the militia. Francisco Alas, the "emperor" of the Mina and Mandinga cabildo in Bayamo and member of the black militia, owned with his wife a small plot of land, three horses, two mares, seven pigs, a gold ring, and over a hundred pesos.[76] Domingo Acosta, the capatáz of the Carabalí Apapa nation, drew upon his connections as a "retired soldier... of the black militia battalion" to request that a military court settle a cabildo dispute.[77] Captain General Someruelos recommended that a "military tribunal" handle the investigation into the financial affairs of the Mina Guagni nation after Esteban Torres and Salvador Ternero emphasized their militia service.[78] When Manuel Blanco became involved in a property dispute with the cabildo Lucumí over selling the nation's house, he hoped to win the case by stressing his volunteer militia service "without receiving a salary or any gratification."[79] The selection of cabildo leaders from the ranks of the colored militia presented colonial authorities with individuals they regarded as loyal subjects of the Spanish crown. By electing leaders acceptable to government officials, the cabildos would suffer less scrutiny. In addition, some nations became entitled to the special privileges of military courts available to their leaders. By selecting militia soldiers for the position of capatáz, cabildos could address the conflicting goals of earning approval from a government that

FIGURE 7.1:
Free Black Militiamen from Veracruz and Havana, 1770–1776. Reproduced courtesy of the Florida Museum of Natural History, Fort Mose Exhibition.

sought to maintain a racial social hierarchy while at the same time better the conditions of those who shared a common African ethnicity.[80]

An examination of the electoral process indicates that female members often guided the affairs of the nation, not the elected capatáz as Cuban officials believed. Because of their numerical superiority among the cabildo's voting members, women frequently decided the selection of new leaders. Forty-two eligible voters participated in the cabildo Carabalí Oquella elections of 1804; thirty-one were women.[81] Although the majority of males voted for Cayetano García as the new capatáz for the cabildo Congo Macamba in 1807, Antonio Diepa won the election because of six females votes.[82] Of the forty-seven votes cast in favor of Juan Echevarría for the position of second capatáz of the cabildo Carabalí Induri, thirty-two came from women, guaranteeing his margin of victory by a ratio of

two to one. The capatáz of the cabildo, Jesús Sollazo, attempted to overturn Echevarría's election on the basis that he was not of Carabalí Induri
ethnicity, "but also because the general customs observed in the cabildos
of this city for the elections of capatáz do not admit the votes of
women."[83] The captain general ruled against the attempt "to not accept
women's votes" for capatáz because it was "contrary to what is daily
observed." The captain general's investigation concluded Sollazo's protest
simply represented a tactic to nullify an unfavorable election.[84] The capatáz of the Carabalí Oquella, Cristóbal Govín, shared Jesús Sollazo's
opinion that female participation in cabildos should be limited because
Lázaro Rodríguez won the election with "only the assistance of Teresa
Barreto's supporters."[85]

   Some cabildo leaders felt threatened by the authority women could
exert in shaping the leadership of African societies, while others recognized their important role in maintaining the unity of nations. In 1805
José Aróstegui of the cabildo Carabalí Osso informed the captain general
of the death of Rita Castellanos, who held the leadership position among
the female members of the nation. Shortly thereafter, Barbara de Mesa
"occupied her place with all the support of the nation for her recom-
mendable" characteristics. Aróstegui requested that the captain general
"give his recognition to Barbara de Mesa as capatáza" so that she could
"govern the women of said cabildo with authority" to ensure "perfect
peace and harmony."[86] Other cabildos not only recognized the important
role of women in governing female members but also acknowledged that
they maintained the unity of the entire nation. The leaders of the Congo
Macamaba nation attributed their inability to resolve disputes by themselves and the need for government officials to intervene to "the death of
Rafaela Armenteras, queen of the nation"; since that event, "the disorder
has increased."[87]

   Not only did females exhibit considerable authority in determining
the cabildos' leaders, they also influenced financial matters. Through
membership dues, renting rooms, collecting alms, and hosting festivals,
cabildos normally held savings from 300 to 1,000 pesos, which represented a significant amount, given that the prices for slaves in Havana
newspapers usually ranged from 300 to 500 pesos.[88] The queen of the
cabildo had the important duty of guarding the safe. When the cabildo
Carabalí Osso became involved in a dispute that required paying a legal
fine, the neighborhood commissioner went to the house of Barbara de

Mesa to "request the safe." José Castillo reported that Barbara de Mesa would not turn over the safe "until she had been threatened with prison."[89] When members of the cabildo Carabalí Oquella challenged the financial expenses of the capatáz, the whole nation went "to the house of Teresa Barreto, queen of said cabildo" to count the money in the safe. The cabildo leaders pulled from the safe "a bag full of money and in the presence of the nation . . . counted 946 pesos."[90]

Most cabildos entrusted the queen to guard their money, but they took precautions to ensure that it would take more than one person to open the safe. With banks unavailable to cabildos, they generally used a safe modeled on the Spanish coffer, which required "three different keys," to prevent one person from making a withdrawal.[91] According to the cabildo Carabalí Induri, the "first capatáz" received a key to the safe, "the second capatáz another" and, adding yet another layer of security, "an elected person in consultation with all the nation" held the third key. The three key holders could open the safe only in the presence of "twenty people, men or women, of the nation," to explain the purpose of the withdrawal.[92] Likewise, the cabildo Congo Macamba also required its safe to be opened in the presence of its members to "avoid future disputes, objections, and suspicions of the capatáz."[93] Despite such measures, money often disappeared from the safe. Tomás Paveda of the cabildo Carabalí Osso suspected the capatáz had withdrawn money without consulting the nation by acquiring the other two keys.[94] The required presence of three key holders could sometimes work too effectively in preventing access to the cabildo's money. On one occasion, a safe could not be opened because the key holder worked "in the countryside."[95] Apparently, this was a common problem; one cabildo required that key holders "should not be absent from the city without leaving the key with a person of known confidence."[96]

Female leaders might hold the duty of guarding the safe, but they did not hold the keys to open it. The Congo Macamba nation stated very clearly that whoever "takes on the task of treasury" would have to be a "black male."[97] Cristóbal Govín, the capatáz of the cabildo Carabalí Oquella, feared that "the funds of the cabildo held by Teresa Barreto, a rebellious woman with bad ideas," would jeopardize the stability of the nation.[98] Govín never suggested that Barreto be stripped of her duty to guard the safe, but he cautioned she should be watched closely. According to Govín, Barreto supported "Lázaro Rodríguez for second capatáz . . . with the design to place him later in the position of first [capatáz]." Govín warned that if this would occur, she "could maneuver... the common money of the nation." Despite Govín holding the title of capatáz, he recognized the power of Teresa Barreto in deciding the affairs of the cabildo when he described her as the person "who moves all of these machinations."[99] Whether through deciding elections or guarding the safe, females decisively shaped cabildo functions.[100]

"Entertainment, Food, and Drink"
Unity through Collective Identity

The cabildos showed remarkable flexibility in maintaining an overall sense of unity despite their divisions. While it is important to emphasize ethnic distinctions, place of birth, legal status, and gender, since the members of the nations themselves made them, it is equally important to recognize that cabildos continued to support the collective efforts of the nation as a whole. As with many organizations representing lower-class interests in a society controlled by a powerful elite, the tension between the specific needs of individual members and the unity of the cabildos created friction within the nations. Nations could recognize dissent within their ranks without causing the dissolution of their societies. This fact indicates that collective needs often superseded individual interests. The nations represented the only institutions that permitted the voluntary grouping along ethnic lines for Africans and creoles, men and women, and slaves and freed persons in Cuba. For a colony most clearly divided between white European masters and black African slaves, cabildos stood in contrast to the racial slave-free paradigm that defined the dominant circles of inclusion and exclusion for most of Cuban society.

Cabildos also broke down the division between rural and urban society. Although the urban cabildo house provided the center for the nation's activities, members represented both the city and countryside. When the cabildo Congo Musolongo elected Augustín Pedroso capatáz in 1806, the rural members of the nation could not travel to Havana to vote. Before Pedroso could assume leadership of the cabildo, however, the nation recognized—in something akin to an absentee ballot—that the members "absent in the countryside agreed with the election of Pedroso."[101] Not only could cabildos break down rural and urban division by both groups participating in elections, but housing could also link the two distinct geographic areas. Free black María Francisca Duarte lived in the cabildo house of the Carabalí Apapa located outside the city walls of Havana. She shared the room on weekends with her husband, who worked in the countryside. "On the first day of the month," according to María Francisca, she paid five pesos in rent to the capatáz of the cabildo when, "as customary, [her] husband came from the countryside."[102] Temporary housing on weekends served to unite rural and urban members of the nation, which likely facilitated their attendance at cabildo functions in the city. In addition, and perhaps more important for María Francisca and her husband, the cabildo house offered temporary marital solitude. The geographic, gendered division of labor often separated spouses of African descent. Females most commonly found employment as market vendors and domestic servants in urban areas, whereas male laborers tended to dominate rural plantations.

The cabildos' cooperative methods of raising revenues and deciding expenditures revealed an emphasis on collective rather than individual goals. From October 1 to December 31, 1801, the cabildo Carabalí Osso raised 576 pesos from membership donations. Apparently, the cabildo did not require a specific amount for all members to pay. Domingo Alcántra made the largest donation, 72 pesos, while Trinidad de Medina contributed the smallest amount, 29 pesos. As only fourteen members, six women and eight men, made donations to the cabildo's safe, it suggests that participation in a nation did not require paying dues. According to Manuel de Jesús, who participated in an unnamed cabildo in Puerto Príncipe, slaves "were poor blacks that could contribute [only] one coin for the festivities" of the nation.[103] The cabildos Carabalí Induri and Carabalí Oquella realized some members could not contribute from their own pockets but could provide money to the nation by begging for alms.[104] Cabildo members represented such diverse economic backgrounds—free landowners, artisans, market vendors, and unpaid slave laborers—that a set membership fee of any substantial amount would have been difficult to collect.

Cabildo revenues were often redistributed back to members. A special meeting of members who had voting rights would decide the financial affairs of the cabildo. Nations commonly provided loans to members and on occasion even purchased freedom for slaves who participated in the cabildo.[105] The account books of the cabildo Carabalí Umugini recorded loans to José María Rebollo, María Dolores Méndez, and Josefa for unspecified reasons in December 1801.[106] In addition, cabildos also offered medical and financial assistance to sick members. The Carabalí Osso paid

FIGURE 7.2: *Day of Kings Celebration in Havana, 1851. From* Album
pintoresco de la isla de Cuba, *(F1763.A4 1851),*
Reproduced courtesy of the Marion duPont Scott Sporting
Collection, Special Collections, University of Virginia Library.

ten pesos to rent a "carriage to take a sick [member] of the nation to the village of Guanabacoa" located on the eastern side of Havana harbor.[107]
Tomás, the king of Carabalí Induri nation, recorded the cabildo giving four
pesos to "Matías Billalta, who was sick."[108] The cabildos also paid for burial
services that normally fell upon the lay brotherhoods of the Catholic
Church.[109] The cabildo Carabalí Oquella paid "eleven pesos for the burial
expenses of Rafaela Melcoleta" in 1804.[110] Loans, medical assistance during periods of illness, or a solemn burial brought the nation together by
pooling its members' limited financial and material resources.

Festivals, more than any other activity, united the nation. Almost all
cabildos held elaborate celebrations on January 6, the Day of the Kings. In
addition, on other religious holidays, Sundays, and to transfer power to a
new elected leader or commemorate the death of a past one, cabildos
hosted gatherings where they performed music and danced. During the
festival days of San Blas in Bayamo in early February, all the cabildos of the

city held gatherings and parades.[111] According to British traveler Robert Jameson, cabildo performances on Sunday could be observed throughout the city of Havana. "At these courtly festivals (usually held every Sunday and feast day) numbers of free and enslaved negroes assemble to do homage with a sort of grave merriment that one would doubt whether it was done in ridicule or memory of their former condition. The gong-gong— (christianized by the name of diablito), cows-horns, and every kind of inharmonious instrument, are flourished on by a gasping band assisted by clapping of hands, howling and the striking of every sounding material within reach, while the whole assemblage dance with maniac eagerness till their strength fails."[112] Jameson's musical preferences caused him to describe the performances as nothing more than crudely fashioned instruments that revealed neither musical talent nor purpose. Perhaps colonial authorities held the same opinion and therefore saw nothing threatening in the collective gatherings.

The view of cabildos as Africans engaged in primitive, savage dances depended, of course, on who witnessed them. When a cabildo member from Bayamo was asked by colonial officials why he participated in the festivals, he told authorities that he had "entered for entertainment, food, and drink because he knows how to work hard and his land is well cultivated."[113] Juan José Moroto of the Lucumí nation, who "grew up in Philadelphia," explained his participation in cabildos as an opportunity to express a collective ethnic solidarity not permitted in North America. Moroto told colonial officials that he "had been raised in North America, where the blacks do not dance in cabildos and are not permitted to have dances, on the days of work they are working and on Sundays they are in the church praying."[114] To hold a dance, the capatáz had to notify the neighborhood military officer and purchase a license. In 1796 military commissioner Juan García fined the Carabalí Apapa nation eight pesos for "dancing in the cabildo" without a license.[115] Although cabildo festivals ultimately required approval from colonial authorities, they allowed Africans to identify themselves as members of an ethnic-based organization by performing rituals and customs they had brought across the Atlantic and transformed in Cuba.

Cabildo dances served to bring the members of the nation together to express a collective identity and solidarity and, at the same time, raise money for the nation. During festival days cabildos often opened their doors to nonmembers. For a small entrance fee, nonmembers of the

FIGURE 7.3: *Day of Kings Celebration in Havana, 1847. These celebrations among the* cablidos de nación *in Havana incorporated dancing and drumming, as in the case of the* batuques *in colonial Brazil (see Chapter 8). From* The Illustrated London News, *(AP4.I5). Reproduced courtesy of the Tracy W. McGregor Library, Special Collections, University of Virginia Library.*

cabildos could become spectators to the dances and ceremonies and pur-chase food and drink. Unfortunately, we do not have a list of the people who attended the cabildos' festivals. Nonetheless, we do know that the nations attracted a wide audience that included not only their own eth-nicity but also other Africans, people of African ancestry born in Cuba, and even curious white observers, according to European travelers.[116] Depending on the size of the festival, the cabildos could raise a substan-tial sum. In March 1808 the cabildo Lucumí Llane collected 57 pesos from entrance fees for a fiesta.[117] The cabildo Carabalí Osso raised 240 pesos over several religious holidays celebrated during Christmas in 1805.[118] The revenues derived from selling what amounted to tickets for cabildo performances helped fund the nation's other activities. Further, the attendance by members of different nations to cabildo houses during festival days provided the opportunity for the diverse African populations in Cuba to share the cultures they held in common. At the same time, the festivals also singled out what made the nations different from one another because of their place of origin.

Conclusion

Members of cabildos chose to join associations to define themselves in cooperation with others who shared a similar ethnicity. In this sense, the cabildos of Cuba show the importance of understanding that Africans in the Americas did not immediately or exclusively adopt a black racial identity. When Africans arrived in Cuba from the trans-Atlantic slave trade, they brought with them their own culture, identity, language, and history. While Europeans most commonly identified the diverse populations of West and Central Africa for convenience as "blacks," cabildos enabled Africans to fashion their own categories for defining themselves that emphasized their ethnicity and geographic provenance. Africans in Cuba participated in cabildos to channel their Old World cultural experiences into an institutional framework to improve their livelihood and identify with their African origins in the New World. Although racial notions of blackness and whiteness undoubtedly represent the most important legacy of slavery in the New World, it cannot be considered the single defining characteristic from the very beginning or even as late as the nineteenth century. The African population in Cuba defined itself, and became defined by others, by cultural, geographic, and linguistic criteria that tended to militate against a broad racial identity. The functions of cabildos did not concentrate exclusively on attacking racial inequalities, but the nations sought to remedy, in one way or another, the grossly unequal position of its members—a position that was common to all people of the African diaspora. By providing a network of alliances and an institutional structure for Africans in Cuba, cabildos helped their members survive in a society based upon racial oppression. Africans in Cuba could define themselves by simultaneously emphasizing both their Old World ethnic origins and their New World racial identity, revealing the strength—not the weakness colonial officials assumed and some present-day observers fear—of cultural diversity.[119]

APPENDIX

Frederika Bremer's Visit to the Cabildo Houses

In this selection Swedish writer Frederika Bremer provides us with a detailed description of her impressions of the Havana cabildo houses she visited in 1851 after spending a year in the United States. Travel accounts, like all sources, have their strengths and weaknesses, as well as biases and honest observations. While Bremer sought to exoticize and portray the cabildo houses as locations of savage dancing and pagan religious practices, her observations also provide key insights into the social and cultural world of Africans in Havana when read carefully. From her selection we learn that the cabildos were concentrated in one part of Havana outside the city walls, where they often controlled the streets on festival days. We are also provided a glimpse into the cabildos' hierarchical leadership structure of kings and queens as well as their fund-raising activities, as Bremer had to pay an entrance fee to attend a dance.

I was, in reality, going to tell you of a visit which I and my two American gentlemen had made to the *Cabildos de Negros*, or to the assemblies of the free negroes of the city. It was not possible for me to go alone. These two gentlemen offered to escort me, and Mr. C., who spoke Spanish like a native, undertook to obtain admission for us, although the free negroes, in general, do not admit of the whites in their society, nor are they by any means so patient or so much under restraint as in the United States.

As these clubs generally meet in the afternoons and evenings of the Sunday, we set off in the afternoon to the street in which the *cabildos* are situated, for they occupy a whole street near one of the toll-gates of the city. The whole street swarmed with negroes, some decked out with ribbons and bells, some dancing, others standing in groups here and there. There prevailed a wild but not rude sort of lawlessness, and on all hands, near and afar off, was heard the gay, measured beat of the African drum. Round the gates of the different halls were collected groups of white people, most of them evidently sailors, who were endeavoring to get sight of what was passing inside; but a couple of negroes, stationed at each with sticks in their hands, kept the entrance closed with good-tempered determination, and did not allow the doors to open beyond half way.

By some means, however, Mr. C. succeeded in getting his head within the door of the Luccomées' *Cabildo*, and then requested permission for *la Signora* to enter. Some negro heads peeped out, and when they saw my white bonnet and veil, and the flowers which I wore—for I adorn myself more with flowers here than in Sweden—they looked kind, and granted permission *per la Signora*, and the gentlemen also who accompanied her were allowed to enter; but the door was immediately closed to various others who wished to thrust in after us.

Chairs were offered to us not far from the door; we were presented to the queen and the king of the assembly, who made demonstrations of good-will, and we were then left to look about us in quiet.

The room was tolerably large, and might contain about one hundred persons. On the wall just opposite to us was painted a crown, and a throne with a canopy over it. There stood the seats of the king and queen. The customary dancing was going forward in front of this seat. One woman danced alone, under a canopy supported by four people. Her dancing must have given great delight—though it was not very different from that of the negro ladies which I have already described—for all kinds of handkerchiefs were hanging about her, and a hat, even, had been placed upon her head. The women danced on this occasion with each other, and the men with the men; some struck the doors and benches with sticks, others rattled gourds filled with stones, and the drums thundered with deafening power. They were apparently endeavoring to make as much noise as possible. While this was going on, a figure was seen advancing with a scarlet hat upon his head, and with a great number of glittering strings of beads round his neck, arms, and body, which was naked to the waist, from which hung scarlet skirts. This figure, before which the people parted to each side approached me, bowing all the time, and as he did so the whole upper portion of his body seemed to move in snake-like folds. Still making these serpentine movements, he stood before me with extended hands, I being not at all certain whether he was inviting me to dance, or what was the meaning of his apparently friendly grimaces, and his great, black, outstretched hands. At length he uttered, with

other words, *"per la bonita!"* and I comprehended that all his
bowings and bedizenment were intended as a compliment to
me, and I made my reply by shaking one of the black hands, and
placing within it a silver coin, after which we exchanged friendly
gestures, and my friend made a serpentine retreat, and began
to dance on his own account, receiving great applause from
the by-standers. A great number of negroes were sitting on the
benches, many of whose countenances were earnest, and
remarkably agreeable. The Luccomées have, in general,
beautiful oval countenances, good foreheads and noses,
well-formed mouths, and the most beautiful teeth. They look
less good-humored and gay than the other negro tribes, but
have evidently more character and intelligence. The nation is
regarded as rich, in consequence of the great prizes which it has
won in the lottery, and this wealth it is said to apply to a good
use—the purchasing the freedom of slaves of this tribe.

These cabildoes are governed, as I have already said, by
queens, one or two, who decide upon the amusements, give
tone to the society, and determine its extension. They possess
the right of electing a king, who manages the pecuniary affairs
of the society, and who has under him a secretary and master of
the ceremonies. The latter presented me with a small printed
card, which gave admission to the *"Gabildo de Señora Santa
Barbara de la nacion Lucumí Alagua."* [Here Bremer adds a
footnote: "The Luccommée nation, like other African tribes,
Gangas, Congoes, &c., are divided into many subordinate
tribes, with their various cognomens, and their various places
of meeting."]

After this, and when we had made a little offering to the
treasury of the society, we took our departure, in order to visit
other cabildoes. And in all cases they were so polite as to give
free access to *la Signora, la bonita,* and her companions. I do
not know whether this politeness is to be attributed to the
negro character, or to the Spanish influence upon it, but am
inclined to believe the latter.

I was received in the *Cabildo de Gangas* by the two queens,
two young and very pretty black girls, dressed in perfectly
good French taste, in pink gauze dresses, and beautiful bouquets

of artificial roses in their bosoms and their hair: they both
smoked cigarettes. They took me kindly each by the hand,
seated me between them and continued to smoke with Spanish
gravity. One of them had the very loveliest eyes imaginable,
both in form and expression. On the wall opposite to us was
a large and well-painted leopard, probably the symbol of the
nation. There were also some Catholic pictures and symbols
in the hall. I here saw a whole group of women moving in a
kind of dance, like galvanized frogs, but with slower action,
bowing and twisting their bodies and all their joints without
any meaning or purpose that I could discover. It seemed to
be the expression of some kind of animal satisfaction; it had
also the appearance as if they were seeking for something
in the dark. And the poor benighted people may be said to
be still seeking—their true life's joy, their life beyond that
of Nature.

They seem, however, to have approached nearer to this
in the States of North America. I thought of that nocturnal
camp-meeting in the forest, by the light of the fire-altars,
and of the melodious hymns which sounded from the camp
of the negroes!

I saw in another *Cabildo de Gangas* that same irregular,
serpentine dance, danced in circles and rows both by men and
women around one another. I saw again, also, in a *Cabildo de
Congos*, the Congo dance, as I had seen it in the bohea at
St. Amelia, and another which seemed to be a mixture of
the Spanish-Creole dance, Yuca and Congo dance. There is
considerably more animation in the latter dances than in the
former, as well as more art and poetical feeling. The symbol
painted upon the wall of this room was a sun with a human face.
Here also were several Christian symbols and pictures. But even
here, also, the Christianized and truly Christian Africans retain
somewhat of the superstition and idolatry of their native land.
The Congo and Ganga nations seem to me born of a more
careless temperament, and have a more animal appearance
than the Luccomées.

I visited two other cabildoes, but did not find any new
features of interest, and, finally, I was heartily wearied by the

noise, and the rattling, and the bustle, and the dust, and the
chaotic disorder in the dancing, and in the movements of their
assemblies. I longed for pure air and clear water, and, to gratify
my longing, Mr. F. drove me in his volante to Havana harbor.

Frederika Bremer, *The Homes of the New World: Impressions of America*,
trans. Mary Howitt (New York: Harper & Brothers, 1853), 2:379–83.

NOTES

The author gratefully acknowledges the critical comments of Joe
Richardson, Joan Casanovas, Albrecht Koschnik, Sally Hadden, Robinson
Herrera, C. Peter Ripley, and Magdalena Chocano, who participated
in the Florida State University History Department Works in Progress
Seminar, February 2002, and Roseanne Adderley and the audience at the
Southwestern Historical Association Annual Meeting, New Orleans,
March 2002. Financial support from the Conference on Latin American
History, the Southwest Council of Latin American Studies, the Institute
of Latin American Studies at the University of Texas at Austin, the Ford
Foundation, the Johns Hopkins University, the Fulbright-Hays Program,
and the Social Science Research Council generously funded research in
Cuba and Spain.

1. "La nación mina guagni contra Salvador Ternero sobre cuentas"
(1794–97), Archivo Nacional de Cuba, Havana, fondo Escribanía
Antonio Daumy (hereafter ANC-ED), file 893, no. 4; I have relied on
the following sources for identifying African ethnicity: Benjamin Nuñez,
Dictionary of Afro-Latin American Civilization (Westport, CT: Greenwood
Press, 1980); John Thornton, *Africa and Africans in the Making of the
Atlantic World, 1400–1800*, 2nd ed. (Cambridge: Cambridge University
Press, 1998), x–xxvi; Philip D. Curtin, *The Atlantic Slave Trade: A Census*
(Madison: University of Wisconsin Press, 1969), esp. 291–98; Jorge
Castellanos and Isabel Castellanos, *Cultura afrocubana: El negro en Cuba,
1492–1844* (Miami: Ediciones Universal, 1988), 1:28–43; idem, "The
Geographic, Ethnologic, and Linguistic Roots of Cuban Blacks,"
Cuban Studies 17 (1987): 95–110; Fernando Ortiz, *Los negros brujos*
(Havana: Editorial de Ciencias Sociales, 1995; orig. pub. 1906), 22–26;
idem, *Los negros esclavos* (Havana: Editorial de Ciencias Sociales, 1975;

orig. pub. 1916), 40–59; Pedro Deschamps Chapeaux, *El negro en la economía habanera del siglo XIX* (Havana: Unión de Escritores y Artistas de Cuba, 1971), 31–46; idem, "Cabildos: Solo para esclavos," *Cuba 7*, no. 69 (1968): 50–51; idem, *Los cimarrones urbanos* (Havana: Editorial de Ciencias Sociales, 1983), 42–47; George Reid Andrews, *The Afro-Argentines of Buenos Aires, 1800–1900* (Madison: University of Wisconsin Press, 1980), 233–34; Frederick P. Bowser, *The African Slave in Colonial Peru, 1524–1650* (Stanford: Stanford University Press, 1974), 346.

2. Throughout this chapter I use the term *nation* as it was used in the Afro-Atlantic world of the fifteenth through the mid-nineteenth centuries, to refer to African ethnicity and not the modern political definition of "nation," linked to the formation of nation-states in the nineteenth and twentieth centuries. For a discussion of the terms *nation* and *ethnicity* as they apply to identity in the early modern world and the African diaspora in particular, see David Eltis, *The Rise of African Slavery in the Americas* (Cambridge: Cambridge University Press, 2000), 244–57; Michael A. Gomez, *Exchanging our Country Marks: The Transformation of African Identities in the Colonial and Antebellum South* (Chapel Hill: University of North Carolina Press, 1998), 2–8; idem, "African Identity and Slavery in the Americas," *Radical History Review* 75 (1999): 111–20; Robin Law, "Ethnicity and the Slave Trade: 'Lucumí' and 'Nago' as Ethnonyms in West Africa," *History in Africa* 24, (1997): 205–19; Paul E. Lovejoy, "Identifying Enslaved Africans in the African Diaspora," in *Identity in the Shadow of Slavery*, ed. Paul E. Lovejoy (London: Continuum, 2000), 1–29; John Thornton, "The Coromantees: An African Cultural Group in Colonial North America and the Caribbean," *Journal of Caribbean History* 32, nos. 1–2 (1998): 161–78; idem, *Africa and Africans*, 183–205. For the ongoing incorrect use of the term *tribe* for African ethnicity and nationhood as part of the pro-colonialist ideology, see Joseph C. Miller, "History and Africa/Africa and History," *American Historical Review* 104, no. 1 (1999): 14–16.

3. Historian Philip A. Howard states the societies were "known as cabildos de naciones de afrocubanos." *Changing History: Afro-Cuban Cabildos and the Societies of Color in the Nineteenth Century* (Baton Rouge: Louisiana State University Press, 1998), xiv. I found the societies described as "cabildos de nación" only in documents from the 1750s to 1830s.

4. Mina Guagni to Capitán General, Havana, April 29, 1794, "La nación mina guagni contra Salvador Ternero sobre que de cuentas del producido del cabildo de la misma nación" (1794) ANC, fondo Escribanía Ortega, (hereafter ANC-EO), file 65, no. 11, fols. 1–1v.

5. "La nación mina contra Juana de Mesa" (1797), ANC-ED, file 673, no. 9.

6. "La nación mina guagni contra Salvador Ternero sobre cuentas" (1794–97), ANC-ED, file 893, no. 4, fol. ? (It is not possible to cite the specific folios of many pages of this document and others in the fondo Escribanía because the pagination has been destroyed by deterioration.)

7. Francisco Ferrer to Capitán General, Havana, January 24, 1794, ANC-EO, file 65, no. 11, fol. 5.

8. Salvador Ternero to Capitán General, Havana, June 4, 1794, ANC-EO, file 65, no. 11, fol. 40.

9. Ibid., fols. 65v, 123v.

10. ANC-ED, file 893, no. 4 , fols. 143–44 (parentheses in original).

11. Ibid., fol. 51v.

12. Ibid., fols. 52–53.

13. Ibid., fol. ?

14. Ibid., fol. ?

15. Robert Francis Jameson, *Letters from the Havana during the Year 1820; Containing an Account of the Present State of the Island of Cuba and Observations on the Slave Trade* (London: John Miller, 1821), 21.

16. See most recently Gomez, "African Identity and Slavery in the Americas," 119; Thornton, "The Coromantees," 161. "Glitters of truth" is from Gomez, *Exchanging our Country Marks*, 33.

17. Eltis, *The Rise of African Slavery*, 244.

18. Ruth Pike, "Sevillan Society in the Sixteenth Century: Slaves and Freedmen," *Hispanic American Historical Review* 47, no. 3 (1967): 344–46.

19. Bowser, *The African Slave in Colonial Peru*, 249–50, 339.

20. Leslie B. Rout, Jr., *The African Experience in Spanish America, 1502 to the Present Day* (Cambridge: Cambridge University Press, 1976), 136.

21. See the numerous petitions in *Indice del Archivo del Departamento General de Policía desde el año de 1812* (Buenos Aires: Imprenta del Gobierno, 1858–60); and for a broader discussion see Andrews, *Afro-Argentines of Buenos Aires*, 142–51.

22. Fernando Ortiz, *Los cabildos y la fiesta afrocubanos del Día de Reyes* (Havana: Editorial de Ciencias Sociales, 1992; orig. pub. 1921), 6; Carmen Victoria Montejo-Arrechea, *Sociedades de instrucción y recreo de pardos y morenos que existieron en Cuba colonial* (Veracruz: Instituto Veracruzano de Cultura, 1993), 14–16.

23. Jane Landers, *Black Society in Spanish Florida* (Urbana: University of Illinois Press, 1999), 109.

24. "El Obispo Morell de Santa Cruz oficializa los cabildos africanos donde nació la santería, convirtiéndolos en ermitas," Havana, December 6, 1755, in Levi Marrero, *Cuba: Economía y sociedad, del monopolio hacia la libertad comercial (1701–1763)* (Madrid: Editorial Playor, 1980), 8:159–60.

25. See Landers, *Black Society,* 108–10 for the overlapping functions of brotherhoods and cabildos in Cuba.

26. Antonio Bachiller y Morales, *Los negros* (Barcelona: Gorgas y compañía, 1887), 114–15; Ortiz, *Los cabildos,* 4–6; Montejo-Arrechea, *Sociedades,* 12–13; Pedro Deschamps-Chapeaux, "Cabildos: Solo par esclavos," *Cuba* 7, no. 69 (1968): 51; idem, "Sociedades: La integración de pardos y morenos," *Cuba* 7, no. 71 (1968): 54; Howard, *Changing History,* 21–25.

27. At the port of Old Calabar and surrounding regions in the Bight of Biafra, an all-male secret society known as Ekpe formed as early as the second half of the seventeenth century. Identified with the leopard, Ekpe members paid dues assessed by their rank in the organization. According to historians Paul Lovejoy and David Richardson, Ekpe society created an "interlocking grid of secret associations [that] served to regulate the behavior of members." "Trust, Pawnship, and Atlantic History: The Institutional Foundations of the Old Calabar Slave Trade," *American Historical Review* 104, no. 2 (1999): 347–49. The secret organization crossed the Atlantic and resurfaced in nineteenth-century Cuba in an altered form in the Abakuá society. Lovejoy, "Identifying Enslaved Africans," 8; Howard, *Changing History,* 48, 53, 68–69, 109–10. The classic treatment of the Abakuá in Cuba remains Lydia Cabrera, *La sociedad secreta de Abakuá, narrada por viejos adeptos* (Havana: Ediciones, C. R., 1959).

28. In the Yoruba Kingdom of Oyo a semisecret organization known as the Ogboni Society advised the king on religious and political matters. Scholars disagree about the founding date of the Ogboni Society and the extent of its influence. However, it is likely that because the war-torn region of Yorubaland funneled thousands of Africans to Cuba in the nineteenth century some knowledge of the organization crossed the Atlantic and influenced the cabildos. Peter Morton-Williams, "The Yoruba Ogboni Cult in Oyo," *Africa* 30 (1960): 362–74; J. A. Atanda, "The Yoruba Ogboni Cult: Did It Exist in Old Oyo?" *Journal of the Historical Society of Nigeria* 6, no. 4 (1973): 365–72; Robin Law, *The Oyo Empire, c. 1600–c. 1836: A West African Imperialism in the Era of the Atlantic Slave Trade* (Oxford: Clarendon Press, 1977), 61.

29. The 1789 Real Cédula declaring free trade in slaves can be found in Archivo General de Indias, Seville, fondo Indiferente General (hereafter AGI-IG), file 2823.

30. Francisco Arango y Parreño, "Representación manifestado las ventajas de una absoluta libertad en la introducción de negros y solicitando se amplíe a ocho la prórroga concedida por dos años," in *Obras* (Havana: Dirección de Cultura, Ministerio de Educación, 1952), 1:98.

31. Las Casas to Pedro Herrera, Havana, May 2, 1791, AGI-IG; "Comunicaciones, oficios, etc. del superintendente de la Isla, al intendente de ejercito y Rl. Hacienda de la provincia para que este envié a las subdelegaciones con puertos Rl. cédula de 20 de Abril de 1804, donde se manda ampliar el comercio de Negros Bozales," Archivo Histórico Provincial de Camagüey, fondo Intendencia de Ejercito y Real Hacienda de la Provincia de Puerto Príncipe (hereafter AHPC-IERH), file 1, no. 5, fols. 1–5; Biblioteca Nacional José Martí, colección Vidal Morales y Morales (hereafter BNJM-Morales), vol. 79, no. 181; David R. Murray, *Odious Commerce: Britain, Spain and the Abolition of the Cuban Slave Trade* (Cambridge: Cambridge University Press, 1980), 11–13.

32. Gloria García, "Importación de esclavos de ambos sexos por varios puertos de Cuba, 1763–1820," in *Historia de Cuba: La colonia, evolución socioeconómica y formación nacional de los origines hasta 1867*, ed. María del Carmen Barcia, Gloria García, and Eduardo Torres-Cuevas (Havana: Editorial Política, 1994), 471–73, table 11; Juan Pérez de la Riva, *El monto de la inmigración forzada en el siglo xix* (Havana: Editorial de Ciencias Sociales, 1979), table 3; David Eltis, *Economic Growth and the Ending of the Transatlantic Slave Trade* (Oxford: Oxford University Press, 1987), 245.

33. Murray, *Odious Commerce*, 19.

34. Bishop of Cuba to His Majesty, Havana, December 6, 1753, Archivo General de Indias, Seville, fondo Audiencia de Santo Domingo (hereafter AGI-SD), file 515, no. 51, also see Fernando Ortiz, *Los negros curros* (Havana: Editorial de Ciencias Sociales, 1986), 212–13.

35. Estimate derived from documentation found in: ANC-EC, file 6, no. 6, file 47, no. 1; ANC-ED, file 336, no. 1, file 398, no. 23, file 439, no. 16, file 548, no. 11, file 583, no. 5, file 610, no. 15, file 660, no. 8, file 673, no. 9, file 893, no. 4; ANC-Escribanía de Gobierno (hereafter ANC-EG), file 28, no. 4, file 123, no. 15, file 123, no. 15-A, file 125, no. 3, file 277, no. 5; ANC-EO, file 3, no. 8, file 6, no. 1, file 65, no. 11, file 494, no. 2; ANC-Escribanía de Valerio (hereafter ANC-EVal), file 671, no. 9873; ANC-Escribanía de Varios (hereafter ANC-EVar), file 211, no. 3114;

ANC, fondo Asuntos Políticos (hereafter ANC-AP), file 11, no. 37; file 12, nos. 9, 14, 17, 27, file 13, no. 1, file 14, no. 1; ANC-Donativos y Remisiones (hereafter ANC-DR), file 542, no. 29; Archivo General de Indias, Seville, fondo Papeles de Cuba (hereafter AGI-PC), file 1433-B, and 1667.

36. Thorton, *Africa and Africans*, 190.

37. ANC-EC, file 147, no. 1, fol. 53v.

38. Ibid., fol. 82.

39. "Pedro José Santa Cruz solicitando nombramiento de Capatáz al Cabildo de la nación Congos Musolongos" (1806), ANC-ED, file 660, no. 8, fols. 1–4.

40. "La nación Caravalí Umugini sobre división con la Osso y con la misma Umugini, y liquidación de cuentas con el capitán Pedro Nolasco Eligió" (1805–6), ANC-EG, file 123, no. 15-A, fol. 9.

41. "Autos criminales obrados en razón de la insurrección que contra los blancos tenían proyectada en Bayamo los negros vosales" (February 8, 1812), ANC-AP, leg, 12, no. 9, fol. 9v.

42. Ibid., fol. 22v.

43. Ibid., fol. 30v.

44. "Expediente seguido por Cristóbal Govín, capatáz de la nación Oquella contra Lázaro Rodríguez, capatáz del la Agro, sobre cuentas" (1799), ANC-EO, file 6, no. 1, fol. 62.

45. ANC-AP, file 12, no. 9, fol. 23v.

46. Francisco Alonzo de Morazan to Someruelos, Havana, June 28, 1811, AGI-PC, file 1667.

47. ANC-AP, file 12, no. 9, fols. 86–87.

48. "Cabildo musolongo sobre nombramientos de capatáz" (1806), ANC-ED, file 548, no. 11, fols. 15v–16.

49. ANC-ED, file 893, no. 4, fol. ?

50. ANC-AP, file 12, no. 14, fol. 12.

51. "Incidente a los autos sobre la conspiración de José Antonio Aponte contra José Herrera y otros por complicidad en aquella" (March 19, 1812), ANC-AP, file 14, no. 1, fols. 182v–83v. According to contemporary J. M. Pérez, the minuet was the most popular dance in 1800. "Siglo XIX: Costumbres de Cuba en 1800 por J. M. Pérez," AOHCH, fondo José Luciano Franco (hereafter AOHCH-JLF), file 214, no. 31.

52. ANC-ED, file 893, no. 4, fol. ?

53. ANC-AP, file 12, no. 9, fol. 109.

54. ANC-ED, file 893, no. 4, fol. 46; "La nación Caravalí Induri sobre nombramiento de capatáz del cavildo del Santo Cristo de Buen Viaje" (1802–6), ANC-EG, file 125, no. 3, fol. ?; ANC-EO, file 65, no. 11, fol. 72.

55. Deschamps-Chapeaux, *El negro en la economía habanera*,. 47–86; also see Rafael Duharte, *El negro en la sociedad colonial* (Santiago: Editorial Oriente, 1988), 91–115.

56. "Juan Nepomuceno Montiel y Rafael Aróstegui como apoderados en la nación Lucumí Llane contra Agustina Zaraza y Antonio Ribero sobre la extracción de pesos que hicieron de la caja de la nación" (1807–10), ANC-EC, file 64, no. 6, fols. 13–15.

57. ANC-EO, file 6, no. 1, fol. 59.

58. ANC-ED, file 893, no. 4, fol. ?

59. Eugene D. Genovese adeptly describes how certain privileges bestowed on slaves such as garden plots and holidays became transformed into rights: *Roll, Jordan, Roll: The World the Slaves Made* (New York: Vintage, 1974), 30–31, 314–15, 535–85, esp. 539, 569, 575. Emília Viotti da Costa explores the battle between master-awarded privileges and slaves' rights within the context of an extensive slave revolt: *Crowns of Glory, Tears of Blood: The Demerara Slave Rebellion of 1823* (New York: Oxford University Press, 1994), 84–85.

60. ANC-EG, file 123, no. 15-A, fol. 21.

61. Howard, *Changing History*, 48.

62. "José Antonio Diepa, capatáz del cabildo nación Congo, sobre que se recojía los memoriales que promovió Cayetano García y socios para despojarlo del encargo de capatáz del cabildo nación Congo Macamba" (1808–9), ANC-ED, file 439, no. 16, fol. 51v.

63. ANC-AP, file 12, no. 9, fols. 68v–69v.

64. Ibid., fols. 13, 44v.

65. ANC-EG, file 125, no. 3, fols. 106–15.

66. Ibid., fol. 115.

67. "José Xavier Mirabal y consortes contra Domingo Acosta y socios sobre pesos, trata del cabildo de Apapa" (1808–30), ANC-ED, file 583, no. 5, fols. 82–v (emphasis in original).

68. ANC-EC, file 147, no. 1, fol. 54v.

69. "Tomás Poveda, Clemente Andrade, Antonio de Prucia, Joaquin de Soto y Antonio María Lisundia contra el moreno José Aróstegui sobre que cuentas de caja del cavildo" (1805), ANC-ED, file 336, no. 1, fol. 40.

70. ANC-EO, file 6, no. 1, fol. 6ov.

71. Thornton, *Africa and Africans*, 199.

72. "Expediente relativo a la renovación de cargos de un cabildo de nación ante las autoridades en la ciudad de Matanzas" ANC-DR, file 542, no. 29, fol. 1; some of the documentation for the Matanzas Carabalí cabildo is published in "Constitución de un cabildo Carabalí en 1814," *Archivos del folklore cubano* 1, no. 3 (1925): 281–83.

73. ANC-AP, file 12, no. 9, fols. 45, 68v, 73.

74. Ibid., fol. 36v; ANC-AP, file 13, no. 1, fol. 101.

75. ANC-EG, file 125, no. 3, fols. 115–v.

76. Archivo Histórico de la Provincia de Granma, Bayamo, fondo Protocolos, (hereafter AHPG-Protocolos), file 11, book 1 (1810), fol. 116v.

77. ANC-ED, file 583, no. 5, fol. 24.

78. ANC-EO, file 65, no. 11, fol. 55.

79. ANC-EC, file 147, no. 1, fol. 41; also see Howard for the link between militia soldiers and cabildo activities, *Changing History*, 31–36.

80. Kimberly S. Hanger observed that in New Orleans the town council often rejected petitions by blacks to hold dances, "but when the free black militia, represented by four officers, submitted its request in 1800" authorities approved it. *Bounded Lives, Bounded Places, Free Black Society in Colonial New Orleans, 1769–1803* (Durham: Duke University Press, 1997), 132.

81. "Expediente seguido por los de la nación Caravalí Oquella sobre nombramiento de segundo y tercero capataces" (1804), ANC-EV, file 211, no. 3114, fols. 9v–12.

82. ANC-ED, file 439, no. 16, fol. ?

83. ANC-EG, file 125, no. 3, fol. 108v.

84. Ibid., fol. 115.

85. ANC-EO, leg, 6, no. 1, fol. 6ov–61.

86. ANC-ED, file 336, no. 1, fol. ?

87. ANC-ED, file 439, no. 16, fol. ?

88. See, for example, *Diario de la Habana*, February 3, 1812, 3, Biblioteca Nacional José Martí, Havana.

89. ANC-ED, file 336, no. 1, fol. 38v.

90. "Expediente de cuentas que produce Tomás Betancourt de las cantidades que han entrado en su poder del cavildo Caravalí Oquella" (1804), ANC-EO, file 3, no. 8, fol. 7v.

91. Ibid., fol. 6v; ANC-EO, file 6, no. 1, fol. 8v; for the Spanish coffer, see Amy Bushnell, *The King's Coffer: Proprietors of the Spanish Florida Treasury, 1565–1702* (Gainesville: University Presses of Florida, 1981), 1, 36, 45.

92. ANC-ED, file 398, no. 23, fol. 3.

93. ANC-ED, file 439, no. 16, fol. ?

94. ANC-ED, file 336, no. 1, fol. 5.

95. ANC-EO, file 6, no. 1, fol. 33v.

96. ANC-ED, file 398, no. 23, fol. 3.

97. ANC-ED, file 439, no. 16, fol. ?

98. ANC-EO, file 6, no. 1, fol. 33.

99. ANC-EO, file 6, no. 1, fol. 30v.

100. Howard, *Changing History*, 40–42.

101. ANC-ED, file 660, no. 8, fol. 4.

102. ANC-ED, file 583, no. 5, fol. 100.

103. "Sobre la conspiración intentada por los negros esclavos para invadir la villa a resultas de la libertad que suponen estarles declaradas por las Cortes Generales y estraordinarias del Retno de Puerto Príncipe," (January 1812), ANC-AP, file 11, no. 37, fol. 58.

104. ANC-ED, file 398, no. 23, fol. 1; ANC-EO, file 6, no. 1, fol. 1v.

105. ANC-EO, file 3, no. 8, fol. 3v; ANC-EC, file 64, no. 6, fol. 60; ANC-ED, file 439, no. 16, fol. 51v.

106. ANC-EG, file 123, no. 15A, fol. 6.

107. ANC-ED, file 336, no. 1, fol. 22v.

108. ANC-EG, file 125, no. 3, fol. 167.

109. ANC-ED, file 336, no. 1, fol. 22; ANC-ED, file 610, no. 15, fol. 2.

110. ANC-EO, file 3, no. 8, fol. 7.

111. ANC-AP, file 12, no. 9, fols. 68v–69.

112. Jameson, *Letters from the Havana*, 21–22.

113. ANC-AP, file 12, no. 9, fol. 23.

114. ANC, fondo Comisión Militar, file 11, no. 1, fols. 456v–58. I would like to thank Gloria García for directing me to this source.

115. ANC-ED, file 893, no. 5, fols. 51–v.

116. Jameson, *Letters from the Havana*, 21–22; Frederika Bremmer, *The Homes of the New World: Impressions of America*, trans. Mary Howitt (New York: Johnson Reprint, 1968; orig. pub. 1853), 2:379–83.

117. ANC-EC, file 64, no. 6, fol. 60.

118. "Tomás Povea, capatáz de los cabildos Carabalí Osso solicitando nombramiento de otra capatáz" (1806), ANC-ED, file 610, no. 15, fol. 2.

119. Howard identifies the same process whereby "members of these organizations manifested a 'consciousness of kind': an identity that mitigated, to a certain degree, differences of language, ethnicity, and customs, an identity that allowed them to discern the common problems all people of color confronted on a daily basis." *Changing History*, xvii.

CHAPTER EIGHT

Cantos and Quilombos
A Hausa Rebellion in Bahia, 1814

STUART B. SCHWARTZ

❧ SLAVE RESISTANCE IN BRAZIL HAS USUALLY BEEN DIVIDED BY HISTORIANS into two parallel but somewhat distinct categories. The first is *marronage*, or running away, and by extension, the formation of runway communities, or *quilombos*. This was a process that was almost continual throughout the history of Brazilian slavery. The second category is rebellion and the far less frequent large slave revolts, usually urban in nature, and especially those that occurred in Bahia in the early nineteenth century. While other aspects of resistance have received some attention as well, these two phenomena, quilombos and revolts, have dominated discussions of slave resistance but usually as distinct activities, as two different strategies for confronting the slave regime. In this chapter I want to reexamine those two aspects of slave resistance at the moment of the Atlantic Revolutions of the late eighteenth and nineteenth centuries, and to examine a case in which they were not simply two variant responses to the oppression of slavery but mutually supporting tactics in the slaves' war against slavery. My emphasis here will be not on what masters thought or did, but what moved the slaves and what may have lay behind their actions.

247

In this study I wish to begin that reexamination by analyzing a previously unknown judicial investigation of a revolt planned by Hausa slaves
in 1814 but betrayed to the authorities and thus stillborn.[1] The organization and plans of this revolt revealed by the judicial inquiry underline a
number of themes common to these Bahian slave risings: the ways in
which urban and rural slaves cooperated and coordinated their actions,
the role of "ethnic identities" and their meaning in a colonial context, the
adherence and participation of nonslaves in these movements, and finally
the role that marronage and quilombos could play in linking and mobilizing the potential sources of slave rebellion.

In the long history of resistance against Brazilian slavery there was,
in fact, nothing quite like the series of revolts and conspiracies that rocked
the city of Salvador and its surrounding agricultural zones between 1806
and 1835. This was a turbulent period, characterized in Brazil by barrack
revolts, the end of colonial rule, independence, a royal abdication, and
general political unrest and instability, intensified by the slave rebellions,
which were themselves a product of those general conditions. The Bahian
slave revolts were usually organized and carried out along ethnic lines, but
sometimes participation and leadership crossed these somewhat artificial
cultural boundaries. They occasionally united in common action slaves
and freedmen and -women. The slave revolts of nineteenth-century Bahia
constituted a series of campaigns or battles in a long war against slavery
or, as one slave called it, a Blacks' War (*uma guerra dos pretos*). The relationship between this war and the tradition of marronage and quilombos
needs to be explored. The Hausa risings of 1814 provide an opportunity
to begin that process.

The Bahian slave rebellions have been explained by a variety of interpretations: religious, structural, political, conjunctural, and ethnic. The fact
that some of the rebellions, like the largest of them, the Malê rebellion
of 1835, had a strong Islamic orientation led to a religious explanation,
but other authors have pointed out that not all the rebels were Muslims
nor were their goals particularly religious. Some authors have argued that
the timing of the rebellions in terms of the broad "Atlantic Revolutions"
(1776–1840) and in relation to the political unrest associated with Brazilian
independence (1822) was in no way accidental and that the rebellions must
be seen in that light.[2] At the same time, the strongly ethnic character of
many of the revolts, organized as they were by various African peoples, the
lack of large-scale participation in them by Brazilian-born blacks (*crioulos*)

and mulattos, and the divisions of color, status, and origin within the Afro-Brazilian communities argue against a unifying theme of ideological Jacobinism among the slaves. That kind of more inclusive political thinking and the example of France seems to have been more important in the republican political movements of the period that involved the free people of color, and even the Haitian example had more impact on them and on the slave owners than it did as a motive for the slaves themselves.

Contexts

The captaincy of Bahia had long been a major terminus of the slave trade, but changes in the Atlantic economy, especially the Haitian revolution of 1792, had created new conditions for the expansion of slavery. In the early nineteenth century about eight thousand to ten thousand Africans a year were arriving at the docks of Salvador. Between two-thirds and three-fourths of these Africans came from the Bight of Benin or what the Portuguese called the Mina Coast. In 1806, for example, 8,037 Minas disembarked in Bahia compared to 2,588 slaves from Angola and Benguela.[3] Bahia had a long tradition of direct trade with that part of the African coast, and many slave owners had developed a preference for workers from this region.[4]

The elimination of Haiti as a sugar producer after the rebellion of 1791 had stimulated the expansion of sugar production in Brazil, and traditional plantation areas like Bahia boomed with the creation of new market opportunities. This expansion was accompanied by an increase in slave imports to meet the needs of plantation labor, and it also resulted in a swelling of the urban slave population in Salvador, the port city, the capital of the captaincy, and the administrative hub of Portuguese government in the region.

By the first decade of the nineteenth century, the captaincy as a whole had a population of over four hundred thousand, of which about one-third were slaves. The city of Salvador had a population of over fifty thousand, about half of them black, another 22 percent *pardos*, and only about a quarter of the population were whites. Slaves made up perhaps 40 percent of the city's population.[5] What distinguished the slave population of Salvador and of the captaincy in general (and most of Brazil as well) and often provoked the comments of foreign observers was the African origins of the majority of the slaves. In this period in Bahia, Africans probably made up 60 percent of the slave population. As the population became increasingly African, it became more imbalanced in terms of sex and age as well because of the imbalanced sex ratio in the trade. By the early nineteenth century, the African-born probably made up about two-thirds of Salvador's slaves. The chances for Bahian male slaves to find a mate and form a family were probably worse in this period than they had been since the sixteenth century. Finally, the age structure of the slave population favored young adults, who made up about 60 percent of the city's slave force.[6] Here was a slave population that was predominantly composed of young, African males, and in the early nineteenth century, increasingly so. Little wonder the growing preoccupation of the slave owners, surrounded by a rising sea of foreign, African-born slaves whose gatherings, drumming, and dances had turned parts of the city into something similar to the "backlands of the Mina Coast."[7] Little wonder, too, the rising tide of slave restiveness and ethnic solidarities within the complex structure of Bahian slave society and the context of traditional resistence.[8]

The normal insecurity of slave society had intensified by the turn of the century. Runaways and bandits made the roads insecure. Manoel de Araújo e Góes, who lived at Engenho Camorogi, some fifteen miles from the town of Santo Amaro in the heart of the sugar country, complained that in the woods on his daily trips to his *engenho* (sugar mill plantation) Santa Anna de Pojuca he was in constant dànger from brigands or "even from his own slaves."[9] He petitioned for the right to bear a brace of pistols. Going about unarmed in the countryside had become dangerous.

These concerns were not unfounded. Maroons were a common problem. Sometimes newly arrived Africans took the first opportunity to flee, joining others who were fed up with what the French consul called the "intolerable despotism" of the slave owners.[10] Fugitive communities dotted the countryside and served as a beacon and refuge for plantation slaves. The interrelationship of the plantations and quilombos and the nature of the threat is made clear in the career profile of Severino Pereira, "captain major of expeditions and assaults of the district of San José de Itapororocas, chief of the effective militia for the control [*reducção*] of escaped slaves and those fortified in quilombos or hideouts"—in other words, a slave catcher. Pereira listed among his services to the "internal security of the people and the dominion of masters over slaves and wrongdoers" various activities revealing of the nature of slave resistance.[11] In 1789 he had attacked a fugitive community made up of slaves who had fled the plantation of Bento Simões de Brito and joined a quilombo in the

Matas de Águas Verdes. In 1791 he had been wounded twice in an attack on a quilombo in the vicinity of Matas do Concavo on the Jacuípe River. His main service had been to lead an expedition of two hundred men against the quilombos of Orobó and Andrahy, which had been, in his words, "committing robbery, murder, sacking houses, stealing cattle, devastating farms, holding up travelers on the roads, inducing other slaves [to escape] and taking them by force for their reproachable purposes."[12] He was particularly proud of his actions against these "enemies of the State of Your Magesty," who had built a strongly fortified position protected by a network of subterranean pits, traps, and stakes—in other words, a strongly fortified permanent settlement.[13] These "services" were typical of the slave hunters of the period.[14] Each district maintained these bush captains (*capitães do mato*), who not only pursued individual runaways but also mobilized posses or militia units to attack fugitive settlements.

While such quilombo activity had been endemic in Bahia since the beginnings of African slavery, governmental concern with them had intensified in the late eighteenth century, especially with the growing number of Africans brought in the post-Haitian revolt agricultural expansion in the captaincy. After 1807, with the tide of revolts, the problem—or at least the fear—became more accute. Many of these quilombos were not far from the centers of population, the towns and plantations, and their members lived by raiding or trading with the nearby populations. By the early nineteenth century, these suburban quilombos in Cabula, Matatu, or Itapoam on the outskirts of Salvador were increasingly integrated into the life of urban slavery, perhaps even serving at times as places of temporary escape for *petite marronage*, centers for the relief and rest for urban slaves.[15] Fugitives from quilombos sometimes entered the city to "fence" their goods, and the relative isolation of the quilombos offered opportunities for Africans to maintain a certain cultural autonomy away from the civil and religious constraints of the dominant society, which suppressed the practice of African religions.[16] The quilombo of Urubu, destroyed in 1826, housed a *candomblé* (African religious cult).[17] The turnover of residents in these suburban quilombos may have been high, but while the settlements themselves were subject to police raids or military attacks, some were able to last for years. Almost invariably after a quilombo's destruction, some of the fugitives would avoid capture and set up a new quilombo, soon joined by new runaways in a dialectic of slave resistance. The formation of quilombos was a chronic problem for Bahian slave owners and a constant tactic of Bahian slaves.

The Hausas among the "Nations"

By the beginning of the nineteenth century the slave population of the captaincy and the city had swelled. Large numbers of Mina slaves were arriving, particularly those groups or "nations" that were called in Bahia Nagô (Yoruba), Gege (Aja-Fon), and Ussá or Aussá (Hausa).[18] To some extent these ethnic designations were colonial creations because they did not recognize African political or religious divisions. Thus Nagôs might all speak Yoruba, but they came from different and often hostile polities. The same could be said of the Dahomeans, called in Bahia Geges.[19] The formation of new identities and "imagined communities" according to these colonial labels was a complex and incomplete process.[20]

The Hausas were also divided by regional origins and by religious differences. The process of Islamization in Hausaland had been violent and incomplete and continued in Bahia as converts continued to be made.[21] Hausas were not the most numerous group in Bahia, and in the city of Salvador itself they constituted only about 6 percent of the slave population, but they had begun to enter the captaincy in some numbers with the other peoples from the Bight of Benin after 1780, and increasingly after the Torodbe Fulani Shehu Usumanu Dan Fodio initiated a jihad in Hausaland in 1804 that resulted in the creation of large areas under Fulani control, and eventually the formation of the Sokoto caliphate. The fighting lasted six years and produced large numbers of defeated captives, Muslims and non-Muslims from the Central Sudan who were sold into the Atlantic trade, mostly through the port of Lagos.[22] Eventually, the Islamic expansion also set off a series of wars within the Yoruba area as some of the Yoruba city-states were Islamicized and new states also appeared.[23] These wars generated thousands of prisoners sold into the Atlantic slave trade. In the early decades of the nineteenth century, however, most of the Muslim slaves arriving at Bahia were Hausas. The German scientists Spix and Martius saw them in Salvador and called them "very black, tall, muscular, and very daring," opinions shared to some extent by the French consul in Bahia, who thought the Hausas to be physically strong and less willing to resign themselves to their captivity than other groups. He also noted that most of them were fighting men who had been enslaved as prisoners of war and that it was rare to see Hausa women in Bahia.[24] His personal observations have been confirmed by modern research.[25]

The Hausas had begun to cause trouble in Bahia as early as 1806 or 1807. A supposed plot of Hausas had been discovered by the governor, the

Count of Ponte (Conde da Ponte), in which Hausas in the city had elected a "governor" who with the aid of a freedman as his secretary had begun to establish contacts with other Hausas on the Recôncavo plantations. Another account noted that "captains" had been appointed in each of the city's districts.[26] Arms had been gathered and the rising, coordinated between slaves in the city and on the plantations, set to take place on Corpus Christi, when vigilance would probably be lax. The Count of Ponte had acted quickly, suppressing the movement, arresting the leaders, and throwing a guard around the public fountains out of fear of the threat of poison.[27] This conspiracy was noted in a royal order and sentence of October 1807 that pointed out that the plot would have violated "not only the rights of their respective masters, but would also disturb the security and public order on which the conservation of states depended."[28] The leaders were executed and ten other slaves publicly flogged. A curfew was imposed on all slaves in the city, and even the movement of freed persons was curtailed.

Neither these early Hausa rebels nor the Count of Ponte were fools. Both realized that while the origins of slave action and organization might be most favored in the fluid, urban world of the port of Salvador, where slaves and freed people mixed freely, the majority of the captaincy's slaves lived in the countryside on the sugar engenhos and cane farms, in the tobacco-growing and food-producing regions, and therefore any hope of success would lie in linking urban plans to a general uprising in the countryside. Thus, from the slaves' point of view contact with the mass of rural workers was essential, and from the government's perspective this was the thing to be most feared. The governor's report of the incident specifically noted that the projected uprising had included not only city slaves but also those of the Recôncavo plantations.[29] The Count of Ponte also realized that a real potential danger of possible linkage lay in the fugitive communities, the quilombos, which often housed runaways from both the city and the countryside. In April 1807, the Count of Ponte had projected the destruction of suburban quilombos in the woods that surrounded the capital, and the Portuguese crown approved this measure to assure the "peace and tranquility of the people."[30] He took a hard-line position on the destruction of quilombos as a potential source of revolt and on any manifestations of African culture like the *batuques* (reunions for drumming and dancing), which might serve to agitate rebellion or further unify slaves along ethnic or religious lines.

An example of the potential danger of the quilombos was not long in coming. During this period a group of Hausa runaways who had fled from Salvador and from the rural estates of the Recôncavo had formed a quilombo on the Rio da Prata, not far from the rural town of Nazaré das Farinhas. In early January 1809 about three hundred fugitives, Hausas and apparently some Nagôs, attacked Nazaré but were repelled and then badly mauled by militia troops two days later, suffering numerous casualties. Hundreds of rebels from Salvador who tried to join the rising were intercepted on the road. Some ninety-five rebels were captured, but many fugitives continued to roam the countryside in small groups, throwing the towns and plantations of the region into alarm, perhaps as far away as Sergipe d'El Rey. Exemplary punishment was meted out once again, and local officials imposed strict curfews, complaining that slaves circulated in the taverns and at batuques without proper supervision by their masters, but despite such measures, in 1810 the government had to suppress yet another revolt.[31] By 1814 the patterns of the early revolts were already well established: ethnic organization, attempts to link city and plantation countryside, contact with quilombos, and government repression.

In February 1814, a new and potentially major revolt erupted just north of the city limits of Salvador at the whaling and fishing stations of Itapoã. A group of perhaps 250 slaves from a nearby quilombo attacked the stations and raised the slaves employed there in revolt. With shouts of "Freedom," and "Death to whites and mulattos," the rebels burned the stations and killed between fifty and one hundred people. Led apparently by a Hausa *malam*, or Muslim preacher, the rebels killed a number of whites and mulattos, attacked Itapoam, burned over a hundred houses, and tried to enlist other slaves to join them. Hoping to spread the revolt, the rebels began to march toward the Recôncavo, the heartland of the sugar plantations. They burned two engenhos on the line of march, seized arms and horses, and killed anyone who opposed their progress. Intercepted by a cavalry contingent at Santo Amaro de Ipitanga, some fifty rebels were killed in the battle itself while others hanged themselves in despair. The usual repression followed: public whippings, execution of four (leaders?), and the deportation of twenty-three men to Angola. Many others were arrested and subjected to brutal and exemplary punishment. Apparently, others escaped into the woods and reformed again a new quilombo in the forests north of the city.[32]

Even while the judicial process proceeded against the rebels of the Itapoã rebellion, word arrived in Salvador in March 1814 of a rising on some of the engenhos of the Iguape region near Cachoeira.[33] Slaves had gathered at Engenho da Ponta with the intention of taking the provincial town of Margogipe, but three Hausa freedmen who had been in contact with them were arrested and the revolt dissipated. It was Hausas again across the Bay of All Saints in the sugar and tobacco region of Iguape and its nearby port town of Cachoeira who seem to have organized this revolt. The city council of Cachoeira had already expressed fears in 1813 of such a rising and had warned the government that Hausa dockworkers were planning something, but the new governor, the Count of Arcos, no particular friend of the slave owners or slavery, had thought their premonitions exaggerated and probably due to their own guilty consciences. The government had done little when the revolt erupted on March 20, 1814. The rebels had planned to gather at the large Engenho da Ponta and then march on the town of Maragogipe. They were intercepted and the revolt suppressed, but the planters were now on their guard and disgusted with what they considered to be the vacillating and permissive attitude of the new governor, so different from that of his predecessor.[34]

The War Continues: May 1814

It is in this context that only two months later, on May 26, 1814, a Portuguese named Joaquim José Correa Passos appeared at the office of the lawyer, Elias Baptista Pereira de Araújo Lasso, to declare that he had learned from a woman from the Mina coast with whom he had illicit relations that Hausa slaves and freedmen were planning another great uprising. Lasso was a lawyer at the regional High Court (Relação da Bahia) and he had been involved in the denunciation of the slave revolt of 1807.[35] On revealing this new plot to the senior criminal prosecutor (*ouvidor geral do crime*), Desembargador Antônio Garces Pinto de Madureira, Lasso was ordered by the governor to continue an investigation in all secrecy and to attempt to discover the meeting place of the plotters, their arms, and their plans.[36] One day later (May 27) another slave owner, José Ferreira da Silva, reported that his Hausa slave Germano and a Guruman slave named Jerônimo had overheard a conversation between other Hausas at the docks in which they spoke of a "war against the whites."[37] In fact, what was said in the exchange was that anyone who joined was a man, and those who refused were women. Ferreira was well informed. He had been involved in the slave trade and could speak a number of the languages of the Mina Coast and had been called upon to read some of the documents (*carteis da guerra*) associated with the rising in February. Lasso convinced Ferreira to have his slave pretend to join the rebels in order to learn of their plans, leadership, and preparations for the rebellion. The lawyer later confirmed the report with another of Ferreira's slaves, promising rewards or even freedom to both slaves for their cooperation. This was done, and Ferreira even provided money to his slave that had been demanded by the plotters to help in the preparations. Ferreira was able to report that his slave had seen two hundred arrowheads (*ferrões*) wrapped in cloth bundles that had been taken to the woods to prepare arrows. Others had been prepared in the home of a blacksmith. Hausa plotters had also told the informant that five barrels full of arrowheads were ready and another barrel was held by the slave of a baker. Ferreira and his slave had witnessed the purchase of two bundles of pipe reeds (*canudos*) that could serve as arrows. The slaves were taking the risk of making such purchases because the revolt was planned for St. John's Day (São João), June 24, and the plotters simply had no time to cut arrow shafts in the woods.

Ferreira and his slave reported that the conspiracy involved "all the Hausa blacks, freed and slave, of this city as well as the Recôncavo." Also, supposedly involved were some mulattos and crioulos from outside the city as well as Indians who "wanted the land that the Portuguese had taken from them." Indigenous "ambassadors" to the plotters who arrived in the city on June 12 and 13 were quickly hustled out of town again to avoid provoking attention. Indians were not that common a sight in nineteenth-century Salvador, and their contact with slaves in the city might have produced unwanted attention.[38]

To this point the plans of the rising seem to fit the patterns of the period. The rebellion was to be initiated at a moment in the secular or religious calendar when the levels of control might be slack: Christmas, Easter, Nossa Senhora da Guia, or St. John's Day being particularly favored. The Eve of St. John was usually celebrated with bonfires, celebration, and fireworks that could disguise the first hostile actions of the plotters. St. John's Day also fell in June, after the *safra*, or harvest, had been completed and a time when slaves may have been less subject to daily supervision. The collaboration here between Hausas both slave and freed indicates that linguistic or ethnic identities seem to have been more important than the juridical distinctions between slave and freed people, but the rebels' plans to incorporate some Brazilian-born crioulos and pardos and even to

FIGURE 8.1: *View of slave and freedmen porters and stevedores who formed the cantos. From Jean Baptiste Debret,* Voyage pittoresque et historique au Bresil, *vol. 2 (Paris, 1834–39).*

mobilize Indians was a curious and somewhat distinctive aspect of the plot. While such cooperation was not common, it was always a possibility. Brazilian-born blacks and pardos might have differences with each other and with the Africans, but cooperation could be forged in times of crisis. Such collaboration was greatly feared by the slave owners. Later João Maciel da Costa wrote, "it is an enormous mass of black slaves and freedmen who ordinarily make common cause."[39]

The investigation revealed that the leadership of the rebellion was centered in the *negros ganhadores.* A large number of urban slaves and freedmen worked in the city as porters, stevedores, and occasional laborers who hired out their services as *negros de ganho,* or *ganhadores.* They gathered at various points throughout the city in organized working groups, or *cantos.* By the warehouses and docks of the lower city, at strategic points on major streets, and near the fountains and plazas, these cantos were established so that anyone needing laborers to move goods or for occasional jobs knew where to look and could negotiate directly with the workers. So cheap and available was this labor that whites, even servants, rarely carried anything. Foreign observers were greatly impressed by the gangs of porters in the Brazilian cities and the call and response songs that accompanied their labor. They gave the city its character. John Luccock saw the street workers in Rio in 1820 and he gave this account:

> Among the people of the lower classes of Rio, the men that carry things in the streets get the attention of visitors not only because of their numbers but because of their habits. They are not really stevedores because those who are paid for their work for themselves are rare; most of them are slaves sent out to work in the streets with an empty basket and some long poles for the service of their masters. They carry heavy objects, hanging them from a chain suspended from the poles supported by a couple of the men. If it's very heavy four, six, or more will form a work group, captained by the most intelligent of them. To give rhythm to their work and coordinate their steps, the leader will sing a short, simple African song, at the end of which the group will respond in a loud chorus. The song will go on so long as the work lasts and with this they make their burden less and cheer up their spirits. I have at times the impression that these people are not insensitive to the pleasures of their memories of the homes they have lost and will never see again. What is certain is that these songs give to the streets a joy that in other ways they are missing.[40]

The message was not always so nostalgic. The Benguela *carregadores* in Alagoas sang:

The snake has no arms,
No legs, no hands, no feet
How does he rise, and we do not
We who have arms,
and legs, and hands, and feet?[41]

Sometimes the foreign observers recognized that the singing was misleading. The German travelers Spix and Martius wrote: "In the city the condition of those who work for a daily wage (240 *reis*) for their masters is

FIGURE 8.2: *Debret observed these men in Rio de Janeiro, but in their
organization and appearance these groups probably resembled
those of Salvador who plotted the still-born rebellion of 1814.*
From Jean Baptiste Debret, Voyage pittoresque et historique
au Bresil, *vol. 2 (Paris, 1834–39).*

very sad. They are considered living capital in action and since their masters hope to recoup their capital and interest payments as quickly as possible, the slaves are not spared."[42] The seeming freedom of the negros de
ganho was also deceptive. Many lived with their masters and were under
their vigilance.

The cantos were organized ethnically, that is, membership was usually controlled by a particular African group or by the colonial equivalent
of ethnicity since some of the categories were regionally or linguistically
defined and did not necessarily imply shared identities. There were
cantos of Nagôs (Yoruba), Aussá (Hausas), Gege (Dahomey), Angolas
(Ovimbundu, Congo, Benguela, and so on), and others. In the cantos,
slaves and freedmen cooperated.[43]

The negros de ganho could move freely within the city without causing suspicion. Their work on or near the waterfront also brought them into contact with the slaves bringing in goods from the surrounding agricultural areas. Moreover, the cantos were organized, usually choosing or electing their own "captains," sometimes in a ceremony held on the streets, the elections being confirmed by the other cantos.[44] This mobility and organization made them ideal centers for plotting rebellion and for active resistance. They seemed to control the streets. In December 1813, when customshouse officials had arrested a black man for theft, members of the canto of the Alfandega had intercepted them on the way to prison and had set the prisoner free, threatening the accompanying officers at knifepoint.[45] The police did nothing to punish them.

The 1814 investigation revealed that the cantos in the lower city at the Cais (docks) de Cachoeira, the Cais Dourado, and Corpo Santo had taken a leading role in the plot, while the cantos of Trapiche Novo, Trapiche Grande, Pezo do Fumo, Terreiro, Paço de Saldanha, and other locales were also involved. African divisions and rivalries were not forgotten, but witnesses questioned were unsure about the level of collaboration. Some testimony claimed that with the exception of the Tapas (Nupe), the other African "nations," the Angolans, Gege, and Nagôs, had not been brought into the conspiracy.[46] João, a later Hausa witness who had been invited to join the conspiracy by his *malungos*, claimed that Antônio, captain of a canto and the leader of the conspiracy, had told him that all the cantos were involved except the Geges.[47] Perhaps Antônio had exaggerated the level of collaboration in order to impress a possible recruit. Whatever the truth, it was clear to everyone that the ethnic divisions or levels of cooperation were crucial in the plans of the rebels and for their hope of success.

Although the enterprise was led from the docks, slaves throughout the city were involved. A Hausa slave of Antonio Coelho da Fonseca who sold tobacco at the canto of the Cais de Cachoeira revealed that other major figures in the plot were José, the slave of a baker in the Baixa dos Sapateiros who had stored or hidden much of the arms, and a Hausa blacksmith, slave of an old black freedman, who forged most of the arrowheads. The informant Germano reported to his master that he had attended a meeting in a shack near the Pilar Church in which ten conspirators, including two freedmen and two of the leading plotters, had met. Apparently, it was at that gathering he had learned the plan of action.

The key element in the plan was a coordination of action between quilombo fugitives and urban slaves. The main point of contact was the Sangradouro woods on the outskirts of Salvador. This scrub forest was extensive and bordered on the smallholdings (*roças*) on the Brotas road, Matatu, the Quinta dos Lázaros, and the Cabula road. This had long been a site of suburban quilombos, one having been destroyed at Cabula in 1807. Apparently, after the uprising at Itapoam in February 1814, a number of the rebels had escaped to the safety of the bush. The plan called for a diversionary tactic. Those fugitives hidden in the woods of Sangradouro would mount an attack on the Powder House at Matatú, and when the troops mobilized to meet that threat, the rising would begin in the city. Coordination between the two groups had been maintained by a crioulo who circulated in the woods, in contact with the fugitives and keeping them apprised of recent developments in the city. Actions were to be coordinated by means of conch shell trumpets, which were widely distributed among the plotters.[48] Plans for the rebellion had spread into the countryside. The slaves at the engenho of Antônio Vaz de Carvalho were enlisted, as were the Hausas at the farm of Manoel da Silva. The plot was well planned and preparations were extensive. Ferreira Silva's slave Germano reported that on June 16 he had been taken to the Sangradouro woods and shown a large pit filled with arms and several bundles filled with gunpowder. There was, however, little mention of firearms. Most of the preparations had been of bows and arrows and here, as in most of the other rebellions, bows and arrows and edged weapons made up the arsenal of the rebels.

The government had acted on June 23, dispatching a small unit of soldiers to the Sangradouro woods to seize the arms. They found over two hundred arrowheads, wood for bows, and bundles of shafts for arrows. João, the Hausa slave of Manoel José Teixeira de Souza, who had informed his master that he had been contacted by Antônio, the captain of a canto who lived at the Fonte de Xixi, to enter the plot, reported that to enlist him, he had been taken to a farm of a widow in Cabeça, on the road to Matatú, near Boa Vista. He claimed to have seen firearms hidden in a sugar crate, African arms (*armas da sua terra*), supplies (*carne de sertão, carne do sol*), and some cattle belonging to the farm owner that would also be used for the rebels. He encountered fifteen blacks, five from the farm and ten strangers, and he learned that there was a great quilombo nearby in Matatú where many of the rebels from the rising in February had gathered along with some country folk (*caboclos*). They had money taken in the

February rising and were apparently well supplied if not entirely unified in their plans. Some wanted the revolt to begin on the Eve of St. John's Day when the noise of the traditional celebrations would cover their first movements. Others like Antônio, the capitão do canto, wanted to wait until July 10, when the numbers of adherents would be greater. Anyone seen on the road to the quilombo would be killed to prevent leaks before the plan could be put into motion. The rebels hoped to seize the Powder House at Matatú, taking what powder they needed and wetting down the rest in order to make it useless to the government's forces. João learned from Antônio that the arms and supplies had been moved from the farm into the woods, and he had worked for much of a day preparing arrows along with other plotters. He claimed to have counted some thirty-seven blacks in the woods. He revealed all this to his master and was dispatched to lead troops to the cache the following morning, but by the time of their arrival, everything had been moved. Whether the plotters had become suspicious of João or he had simply led the troops on a wild goose chase was unclear. Nothing could be found.

The government was not through. Manoel, a twenty-six-year-old apprentice blacksmith, slave of Caetano Soares, was questioned on June 27. Shown two types of arrowheads, he was asked if had made any like them and who had commissioned them and provided the iron. He answered that a Hausa who lived in the lower city, called Jatao in his own language, had asked for them and that he had made ten of them, four of one type, six of the other, from old nails. Manoel claimed he did not know Jatao's Portuguese name, his master's name, or his residence. He was either protecting his accomplice or reflecting the reality that an African world existed in Bahia in which the labels and categories of colonial society did not necessarily apply.

The plot of May 1814 was in some ways a continuation or extension of the rising of February and even involved some of the rebels from the earlier movement. Some slaves invited to join the conspiracy were told that many refugees from the February battle as well as new recruits were hidden in the woods, including "the Muslim priest that they said had been killed in the attack at Itapoã" (*o sacerdote Malamim que sedezia morto no combate da entrada da Itapoam*). To what extent this was a rumor designed to mobilize further cooperation, especially from Muslims, is unclear, but a desire by the rebels of February to continue their struggle from the suburban quilombos is obvious. Whatever the truth of the claim, the plot of

May 1814 had gone beyond ethnic and religious limitations and had sought to draw crioulos, pardos, and even Indians into the movement.

In the process of resistance, Africans sought to draw on institutions or cultural features that might serve as bases of organization. These might be African in origin, such as the batuques, or dance meetings, or candomblés destroyed by police authorities, or they might be colonial institutions like religious brotherhoods or the black and mulatto militia units, adapted and transformed or simply mobilized by slaves and freedmen.[49] As the number of Africans in Bahia swelled, and especially as the tide of rebellion rose, colonial authorities and slave owners increasingly sought to restrict, control, or eliminate those cultural features that brought slaves together or were African in nature. Candomblés became a major police concern, with cult centers raided in Cachoeira in 1785 and Assu in 1829. The control of batuques became a topic of heated controversy between those who saw them as a breeding ground for rebellion and slave autonomy and those, like the more lenient governor, the Count of Arcos, who felt that such gatherings or the election of "kings" by slaves and freed persons during certain festivals made slavery more bearable and kept the "nations" divided.[50] In general, however, the trend was to crush these seeming manifestations of African culture or autonomy. Quilombos also fell into that category, but by their very nature it was impossible to stamp them out. Institutions that were not so overtly African or that were constitutive of colonial culture and society and served to integrate slaves and freed persons into that society were less likely to be targeted for repression. It was hard to do so. Black brotherhoods, colored militia troops, and cantos were too much a part of colonial reality. A later municipal attempt to impose municipal control over the cantos in 1857 met with stiff resistance and a strike by the slave workers.[51] Despite the role the cantos had played in the 1814 planned revolt, there is no evidence that their activities were more controlled or that their ethnic basis was challenged.

The abortive rising of May 1814 shows clearly that Africans had found in the cantos and the quilombos two potential bases for the mobilization of resistance. For different reasons, both offered a certain freedom of operation and a potential to focus resistance. The plotters of May 1814, like their predecessors and those who followed in the next two decades, realized that linking urban and rural risings was the best hope of success, and the quilombos seemed to provide points of contact that could facilitate this cooperation. Like a tree scattering its seeds, many of the revolts produced new quilombos as rebels avoided capture and sought new spaces for life and action. After the 1814 revolts in Bahia a slave rising in Alagoas in 1815 was forestalled when the government raided a nearby quilombo and seized a cache of arms.[52] A worried batallion commander in Sergipe in 1827 noted the marauding fugitives increased their numbers and contaminated those still in slavery. His response was to terrify plantation slaves, but he warned of terrible consequences.[53] Slave owners had always recognized the threat that quilombos presented to the slave system, but in a period of political agitation and rebellion both they and the slaves came to see quilombos as the keys to the success or failure of rebellion.

APPENDIX

Declaration of Manoel José Teixeira

Throughout the Americas, the most common records we have of slave resistance and revolt come from the judicial proceedings that were used to investigate and punish those responsible. The testimony in such trials, whether given by slave owners, by slaves who had refused to join the movement, or by the rebels themselves, was often self-interested and must be read with caution, but often this information is all that remains of revolts, and especially of revolts that were planned and never realized. In this case, the slave owner Manuel José Teixeira recounts in detail for the ouvidor geral do crime, the senior judge on criminal matters, what he supposedly learned from his Hausa slave. The testimony seems to have the ring of truth because of the details it provides about ethnic rivalries among the slaves, the organizations of the cantos, or urban work groups, and the plans to link the movement to the quilombos, or escaped slave communities on the periphery of Salvador.

Act of Ratification Made by Manoel José Teixeira to the Declaration He Made.

On the 25th of June 1814 in this city of Salvador of the Bay of All Saints in the residence of the desembargador, ouvidor geral

do crime Dr. Antônio Pinto de Madureira, professed knight in
the Order of Christ where I, the scribe, came called by his order;
Manuel José Teixeira, resident in São Miguel, appeared. . . .
The said judge said that having declared verbally on the 20th
of the present month certain facts in respect to the continuation
or new convulsion of the slaves of this city with information
acquired from his Hausa slave named João, of whose participation the judge has made appropriate use, it is now necessary that
he [Manoel José Teixeira] declare and ratify these statements in a
legal document, to which end he has been called to the judge's
presence so that he can do so under oath to the Holy Evangels.
Having been sworn under oath, he said he well remembers what
he declared because of his zeal and not as an act of passion or
hate, and he ratifies this in the following manner. That being
the owner of a slave named João Hausa, this slave without any
coercion whatsoever reported that some of his buddies [*malungos*]
and particularly the black, Antônio, captain of the canto, resident
at the Xixi Fountain, invited him to enter a seditious conspiracy
with others who tried to sway him to their opinion; they took
him to a small farm [*roça*] of a widow near the beginning of the
small road that goes to Matatu near Boa Vista where he was
shown firearms in a sugar crate in a room, arms from his
land, dried meat [*carne do sertão e carne de sol*], some cows that
belonged to the owner of the farms that he was told would also
serve as supplies; and finding there fifteen blacks, five of the
farm and ten who were not, he also certified that there was a
great quilombo above Matatu where there were many from the
past revolt and some *caboclos* [Indians or mestiços]. They had
money stolen in the last revolt and their plan was to break out
on the eve or day of Saint John under cover of the usual noise
of such days; the first step was to kill the guard of the armory
[Casa da Pólvora] of Matatu, take there what they needed and
ruin the rest with water; others wished the war to begin on the
10th of July so they could gather together the largest number of
blacks; the captain of the canto said that the blacks of Trapiche
Novo, Trapiche Grande, or the Tobacco Scale, some of the
merchant Cunha, of Friandes, and almost all the cantos of all
the nations except the Geges were all ready. They were ready

to kill everyone encountered on the road all the way to the
quilombo in order that no one in the city became aware. Given
this statement, he learning of such a grave situation, he told his
slave to go with them in order to learn as much as he could,
so that he, the witness, might be given proper warning and make
a statement to the judge as a loyal vassal. The slave continued
in contact with the captain of the canto, who told him on
Wednesday the 22nd of the present month that there was news
and that everything had been taken from the farmhouse and
taken to the Sangradouro woods because there had been some
searches made; some weapons were hidden, but those from the
house had been carried further away and the slave was taken
there where he saw everything that had been in the farmhouse
and in addition, four bearded blacks attaching arrowheads to
reeds that would be used as arrows in whose service the said
slave of the witness worked almost the whole day, having brought
a basket of meat manioc flour so that going in the morning,
he returned only after five in the afternoon, promising to steal
something from the witness and some weapons to return once
and for all on Thursday the 23rd of the present month. The
judge, learning of this, then required the slave to reveal the place
on Thursday in the company of the adjunct scribe of this court,
Honório Fidelis Barreto, who accompanied a senior military
official responsible for the investigation and arrest. The party
left at eight in the morning in the company of the slave who
served as a guide, nothing was found, and he the witness does
not know why, being certain of what he had discovered and in
the truthfulness of his slave who had reported well and loyally
because he believed it his responsibility, as the witness said and
declared. The said judge ordered this act made, to which I the
scribe attest.

Signed by the witness and the judge. I, Germano Fereira
Barreto, Scribe, recorded and signed.

Arquivo Nacional da Torre do Tombo, Lisbon, Casa Forte, 78, no. 11.

NOTES

1. Autos sobre o levantamento de negros projectado na Bahia (1814), Arquivo Nacional da Torre do Tombo, Lisbon (ANTT), Casa Forte, 78, no.11. The plot is mentioned in both Décio Freitas, *Insurreições escravas* (Porto Alegre: Editora Movimento, 1976) and Clóvis Moura, *Rebeliões da senzala: Quilombos insurreições guerrilhas*, 3rd. ed. (São Paulo: Livraria Editora Ciências Humanas, 1981). The two accounts are very similar, although neither author cites the source of the description. They are probably based on the brief description in Pierre Verger, *Fluxo e refluxo do tráfico de escravos entre o Golfo do Benin e a Bahia de Todos os Santos* (São Paulo: Editora Corrupio, 1987), 331.

2. João José Reis, "Um balanço dos estudos sobre as revoltas escravas da Bahia," in *Escravidão e invenção da liberdade*, ed. João José Reis (São Paulo: Brasiliense, 1988), 87–142, provides a review of the literature. The Atlantic Revolutions theme is developed by Eugene D. Genovese, *From Rebellion to Revolution* (Baton Rouge: Louisiana State University Press, 1979). I have noted the difference between slaves and freed people in Brazil in Stuart B. Schwartz, *Sugar Plantations in the Formation of Brazilian Society: Bahia, 1550–1835* (Cambridge: Cambridge University Press, 1985), 468–88. Reis makes an error when he claims that slaves in Rio were arrested in 1805 for wearing cameos with the image of Dessalines. The document in question states that those arrested were not slaves but freedmen (*cabras e crioulos forros*) in the militia. See João José Reis, *Slave Rebellion in Brazil* (Baltimore: Johns Hopkins University Press, 1993), 48; cf. Luiz Roberto de Barros Mott, "A escravatura: A propósito de uma representação a El Rei sobre a escravatura no Brasil," *Revista do Instituto de Estudos Brasileiros* 14 (1973): 127–36.

3. Arquivo Histórico Ultramarino, Lisbon (AHU), Bahia, doc. 29,773. In 1803, 6,437 Africans landed at Salvador, 2,180 or one-third of whom came from Angola. See Arquivo Publico Municipal do Salvador, Visitas das embarcações vindas d'Africa, 1802–29, vol. 182.1.

4. Felipe Nery to Antônio Estes da Costa (Pernambuco, August 22, 1812) stated that "Minas were the best here." Biblioteca Nacional, Lisbon (BNL), Fundo Geral, box 224, nos. 31–33.

5. See the discussion in Reis, *Slave Rebellion*, 5–7. A more extensive discussion with excellent figures for 1808 is provided by Katia M. de Queirós Mattoso, *Bahia, século XIX: Uma província no Império*

(Rio de Janeiro: Nova Fronteira, 1992), 82–87. For the mid-nineteenth century, see Anna Amélia Vieira Nascimento, *Dez freguesias da cidade do Salvador* (Salvador: FCBa, 1986).

6. Maria José de Souza Andrade, *A mão de obra escrava em Salvador, 1811–1860* (São Paulo: Editoria Corrupio, 1988). In a sample of 2,461 urban slaves, 1,456 (59 percent) were listed as young (*moço*) or still young (*ainda moço*). Children made up only 17.5 percent (431). New writings on African ethnicity in Brazil are found in "Rethinking the African Diaspora: The Making of the Black Atlantic World in the Bight of Benin and Brazil," ed. Kristin Mann and Edna G. Bay, special issue, *Slavery and Abolition* 22, no. 1 (2001). Mann and Bay also available in book form.

7. Citizens of Bahia to the king (1814), printed in Carlos B. Ott, *Formação e evolução étnica da cidade do Salvador*, 2 vols. (Salvador: Manu, 1957), 2, 103–9. There is a translation in English in Robert E. Conrad, *Children of God's Fire: A Documentary History of Black Slavery in Brazil* (Princeton: Princeton University Press, 1983), 401–6.

8. See my fuller discussion in Schwartz, *Sugar Plantations*, 474–75.

9. Petition of Manoel de Araújo e Góes (July 19, 1792), AHU, doc. 24.600.

10. All six of the Nagô runaways being held in jail in 1831 were described as either *boçal* (unacculturated) or not knowing their master's name. See "Relação dos escravos fugidos," Arquivo Público da Bahia (APB), Presidência da Província, folder 2270 (1831); Barbara Marie-Charlotte Wanda Lasocki, "A Profile of Bahia 1820–1826 as seen by Jacques Guinebaud, French Consul General" (M.A. thesis, University of California, Los Angeles, 1967), 21.

11. Diz Severino Pereira (1798), APB, Ordens Régias 86, 242–45.

12. Ibid. A description of the destruction of these two quilombos and the flight of the survivors to yet another settlement is found in a letter of the governor, Fernando José de Portugal, to Rodrigo de Sousa Coutinho (Bahia, April 6, 1797), in Ignacio Accioli de Cerqueira e Silva, *Memórias históricas e políticas da Província da Bahia*, 6 vols. (Bahia: Braz do Amaral, 1925), 3:227.

13. For a view of such a network developed by another quilombo, see Stuart B. Schwartz, *Slaves, Peasants, and Rebels: Reconsidering Brazilian Slavery* (Urbana: University of Illinois Press, 1992), 103–36.

14. For example, see the petition of Francisco Xavier Soares Bandeira, capitão de entradas e assaltos, freguesia de Nossa Senhora de Oliveira, Santo Amaro, who listed his efforts in an attack on "a great quilombo of rebellious slaves in the forests of the town of Cachoeira." APB, Cartas ao Governo 218 (Bahia, September 2, 1809).

15. Reis, *Slave Rebellion*, 41.

16. On this repression see Luiz Mott, "Acontundá: Raízes setecentistas do sincretismo religioso afro-brasileiro," *Anais do Museu Paulista* 31 (1986): 124–47; João José Reis, "Magia Jeje na Bahia: A invasão do calundu do Pasto de Cachoeira, 1785," *Revista brasileira de história* 8 (1988): 57–82.

17. Reis, *Slave Rebellion*, 55–56.

18. The classic works on African "nations" in Brazil are now outdated but still useful. See Nina Rodrigues, *Os Africanos no Brasil*, 5th ed. (São Paulo: Homero Pires, 1977); Artur Ramos, *As culturas negras no novo mundo* (Rio de Janeiro: Civilização Brasileira, 1938).

19. On the Gege see Reis, "Magia Jeje," 68–69.

20. The most complete treatment of the "nations" is Mary Karash, *Slave Life in Rio de Janeiro, 1808–1850* (Princeton: Princeton University Press, 1987), 3–28.

21. Rodrigues, *Os Africanos*, 109.

22. See Mervyn Hiskett, *The Sword of Truth: The Life and Times of Shehu Usuman dan Fodio* (New York: Oxford University Press, 1973); M. G. Smith, "The Jihad of Shehu Dan Fodio: Some Problems," in *Islam in Tropical Africa*, ed. I. M. Lewis (London: Oxford University Press, 1966), 408–19. See Paul E. Lovejoy, "Background to Rebellion: The Origins of Muslim Slaves in Bahia," *Slavery and Abolition*, 15, no. 2 (1994): 150–80.

23. Robert S. Smith, *Kingdoms of the Yoruba*, 3rd ed. (Madison: University of Wisconsin Press, 1988), 125–40.

24. Johann von Spix and Karl von Martius, *Viagem pelo Brasil*, 3 vols. (São Paulo, 1961), 2:171–72. Francis de Castelnau, *Renseignements sur l'Afrique centrale et sur une nation d'hommes à queue que s'y trouveraient d'apres le rapport de nègres du Soudan. esclaves à Bahia* (Paris: P. Bertrand, 1851), 8, cited in Verger, *Fluxo e refluxo*, 331.

25. Lovejoy, "Background," 160–65.

26. Verger, *Fluxo e refluxo*, 332.

27. Untitled MS volume, Instituto Histórico e Geográfico Brasileiro (IGHB), box 399, doc. 2, 287–88. This is a curious volume on rebellions and civil disturbances in Bahia. It includes a long chapter entitled "Relação da Francezia formada pelos omens pardos da cidade da Bahia no anno de 1798." See the account by the governor in Count of Ponte to Viscount of Anadia (Bahia, July 16, 1807), in Accioli, *Memórias*, 3:228–30.

28. Count of Ponte to Fernando José de Portugal (Bahia, May 17, 1808), Arquivo Nacional, Rio de Janeiro (ANRJ), I-JJ-317, fols. 205–6. The appended *orden regia* (October 6, 1807) speaks of the "sedição projetada pelos negros aussás."

29. Count of Ponte to Viscount of Anadia (Bahia, July 16, 1807), Accioli, *Memórias*, 3:228–29.

30. Viscount of Anadia to Count of Ponte (Mafra, June 27, 1807), Biblioteca Nacional, Rio de Janeiro (BNRJ), I-31–27, 1.

31. Joaquim Ignacio da Costa, juiz ordinário de Maragogipe to governor (January 31, 1809), APB, Cartas ao Governador 216.

32. Schwartz, *Sugar Plantations*, 482–83; Reis, *Slave Rebellion*, 48–49, provides details. A long letter from the Bahian merchants to the crown reporting the events of February 1814 and suggesting preventative measures is published in Ott, *Formação e evolução étnica da cidade do Salvador*, 2:103–8. It appears in an English translation, which contains a number of errors, in Conrad, *Children of God's Fire*, 401–6. See also BNRJ, II–34, 6, 57.

33. Schwartz, *Sugar Plantations*, 483. See also João José Reis, "Recôncavo rebelde: Revoltas escravas nos engenhos Baianos," *Afro-Ásia* 15 (April 1992): 105–7.

34. I have written about the divergence of opinion and actions of the Count of Ponte and the Count of Arcos in Schwartz, *Sugar Plantations*, 484–85. See also Reis, *Slave Rebellion*, 49–51.

35. See Count of Aguiar (Rio de Janeiro, January 16, 1811), in Accioli, *Memórias*, 3:231.

36. Pinto de Madureira was a rising legal star in the captaincy. Member of an important planter family, he eventually became a judge of the Supreme Court (Casa da Suplicação) in Rio de Janeiro. His sister owned Engenho Aramaré in the Recôncavo. See Antônio D'Oliveira Pinto da França, *Cartas baianas, 1821–24: Subsídios para o estudo dos problemas da opção na independencia brasileira* (São Paulo: Companhía Editora Nacional, 1980).

37. The designation "Guruman" is probably the people called by the Portuguese "Galinhas," and sometimes referred to as Gurunxi. They were also Muslims and were closely associated with the Hausa. Like them they were thought to be rebellious and unsubmissive slaves. See Ramos, *As culturas*, 216.

38. The Bahian census of 1808 listed 5,663 Indians living as part of colonial society. See Mattoso, *Bahia*, 82.

39. João Maciel da Costa, *Memória sôbre a necessidade de abolir a introdução dos escravos africanos no Brasil* (Coimbra, 1821), 21.

40. John Luccock, *Notes on Rio de Janeiro and the Southern Paris of Brazil: Taken during a Residence of Ten Years in That Country from 1808 to 1818* (London: Samuel Leigh, 1820).

41. Abelardo Duarte, *Folclore negros nas Alagoas* (Maceió: DAC, 1974), 221–37, provides the text of other shouts and songs used by *ganhadores do canto* in various Brazilian cities.

42. Spix and Martius, *Viagem pelo Brasil*, 2:172. In 1837 it was estimated that the daily wage for a working slave was 320 réis which, with eighty-one Sundays and saints' days removed, came to 90,880 réis. Food costs for maintaining the slave was 160 réis per day, or 58,400 réis a year, to which 7,480 réis for clothing and health care had to be added. This left a profit to the owner of 25,000 réis, but this did not take into account days missed for illness, punishment, running away, etc. Since a working unskilled slave cost about 400 réis and the minimum rate of interest was 6 percent, an owner could just about break even. See the discussion in Federico Leopoldo C. Burlamaqui, *Memória analytica acêrca do commercio d'escravos e acêrca da escravidão domestica* (Rio de Janeiro, 1837).

43. On cooperation between the two groups, see Leila Mezan Algranti, *O feitor ausente: Estudos sobre a escravidão no Rio de Janeiro, 1808–1822* (Petrópolis: Vozes, 1988), 121–31.

44. João José Reis, "A greve negra de 1857 na Bahia," *Revista da USP* 18 (1993): 8–29.

45. Citizens of Bahia to king (1814), 104.

46. In later testimony by the slave João Aussá, he stated that he had been told that the cantos of other nations, with the exception of the Geges, had also been involved. "Autos sobre o levantamento," 19.

47. *Malungo* was a term of fictive kinship generally applied to another African who had come to Brazil in the same slave ship. The term eventually came to mean simply a friend.

48. "Os signaes que tem destinado para o levante sao huns buzios dos quaes já estão prevenidos e com bastante porção," ANTT, Casa Forte, folder 78, no. 11, p. 5.

49. On the destruction of the candomblé of Assu, see João José Reis and Eduardo Silva, *Negociação e conflicto* (São Paulo, 1989), 32–61.

50. The local magistrate of Maragogipe complained in 1809 that the slave owners gave too much liberty to slaves by allowing batuques that scandalized religion, the state, and public order (APB, Cartas ao Governo 216). The Count of Arcos, governor of Bahia, believed that the best guarantee of tranquility in Brazil's cities was the disunity of the Africans, which was promoted by the batuques. Slave owners denounced his policy as dangerous and wrong. For a partial defense of Arcos, see Marquês de Aguiar to Count of Arcos (Rio de Janeiro, June 6, 1814), BNRJ, II-33, 24, 29. On the election of "kings," see Elizabeth Kiddy, "Who Is the King of the Kongo? A New Look at African and Afro-Brazilian Kings in Brazil," in *Central Africans and Cultural Transformations in the American Diaspora*, ed. Linda M. Heywood (Cambridge: Cambridge University Press, 2002), 153–82.

51. Reis, "A greve negra," 17–29.

52. Luiz Antônio da Fonseca Machado ao Governador (Sergipe de El-Rey, September 1, 1815), APB, Cartas ao Governo 229.

53. Luis Mott, "Violência e repressão em Sergipe: Noticia das revoltas escravas século XIX," *Mensário do Arquivo Nacional* 11, no. 5 (1980): 13.

CHAPTER NINE

"The Fruit of Freedom"

Slaves and Citizens in Early Republican Argentina

SETH MEISEL

Never have you dawned
happy Buenos Aires, with a clearer day
than that on which you learned
to convert weeping into happiness
of so many redeemed from the heavy
yoke of slavery that they had carried. (1807)[1]

⚘ IN 1831, SHORTLY AFTER FIGHTING ENDED IN ONE OF ARGENTINA'S MOST bloody civil wars, Manuel Liendo, a slave from the province of Córdoba, submitted a petition to Estanislao López, the most prominent commander of the recently victorious Federalist forces, inviting him to consider "if I am worthy of enjoying the fruit of freedom." He laid out his case before the military hero, explaining that he had joined the insurgency against the ruling Centralist Party inspired by López's own example of generously abandoning the tranquility of his home in neighboring Santafé province to spearhead the liberation of Córdoba. His petition states, "[P]ossessed of the most vehement desire for the prosperity of the fatherland . . . I resolved to die before accepting the denigrating servitude to which the [Centralist] rebels had reduced it and animated by these noble sentiments I offered my services." Like López, Liendo found that his patriotic ideals placed him in harm's way. Yet, though wounded and imprisoned, the slave soldier remained resigned to "suffer even more for that cry of liberty that so rouses the human heart (although I have not experienced it)."[2] Shared ideals, political fortunes, and the undeniable aspirations of the human condition united López, Liendo, and their Federalist compatriots. His petition, therefore, concluded with his request to share in the "fruit" of their labors and live free in the society his sacrifices helped to bring into creation.

Liendo's bid for freedom reminds us that of the many strategies employed by slaves to escape servitude—the path of accommodation, of appealing to what slaveholding society embraced as its most flattering ideals—could often prove successful. Leveraging free society's own resources in order to secure their liberty, however, demanded that slaves acquire profound insight into the potential allies, institutions, and traditions that might be enlisted on their behalf. How otherwise can we account for Liendo's faith that his petition would be read, that his wartime melodrama might sway López to recommend his manumission, or simply that a literate intermediary could be entrusted to record his story in such a compelling fashion? Similarly, we learn a good deal about the changing place of human bondage in postcolonial Argentina by considering why one of the nation's most powerful authorities would entertain such a solicitation from a slave (and likely a runaway, as Liendo offers no indication that he had his master's permission to offer his "services"), grant it, and thus implicitly endorse the petition's argument that a slave's servile status did not preclude his possessing an independent political consciousness.

Liendo and López understood quite well their respective roles in this exchange. Drawing on the precedent of nearly a generation of similar negotiations between Argentine slaves and national authorities over the conditions and quality of citizenship in the new republic, Liendo knew that it sufficed to point to his actions on the battlefield as the proof the governor needed of his ideological convictions and thus the slave's ability to participate as a useful member of free society. The alchemy of military service could make slaves into patriots and patriots into free men.

Liendo's is by no means an isolated case. In the first half of the nineteenth century, thousands of Spanish American slaves won their freedom by joining the ranks of the Independence armies, and the promise of emancipation was also extended to slaves who served in the internecine conflicts that afflicted the region into the 1850s. Military service became a path to liberation that, while not without precedent, greatly expanded the opportunities for black males' manumission after 1810.[3] Revolutionary and national leaders' resolution to enlist slaves into the armed forces was largely dictated by a chronic need for manpower. Freeing those slave recruits, however, entailed an acceptance of larger social and political changes. Government-sponsored manumissions established society's prior claim to a slave's labor and allegiance, confirmed that military service served as evidence of the slave-soldier's capacity to assume the duties of citizenship, and thus gave state sanction to the freeman's integration into postcolonial society. Indeed, in the most optimistic visions, the new-style army itself became a vehicle for transforming the colonial society of estates into a new democratic community composed of men who in their military and civic actions exemplified the kind of public virtues that might make possible a government based upon the "general will."

This insistent linkage between slave emancipation and Argentina's emerging republican political culture became enshrined in postcolonial rhetoric, rituals, and social reforms. As slave recruits were being mustered into the Independence armies, the newly adopted "national march" of 1813 proclaimed,

> *Hear mortals the sacred cry*
> *Liberty, Liberty, Liberty*
> *Hear the cry of broken chains*
> *See noble Equality enthroned.*

Two years later, Buenos Aires celebrated Independence Day by inaugurating a statue of Redeemed Africa, whose dedicatory plaque read,

> *Ever since the American*
> *with his proud liberty*
> *compassionate and generous*
> *bestowed this precious gift*
> *upon the unfortunate African.*[4]

As late as 1889, when Argentine society was being transformed by a wave of European immigrants, residents of cosmopolitan Buenos Aires, *porteños*, could also proudly point to the new monument of the slave soldier Falucho, killed by Spanish forces in 1822 for refusing to surrender the fort of Callao, Peru. Falucho's story had been popularized (some say invented) nearly forty years earlier by Bartolomé Mitre, historian and president of Argentina (1862–68), in a conscious effort to bring to the public's attention the patriotism of the nation's unknown soldiers: "so many obscure sacrifices, so many modest martyrs, so many anonymous heroes!" This slave's bravery, Mitre editorialized, should gladden any country that could "inspire such sentiments in the heart of a rough and obscure soldier."[5] A generation later, porteños again chose to express their own patriotism in honoring not only Falucho, "but also his intrepid and loyal race: these valiant blacks that were the principal base of the Argentine infantry that brought at bayonet point the advanced ideas of our social and political regeneration."[6]

In praising their "redemption" of slaves and black soldiers' embrace of the independence cause, Argentines also reflected upon their own emancipation from monarchical rule. The refrain that all colonial subjects had been "enslaved" by Spanish tyranny was a constant one in the rhetoric of the period. In the Independence Day sermon delivered in the Córdoba cathedral in 1814, the patriot cleric Gregorio Funes called upon parishioners to reflect on the "three hundred years of shameful slavery" that had only recently come to an end. "Freedom, I repeat, is the first right of man. Unfortunate is the slave that does not dare to say its name!"[7] From the same pulpit five years later, his colleague, Miguel Calixito del Corro, denounced the despotism of King Ferdinand VII in treating the inhabitants of the viceroyalty as a "tribe of slaves" instead of the "virtuous citizens" they had proven themselves to be.[8] Just as Argentines had awoken from a "deep lethargy" to discover their own talents and dignity, many believed that slaves could be a part of this national "regeneration." Indeed, as interpreted by patriot leaders, the seed of their nationhood could be found in the shared determination to create a new society that reached out to the victims of the old regime. The humanitarian sentiments that underlay the measures, they argued, demonstrated Argentines' identification with the liberal ideals of the time and thus their capacity for self-government.

Central, therefore, to Argentine slave soldiers' ability to win their freedom was the importance of their military services as well as new ideas of nationhood. Liendo's petition illustrates his familiarity and engagement with the political ideals of his day. Like slaves throughout the region in their dealings with political officials, the courts, and their own commanders, he emphasized his role in defending the "fatherland," appealing to the ideal of the soldier-citizen in order to secure recognition of his military efforts as well as the rights and privileges due to public-spirited men.[9] Slaves' efforts served to convert an ideological moment into concrete actions that undermined Argentine slavery and caste privileges. The road to freedom through military service was, of course, one that took an enormous toll on Afro-Argentines and their families. Moreover, it was a individual strategy that never directly challenged elite control or the institution of slavery. Nevertheless, the state's need to cultivate a bond with its soldiers and black soldiers' own negotiation for a place in the new order eroded many aspects of the inherited colonial order, and in the process fundamentally shaped the meaning of freedom in the new nation.

Slavery in the Río de la Plata

Spanish settlers brought African slaves to the Río de la Plata region in 1536, the year that Pedro de Mendoza established a South Atlantic foothold in Buenos Aires. Slavery endured until 1853. Argentina's first constitution, ratified in that year, abolished slavery and laid the foundations for the modern nation. It was the final century of slavery, however, that most significantly shaped the boundaries of citizenship in Argentina. In the early centuries, few of the African slaves who arrived in this isolated outpost of the Spanish colonial empire remained. The majority were transported inland and sold in the far more dynamic markets of the southern Andean silver mining centers. In the underdeveloped and sparsely populated territories that would become Argentina, demand for slaves remained concentrated in the small urban elite and middle sectors, which employed slaves in domestic service and as artisans. The only large-scale rural enterprises relying on slave labor were the ranches owned by the Jesuit order.[10] In 1767 the Spanish imperial state expelled the Jesuits and sold off their slaves. Despite the region's chronic labor shortage, the Jesuits' precedent was not replicated.

After 1776 the administrative and commercial colonial decrees known as the Bourbon reforms transformed the region and slavery's place in it. These measures created a new viceroyalty, the Río de la Plata, with its capital in Buenos Aires, and expanded the possibilities for legal trade with Spain. While the port of Buenos Aires emerged as the principal entrepôt for European goods in the Spanish South Atlantic, the Bourbon's reinvigoration of silver mining stimulated Argentine rural production in the

interior to supply the Andean boomtowns. The combined rural and commercial prosperity increased the demand for African slaves.

The last generation of slaves to live under Spanish colonial rule experienced three often contradictory trends. First, their numbers rose dramatically, reaching approximately 28–29 percent of the population in major
cities such as Buenos Aires and Córdoba, less than half that in the countryside.[11] As in the past, most slaves found themselves working in domestic
service, as unskilled labor, and in the crafts. Slave artisans worked under the
supervision of their masters, were rented out to other shop owners or, like
many unskilled laborers, were frequently allowed to secure their own
income and subsistence in return for regularly delivering a stipulated sum
to their masters. The latter arrangement gave slaves a remarkable degree of
personal liberty, though at the cost of having to bear the risk of earning
their livelihood and additional income for their owners.

Second, an increasing number of slaves won their freedom. On the
eve of Argentine independence in 1810, Buenos Aires's masters manumitted 1.3 percent of their slaves. These figures are quite modest, though
they are three times the annual manumission rate of 1778.[12] Significantly,
in 60 percent of these manumission cases Buenos Aires slaves achieved
their own and their family members' freedom by investing their hard-won
savings in "self-purchase"; masters released less than one-third of their
slaves from servitude without compensation.[13] Afro-Argentines at the end
of the colonial period, therefore, inhabited a social world where many in
this growing community lived in the indeterminate border zone between
bondage and freedom. There were slave artisans and street sellers who
enjoyed significant personal autonomy and perhaps the aspiration to
attain self-purchase. Other slaves, almost 11 percent of those manumitted, had been granted "conditional" freedom by their owners, a promise
of liberty at a future date in return for their continued good service. Still
other slaves had gained their own freedom yet worked collectively to
redeem enslaved kin.[14] The efforts by Afro-Argentines to expand their
independence within and outside of slavery and the continued importance
of slave masters' power in limiting their efforts even when they were
legally emancipated conditioned the black experience in colonial society.
However, the growing economy increased possibilities for manumission,
giving rise to limited examples of economically successful free blacks and
mulattos, a trend that threatened to blur the identification between slave
origins, color, and social status.

Third, the growth of the slave and freeman community precipitated a backlash. The rumors of sedition in 1794, which linked a small circle of French residents of Buenos Aires with a supposed slave rebellion, point to the growing anxiety about the increasing African presence in the Río de la Plata.[15] Equally important, colonial officials posted new legislation, or reiterated older regulations, in order to police more scrupulously the boundaries of racial privilege. This effort to secure the racial basis of the viceroyalty's social hierarchy was made manifest in sumptuary laws that prohibited blacks and mulattos from wearing imported textiles and jewelry, regulations that barred nonwhites, *castas*, from access to higher education or the ability to stand for municipal elections, and new imperial prohibitions on racially mixed marriages.[16] At the same time, Spanish immigrants were attracted to the Río de la Plata in search of new opportunity and worked to exclude castas from the trades or block their participation in guild governance. Authorities often supported these initiatives, observing the prejudice in the Río de la Plata against working in the crafts because the "mechanical arts makes those who exercise them vile, as artisanry is linked to people of vile condition: slaves, blacks, mulattos and *zambos*."[17] In this view, only limiting casta prevalence among skilled manual workers would encourage whites to become craftsmen and thus raise the occupations' social prestige. These proposals ultimately failed, in part because the livelihood of a wide sector of the free population depended upon the income generated by their slave artisans. The measures, however, are indicative of late colonial attempts to arrest the gains of freemen and deny castas a place among the "decent people" (*gente decente*) in the social order.[18]

Cofradías for both enslaved and free Africans flourished during these same years. Organized around Catholic observance as well as mutual support for members, the cofradías created a space within colonial society for blacks to form new diaspora communities around shared cultural and ethnic traditions. Their religious festivals, in particular, provide testimony to slaves' efforts to preserve an African identity even in the framework of colonial institutions. Celebrations, known as *tambores* or *tangos* but most commonly as *candombes* centered around public dances, drum ceremonies, the election and crowning of a "king" and, archeological evidence suggests, the practice of rituals associated with ancestor cults. While colonial authorities at times attempted to suppress elements of the candombes (the dancing was often regarded as obscene, the sacred drumming as barbaric, and the election of black "kings" as potentially subversive), cofradía leaders assured the government that they would contain any hint of disorder. They also reminded the crown's representatives of the many military services the black population of Buenos Aires had provided on the viceroyalty's hostile frontiers, for which official permission to hold their candombes was a just reward. Cofradía membership did draw upon existing "ethnic" identities, most importantly the Congo and Angola "nations," and tended to reinforce those cultural ties. Initiatives by freed blacks, and especially lighter-skinned mulattos, to form their own cofradías, however, demonstrate that the viceroyalty's social hierarchies also shaped identities in the Afro-Argentine community.[19]

The year 1806 marked an inflection point. In the following half century, war and the politics of nation building would be crucial factors in undermining slavery and determining the sociopolitical status of Afro-Argentines. Where the commercial prosperity of the viceroyalty had led to higher slave imports, social fluidity, and anxious attempts to stabilize race relations, after 1806, slaves' lives, like those of all Argentines, were primarily shaped by the demands of war. In particular, the chronic political and social instability of this period meant that, faced with a divided society, Argentine leaders sought to secure internal allies, and in the process they were often forced to admit profound transformations. The practice of enlisting slave men as soldiers and granting them their freedom in return for military service stands out. By creating a new, state-sponsored path for manumission, it illustrates how the militarization of society offered unprecedented opportunities for Afro-Argentines to win their freedom and negotiate the quality of postcolonial citizenship.

Significant participation of slaves in Argentina's wars began in 1806 and 1807 when many Buenos Aires slaves joined the popular campaigns to repel two British expeditions. By 1813, in the fourth year of the war against Spanish imperial rule, faced with royalist victories and resistance in the free population to military service, authorities of the United Provinces of the Río de la Plata decreed a levy of slaves throughout the territories under their command and would continue the practice until national authority collapsed in 1820. Altogether, some four to five thousand slave soldiers served in Argentina's Independence War.[20] Thereafter, the semiindependent provincial states sporadically resorted to incorporating slaves into the ranks during the next thirty years of civil wars. The welcome given to slaves as soldiers, and the consequent civil equality recognized as an essential right of combatants, thus converted the conflict to determine the status of slavery and freedmen in postcolonial society into one of the central, if unanticipated, dynamics of the American fight for nationhood.[21]

By the 1820s, with independence secured, governing elites in Spanish South America did work to curtail the reach of the social pacts forged during the revolutionary decade. Limiting the destabilizing impact of black soldiering on race relations in societies where slavery, though weakened, endured and slaveholders remained influential, coincided with the conservative aims of early national authorities. As in Argentina, this retrenchment was often stymied, as regional and ideological divisions led the countries' leaders to mobilize slaves time and again.[22] Chronic political conflict thus kept alive the legacy of the Independence pledge of citizenship in exchange for military support during the intervening three decades before Argentina's 1853 abolition, embedding the concept firmly in the inchoate political culture. Aspiring authorities found it an expedient precedent; slaves incorporated it into an expanding repertoire of strategies for increasing their freedoms.

We can appreciate the impact of these changes in the declining slave population, in both absolute and relative terms, for the important province of Córdoba. A census conducted shortly after the establishment of the viceroyalty in 1778 recorded 6,338 black slaves in the future province, composing 29.1 percent of the urban population and 11.5 percent of the countryside. By 1813 the total numbers had risen only slightly, to 7,060, and were 24.6 percent and 7.25 percent of the urban and rural population. After this date, their numbers began to fall precipitously, to 10.4 percent of the inhabitants of the capital and 3.9 percent of its hinterland (3,952 total) in 1822 and 3 percent and 1.1 percent respectively in 1840, when 1,424 black Cordobans remained in bondage and 685 were classified as *libertos* (slaves who by law would be freed at adulthood).[23]

Creole Patriotism

When Manuel Liendo wrote to Estanislao López about his military exploits, he drew upon a tradition that had been firmly established in the Río de la Plata. Already in 1807, porteño slaves wrote to colonial authorities, or had their commanders submit petitions on their behalf, to recount their participation in the second expulsion of British troops from the capital. Ilario Armando, for instance, expressed the "loyalty and love" that moved him to join the dangerous battle rather than have the "misfortune to see the fatherland delivered to an alien and enemy domination."[24] The slave Ignacio also enumerated his efforts on behalf of the defense of his city "where," he wrote, "I completely fulfilled the duties of a good citizen."[25] While imperial troops stationed in the port had been overwhelmed by only modest English numbers, the city's recapture was directed by a variety of new local leaders who mobilized popular forces, including slaves. These events led to a blossoming of creole patriotism that in its optimism was more than willing to accept and reward slaves' protestation of their own stake in local society.

Most dramatic were the very public efforts of the Buenos Aires *Cabildo* (referring here to the city council, rather than an ethnic association) to reward those affected by the conflict. A pamphlet it commissioned explained its determination to: "not pardon cost nor expenditure that might contribute to aid the infirm widow and the orphaned children of those who died for such a noble cause, nor that so many of its inhabitants who, mutilated and useless in a clear testimony of their patriotism, might be exposed to indigence and mendacity."[26] Wounded slaves were included in these pensions, manumitted for their sacrifices, after the municipality bought their freedom, "giving them, consequently, the liberty that they purchased at the price of their own blood."[27] It is fair to view this act as a response to slave owners' demands for damage to their valuable property. However, it is important to note the cabildo stressed its obligation to slave soldiers, not their masters, and recognized slaves' political personality despite their status as chattel.

For the remaining slave soldiers, the cabildo staged a public lottery to select twenty-five who would be freed with treasury funds, while an additional five soldiers deemed exceptionally worthy would be handpicked for emancipation. Scheduled for the afternoon of the king's birthday, the lottery was evidently the main public event sponsored to honor both the monarch and the city that defended his patrimony. A pamphlet the cabildo issued commemorated the occasion with a detailed account of the festivities.[28] The care taken to choreograph the lottery alerts us to the ideological weight that municipal authorities assigned to this act and hoped to impart to the lottery participants, the public audience, and the pamphlet's readership.

Convoked by posted notices, slave soldiers, their families, and a large audience gathered for the function in Buenos Aires's principal plaza at the foot of the cabildo's offices. There, a richly decorated dias reserved well-appointed chairs for the colony's dignitaries, while the sovereigns' portraits, symbolically presiding over the event, hung above them. The flanks of the plaza were lined by the infantry corps that had been engaged in the recent battles, and at the far end stood the cavalry. Buenos Aires's elite observed from the surrounding balconies. As the drawing grew near, military bands and chapel choirs offered musical accompaniment. Finally, occupying the plaza was the crowd of slave soldiers, family, and friends who, the pamphlet narrates, "enchanted with the imminent hope of liberty, had adorned themselves in their own manner."[29]

Once the lottery began, each winner was individually announced to the assembly and, amid the cheers of "Long Live the King" and choral song, carried from the crowd on the shoulders of his military companions to the dias to receive his certificate of freedom. He then returned to the plaza but, significantly, now took his place standing alongside the ranks of the free *pardo* and black (*moreno*) militia troops. In recounting this episode, the cabildo evidently sought to convey the solemnity of the proceedings as well as the acclaim of the spectators at seeing a deserving slave released from servitude. Indeed, the Patricians Militia corps was so moved that after the allotted thirty names had been announced, its officials stepped forward to sponsor the selection of two additional manumissions in proof of its appreciation. Addressing those "valiant slaves" in a pamphlet that it also distributed to immortalize the lottery, "Demonstration of Gratitude that the Patrician Corps of Buenos-Ayres Makes to the Slaves Distinguished in the Defense of this Capital," the corps apostrophized, "you accomplished deeds worthy of our imitation." Joining the slaves in the high emotions of the day, it recalled: "you yourselves have been witnesses to the joy that we have all had upon seeing the considerable number of dignitaries who presented themselves that afternoon for the lottery of your freedom; you yourselves have seen the pomp, the military formation, and the decorous ostentation approved by our most dignified magistrates to . . . solemnize the most tender, demonstrative presentation that has ever been seen."[30] Other Buenos Aires notables followed the Patricians' lead until seventy of the seven hundred slaves who were able to submit the requisite certificates from their military commanders and masters were granted their freedom. Afterward the music and bright lights continued for several hours.

A poem published in that year also celebrated the lottery as an example of Buenos Aires's generosity. According to the author, Buenos Aires had surpassed the classical models of both Rome and Athens in passing humane laws. To his fellow citizens he applauded,

You have found the secre
For augmenting zealous defenders
As you have paid so well.[31]

The lottery and its literary afterlife seem excessive in their extrava-
gant claims of slave nobility and self-satisfaction in Buenos Aires's generosity. The poet may have been closest to the mark in simply noting the
colony's wise decision to free and co-opt slaves who had experienced com-
bat. Certainly, the choice of a lottery to reward a select portion of slaves
who had fought for the city seems evidence of the cabildo's efforts to contain the social impact of mass mobilization even while dramatizing the
social debts incurred during the invasion. We can only imagine the skep-
ticism of the city's "valiant defenders" who remained in servitude, having
their fate determined by chance, or their evaluation of the cabildo's excuse
that it lacked funds to free all deserving soldiers. Nevertheless, for both
free and slave, this ceremony and its attendant propaganda did show the
way in which military service could work to bridge the status of a slave to
his newfound responsibilities as a free subject of the crown.

Indeed, the patriotic literature of the period exulted in the solvent of
wartime experiences for uniting slave and master. One early epic poem
commemorating those days, "Romance of the Glorious Defense of the
City of Buenos-Ayres," highlighted the role of the colony's slave soldiers:

What prodigies of valor
what heroic exploits they made
these slave vassals
before the eyes of the entire world!

As evidence, it offered the example of a slave who saw his commander,
José Domingo Urien, mortally wounded and exacted swift revenge on the
offending English soldier by lancing him through his chest. Urien, the
poem narrated, witnessed this action from where he lay prostrate on the
ground and turned to "his liberator," saying, "[S]on, look for me later /
in my house, for you are free."[32] Similarly, the mulatto Pablo Ximenes
was manumitted by his master after he was able to kill two British soldiers
and then carry an injured comrade to the hospital, an act, the poem
affirmed, that reflected honor and virtue on both master and former
slave.[33] This poem's inversion of the roles of "liberator," its assurance of
the unity of affections that bound all Buenos Aires's fighting men, and the

grand gestures it finds in slaves and masters alike suggested the kind of possible postwar community that might be forged from such like-minded individuals. Similarly, the future author of Argentina's national anthem, Vicente López y Planes, wrote a poem, "The Heroic Triumph," which also emphasized the cross-racial coalitions that united porteños against the British invaders: "through an infinite number of streets, one sees the illustrious youth run from the neighborhoods, bringing their brio, their heroic valor, their enthusiasm, the Indian, the quadroon, and the son of the browned inhabitant of Ethiopia."[34] This poem, like the other examples, seems determined to stamp on public memory a vision of the city's heroic days grounded in porteños' self-recognition of their commonality.

To be sure, there are more than sufficient counterexamples that illustrate the anxiety that these events provoked among colonial whites and their attempts to arrest social change. The pamphlet that the Patrician Corps had published to praise the lottery and its own subsidy of two slaves' freedom ended with a gentle reminder to the slaves it had patronized: "You should apply yourselves to the work of your crafts, which is the most opportune method to save yourselves from vices that are the infallible consequences of laziness. . . . You were the object upon which fell the demonstration of gratitude of the Patricians of Buenos-Ayres, you should make sure that in your successive actions you are never an object of reprimands and abomination for this corps that is so proud of having freed you."[35]

The cabildo also published a petition that the slave Manuel Antonio Picabea had submitted to municipal authorities seeking a pension for his military services. Picabea explained that he had not entered into the lottery as his mistress, an elderly widow, depended on his earning and his love of her made him "resist against his own good." The subsequent investigation by a neighborhood official conveyed his "admiration upon finding a slave of such lofty sentiments," and the cabildo agreed to a reward of fifty pesos for Picabea and to disseminate this account "in order that the public might know about such an extraordinary act."[36] Slaves bound by ties of affection to their masters and freedmen who assumed their natural place in the colonial order were doubtless models that the viceregal authorities hoped would curtail more profound challenges to the caste system.

For the next decade, however, the militarization of the region would provide greater leverage for those who sought social change than for the defenders of social stability. In 1807, for instance, the viceroy, Santiago

Liniers, moved by a well-founded fear of the continuing British military threat, decided to refound the city's militia divisions by allowing each to select its own commanders. The Córdoba priest Gregorio Funes described the 1807 militia officers' elections as follows: "In these assemblies, the diversity of prerogatives that professions and fortunes gives disappeared, because, moved by love of the fatherland, all put themselves on the same level and allowed merit alone to find them a place. It was a scene worthy of philosophy to see wealthy men as foot soldiers under the orders of a poor laborer, but even more to see the valiant black shoulder to shoulder with his master who for his deeds gave him liberty."[37] Funes's comments make clear how the patriot historian and the king's representative could both celebrate the nature of the new institution. Public elections of the new officer corps permitted the crown at once to reward its most ardent defenders and to harness popular energies to imperial interests through militia service. However, as Funes and other Independence era leaders would recognize, this new-style militia also contained the germ of a new society where, in a short span, centuries of inherited social hierarchies were inverted by the meritocracy of patriotism.[38] He was not alone in his sentiments. Already in 1801, the Enlightenment-inspired editor of the *Telégrafo mercantil* newspaper had attacked the caste system as against the colony's collective interests in depriving "the arts and sciences of learned professors, the King of valiant and devoted soldiers, and the state and country of the society of citizens who could serve it most usefully and splendidly." He could even imagine a day in which Buenos Aires might see "leading soldiers into battle the very people whose grandfathers had been slaves."[39]

These comments remind us of the degree to which early republican authorities clearly drew upon late colonial precedents that were themselves influenced by models of nation building from the late-eighteenth-century Atlantic world. This connection between Argentina's colonial and early national experience reveals the impact of Enlightened absolutist reforms on society. Even before the English invasions, colonial administrative and military reforms, stimulated in large part by imperial rivalries, had sought to impose a new model of authority that called upon heightened levels of civic participation to strengthen both empire and crown. As Spain's ministers expanded colonial armies throughout the empire, they remained committed to maintaining the traditional prestige of the military profession even as the ranks became increasingly open to new social classes. The irony, of course, is that while the status prized by the king's soldiers was the classic expression of the corporate vision of society, the monarchy's determination to grant the special privileges and immunities to an ever-broader spectrum of men blurred the identification of high social status with political privileges. To the consternation of the local (creole) elite, men of otherwise low social status came to enjoy the high rank accorded military men.[40] This was particularly evident in coastal and frontier areas of the Spanish American empire, where free blacks were drawn into military service and loyal slaves occasionally manumitted by the crown for their meritorious actions.[41]

Emancipation and Argentine Republicanism

This colonial precedent would become increasingly important after 1810 as the pressures rose to mobilize society on a vast new scale for the Independence struggle. Colonial authorities had also employed slave soldiers, but only after 1810 was recruitment explicitly linked to citizenship and the enjoyment of the rights enjoyed by free men. The decision to enroll slaves in the revolutionary armies and emancipate them at the end of their service was therefore a distinguishing mark of the early republic. General José de San Martín, who heavily recruited slaves in the western provinces, proclaimed to his troops before they marched on to liberate Chile, "Soldiers, six days ago you were slaves and now you are citizens." As further motivation he read to them a letter supposedly written by Santiago merchants that revealed their designs to sell the Afro-Argentines who might fall prisoners for a boatload of sugar. "Look companions," he warned, "at the fortune that the tyrants of Chile reserve for you."[42] Not surprisingly, some of the strongest bonds between the inchoate state and the newly liberated population were often forged with Afro-Argentines. Slave recruits in particular were notable for their success in pressing their claims for government recognition of their sacrifices on the battlefield, appealing to their corporate identities as soldiers in order to achieve significant individual benefits.

In the Río de la Plata, as throughout much of the Atlantic world of the nineteenth century, armed service became an engine of social modernization as states found traditional hierarchies an obstacle to increasing military manpower or their base of support. When wedded to the republican ideology of the Atlantic Revolutions, this found expression in the soldier-citizen ideal. In this conception, a politicized soldiery was the key to nation building, as the republican emphasis on civic and military participation made clear that citizenship was a learned activity that engendered the kinds of new identities, values, and capacities that made a government based on "the will of the people" possible.[43] Revolutionary pamphlets and newspapers, sermons and speeches, public ceremonies and newly composed rituals served to disseminate these ideas to a wide audience, thereby expanding the "repertoire" of ideological tools available to popular groups for deepening the political and social reforms of the postcolonial era.[44]

As slave recruits were keenly aware, the word *emancipation* had profound resonance in Argentina's early-nineteenth-century political culture, linking slaves' freedom with the emerging character of the nation. It was at the same time a framework by which Argentines interpreted their own political release from imperial tyranny, a shared ideal that Argentines could perceive in each other in moments of collective self-recognition, and a national objective to create, over time, a society free of human bondage. As a society with slaves and slave owners, in which humans were bought and sold and slaves continued to enter the country though a variety of subterfuges until the 1830s, Argentina's embrace of the idea of emancipation was also, of course, one full of contradictions.[45] The enduring importance throughout the century of an individual's socially perceived race in determining opportunities for advancement, for instance, attests to how the Argentine elite cleaved to an ideal of "natural hierarchies" in organizing social relations.[46] Nonetheless, the emancipatory tradition was a source rich and deep enough that it continued to percolate upward in this era of political turbulence, providing slave soldiers and their allies with ideas and practices that they could draw upon in order to realize the promise of an Argentine nationhood founded upon an increasingly open political community.

Revolutionary leaders embraced the goal of ending slavery from the earliest days of the Independence movement. The "slavery" they referred to, however, was the political subjugation of Spain's colonial subjects. This theme was a constant refrain in the Buenos Aires government's official publication, *La gazeta de Buenos-Ayres*. As one article expressed it, the inhabitants of the Río de la Plata had been no more than "humiliated, enviled, degraded under the arbitrary government of Spain...and it was necessary to confess ourselves slaves."[47] A letter to the editor therefore offered praise to the "happy revolution that brought us out of that stupid indifference that characterizes enslaved peoples . . . as the servile do not discuss their fate and allow themselves to be led like vile flocks. . . . Despotism made us servile because fear weighed down the springs of our soul: freedom will make us citizens."[48] Similarly, the Córdoba press in the 1820s lauded new public education initiatives that would end ignorance and fear, the "fruit of slavery," and allow citizens to appreciate the benefit of obeying laws that served the commonweal.[49]

In equating the birth of republican citizenship with the formation of the Independence governments, authorities offered the viceroyalty an interpretive lens for understanding the meaning of the political changes after 1810 and reinforcement for their own legitimacy. To the degree that they were successful on either of these counts, the claim that the new regime would end political slavery also served as a mobilizing ideology, a call to arms for Argentines to defend their freedoms and extend them to Spanish subjects throughout the continent. The porteño troops that marched in July of 1810 on the city of Córdoba were reminded by their commander, "Soldiers, you are going to free them from a shameful slavery." Independence leaders seemed to trust in the appeal of this message, including it in almost all public proclamations made to their fellow provinces. In the Bolivian city of Cochabamba, the colonel Francisco del Rivero assured inhabitants that while imperial officials had considered them all slaves, their Argentine "brothers" who deposed Spain's agents regarded them "as men, that in proportion to their merits" would excel in the new society. Chileans were reminded, "[Y]ou are not slaves, no one can rule you against your will. . . . Nature made us all equal."[50]

Disseminating these ideas played a significant role in the 1810s project to create a political community that, from Buenos Aires's point of view, needed to be convinced of its ability to participate in its own affairs, but once this lesson had been absorbed, would actively defend its self-determination and the regime that represented its newfound power. There were many lessons in republican socialization, however, to learn along the way. In December of 1810, for instance, arguing that it was with ostentatious pomp and circumstance that the "former despots enslaved their subjects," the Buenos Aires government prohibited high-ranking authorities from wearing any distinctive dress or receiving special seating and toasts in public events so that common men could understand the new character of its leadership.[51] Three months later, the central government decided to allow popular elections of provincial authorities, noting

that while before it had feared that "slave subjects do not have a fatherland nor love of the public good," the revolutionary tutelage had borne
results and it was now confident that the "best fruit of this revolution con-
sists in making the peoples appreciate the advantages of a popular government." A letter to the editor echoed these sentiments, imagining that
in republican Buenos Aires, while a poor man might find in his house
many signs of his misery, he need only walk into the street to "see his dignity, find his throne, and remind himself of his sovereignty," and if he
might come upon a rich neighbor there, he need only "remind himself of
the political equality that was between them, he and his fellow citizen."[52]

By 1813 military setbacks and political resistance to Buenos Aires's
centralized authority forced the revolutionary regime to expand its base of
support. In the process, its rhetoric and reforms came to explicitly link the
viceroyalty's anticolonial struggle with the emancipation of Afro-Argentine
slaves. The "free womb" law, which freed at adulthood slaves born after
January 31, 1813, was passed as one of the first acts of the newly constituted
General Assembly. This gradual emancipation helped resolve the contradiction, the decree explained, "in the same communities that with tenacity
and effort walk toward their freedom, there might remain more time in
slavery those children that are born in the United Provinces of the Río de
la Plata."[53] Thus, without impinging on individuals' property rights, the
measure would ensure that slavery would be "extinguished successively
until this miserable race is redeemed and made the same as all other classes
of the state and [show] that nature has never formed slaves but men."[54]
Other liberal reforms followed that helped distance the new society from
the old regime: it abolished indigenous tribute and declared Indians equal
to other citizens, publishing the decree in native languages; made torture
illegal; and ended the Inquisition. In a fitting gesture to celebrate
Independence Day that year, May 25, the General Assembly proclaimed the
end of the slave trade, an appropriate landmark as the Independence armies
now began to incorporate Argentine slaves. It was, the local press would
argue in 1823, "a law that did honor to those that dictated it and filled with
glory that country that adopted it."[55] A generation later, with the defeat of
the dictatorship of the Buenos Aires governor, Juan Manuel de Rosas, the
1853 Constitution would finally provide for complete abolition. This
moment of self-definition again saw in the fate of slavery a reflection of
Argentina's political progress: "Slavery has succumbed among us one
moment after the tyranny collapsed."[56]

Self-congratulatory about the liberal pedigree that they could lay claim to as a result of this legislation, postcolonial governments reinforced the identification of Argentine nationhood with the end of human bondage in patriotic celebrations. Beginning in 1812 and continuing into the 1820s, authorities in Buenos Aires and in Córdoba province marked the May 25 commemoration with a public lottery in which a small number of slaves were chosen to be freed.[57] In 1825 a Córdoba newspaper wrote of the joy the assembled lottery crowd shared with the slaves who had been freed with public funds. In the slaves' manumission, the editorial noted, one perceived "the enthusiasm, the patriotism upon seeing the source of this benefit and other sentiments that were revealed from within the slaves drew the attention of the men of state. It is not possible that anyone with good sentiments not feel himself moved by the cause of humanity!"[58] The patriotism that observers found in the new freedmen, and the free community's show of commitment to gradual abolition, helped to consolidate the vision of Argentina as a society in which slavery's days were numbered. "The diminution of the slaves is already being felt and [their] total extinction should be promoted as soon as possible," an article reported in 1823, calling at the same time for new regulations to govern domestic service now that porteño households were increasingly being staffed by free men and not slaves.[59] In order to hasten and channel this process, the Liberal government of Bernadino Rivadavia in Buenos Aires established new African Associations between 1821 and 1823, mutual-aid societies for Afro-Argentines that would lend funds for members to purchase their manumission and provide educational and religious services to facilitate their transition into free society.[60]

Slave Soldiers and Their Allies

It was in this ideological and political context that Argentine slave soldiers demanded that their actions on the battlefield be understood as signs of their steadfast patriotism. In proud narratives of the engagements, generals, and years of service that they had known, they sought recognition from authorities of their rights to civil liberty as well as, often enough, the state's help in freeing their family members.[61] Slave soldiers' strategy of petitioning authorities for freedom became crucial after 1816 when Congress limited making slaves "citizens only after they might have bought this precious gift at the price of their military actions."[62] During the civil wars of 1820–53 when central authority collapsed, the practice of offering freedom upon recruitment or only after the completion of their service varied according to local circumstances. Slave soldiers therefore became adept at pursuing freedom by presenting provincial governors with their particular political vitae. In doing so, they countered the traditional view that slaves were not political beings because, as property, their minds, like their bodies, belonged to their owners. Soldiering, however, had endowed them with a political personality. Indeed, to dispel one fiction they cloaked themselves in another: the fond hope, announced time and again by the province's leaders, that soldiers' actions under their leaders' command was a testament to their loyalty. In these petitions, soldiers' tales became protestations of fealty, told by men of decision whose lives demonstrated that they were fully worthy of the benefits that the government had long held out as belonging to those who helped to create the new order.

These moments of high emotions in which the promise of a better society was briefly crystallized in the call and response of the soldiers' act of petitioning and the governor's dispensation were indicative of larger sociopolitical transformations that also worked to ratify the new understandings. Indeed, it is noteworthy the extent to which early republican governments began to erode caste privileges in an attempt to win the favor of their Afro-Argentine recruits. During the early 1810s many militia and veteran regiments were, for the first time, integrated. Black officers won the right to be addressed by the honorific "don" and in several cases could even be found commanding white troops.[63]

Integration and increasing status into the white world was not, of course, the only identity that Argentine slaves sought. In Buenos Aires, the African Associations that Rivadavia established resisted government supervision and instead employed the organizations to reinforce kinship ties and community traditions. Indeed, as in the colonial period, they often were willing to trade political and military support in order to gain official patronage of their cultural organizations. One prospective association leader thus wrote to a Buenos Aires political boss, "We, the individuals who are going to form this society, are all militiamen of the active militia. We are decided supporters of order and constituted authority."[64] Governor Juan Manuel de Rosas was notable for his cultivation of the African Associations, attending candombe performances and receiving association leaders at his home, practices that Oscar Chamosa argues "clearly resemble rituals of homage between village elders and kings in Africa."[65] However, if the associations were efforts to adapt African practices to the diaspora, the cohesion of the groups was threatened by internal rivalries as well as the conflictive politics of the time. The original associations gathered in their societies various "nations" and African ethnicities. Members valued the associations as a way to fulfill the obligation to honor their ancestors. Thus, the associations tended to fragment over time as aspiring leaders established new lineages as the basis for their communal identity. Toward this end, new leaders had to win the sanction of Rosas's local police chiefs, cementing ties of patron-client between the Buenos Aires state and the growing number of African Associations, which grew to more than fifty by midcentury.[66]

In Córdoba, the most concerted attempt to win the allegiance of the province's considerable black and freedman population was under the Centralist governor José María Paz (1829–31). Surrounded by a hostile countryside and desperate for additional support, Paz made a special effort to bring urban black artisans to his side. His cultivation of urban blacks began with a promise that at the war's conclusion, he would emancipate slaves who had been conscripted into his forces by an October 1829 decree.[67] Paz also founded a new militia battalion of urban artisans, principally composed of castas, that linked militia support with substantial psychosocial benefits for Afro-Argentines. The innovation was clear when he replaced the white silversmith Cayetano Álvarez, who had, as nominal head of the artisan community (that is, master artisan of the most prestigious guild), formally commanded the urban militia, with the mulatto army officer and former slave Lorenzo Barcala. The nineteenth-century historian Domingo Sarmiento explained this as a deliberate move to provide Paz's administration with "an interpreter who should explain his ideas and objects to the common people."[68] While Sarmiento's characterization perhaps overstates the explicit mediating function Barcala played, certainly his appointment broke with the convention by which casta troops were, in traditional colonial fashion, led by white officers.

Moreover, Paz openly defended his casta officers, who suffered the stigma of their color and their slave births, against public incidents of social prejudice.[69] Paz demanded proper respect for his officers. For his black and mulatto soldiers, he made militia service the basis for providing them with access to previously denied social privileges. Arguing that it was inconsistent that castas served in the militia and yet were denied entrance into public schools, much to the detriment of artisan skills, he

FIGURE 9.1:
Lorenzo Barcala
(1795–1835). Born
a slave in Mendoza
province, Barcala
rose to be a colonel.
Reproduced courtesy of
the Archivo General de
la Nación, Dpto. Doc.
Fotográficos, Argentina.

ordered the schools opened to all social classes and established two government scholarships to support talented castas in the university.[70] In
another case, he overruled the objection of a local priest to the marriage
of one his black soldiers to a white woman. For other casta recruits he
extracted a concession from the church for lower nuptial fees in order that
poverty might not constitute an obstacle to marriage.[71]

The success of Paz's efforts can be gauged by the loyalty of black
artisans to the Centralist cause when the Centralists briefly regained control of Córdoba in late 1840. According to Sarmiento, Barcala's efforts
had not been in vain: "the lower classes were transformed by the magic
of his power; and the officers and soldiers of his training were remarkable

for their good behavior, decent dress, intelligence and love of liberty."[72] Marching under a banner that bore Barcala's name, the black infantry battalions defended the city and many followed the Centralists in their retreat to the north. Even the victorious Federalists commented on the adhesion of the urban castas to the defeated Centralists. As the army commissary discovered quickly in 1841, the deaths and forced emigrations that the artisan population suffered constituted a severe drain of essential craftsmen for the province. Outfitting troops proved much more difficult after the 1841 conflict due to the loss of their skilled hands and the breakdown of the guild organizations.[73]

Their close identification with Centralists may be the cause behind the second substantial attempt to mobilize Córdoba's slave population: the creation of the López Squadron in the early 1850s of a new regiment headed by the governor's son, José Vicente López. Recruits for this regiment drew mainly from the population of libertos. Largely rural young men, they seem to have been regarded by López as a human resource on which the state had first claim, as it was the government that had provided for their liberty. The end result of the López Squadron was further to undermine the slave regime in the province. Though the regiment seemed to make no attempt to raise the social status of its soldiers or to allow for mobility of castas into the officers' ranks, it did contribute to the liquidation of the remnants of slavery, as its commander constantly found himself obliged to respond to his soldiers' requests to use military funds to help redeem their wives from slavery.[74]

Córdoba's treatment of its slave soldiers was hardly unique in the Río de la Plata and illustrates in many ways the nature and limits of power in the early national regimes. The recruitment of slaves responded primarily to the need of aspiring leaders, of all political stripes, to create a new base of power independent of local men of property. For example, in order to liberate his "Eastern State," the Banda Oriental caudillo, José Gervasio Artigas abolished slavery in 1814 and also reached out to the rural poor. He was already in open opposition to Buenos Aires; his emancipatory measures were crucial in his attempt to gain support for a complete break with the United Provinces. Later, after the Portuguese crushed his experiment, the reimposition of slavery by the victors and the subsequent promise of emancipation by insurgents would be a constant dynamic in the struggle for control of early Uruguay.[75]

General José San Martín, fundamentally dependent on Buenos Aires to help him mount his campaign across the Andes, found it necessary to respect the regime's laws but also expedient to recur to slave enlistment. No radical reformer, the general nonetheless encouraged rumors in the Cuyo provinces of an imminent abolition in order to intimidate owners into presenting their slaves to his armies for later compensation.[76] San Martín's career was marked by his single-minded mission to destroy Spanish power on the continent. He stepped back from completely militarizing Mendoza's society and economy only for fear of utterly alienating both his supporters in Buenos Aires and the local elite. In enemy territory, however, "the Liberator" would aggressively recruit slaves with the promise of emancipation. He abolished the slave trade, extended the "free womb" law, and confiscated Spaniards' slaves, incorporating them in his troops.[77] These measures allowed San Martín to polarize the Pacific coast societies and create an army capable of finally demolishing the Spanish Empire.

In the Argentine revolutionary experience, slave emancipation was linked to the enjoyment of civil rights only through the agency of military service. That is, it was by becoming soldiers that ex-slaves became citizens. San Martín's liberated Chile is an example. The decree that freed slave soldiers spoke in broad terms of "extinguishing the degradation of man." Yet beyond these lofty principles it concluded that it could trust in the enthusiasm of enlisted slaves to use the "robustness of their arms" to save the fatherland that freed them if only "so that they might not fall in the hands of a tyrant who would return them to the awful condition from which they have been extracted."[78]

Argentina and the lands it helped to free were nations born through the work of new armies brought into being by a determined military leadership. This was a leadership often inspired by the influential models of the revolutionary Atlantic, with its ideal of the nation in arms. Yet, more than revolutionary France or the United States, these were clearly nations that were works in progress. The revolutionary generals who hoped to begin the work of nation building saw as their first priority the task of assembling and arming those men who would create the nation. Revolutionary Argentina, therefore, tended not to issue decrees on the universal rights of man or to propose sweeping measures to abolish caste and corporate distinctions. Instead, it offered unprecedented benefits for those soldiers who fought under its flag. Only in outlying regions where Argentine armies entered as a conquering force, or in the case of Artigas, who radicalized his movement in a bid to establish an independent base of

FIGURE 9.2: *"Blacks of the Rosas Federation" (Negros Federales). This painting by the Uruguayan artist Pedro Figari (1861–1938) is one of his many illustrations of the black community's festivities in nineteenth-century Río de la Plata. From* Figari: Cielos, Fiestas, Ceremonias, *Plate 23 (London: Wildenstein and Co. Ltd, 1972).*

support, did these leaders broaden the social transformation in order to mobilize support in virgin territory.

General Paz's cultivation of urban blacks clearly fits in this tradition. In the competition for support during Córdoba's bloody civil war, black recruitment became the wedge by which the Centralists began to pry open the identification between caste and civil status. Paz's government had relatively little to offer the majority of the province's slaves as slaves. But for his black soldiers, he offered opportunity and respect in return for their adherence to his cause. In turn, however, his alliance with the castas gave them a role in shaping the outlines of the society that together they briefly upheld.

Neither Paz nor the Buenos Aires governor Juan Manuel de Rosas envisioned a program of social change. In each case, however, under the pressures of war, their search for a constituency and for loyal soldiers led them inevitably to the Afro-Argentine community, a visible and legally distinct minority for whom the governors' patronage did indeed signal a social change. Even without an Argentine emancipation proclamation, black soldiering sapped all vitality from the institution of slavery, a transformation none of these governors consciously sought but which their policies nonetheless produced. It remained for a later generation of nation builders after the 1860s to find these cross-racial and cross-class alliances increasingly unnecessary in a country shaped by strong central government, Liberal reforms, and waves of European immigrants, all of which allowed Argentina to finally bury its disorderly past.

APPENDIX

Francisco Rodrigues Solicits his Freedom

Service in the armed forces as a path to freedom was not one that slaves chose lightly, even when they had the ability to choose. Slaves who fought in Argentina's civil wars, for instance, faced the danger of fighting on the losing side. When the ironsmith Francisco Rodriguez wrote to Cordoba's Federalist governor in 1836, therefore, he was at pains to clarify the blind obedience to his master and commanders that compelled his participation in the enemy Centralist armies seven years earlier. Indeed, in Rodriguez's argument, even though urban black artisans formed one of General José María Paz's principal bases of support, it was his master who had supported the Centralist cause by donating his slave, and thus had forfeited his ownership. In the end, Rodriguez did win the right to purchase his freedom, a practice that also existed in the colonial period. So what changes had Independence brought? Most notable was the way in which war made property rights unstable as slaves' military services increased the willingness of the state to assert its own interests. Equally important was a shift in sympathies. A time-honored practice such as self-purchase was now interpreted by local elites who intervened in this case as an affirmation of Argentina's republican principles. As his petition shows, Francisco, biding his time, seems to have understood this.

Long Live the Federation!
Excellent Señor:
Francisco Rodriguez, native of this [province], *moreno* slave of the deceased cleric don Emilio Rodriguez and upon his death remained in the same captivity under a sister of his named doña Manuel Rodriguez, who I have served until now with great respect, submit and say:
 That in the time of the Centralist administration, I was handed over with pleasure by my master don Segundo Martinez into armed service in the army of the execrable General Paz, in which I found myself in the battle of La Tablada and in that of Laguna Larga as a soldier, obeying those commanders in all that they ordered me pertaining to my service. After having returned from the last battle they put me to work in the arms workshop in my craft, which is that of ironsmith, where I remained until that army was dissolved.
 Excellent Señor, after several months in which this [province] was under the command of the Federation, my above-mentioned master recovered me and let me know that he had sold me to the master of my workshop, don Francisco Leje, the master with whom I have remained about two years, more or less, working in the forges without any salary more than said don Francisco gave to me, which was the occasional hour for me to make some small piece for myself. . . .
 [Rodriguez then explains that he is not certain whether he was indeed sold to Leje or if Leje is simply paying Martinez his salary and that currently Martinez is attempting to sell him. Nevertheless, he argues:] I should be freed as I was voluntarily handed over to the Centralist party so he has no rights over me, for unless God had chosen not to allow me to die in those battles there would have been no servant to sell nor any wages to earn for none of those whom I have served with my personal work in my craft. I am an unfortunate with nowhere to turn my eyes but to you, and as I was handed over to the fatherland, he

[Martinez] has no dominion over me, only the authority of Your
Excellency or the service of the state.

Archivo Histórico de la Provincia de Córdoba, notarial records 2,
file 130, 13, 1836.

On *January 4, 1836 the governor, Manuel Lopez, ordered the suspension
of Rodriguez's sale, while Martinez requested a personal audience with the governor to clear up the matter, which was accepted as long as the defensor of pobres,
Carlos Tagle, was also present. On February 3 the governor decided to allow
Rodriguez to purchase his freedom and ordered his assessment which, for a
healthy thirty-one-year-old male ironsmith, was calculated at 250 pesos. When,
on February 9, the defensor de pobres protested this assessment as unjust when
considering the freedom of a man, the assessor clarified that while Rodriguez was
one of the best ironsmiths around, he had the defects of frequently being drunk
and suspected for his involvement in petty crimes, but in accordance with the natural equality in the tendency or spirit of the current national law on this matter
and the republican principles of which we boast . . . he believed the price was fair.*

NOTES

I am the grateful beneficiary of research support from the Institute on
Race and Ethnicity, University of Wisconsin System, and the Gilder
Lehrman Institute for the Study of Slavery, Abolition, and Resistance,
Yale University; their assistance was crucial in allowing me to bring this
chapter to completion.

1. *Poema que un amante de la patria consagra al solemne sorteo celebrado en la
plaza mayor de Buenos-Ayres, para la libertad de los esclavos que pelearon en su
defensa* (Buenos Aires: Real Imprenta de los Níños Expósitos, 1807), 1.

2. Archivo Histórico de la Provincia de Córdoba, Hacienda, 1831, vol. 378,
fol. 254.

3. George Reid Andrews, *Afro-Latin America, 1800–2000* (New York: Oxford
University Press, 2004), 57.

4. Núria Sales de Bohigas, "Esclavos y reclutas en Sudamérica," *Revista de
historia de América* 70 (July–December 1970): 287; Carmen Bernard,
"La población negra de Buenos Aires (1777–1862)," in *Homogeneidad*

y nación con un estudio de caso: Argentina, siglos XIX y XX, ed. Mónica
Quijada, Carmen Bernard, and Arnd Schneider (Madrid: Consejo
Superior de Investigaciones Científicas, Centro de Humanidades,
Instituto de Historia, 2000), 126.

5. Bartolomé Mitre, *Episodios de la revolución* (Buenos Aires: Editorial
Universitaria de Buenos Aires, 1960; orig. pub. 1857), 31. For doubts
about the existence of "Falucho," see Pedro Olgo Ochoa, "El invento
de Falucho," *Todo es historia* 4, no. 41 (1970): 32–39.

6. M. F. Mantilla, "Los negros argentinos: El monumento a Falucho,"
Revista nacional 10 (1889): 174.

7. Gregorio Funes, *Oración patriotica que por el felix aniversario de la
regeneración política de la América Meridional Dixo el Decoro don Gregorio
Funes Dean de la iglesia catedral de Córdoba del Tucumán en la de Buenos-Ayres,
el día de 25 de Mayo de 1814* (Buenos Aires: Real Imprenta de los Niños
Expósitos, 1814), 3, 14.

8. "Oración que djio en la Catedral de Cordoba su Canónigo magistral
Dotor [*sic*] don Miguel Calixto del Corro el día 25 de Mayo de 1819,"
in *El clero argentino de 1810–1830: Oraciones patrióticas*, ed. Adolfo P.
Carranza (Buenos Aires: Museo Histórico Nacional, 1907), 1:305.

9. Peter Blanchard, "The Language of Liberation: Slave Voices in the Wars
of Independence," *Hispanic American Historical Review* 82, no. 3 (2002):
501; Camilla Townsend, "'Half My Body Free, the Other Half Enslaved':
The Politics of the Slaves of Guayaquil at the End of the Colonial Era,"
Colonial Latin American Review 7, no. 1 (1998): 107.

10. David Rock, *Argentina, 1516–1987: From Spanish Colonization to Alfonsín*
(Berkeley: University of California Press, 1987), 23; Nicholas Cushner,
*Jesuit Ranches and the Agrarian Development of Colonial Argentina,
1650–1767* (Albany: SUNY Press, 1983).

11. Emiliano Endrek, *El mestizaje en Córdoba, siglo XVII y principios del XIX*
(Córdoba: Universidad Nacional de Córdoba, Dirección General de
Publicaciones, 1966), 12; Bernard, "La población negra," 95.

12. Lyman Johnson, "Manumission in Colonial Buenos Aires, 1776–1810,"
Hispanic American Historical Review 59, no. 2 (1979): 277.

13. Ibid., 262. In Córdoba, this ratio was reversed. One-quarter of slaves
gained freedom through self-purchase and the rest were freed by their
masters, often with conditions. See Robert J. Turkovic, "Race Relations
in the Province of Córdoba, Argentina, 1800–1853" (Ph.D. diss.,
University of Florida, 1981), 168. The contrast may lie in the higher

number of native-born slaves in the interior and the kind of paternalistic relations they enjoyed, which Johnson found to be related to a higher incidence of owner-initiated manumissions (Johnson, op.cit., 270).

14. Johnson, "Manumission," 261–63, 275.

15. Victor M. Uribe-Uran, "The Birth of a Public Sphere in Latin America during the Age of Revolution," *Comparative Studies in Society and History* 42, no. 2 (2000): 432.

16. Endrek, *El mestizaje en Córdoba*, 7, 40–44; Bernard, "La población negra," 97.

17. Endrek, *El mestizaje en Córdoba*, 74.

18. George Reid Andrews, *The Afro-Argentines of Buenos Aires, 1800–1900* (Madison: University of Wisconsin Press, 1980), 32; Lyman Johnson, "The Development of Slave and Free Labor Regimes in Late Colonial Buenos Aires, 1770–1815" (Occasional Paper, no. 9, Latin American Studies Consortium of New England, Center for Latin American and Caribbean Studies, Storrs, CT, February 1997), 12.

19. This paragraph is based on the discussion in Carmen Bernard, "Entre pueblo y plebe: Patriotas, pardos, africanos en Argentina (1790–1852)," in *Blacks, Coloured and National Identity in Nineteenth-Century Latin America*, ed. Nancy Priscilla Naro (London: Institute of Latin American Studies, 2003), 64–66.

20. Andrews, *Afro-Latin America*, 62.

21. Sales de Bohigas, "Esclavos y reclutas en Sudamérica," 335.

22. Andrews, *Afro-Latin America*, 66.

23. Turkovic, "Race Relations in the Province of Córdoba," 73, 77, 79, 83.

24. Bernard, "La población negra,"123.

25. Silvia C. Mallo, "La libertad en el discurso del estado, de amos, y esclavos, 1780–1830," *Revista de historia de América* 112 (1991): 128.

26. *Relación circunstanciada de los premios de la libertad que ha concedido el M.I.C. de la capital de Buenos-Ayres a la esclavatura de ella, por el merito que contrajo en su defensa del dia 5 de Julio del presente año de 1807* (Buenos Aires: Real Imprenta de los Níños Expósitos, 1807), 2.

27. Ibid.

28. Ibid., 4.

29. Ibid., 6.

30. *Demonstración de gratitud que hace el cuerpo de patricios de Buenos-Ayres a los esclavos distinguidos en la defensa de esta capital* (Buenos Aires: Real Imprenta de los Níños Expósitos, 1807), 1–2.

31. *Poema que un amante de la patria consagra al solemne sorteo,* 1.

32. *Romance de la gloriosa defensa de la cuidad de Buenos-Ayres* (Buenos Aires: Real Imprenta de los Niños Expósitos, 1807), 27.

33. Ibid., 28.

34. Bernard, "Entre pueblo y plebe," 72.

35. *Demonstración de gratitud que hace el cuerpo de patricios,* 3.

36. *Muy ilustre cabildo* (Buenos Aires: Real Imprenta de los Níños Expósitos, 1807), 1–2.

37. *Ensayo de la historia civíl de Buenos Aires, Tucumán y Paraguay.* 2nd ed. (Buenos Aires: Imprenta Bonarense, 1856).

38. Steven Mintz, "Models of Emancipation during the Age of Revolution," *Slavery and Abolition* 17, no. 2 (1996): 5–7, 13–14.

39. Quoted in Andrews, *Afro-Argentines,* 47.

40. Lyle N. McAllister, *The "Fuero Militar" in New Spain: 1764–1800* (Gainesville: University Presses of Florida, 1957), 35.

41. Peter M. Voelz, *Slave and Soldier: The Military Impact of Blacks in the Colonial Americas* (New York: Garland, 1993), 433; Jane Landers, *Black Society in Spanish Florida* (Urbana, University of Illinois Press, 1999), 39; Kimberly S. Hanger, *Bounded Lives, Bounded Places. Free Black Society in Colonial New Orleans, 1769–1803* (Durham, NC: Duke University Press, 1997), 48.

42. Sales de Bohigas, "Esclavos y reclutas en Sudamérica," 292.

43. R. Claire Snyder, *Citizen-Soldiers and Manly Warriors: Military Service and Gender in the Civic Republican Tradition* (Lanham, MD: Rowman & Littlefield, 1999), 3; Morris Janowitz, "Military Institutions and Citizenship in Western Societies," *Armed Forces and Society* 2 (February 1976): 190.

44. This concept is drawn from Charles Tilly, "How to Detect, Describe, and Explain Repetoires of Contention" (Working Paper Series, no. 150, New School for Social Research, New York, October 1992).

45. Andrews, *Afro-Argentines,* 54–57.

46. See, for instance, the review by Jonathan Brown, "The Bondage of Old Habits in Nineteenth-Century Argentina," *Latin American Research Review* 21, no. 2: (1986) 9–17 and evidence for growing racial tolerance in Jeffrey Shumway, "'The Purity of My Blood Cannot Put Food on My Table': Changing Attitudes towards Interracial Marriage in Nineteenth-Century Buenos Aires," *Americas* 58, no. 2 (2001): 201–20.

47. *Gazeta de Buenos-Ayres*, December 27, 1810, 457.

48. *Gazeta extraordinaria de Buenos Ayres*, November 20, 1810, 1–5.

49. *El montonero*, January 28, 1824, 27.

50. *Gazeta extraordinaria de Buenos Ayres*, August 11, 1810, 5; February 18, 1811, 82–83; March 5, 1811, 97.

51. Ibid., December 8, 1810, 33–38.

52. *Gazeta de Buenos-Ayres*, February 14, 1811, 549, 559.

53. Quoted in José Carlos, Chiaramonte, *Cuidades, provincias, estados: Orígenes de la nación Argentina* (Buenos Aires: Ariel, 1997), 148.

54. Ibid. See also Andrews, *Afro-Argentines*, 47–48.

55. *Teatro de la opinión*, March 12, 1824, 699. This editorial was calling attention to the loopholes in the slave trade prohibition.

56. "Libertad de los esclavos," *La libre navegación de los ríos* (Corrientes), November 30, 1853, 1.

57. David Bushnell, *Reform and Reaction in the Platine Provinces, 1810–1852* (Gainesville: University Presses of Florida, 1983), 143; Hans Vogel, "Fiestas patrias y nuevas lealtades," *Todo es historia* 25, no. 287 (1991): 47; Archivo Histórico de la Provincia de Córdoba, Gobierno (AHPC-G), 1825, vol. 88, fol. 405.

58. *El desengandor*, June 5, 1825, 105. See also "Córdoba," *Congreso argentino*, April 14, 1826, 31.

59. "Policia," *El correo de las provincias*, January 23, 1823, 74.

60. Andrews, *Afro-Argentines*, 143–44; Pilar González Bernaldo de Quirós, *Civilidad y política en los orígenes de la nación Argentina: Las sociabilidades en Buenos Aires, 1829–1862* (Buenos Aires: Fondo de Cultura Económica, 2000), 113–14.

61. AHPC-G, 1826, box 93, fol. 509; Archivo Histórico de la Provincia de Córdoba, Escribanías, 1836, file 78, 17.

62. Sales de Bohigas, "Esclavos y reclutas en Sudamérica," 291.

63. Turkovic, "Race Relations in the Province of Córdoba," 218.

64. Quoted in Oscar Chamosa, "'To Honor the Ashes of Their Forefathers': The Rise and Crisis of African Nations in the Post-Independence State of Buenos Aires, 1820–1860," *Americas* 59, no. 3 (2003): 360.

65. Ibid., 364.

66. Ibid., 347, 364.

67. AHPC-G, 1830, vol. 114, fol. 89; Notas de Contaduría, 1829–31, October 9, 1830; Turkovic, "Race Relations in the Province of Córdoba," 255–56; Instituto de Estudios Americanistas, Universidad Nacional de Córdoba, Argentina, #5532.

68. Domingo Faustino Sarmiento, *Life in the Argentine Republic in the Days of the Tyrants; or, Civilization and Barbarism*, trans. Mrs. Horace Mann (New York: Hafner Press, 1868), 166.

69. Lucio Funes, "El Colonel Barcala," *Revista de la Junta de Estudios Históricos de Mendoza* 7 (1937): 131, 140; Ignacio Garzón, *Crónica de Córdoba* (Córdoba: Alfonso Aveta, 1892), 2:231; Turkovic, "Race Relations in the Province of Córdoba," 218; Andrews, *Afro-Argentines*, 137.

70. Garzón, *Crónica de Córdoba*, 2:350. Race-blind admission to public schools was revoked when Paz fell and not restored until 1852: *Compilación de leyes, decretos y acuerdos de la Excma: Cámara de Justicia y demás disposiciones de carácter público dictadas en la Provincia de Córdoba desde 1810 á 1870* (Córdoba: Legislatura de la Provincia de Córdoba, 1870), 1:170.

71. AHPC-G, 1830, vol. 115, fol. 530; 1831, vol. 126, fol. 590.

72. Sarmiento, *Life in the Argentine Republic*, 249.

73. AHPC-G, 1841, vol. 175, fols. 233, 377.

74. Turkovic, "Race Relations in the Province of Córdoba," 254; AHPC-G, 1846, box 200, fol. 542; 1848, box 210, fol. 230; box 211, fol. 392; vol. 214, fol. 330.

75. Rock, *Argentina*, 91; Sales de Bohigas, "Esclavos y reclutas en Sudamérica," 281.

76. Eduardo B. Astesano, *San Martín y el orígen del capitalismo argentino* (Buenos Aires: Ediciones Coyoacán, 1961), 58.

77. Tulio Halperín Donghi, *Revolución y guerra: Formación de una élite dirigente en la Argentina criolla* (Buenos Aires: Siglo Veintiuno, 1972), 250–52; Sales de Bohigas, "Esclavos y reclutas en Sudamérica," 314.

78. Sales de Bohigas, "Esclavos y reclutas en Sudamérica," 295.

Glossary

Alcalde   City councilman and magistrate

Audiencia   High court of Spanish America; also the territorial unit
served by that court

Batuque   Reunion for African drumming and dancing in Brazil

Bozal   Recently imported African, non-Spanish speaking
and unassimilated

Cabildo   Town council in Spanish America; ecclesiastical council

Cabildo de nación   Ethnic organization of Africans and
their descendants

Candomblé   Afro-Brazilian religion

Canto   Work group in Brazil, organized by ethnicity

Capatáz   Overseer of a plantation or of a gang of slave laborers;
also the steward of a cabildo de nación

Casta   Person of mixed ancestry

Cédula   Royal decree

Cimarrón   Runaway slave

Coartación   System of self-purchase for slaves

Cofradía   Lay confraternity or religious brotherhood

Encomienda   Grant of the labor or service of Indians

Engenho   Sugar mill plantation

Feitoria   Portuguese trading factory

Hacendado   Owner of a large estate

Hacienda   Royal treasury; also a large landed estate

Ladino   Spanish-speaking Catholic of African descent

Liberto   Freed slave

Marronage   Slave flight

Mayordomo   Manager, foreman; also the leader of a cabildo de nación

Mestizo (or mestiço)   Person of Indian and European ancestry

Moreno   A black, usually free

Mulato   Person of black and European ancestry

Negro de ganho   Black laborer who hired himself out for wages

Oidor   Judge on the high court in Spanish America

Ouvidor   Judge on the high court in Brazil

Palenque   Runaway slave community in Spanish America

Pardo   Mulatto, usually free; any person of color

Qadi   Judge

Quilombo   Runaway slave community in Brazil

República y común   Republic and commonwealth

Ulamā   Scholarly community

Vecino   Property-owning permanent resident of a city

Zambo   Person of Indian and black ancestry

Contributors

Dr. Matt D. Childs is assistant professor of
history at Florida State University.

Dr. Lynne Guitar is resident director of the
Council on International Education Exchange
Program in Santo Domingo, Dominican Republic.

Dr. Jane G. Landers is associate professor of
history at Vanderbilt University.

Dr. Paul E. Lovejoy is Distinguished Research
Professor of History at York University.

Dr. Seth Meisel is assistant professor of history at the
University of Wisconsin at Whitewater.

Dr. Matthew Restall is professor of history at
Pennsylvania State University.

Dr. Barry M. Robinson is assistant professor of
history at Samford University.

Dr. Stuart B. Schwartz is George Burton Adams
Professor of History at Yale University.

Dr. Renée Soulodre-La France is assistant professor of history at
Kings's University at the University of Western Ontario.

Dr. John K. Thornton is professor of
history at Boston College.

Index

≈

Italicized numbers indicate illustrations.

marronage, 247. *See also* petite
marronage
Martius, Karl von, 252, 258–59
Matamba, 84–85
Matamba, Portugal and, 91
Matosa, Francisco de la, 126
Mayas, 164
McFarlane, Anthony, 188
McKee, Larry, 115
medieval slave codes, 2, 6–7, 29,
112–13, 132. *See also* corporatism,
black Africans and
Mendoza, Antonio de, 118
Mendoza, Pedro de, 277
Menéndez de Avilés, Pedro, 118
Menezes, Bernardo de, 101–3
Mesoamerica, black Africans in, 3–4
Metcalf, Alida, 190
Middle Passage, 1, 42, 63, 148–49,
167n3
military service, manumission and,
6, 275
militiamen, Veracruz, *131, 223*
Miller, Joseph, 116
Mina Coast, 24–25, 249
Mina Guagni cabildo, 217; creoles
and, 209–12; functions, 210
Mina people, 23, 28
*Mi'raj al-su'ud—The Ladder of Ascent
towards Grasping the Law concerning
Transported Blacks* (BÇbÇ), 10,
30–33
Mitre, Bartolomé, 276
mobility of black Africans in New
Spain, 156–59, *157*
Montejo, Francisco de, 149–50
Montesinos, Antonio de, 43

Morell de Santa Cruz, Bishop, 214
Morocco, 4, 13–16, 22, 29, 35n6
Muhammad, Askia, 22
Muslims, 2, 19–20, 22–23, 26–29,
248; slave trade and, 26–29.
See also Islam
Musolongo cabildo, 218

Nagô (Yoruba) nation, 252
Ñanga. *See* Yanga (Ñanga)
Ñanga, Gaspar, 128–29
"nation," definition of, 237n2
Ndongo, 86
New Laws of 1542, 51
New Spain, black African
population, 118–19
Nicuesa, Diego de, 43
Njinga, Queen, 84–85, 90, 99
Nuestra Señora de Guadalupe de
los Morenos de Amapa, 132
Nuestra Señora de la Merced
brotherhood, 119–20
Nuestra Señora del Pilar, 151
Nueva Granada, 175–76
Núñez de Balboa, Alonso, 43

Ocampo, Dieguillo de, 41
Ogboni Society, 239n28
Ojeda, Alonso de, 43
Ovando, Nicolás de, 45, 117

Paiua, João de, 101–3
palenques, 114, 116
Palmares, 143n47
Panama, Joseph de, 130–31
Parada, Antón de la, 124

Valladolid, Juan de, 113
Vaquero, Juan, 41
Vasconcelos, Mendes de, 89
Vásquez de Ayllón, Lucas, 43
Velasco, Luis de, II, 118, 120, 125, 133
Velásquez, José Díaz, 211
Velázquez, Diego, 43
vida política, 116–17
Villalpando, Captain, 41
Villavieja hacienda, 183–87; slave
    petitions, 196–200

Williams, Peter, 158
Wolof people, 50

Ximenes, Pablo, 284

Yanga (Ñanga), 108n42, 121–23,
    124–28, 127–28; "Conditions
    for Peace," 133–35
Yebra, Pedro de, 124
Yoruba, 23
Yucatan: Central Mexico and,
    173–74n46; demography, 151–52,
    168n10; slave trade in, 158–60, 161

Zúñiga, Pasqual de, 183

CPSIA information can be obtained
at www.ICGtesting.com
Printed in the USA
BVHW070725250819
556729BV00001B/220/P